# Solving
# Cyber Risk

# Solving Cyber Risk

*Protecting your company*
*and society*

ANDREW COBURN
ÉIREANN LEVERETT
GORDON WOO

WILEY

For general information on our other products and services or for technical support, please contact our Customer Care Department within the United States at (800) 762-2974, outside the United States at (317) 572-3993, or fax (317) 572-4002.

Wiley publishes in a variety of print and electronic formats and by print-on-demand. Some material included with standard print versions of this book may not be included in e-books or in print-on-demand. If this book refers to media such as a CD or DVD that is not included in the version you purchased, you may download this material at http://booksupport.wiley.com. For more information about Wiley products, visit www.wiley.com.

*Library of Congress Cataloging-in-Publication Data*

Names: Coburn, Andrew (Andrew W.), author. | Leverett, Eireann, author.
    | Woo, G., author.
Title: Solving cyber risk: protecting your company and society / Andrew
    Coburn, Eireann Leverett, Gordon Woo.
Description: Hoboken, New Jersey: John Wiley & Sons, Inc., [2019] | Series:
    Wiley finance series | Includes bibliographical references and index. |
    Identifiers: LCCN 2018035611 (print) | LCCN 2018037247 (ebook) | ISBN
    9781119490913 (Adobe PDF) | ISBN 9781119490920 (ePub) | ISBN 9781119490937
    (hardcover) | ISBN 9781119490913 (ePDF)
Subjects: LCSH: Computer security. | Data protection.
Classification: LCC QA76.9.A25 (ebook) | LCC QA76.9.A25 C577 2019 (print) |
    DDC 005.8—dc23
LC record available at https://lccn.loc.gov/2018035611

Cover Design: Wiley
Cover Image: © iStock.com/scyther5

Printed and bound in Great Britain by TJ International Ltd.

10 9 8 7 6 5 4 3 2 1

# Contents

# About the Authors

The three authors worked together on the development of the leading cyber risk analysis model being used by the insurance industry today, and in the development of scenarios for regulating cyber risk. They are each specialists in different fields of risk and cyber technology.

## ANDREW COBURN

Andrew is a specialist in risk, and is the architect of the Cyber Solutions risk model marketed by Risk Management Solutions, Inc. (RMS), the leading cyber risk model being used in the insurance industry today. He is a senior vice president of RMS and one of the main contributors to the creation of commercial catastrophe risk models over the past 25 years. His previous books include *Earthquake Protection* (John Wiley & Sons). He is also a Director of the Cambridge Centre for Risk Studies (CCRS), based in the business school of the University of Cambridge, where he has coordinated the cyber risk research program and been the lead author on a number of CCRS cyber risk publications, which have been highly cited. Cyber risk scenarios developed at the CCRS have been adopted as stress tests by industry regulators. He is a frequent speaker at conferences on risk and financial services.

## ÉIREANN LEVERETT

Éireann is an ethical hacker with many years of experience in cyber security and the impacts of computer security failures and accidents. He is the founder of Concinnity Risks Ltd and a Senior Researcher on Cyber Risk at the Cambridge Centre for Risk Studies (CCRS) at the University of Cambridge. He has experience of compromising the security of organizations, and assisting them to improve their security postures through a variety of short- and long-term methods. While his background is in artificial intelligence (AI) and computer security, he has increasingly taken an interest in a risk-centric view of computer security, and how markets can help or hinder progress in defending the internet. He is a member of the Forum of Incident Response and Security Teams (FIRST; https://www.first .org), and regularly speaks at incident response and hacker conferences.

## GORDON WOO

Gordon is a catastrophist with Risk Management Solutions, Inc. (RMS), focusing mainly on complex man-made insurance risks such as terrorism and cyber risk. Profiled in *Newsweek* magazine, he was described as one of the world's leading catastrophists. He has 30 years of experience in catastrophe risk consultancy, advising financial institutions, governments, and major corporations. He was educated at Cambridge University, with degrees in mathematics, theoretical physics, and computer science. He is a visiting professor at University College London, and an adjunct professor at Nanyang Technological University, Singapore. He is the author of the books *The Mathematics of Natural Catastrophes* and *Calculating Catastrophe*, published by Imperial College Press.

# Acknowledgments

The authors are fortunate to be supported by some great teams who have helped them carry out much of the work presented in this book. We have tried to acknowledge individual contributions wherever possible, but we would like to acknowledge specifically the inputs of:

### Cambridge Centre for Risk Studies
We have had the support of some of the best and brightest at the Cambridge Centre for Risk Studies, a world-leading research center at Judge Business School, University of Cambridge. We are particularly grateful to the Executive Directors: Simon Ruffle, Professor Danny Ralph, and Dr Michelle Tuveson, and to the cyber risk research team: Dr Jennifer Daffron at stroke, Jennifer Copic, Tamara Evan, Kayla Strong, Andrew Smith (Drew to his risk colleagues), Kelly Quantrill, James Bourdeau, Tim Douglas, and Dr Andy Skelton. We are particularly indebted to Olivia Majumdar for her help in getting this book under way.

We are also indebted to the companies that have sponsored the research into cyber risk at the Cambridge Centre for Risk Studies, including Lockheed Martin, Lloyd's of London (with particular thanks to Trevor Maynard for his support and encouragement), AXA XL, Pool Re, Citigroup, American International Group (AIG), Risk Management Solutions, Inc. (RMS), and all the other supporters that have included cyber risk within the range of multi-threat risk research.

### Risk Management Solutions, Inc.
We very much appreciate the support of our colleagues at RMS in the cyber model development team, particularly the business leadership of Dr Mohsen Rahnama, Peter Ulrich, Adam Sandler, Tom Harvey, and Kathleen Maloney, and the model development team, ably led by Dr Christos Mitas, Dr Hichem Boudali, Chris Vos, John Agorgianitis, Dr Malik Awan, and Simon Arnold. We appreciate the RMS team allowing us to use data from the RMS Cyber Loss Experience Database in various chapters of the book. We are of course particularly grateful to Dr Robert Muir Wood, who has created a culture of curiosity and

innovation at the company, from which we all benefit. We are grateful to Hemant Shah, founder of RMS, for his support of research, tolerance of enquiry, and vision for new risk management frameworks, and to Karen White, CEO, for her emphasis on cyber risk analytics in the future of the organization.

We are also grateful to all the RMS clients who have worked with us over the past few years, helping us understand the nature of cyber risk from their experience, perspectives, and claims data.

**Cambridge Computer Laboratory, University of Cambridge**
We also gratefully acknowledge the inputs and assistance of our colleagues at the Cambridge Computer Laboratory and Cambridge Cybercrime Centre, including Director Dr Richard Clayton, Graham Rymer, Professor Frank Stajano, Professor Ross Anderson, Rob Watson, Dr Alice Hutchings, Professor Jon Crowcroft, and Professor Ian Leslie.

There are a number of hackers and members of the incident response community who contributed to these ideas either directly or indirectly, and either as individuals or as companies doing good work. In no particular order, we thank Sid Rao, Reid Wightman, Matt Erasmus, Erin Burns, Louise Stanhope, Baiba Kaskina, Silje Endsjo, Thomas Dullien, Marion Marschalek, Marie Moe, Alexandre Dulaunoy, Raphael Vinot, Thais Moreira Hamasaki, Aristotle Tzafalias, Arrigo Triulzi, Bruce Stenning, Aaron Kaplan, Thomas Schreck, and Jens Wiesner, with special thanks to Colin Cassidy for going on the full journey.

Finally, but by no means least, we would like to acknowledge the support (and tolerance) of our partners and families in the writing and production of the book. Many thanks, Helen (enjoyed the drinks on the riverbank boring you about hackonomics); Fatma and Mehmet (penguins); and Victoria.

# Solving
# Cyber Risk

# CHAPTER 1

# Counting the Costs of Cyber Attacks

## 1.1 ANATOMY OF A DATA EXFILTRATION ATTACK

### 1.1.1 The Plan

The year 2012 had been good for a small group of cyber hackers. They called themselves '*Rescator*', after the noble and mysterious pirate character in the *Angelique* series of French historical romantic films popular on television in Eastern Europe and Russia. The *Rescator* team specialized in scamming the credentials from credit cards and selling the details for around a 10th of a bitcoin each (approximately $1 in 2012) on sites in the dark web and other black market outlets, such as the Russian 'octavian' marketplace.[1] As they counted their takings in early December 2012, they watched a YouTube meme about the preholiday shopping frenzy taking place in the United States, set to the tune of 'Good King Wenceslas' played on cash registers, a parody of consumerism. *Ker-ching!* Inspired, their planning began in earnest, reinvesting their profits to go for the jackpot: a major theft of US credit card information during next year's holiday spending spree. They could not have known just how successful they would be, and that they were about to commit the biggest theft of credit card data in human history.

### 1.1.2 The Malware

*Rescator* began by buying a malware kit from one of the underground forums to create a RAM scraper, similar to other point-of-sale (PoS) hacking malware known as BlackPOS, but significantly more sophisticated.[2] The *Rescator* software later became known as *Kaptoxa*, Russian slang for potato. In the point-of-sale terminals that were standard in US shops in 2013, when a shopper swiped a credit card through the card reader, the

1

information was read from the card's magnetic stripe, and under Payment Card Industry-Data Security Standard (PCI-DSS) rules, the data was encrypted immediately. This protected it at rest while stored on the local device's hard drive, and in transit when it was transmitted to the back-end servers for processing. The 2013 point-of-sale systems had a vulnerability: the card details were read into the computer's temporary memory (RAM) and encrypted while in memory. The malware RAM scraper could detect and copy the credit card details at the microsecond just before the data was encrypted, and send it to a server that *Rescator* would configure to receive the stolen data.

### 1.1.3   Finding a Way In

Armed with their *Kaptoxa* Trojan horse, the *Rescator* team mapped out a plan to insert it into point-of-sale systems in companies in the United States. They drew up a hit list of the largest retailers that process large volumes of credit card transactions. However, as they went through the list, they found a snag: these big retail companies were all investing heavily in new security systems. During 2012 and throughout 2013, most of the big-name US retailers announced or implemented new installations of malware and data exfiltration detection services – various vendor security systems to prevent unauthorized access to IT systems, to sweep networks for malware, and to monitor traffic on the network to detect suspicious packets that could be data being stolen.

### 1.1.4   Using Suppliers with Authorized Access

*Rescator* started to work on finding ways to get around these defenses. Instead of directly targeting the retail companies themselves, they started researching their suppliers and counterparties, particularly anyone who might be granted access into the retailers' information technology (IT) systems.

In September 2013 they hit the bull's-eye. An employee at Fazio Mechanical Services fell for one of their phishing attacks by opening an attachment on an unsolicited email enabling another piece of spyware, *Citadel*, a password-stealing Trojan, to infect Fazio's IT network.[3] Fazio Mechanical Services had an impressive client list of major US retailers in and around Pennsylvania, providing them with refrigeration and heating, ventilation, and air-conditioning (HVAC) systems, servicing their cold stores for frozen foods, and managing the energy usage and temperatures of large retail outlets. Fazio had access into the IT networks of its customers to enable it to monitor, troubleshoot, and control their refrigeration plants and HVAC systems.

Most significantly of all, the Fazio customer list included stores belonging to Target Corporation, a major discount store operator and second only to Walmart in US retail size. Target operated 1793 stores across 47 states in 2013, and had revenues of $72.5 billion.

### 1.1.5  Installing the Malware

Using their password-stealing Trojan, the *Rescator* team was able to obtain the credentials of the Fazio operators who routinely logged in through the firewall of Target Corporation into its IT network to monitor the Target refrigeration and HVAC systems. During the Thanksgiving holiday in November 2013 when most of the company was closed, they used these access codes to log in to the Target IT network and install their RAM-scraping malware on a few point-of-sale systems in Target stores. They took a couple of days to check that it worked, carried out systems checks, and waited to see if it would be detected. The *Kaptoxa* malware was sophisticated enough to be invisible to some of the best anti-malware systems in use at that time. Target was running 40 different commercial anti-malware tools, sweeping its networks and point-of-sale systems, and looking for any software that matched suspicious signatures. None of the systems identified the *Kaptoxa* installations as malicious.[4]

When the *Rescator* team found that their software had succeeded in evading the anti-malware sweeps, they returned and overnight pushed their malware to as many of Target's point-of-sale systems as they could reach.

### 1.1.6  Harvesting the Data

The pre-holiday season was indeed busy. Shoppers flocked into Target stores for their holiday gifts, appliances, and supplies. In a period from November 27, to December 15, 2013, the *Kaptoxa* malware on the point-of-sale systems in Target stores across the United States captured the details of transactions from 40 million debit and credit cards. An additional overlapping customer database that contained names and addresses of 70 million people was also stolen. It was the largest cache of credit card data that had ever been stolen.

The *Kaptoxa* malware cached the data it was stealing locally at each point-of-sale terminal. Every seven hours it checked the local time, and if it was between 10 a.m. and 5 p.m. it would send the data over the busy network traffic to an internal host on a compromised server inside the Target network. From there, the *Rescator* team used a series of remote file transfer protocol (FTP) transfers to retrieve the intercepted information, amounting to around 11 Gb of data. The stolen data transfers went to a number of 'drop' locations – servers in Russia, the United States, and Brazil that the *Rescator* gang controlled.[5] These were computers in unsuspecting organizations that had also been hacked, giving the gang the ability to store the data there temporarily before moving the data on to a destination source, and masking their tracks.

### 1.1.7   Selling the Stolen Data

The gang moved quickly, trying to sell the stolen credit card details before the hack was discovered. They made the data available on their own marketplace website, as well as auction sites on the dark web and black market private dealerships. They sorted the stolen cards into categories, offering them for sale in blocks, such as 'Tortuga' and 'Barbarossa'. These were bought by other black market fraudsters to create new counterfeit cards mainly for use in shopping in stores for items than could be easily resold, classifying them by ZIP code to enable the fraudsters to shop locally like the real card owner to lessen suspicion. These card details contained full transaction information and verification details and were offered for prices around $20. They also offered non-US cards, chip-and-PIN (Europay, MasterCard, Visa [known as EMV cards]), and platinum or premium cards that were sold at higher prices, up to $120.[6]

### 1.1.8   Buy Back and Discovery

The sites where credit card information is offered for sale are routinely monitored by fraud detection officers from the card companies and major banks. It is a poorly-kept secret that the banks themselves buy back some of the card details on offer to take them off the black market and protect their cardholders. Banks may in fact be some of the best customers of credit card hackers. Around December 15, the bankers who were buying back their cardholders' details noticed that large volumes of new credit card details were appearing on the black market, with one thing in common – they had all made a purchase at Target in the past few days. They called Target. Some of them also spoke off the record to a cyber security journalist, Brian Krebs, who may have broken the news story on his blog on December 18.[7] Target's forensic teams and their security consultants identified and removed the malware from the infected point-of-sale systems in a few hours, and began a full internal systems security audit and investigation. The investigation took many weeks to complete.

### 1.1.9   Disclosure

Target Corporation made a formal announcement of the data breach on December 19, 2013, saying that the matter was under investigation and that Target was now working with law enforcement authorities and financial institutions.[8] US state regulations for the protection of personal data require companies that have a data breach to disclose it publicly and promptly, and to take steps to notify the individuals whose personal data has been compromised. Target's website providing information about the breach, and its customer service hotlines, became overloaded as the company began to assist customers with questions about whether they might have been compromised and what to do about it. Target had to hire additional customer service personnel to deal with the surge in worried calls.

### 1.1.10  Customer Management

The first question of any of Target's customers is 'Was my card information stolen?' Not all of the point-of-sale terminals had been infected, and it wasn't initially clear how long the interceptions had been going on. The forensics to understand the extent, duration, and transactions that might have been compromised took several days to unravel. Target worked with banks to have millions of compromised cards stopped and reissued.

Customers' main fears in response to having their card and personal details stolen are that their cards could be used in fraudulent payments, that they could lose money from their bank accounts, and that their own credit histories and ratings could be impacted. Target offered credit monitoring for a year to each person whose details were stolen. There is also a potential for a secondary fraud, where a criminal armed with the stolen personal details contacts individuals and tricks them into false payments or more disclosures. Target offered advice to counter secondary fraud, including changing account passwords and insisting on ring-backs for unsolicited phone calls.

### 1.1.11  Target's Costs

Target's direct costs from the breach reached over $200 million, and took several years to accrue. In 2015, Target paid out $40 million to banks and credit unions that lost money, paid out to buy back card data, or incurred further loss resulting from the data breach.[9] A consumer class action was settled at $10 million to establish a fund for victims of the data breach, with individual customers able to claim up to $10,000 if they could provide satisfactory evidence of their losses and costs incurred. Victims were also allowed to apply for up to two hours of their 'lost time', billable at $10 per hour. Allowable costs include reimbursed charges on their credit cards, fees for hiring a professional to correct a credit report, late and declined payment fees, and other costs incurred as a consequence of the breach.[10]

Target came to a $18.5 million collective settlement for the regulatory fines with the state attorney generals in the 47 states where it had stores in 2017, the largest payout being $1.4 million for California, with 7.7 million affected Target customers. An additional component of the regulatory settlement ensured that Target implemented a comprehensive information security program, overseen by an independent, qualified third party, and employed a chief information security officer, reporting to the chief executive and board.

### 1.1.12 Strategic Impacts on Target Corporation

The data breach had additional consequences for Target Corporation. The chief executive resigned in May 2014, following the chief information officer in March. Profits for the quarter following the breach dropped by 46%, and contributed to a reduced profit for the year.[11] The damage to the company's reputation caused a reduction in visits to its stores. Target attempted to offset this with a 10% discount offer immediately after the breach, but customer confidence was not easily restored, and Target continued to struggle for some months. Consequential costs of the impact on Target's revenues in the year that followed the breach are harder to gauge, but some estimates suggest it could have been between $1 billion and $2 billion, more than five times the direct costs and between 1.4% and 2.8% of Target's annual revenue.

Share prices dropped several times in response to various stages of disclosure about the breach, initially falling 11% in the weeks after the breach, recovering around 7% with a comforting financial outlook reporting in the following quarter of 2014, and falling again with various settlements and payouts as they were resolved over the following years. Some analysts see the data breach as having undermined confidence in the company's strategic direction, as it tries to promote in-store experience to compete with e-commerce retailers.

### 1.1.13 And the *Rescator* Team?

Nobody was ever caught or prosecuted for the Target cyber hack. Two petty criminals were caught in possession of 112 derived fraudulent credit cards, but to date none of the perpetrators. Target Corporation was not the only victim of point-of-sale malware during the holiday period of 2013. Neiman Marcus and three other retailers reported credit card intercepts. The illegal marketplaces, including *Rescator*'s own marketplace, where the stolen credit cards were offered for sale, were abandoned shortly after the publicity broke.

It is difficult to know how much money the *Rescator* gang made from the operation. A conservative estimate might be $50 million: a long way from the $2 billion it cost Target. The *Rescator* gang, named for a mysterious pirate, has vanished with its treasure, back to the seven seas.

### 1.1.14 Fallout

The consequences of the Target data breach have been profound. Point-of-sale systems have been largely redesigned, and the key vulnerability has been addressed. It is no longer acceptable practice to have point-of-sale systems accessible through the same IT network as HVAC controls and other general activities accessed by a broader, less secure community. Data encryption practices have become more widespread, and verification processes have become more secure. Hacks like these have accelerated the take-up of chip-and-PIN (EMV) credit card technology in many countries of the world, which cuts card-related theft by up to 70%. It is highly unlikely that a cyber hack using the same exploits and techniques as the Target data breach will be seen again.

But it doesn't mean that new techniques won't be used to carry out a similar scale of cyber attack in the future.

## 1.2 A MODERN SCOURGE

### 1.2.1 Types of Cyber Losses

The Target Corporation data breach in 2013 was a high-profile cyber attack that caused a variety of losses and business impacts on one of the largest companies in the United States. However, it was only one of many successful cyber attacks that year; 2013 was a record year for data exfiltration events in the United States. There were 31 reported breaches that year where a US company lost a data set of a million personal records or more, and over 640 US companies reported a loss of more than a thousand personal data records.

Historically, 2013 looks to have been a peak year for the number of US data breach events, as US companies have improved their data security, and incident rates have dropped in the years since. However, all over the rest of the world, the number of data exfiltration incidences has been steadily increasing – the types and severities of attacks seen in the United States since 2005 are now occurring in many other countries.

Data exfiltration attacks are only one of the ways that cyber attacks cause loss to individual organizations and to society as a whole. Most organizations of any significant size report having to deal frequently with cyber incidents of many different types – attempted attacks, probes, phishing approaches, suspicious software detection, unusual network traffic. Sometimes these result in a 'cyber loss' – the organization is compromised in some way and incurs costs through payouts or business disruption. Of course even dealing with attempted attacks has a business cost (which we will come back to later), but in general we refer to a 'loss' as being a cyber incident that results in an organization having a significant unexpected financial payout or an episode of business disruption that prevents the generation of expected revenues. The next chapter describes and defines the losses that can be caused by the various types of cyber incidents, including data exfiltration, so costly to Target, as well as contagious malware, extortion, financial thefts, denial of service attacks, failures of networks, and outages of providers. We also try to define the range of severities of these different types of loss, and a threshold of severity that we might consider as significant, which we use to define 'loss' incidents in this book. In our third chapter we describe the loss processes that can occur from cyber attacks to physical systems and devices.

### 1.2.2   The Direct Payout Costs of a Cyber Attack

A cyber attack that succeeds in penetrating the defenses of an organization can cause losses in various ways. As illustrated in the example of the data exfiltration attack on Target Corporation, the $200 million in direct costs consisted of losses from several different sources.

A company suffering a cyber attack can expect to incur direct payout costs in a number of different areas, depending on the type of attack and the magnitude and characteristics of the attack. Costs of different types of attack are described in more detail in Chapter 2. Types of direct payout costs include:

- The response and forensics costs of the IT security team, both internal personnel and typically involving external consultants, that has to diagnose what happened as quickly as possible and render the system safe from further exploitation. New technology, equipment, software, and systems may need to be purchased to remedy vulnerabilities.
- Compensation for people whose personal data is compromised, including costs of notification, managing their enquiries and providing customer support, providing credit watch services, and payouts for any losses these individuals may suffer.
- Fines that may be imposed by regulators.

- Legal costs to defend any litigation that might be brought against the company, including the costs of settling the action or losing the case and paying damages or even punitive awards.
- Losses from the theft of financial assets – currency, transfers, trading value – which is the motivation behind many attacks.

### 1.2.3 Operational Disruption Causing Loss of Revenue

Costs are also incurred to the affected company from the disruption to business operations resulting from the attack, particularly lost revenues from commercial activities that are unable to be performed. Operational disruption can last for several hours or days and affect many parts of an organization. Surveys of corporate security executives show that breaches impact more than a third of a company's systems in around 40% of cases and more than half of systems in 15% of cases. They disable operational activity, including revenue generation, for more than 9 hours in 35% of cases and for durations of 24 hours or more in 9% of cases.[12] Operational disablement of systems can result in revenue loss to many different business processes, and each organization is different. Losses can occur from suspending customer purchasing activities, such as e-commerce or point-of-sale technologies; provision of services, such as hosting applications; fulfillment of orders; manufacturing or creation of products for sale; and interruption of the business process supply chain. These losses of revenue that can be directly attributed to the interruption of systems caused by the cyber attack are often included in direct costs estimates of a cyber attack.

### 1.2.4 Consequential Business Losses from a Cyber Attack

The consequential business losses from a data breach can be more severe than the direct costs. The company's reputation is damaged. Senior executives resign. Customers lose trust and transfer their business elsewhere. Revenues dip, and market share is lost to competitors. Studies show typical churn rates of around 7% of a company's customers after a data breach, and 31% of consumers have discontinued a relationship with an organization that has suffered a data breach.[13] Around a third of companies that experience a breach have reportedly suffered revenue loss, around 12% reported losses greater than 20% of their annual revenue, and just over 1% lost more than 80% of their annual revenue.[14] These companies also reported customer desertion and significant losses in business opportunities as a result of the breach.

Companies that suffer a costly cyber attack typically see their stock prices marked down.[15] Analysis of historical cases shows that companies see their share prices reduced by an average of 5% after a data breach attack.[16] Stock price reductions can be short term while the market waits to see how the company will be affected, but in cases where the consequences prejudice the organization's business model or long-term profitability, investors can mark them down significantly and for a long period.

A major cyber attack can cause a company to have its credit ratings downgraded.[17] Companies seen as a credit risk lose suppliers as well as customers, and find it more expensive to borrow capital and fund their cash flow. Credit rating downgrades indicate to the public that a company is in distress, and can hasten a company's decline and threaten its viability.

These combined effects have meant that some companies have declared bankruptcy following cyber attacks.[18] Companies that have had their intellectual property (IP) stolen have found themselves outcompeted in the market, leading to their long-term failure.[19]

The viability of a company can also be threatened in other ways if the consequences of the attack are severe enough. There have been cases where class-action litigations brought against a company for its data breach liabilities far exceed the capital valuation of the company.[20] Companies have been devalued in merger and acquisition negotiations because they suffered data breaches.[21] The impact of experiencing a data breach can go far beyond the direct costs, and can impact the brand, the reputation, and the viability of the company itself.

### 1.2.5  Cyber Attack Economic Multipliers

Finally, the effects are not isolated to the individual organization that is attacked. The consequences are also felt by the company's suppliers and trading partners, investors, financiers, and other counterparties. They in turn sell less to the affected company and reduce their revenues, or they lose part of their investment value, loans returns, or earnings. Companies are part of a network of commerce, and the failure or reduction in performance by one company has consequential effects on others. Economists term this the multiplier effect, or 'financial spillover'. Cyber attacks have a clear multiplier effect on the economy as a whole.

In an analysis that the authors published in 2014, we assessed the economic multipliers of cyber attacks by tracking the connectivity of companies in the global economy.[22]

Figure 1.1 shows a network diagram of around a thousand of the largest enterprises in the global economy, sized by their annual revenue, with the

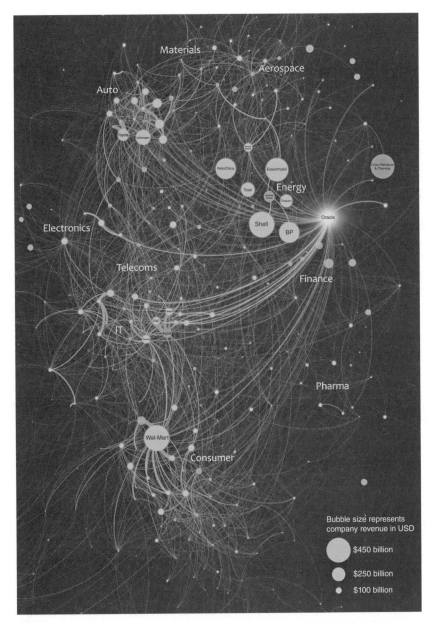

**FIGURE 1.1** Trading interconnectivity of major companies in the global economy. Cyber losses can cascade through the economy to create a multiplier effect for economic costs. Oracle, a market-leading provider of databases, is highlighted to illustrate an example of the key role played by providers of information technology in the global economy.
*Source:* CCRS (2014a).

trading relationships between them shown by the thickness of the line, and the direction of payment flowing counterclockwise. The reduction in annual revenues of any of these large corporations has a consequential effect in reducing their requirement from their suppliers and curtailing their ability to purchase from trading partners. Fluctuations in quarterly reported revenue (from whatever cause) affect trading partners when change exceeds around 10% of expected annual revenue, with greater increases having disproportionately larger effects on their counterparties. The number of trading partners and the depth of trading relationships influence how these impacts spread through the trade network. For a medium-to-large company losing around 20% of its annual revenue (something that occurs in around 12% of data breach cases), we estimate the economic multiplier to be around 1.6 – i.e. the suppliers and customers collectively lose an additional total of 1.6 times the losses that the company itself loses in a cyber attack.

For example, if a company with a $1 billion turnover suffered a data exfiltration event of 20 million personal records, it would face direct costs of around $50 billion, combined with consequential business costs by subsequently losing around 20% of annual revenue ($200 million), and its suppliers and counterparties suffering collective losses of 1.6 times this ($320 million). The total cost of this example of a single data breach on the overall economy is $570 million, more than 10 times the direct costs. Fully recognizing the economic costs of cyber attacks is important in assessing the value of measures to reduce cyber risk.

The economic multiplier increases if several companies suffer losses at the same time. If several of the impacted companies share a supplier, then they may all reduce their volume of orders to that supplier and cumulatively inflict a large enough loss to the supplier to cause it to have financial difficulties, with knock-on effects to its own suppliers and trading partners. This cascade of effects through the economy is known as a systemic shock. This is what makes cyber catastrophes such a concern.

## 1.3 CYBER CATASTROPHES

A cyber catastrophe is an event that causes substantial losses to many organizations. For many years people have predicted a 'cyber 9/11', a 'cyber Pearl Harbor', or a 'cyber Black Swan'. These predictions identify the issue of the potential for strategic surprise from an unexpectedly large cyber catastrophe.

We define a cyber catastrophe as a cyber incident (a criminal campaign, a malware attack, or a major malfunction) that results in significant direct costs and consequential business losses to many (more than 10, but could be many thousands) multinational or very large premier organizations, or very many (more than a thousand) small and medium-size enterprises.[23] In addition to being a shock event, a cyber catastrophe can also be a general trend of slow losses and reduced economic revenues.

### 1.3.1 *NotPetya* and *WannaCry* Cyber Catastrophes

*NotPetya* and *WannaCryptor* malware attacks are profiled in more detail in the next chapter. These are examples of cyber catastrophes at the relatively low end of the potential magnitude scale.

The *NotPetya* virus release in June 2017 penetrated at least 8,000 computer networks, infecting many hundreds of thousands of individual devices, in organizations across 65 countries. More than 300 public companies declared losses to their quarterly results as a result of their infections from *NotPetya*, several reporting losses of hundreds of millions of dollars. The direct and consequential business losses to the infected organizations is estimated to have exceeded $10 billion.[24]

The *WannaCry* ransomware attack in May 2017 was more widespread, but less severe overall. It caused more than 300,000 infections, mainly smaller businesses, but the impact did disrupt the operations of some major organizations, including healthcare providers whose patients were put at risk. The combined losses to the infected businesses are estimated to have been several billion dollars.[25]

### 1.3.2 Near-miss Cyber Catastrophes

These events and others in recent history demonstrate that cyber catastrophes have the potential to disrupt many businesses worldwide simultaneously. In fact, these recent events can be seen as 'near misses'. They were bad-enough events, but could have been even more severe with only minor changes in the way they occurred. Our counterfactual analysis of the *WannaCry* timeline, described in more detail in the next chapter, suggests that the *WannaCry* event could have been many multiples of its actual cost if it had occurred three months earlier and had not included a kill switch in its software design.

There have been several other cyber events that had the potential to become truly systemic, and to inflict widespread disruption and business losses on thousands of organizations. These might be considered as early warning indicators of potential cyber catastrophes. They include:

- A cyber heist operation on banks by penetrating the Society for Worldwide Interbank Financial Telecommunication (SWIFT) financial transaction system impacted more than a dozen national and international banks (August 2016), resulting in the theft of $81 million, but the theft of a billion dollars was attempted and narrowly thwarted. The heist compromised a secure 'network of trust': the SWIFT financial system, used by 11,000 banks, any or all of which could potentially have been robbed.

- A distributed denial of service (DDoS) attack on Dyn, a provider of Domain Name System (DNS) and internet optimization services (October 2016), caused disruption to thousands of its internet service company customers in Europe and North America. The attacks caused service losses of several hours during a single day to many leading e-commerce businesses. It highlighted the vulnerability of DNS infrastructure supporting the digital economy, and indicates the potential for cyber catastrophes to disrupt global e-commerce.

- An outage of the Amazon Web Services (AWS) Simple Storage Service (S3) for five hours affected 148,000 websites and nearly a quarter of all AWS cloud users (March 2017). Cloud service providers (CSPs) like AWS, Google Cloud Platform, Microsoft Azure, and IBM Bluemix tend to have very low failure rates, but the dependency of so many businesses on these leading CSPs means that if there were to be a failure then there is potential for a CSP outage to disrupt many thousands of cloud-reliant businesses.

- The release of stolen National Security Agency (NSA) and Central Intelligence Agency (CIA) cyber toolkits by a cyber hacking group calling themselves *ShadowBrokers* was a game changer by making highly professional cyber weaponry available to less skilled amateur hackers (August 2016 and April 2017). The releases included 15 'zero day' exploits for common software in use, and 24 other tools. The toolkit provided the keys to unlock the firewalls of 30% of all global corporations. These exploits were incorporated into the malware of *NotPetya* and *WannaCry*, but also illustrates how tools could suddenly become available to bypass the apparently impenetrable security systems operated by most of the major international companies.

- A security bug in widely used open-source database MongoDB meant that ransomware *Harak1r1* was able to access data in 'tens of thousands' of MongoDB installations and deny them access until payments were made (January 2017). 'Many' MongoDB servers were reported extorted. This raises the specter of industry-standard software in use by large numbers of organizations suddenly failing or causing losses simultaneously as a result of an internal software bug or vulnerability.

There has not yet been a truly catastrophic cyber event that has cost the economy hundreds of billions of dollars. It is human nature to dismiss

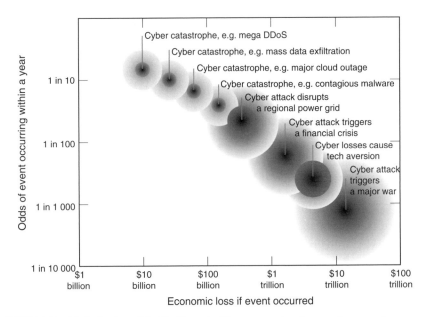

**FIGURE 1.2**　Global cyber risk: likelihood of loss occurring from cyber attacks.
Source: Authors (2018).

possible dangers before an event has actually occurred. But there are reasons to believe that future cyber events are possible that could inflict individual costs of hundreds of millions or even billions of dollars to thousands of major businesses, and inflict crippling losses on large numbers of small and medium-size enterprises. These events, described in the following section and illustrated in Figure 1.2, would have a heavy impact on the economy and on society in general. The likelihood of a future societal catastrophe from cyber attacks is one of the strongest justifications for taking more action to solve cyber risk.

### 1.3.3　Is Cyber Threat Systemic?

The concept of cyber threat having the ability to scale up to cause systemic losses to thousands of organizations, with potential to cause catastrophic consequences for our society and our economy, is better accepted now, but the recognition of this potential is relatively recent. This led people to assume that cyber threat is predominantly characterized by separate loss events at individual organizations, and is limited in its ability to propagate more broadly. Only a few years ago there was still debate about whether the emerging threat from cyber risk is truly systemic, and the extent to which cyber risk could scale.[26]

Part of the authors' research has been assessing the risk of extreme events for regulators, governments, insurance companies, and corporations.

### 1.3.4 Potential Cyber Catastrophes

There are several ways in which cyber catastrophes could occur. We have developed plausible scenarios that are used as stress tests by organizations in their cyber protection planning. In the next chapter we include a 'severe but plausible' cyber catastrophe scenario for each of the cyber loss mechanisms described. It is possible that next year could see the number and severity of data exfiltration incidents increase by an order of magnitude, as a result of a concerted campaign by criminals armed with a new toolkit of exploits to penetrate the security systems of multiple multinational companies.[27] Another potential cyber catastrophe scenario is a contagious ransomware virus that achieves infection rates much higher than anything previously seen, and is both destructive and disruptive to business activities across large numbers of organizations, of all sizes and nationalities.[28] It is possible that denial of service attacks could increase in volume and intensity and target major e-commerce platforms to immobilize many of them for much longer than has been achieved before.[29] A major cloud service provider could suffer an outage on a scale and duration that exceeds anything previously recorded, causing hundreds of thousands of its customers difficulties in sustaining their cloud-dependent business activities.[30] Industrial control systems could be hacked, damaging and disabling manufacturing and processing operations in large numbers of plants.[31]

For each of these, the analysis considers the practical constraints of attack vectors, the capabilities of attackers, how many organizations could potentially be impacted, and what limits there might be to the severity of the consequences. In each case there are typically factors that constrain the number of organizations that a potential cyber loss process might impact. For example, to penetrate a large number of companies, a 'zero day' exploit operates on a particular software system, so only the companies operating that software system would potentially be affected by that exploit. The market share of industry-standard software systems becomes a determinant constraint on the number of organizations that might be affected. Other constraints include the expected response by the security community to detect, protect, and respond quickly to limit the extent of the impact of any event.

These scenarios estimate the numbers of affected operations and loss costs across the population of organizations in an economy such as the United States. Although large numbers of small and medium-size organizations are affected in these scenarios, the main driver of cost to the economy is the impact on large and premier companies. Scenarios where 15–20% of large companies are impacted are feasible in several of the loss processes. It is possible to envision extreme scenarios where as many as 50% of large companies could be hit, under pessimistic assumptions about the resources and skills available to the attackers, and how different defense and response strategies by the community of security specialists might play out. These scenarios result in direct loss and operational disruption costs to the population of US businesses of many tens, and in some extreme cases hundreds, of billions of dollars. These catastrophe scenarios would not be confined geographically to the United States. Similar losses could be expected in companies affected in other developed economies, including Europe, Australasia, India, China, Japan, and Southeast Asian markets. The direct costs would be exceeded by the consequential losses of earnings to these businesses, and as noted earlier, by the multipliers on the economic impact from their effects on suppliers and customers and the economic trading network.

### 1.3.5    Cyber Catastrophes Could Impact Infrastructure

There is even greater potential economic impact from cyber catastrophe scenarios that target key components of the infrastructure, rather than the organizations themselves. We have analyzed scenarios where cyber attacks could disable the power supply in different countries. In 2014 and 2015 when we published these analyses, the idea that foreign agents could potentially attack the power supplies in another country appeared far-fetched, until cyber attacks on the Ukraine power grid in December 2015 left 80,000 people without electricity.[32]

A potential cyber attack could damage and disable multiple power generators in the United States electricity grid. The US grid is compartmentalized into interconnected regions, and the spinning reserve capacity needs to be depleted before cascading failure can occur. A cyber attack that used known vulnerabilities to damage 50 generators in the most populous Northeastern region of the United States could result in loss of power to 90 million people, with reconnection for most of them taking a day or two, but full restoration taking between two and four weeks.[33] This results in disruption to businesses in the region, most significantly on the commercial and industrial sectors that are most reliant on power for their business activities. We estimate the total economic impact of such an event at between $243 billion and, under extreme pessimistic assumptions, over a trillion dollars of lost output from the US economy.

A similar analysis of a future cyber attack on the power distribution system of the United Kingdom, a much smaller country and economy and with a different type of power grid architecture, produces a regional power supply outage that affects between 9 million and 13 million electricity customers.[34] The knock-on effects include disruption to transportation, digital communications, and water services. The attack results in an estimated loss of between $70 billion and $628 billion to the UK economy.

These scenarios demonstrate that cyber attacks on infrastructure have the potential to generate very substantial shocks to the economies of the countries attacked, and are among some of the most severe consequences of cyber risk to our society.

### 1.3.6   Could a Cyber Catastrophe Trigger a Financial Crisis?

Cyber attacks and technology errors could potentially trigger a future financial crisis. Flash crashes have been seen on trading exchanges as a result of trading algorithm malfunctions, cryptocurrencies have been hacked and destabilized, and major financial trading systems have been cyber attacked and plundered. There are genuine fears that a future cyber attack or cyber-enabled fraud could trigger a confidence crisis in the markets that would spread through the financial system and result in a worldwide financial crisis with severe negative impacts on the global economy.[35] Others disagree, arguing that the financial system is resilient to shocks of this type.[36] Even a small financial crisis can wipe hundreds of billions of dollars of value off the market capitalization of listed companies, and can result in reduced output from national economies for years.[37] If a major cyber attack succeeded in stealing from large numbers of financial services companies and caused a crisis of confidence by investors in their banks or the values of their financial assets, then the ensuing financial crisis could be more costly and disruptive to society than many other types of cyber incidents.

### 1.3.7   The 'Cyber Catastrophe' of Tech Aversion

One of the worst outcomes from high levels of continued cyber losses or severe cyber catastrophes is the possibility that the general public might lose confidence in information technology, and distrust its ability to deliver benefits that are greater than its risks of security breaches. Surveys of consumers show that there is ambivalence about trusting technology. Many see the advantages, but are wary about third parties failing to protect or respect their data privacy. They fear cyber attacks that will cause them losses and so are reluctant to rely on digital bank accounts, transact online, or embrace further innovations that could be to their benefit. Various names have been used for this phenomenon, including 'tech aversion', 'e-luctance', 'cyber malaise', and 'technophobia'. This could be responsible for the most severe of all of the economic costs of societal cyber risk by threatening future productivity gains from the digital economy.

The past half-century of economic growth has been driven by a combination of factors, including globalization of trade, financial deregulation, innovation, education, and rapidly improving productivity levels. Global economic output doubled in the period between 1970 and 1985, and has doubled again from 1985 to present-day levels, marking the period of fastest economic growth in human history. This has delivered unprecedented prosperity for the mainstream populations of the developed economies. A major contribution to this economic growth has been the improvement of productivity delivered by information technology. Although there are different views on the contribution of IT to productivity, some economists have suggested that up to 40% of US productivity growth between 1995 and 2002 can be attributed to IT.[38] IT is an enabling technology that allows businesses to improve their output at decreasing costs.

Many analysts predict that we are about to embark on another period of productivity improvement – a 'fourth industrial revolution' – enabled by Big Data, artificial intelligence, robotics, and machine learning. Phrases like 'data is the new oil' underpin a view that information is increasingly enabling accelerated economic growth.

Our analysis of this scenario considered the sectors of the economy that would most suffer from tech aversion and rated the IT business process criticality of operations to key technologies.[39] Productivity losses, consumer confidence, capital investment levels, and consumption indexes were stressed in macroeconomic modeling of the consequences of a 'tech-averse' future. The global economy lost between $4.5 *trillion* and $15 *trillion* over a five-year projection, depending on the assumptions made.

## 1.4  SOCIETAL CYBER THREATS

### 1.4.1  Cyber Threats to Democracy

Cyber activities and the capabilities of hacker groups not only add a significant burden of cost to our economies but also pose a threat to the functioning of our society. Fake news, chatbots, and the manipulation of social media are now commonplace in democratic election campaigns, and may have influenced the outcome of key elections.[40] The permeation of false rumors can manipulate public opinion, electorates, stock prices, and currency markets. Politically motivated attacks and manipulation can undermine the legitimacy of our democratic processes and our confidence in truth, the veracity of sources of information, and our ability to differentiate between realities and lies. As marketing agencies increasingly set up botnets to endorse products through false accounts in social media, and fake news reports try to manipulate financial markets, the public becomes increasingly confused, distrusting, and wary of information. This has a social cost and will be rectified only with better codes of digital ethics, abilities to detect and differentiate veracity, and capabilities to deter and prevent interference in democratic practise.

### 1.4.2  The Cyber Threat of Triggering War

The best-resourced cyber teams are state-sponsored cyber warriors who are increasingly active in testing their techniques by penetrating the organizations of other countries. In Chapter 5 we list some of the 91 national cyber operations teams that are active today. At least 20 of these are potentially antagonistic to Western democracies.

One of the greatest threats that cyber capabilities pose is the potential to trigger conflicts that could rapidly escalate into conventional military warfare. Cyber intrusions into private-sector or non-military organizations have occurred where the perpetrators are suspected to be foreign state–backed operations teams. Typically these ops teams are spying on industrial secrets, stealing funds for impoverished regimes, exploring weaknesses in military systems, and probing and learning about vulnerabilities in the infrastructures and economies of their potential future enemies. So far, disruptive and damaging cyber attacks by foreign operatives are tolerated by national security agencies – partly because of the difficulties of attributing with certainty who carried out the attacks. Most nations that suffer incursions from the cyber ops teams of foreign countries have developed offensive capabilities for retaliation, and for first-strike options.

It is still of course against international law for cyber ops teams to carry out attacks that damage assets in another country, but several western democracies, including the United States, UK, Germany, and Australia, have now passed laws giving their own cyber ops teams the authority to carry out cyber offensive activities in foreign jurisdictions. Some of these have gone public with their capabilities, including the ability to make another country's warplanes, ships, and missiles malfunction, and cripple national infrastructure and the data and communications systems of potential enemies.[41] In 2016, NATO decided that a cyber attack on any member country would constitute an attack under the provision of Article 5, the mutual defense guarantee, that would trigger collective response, including options for retaliation with conventional military weapons.[42]

For many decades, the military dominance and balance of the super-powers has largely prevented armed conflicts – the frequency of international wars is at its lowest for several centuries. However, cyber power has changed this equation and is highly asymmetric. Nations like North Korea that cannot match the military firepower of the superpowers, now have extensive cyber ops capability. The existence of national cyber ops teams, both as an extension of military capability and as national security protection, makes the possibility of international cyber retaliatory strikes a lot more likely, and these have the potential to rapidly escalate into a conventional military conflict. Future geopolitical conflicts are likely to have an entire theater of war in cyberspace. Much of the conflict in Ukraine from 2014 onwards has featured cyber attacks on military and civilian infrastructure and data systems targets that support the military offensives, with suspected Russian involvement. The Ukraine conflict is cited as a template for future wars.

If cyber attacks can trigger wars between nations, then this may be the biggest risk of all. The greatest risks to society, the economy, and our well-being overall have historically come from the threats of war. Wars in the last century alone have caused millions of deaths, the loss of trillions of dollars of economic output, and the biggest disruption to society. In our analysis of possible costs to the global economy from even a contained conflict between two advanced economies, our estimates ranged from $17 trillion to $32 trillion.[43] If cyber capability and our tolerance of low-level cyber attacks by one country against another make wars more likely, then the societal risk from cyber threats has a longer tail – i.e. the extreme severity of low-likelihood outcomes might be more costly to society – than people might realize.

## 1.5  CYBER RISK

### 1.5.1  Risk Terminology

Risk means the likelihood of loss. We quantify risk by assessing the probability of a specified severity of loss within a given time period. For example, the odds of a large US healthcare company experiencing a cyber attack that causes it direct costs of $10 million or more in the next 12 months would be around 1 in 100. Its chances of having a more severe event that causes a higher level of cost, say $100 million, are much less likely: around 1 in 700. The more severe the event, the less likely it is. There is a continuous scale from low levels of cost to the most severe, and at each level of loss there is a corresponding range of likelihood, with the low levels being most common and the most severe being least likely.

This relationship between loss severity and likelihood, known as the 'risk profile', the 'frequency-severity distribution', or the 'loss exceedance probability curve', is the measurement of risk, and is how risk managers assess and think about risk. This is how the term *risk* is used within this book. We use the term *threat* to mean the likelihood of an attempted cyber attack on your organization (and levels of attacks going on in the environment), and in risk terminology your 'vulnerability' means the chances of your company suffering a loss from an attempted attack (which is slightly more general than the IT security technical meaning of a 'vulnerability' being an error in software that can be exploited by a hacker).

The risk profile can be used to assess the average loss rate over time that you might expect from all the different likelihoods and severities of future cyber attacks. This is known as the 'expected loss', and is the equivalent of how much you would need to put away in savings each year to pay for all future cyber losses. Perhaps more importantly, it tells you the likelihood of an event occurring that would result in an 'unacceptable' level of loss to your organization.

### 1.5.2    A Framework for Risk Assessment

It is useful to calculate your risk profile in this way, even though there are large uncertainties in the estimation of likelihood of future cyber losses. Risk varies over time, and for different environments in which organizations operate. Most organizations experience many attempted cyber attacks, and with good security systems in place, their vulnerability rates are low, so the chances of experiencing a cyber loss in any given period are relatively small. However, some cyber attacks do succeed and losses occur. We note the losses that occur across the entire population of organizations, and observe how often and how severely they happen to companies that are similar to yours, even if you yourself have not experienced a loss. You could experience a future cyber loss as a result of unknown vulnerabilities in your trusted systems, attacker ingenuity using techniques you have not foreseen, failures in your security processes, human error, malicious insiders, alignment of multiple unexpected events, or other unpredictable circumstances. We try to capture this in the framework of assessing the risk profile of the frequency and severity of potential cyber losses for an organization.

### 1.5.3 Risk Tolerance of Your Organization

Some companies may tolerate the occasional minor loss from cyber attacks. In fact, it may be too costly relative to the value to make an organization invulnerable and to prevent any cyber loss occurrence at all. But most companies want to avoid having a severe loss above a certain threshold, particularly one that will cause reputation damage, lead to missing earnings targets, materially damage the balance sheet, trigger a rating downgrade, or threaten the viability of the organization itself.

The point of estimating a cyber risk profile for an organization is to assess the value and effectiveness of measures taken to reduce the risk of an unacceptable loss. Each organization has its own risk tolerance and, implicitly or explicitly, manages its businesses to this tolerance, investing in security or imposing procedural change to reduce risks that are unacceptable. We believe that risk management decisions should be based on objective assessments of risk, and be as evidence-based as possible. You should be able to estimate how various security measures and risk mitigation processes will affect your risk profile, and to justify their implementation by how much they will reduce the risk of unacceptable loss. This book sets out a framework for risk assessment and tries to provide information that will help you make some of the estimates you need to assess the risk profile of your organization.

Cyber risk profiles vary significantly from one organization to another. The main attributes of an organization, its size and the types of activities it engages in, provide a benchmark for the base level of risk of enterprises of that type. There are many individual characteristics, however, that make a difference to an organization and determine how far above or below it is relative to the average risk rate of its peer group.

### 1.5.4 Risk of Cyber Catastrophes

In addition to the potential for a severe loss to an individual organization, there is the potential for multiple organizations to be impacted in a single event, which we have termed a cyber catastrophe. The likelihood of cyber catastrophes is an important factor in determining how much effort we, as a society, should put into reducing cyber risk. The risk of a catastrophe occurring is relatively low, but the potential impact could be very severe on our economy, living standards, and way of life. It similarly ranges in a continuum of severity, from events like *WannaCry* and *NotPetya* that cost billions of dollars through to potential scenarios where cyber attacks could cost the economy trillions of dollars and destabilize our way of life. We consider these as risk curves too, with the severity of events ranked against how probable we think they might be, illustrated in Figure 1.2.

## 1.6 HOW MUCH DOES CYBER RISK COST OUR SOCIETY?

In this book, we argue that the costs to our economy and disruption to our way of life being posed by cyber attacks are unacceptable, and that they can be reduced and managed to acceptable levels with collective action, individual responsibility, and appropriate resourcing. Cyber risk is a relatively new risk, and is different from the types of risks that society has faced, and dealt with, in the past.

To know how to manage it, we first need to know how much of a problem it is. Measuring a problem as objectively as possible allows us to make rational decisions about protection and resources.

### 1.6.1 Collecting Information on Cyber Loss Incidents

It is difficult to estimate exactly how much cyber loss incidents cost our society. Some of the losses, particularly those suffered by private companies, are kept confidential. However, many are reported and are on the public record. Any data breaches that compromise personal information are now required to be officially notified and publicized. Incidents that affect shareholders or have wider implications usually find their way into media reports. Larger losses tend to become public. In addition, insured companies claim cyber losses from their insurers, and the authors have worked with insurance companies that have shared their confidential claims statistics. So we believe we have a fairly good representation of the level at which cyber activity is occurring, and can be relatively sure that we have a fairly complete record of the largest events that happen.

For this book we are grateful to Risk Management Solutions, Inc., for the use of its Cyber Loss Experience Database, which is one of the most comprehensive compilations existing; it has identified some 60,000 cyber loss incidences in organizations worldwide from 2007 to 2018, and records hundreds of new events each month.[44] We compare this with the population of organizations that could potentially suffer a cyber loss of these types, derived from census statistics. We take the average rates and patterns of cyber occurrence seen over the past five years and trend them to estimate the annual cost to the global economy at 2019 values.

### 1.6.2 Incident Rate in Advanced Economies

This analysis suggests that in the most advanced economies at least 1% of large companies (those with more than 500 employees) suffer a large and disruptive cyber loss once a year on average. There are also many additional cyber loss incidents that occur to smaller and medium-size companies, of lesser magnitude and cost. Very large losses occur much less often than smaller losses, but when they do, they result in destabilization of a business, which can lose revenues over the following months as a result of the event, and with consequences for the company's suppliers and counterparties.

### 1.6.3 Costs of Cyber Attacks to the US Economy

We estimate that in United States the direct costs of payouts and operational disruption to organizations from cyber attacks is averaging around *$20 billion a year*. A further *$225 billion of lost revenues* is suffered by businesses that are impacted so severely that they suffer consequential business loss. Their trading partners and counterparties suffer as a result, and add a further $270 billion of economic loss. In total we estimate that cyber losses cost over *$500 billion a year to the US economy*, which is around *2.5% of US gross domestic product (GDP)*.

### 1.6.4 Cyber Risk Levels Across the World

Cyber losses in the United States are mirrored by similar losses around the world. Cyber loss is a unique problem in that it is not geographically bounded. Cyber losses have been recorded in more than 150 countries. The number of losses that occur varies significantly from country to country, but this is rapidly converging as nearly all major economies of the world see their information technology systems and data resources come under attack. The costs of cyber events vary significantly in different jurisdictions. Figure 1.3 shows our mapping of the cyber risk across 200 countries, measured by frequency and severity of loss occurring in these economies.

Cyber risk is still highly concentrated in the most IT-dependent economies. We estimate that 90% of all cyber loss by value currently occurs in 18 countries, which between them contribute around 50% of the world's GDP. Around 60 countries account for 99% of cyber loss.

### 1.6.5 Global Costs of Cyber Attacks

Taking the loss incidence rates across the affected countries, and taking the costs of different types and severities of cyber loss in those jurisdictions, we

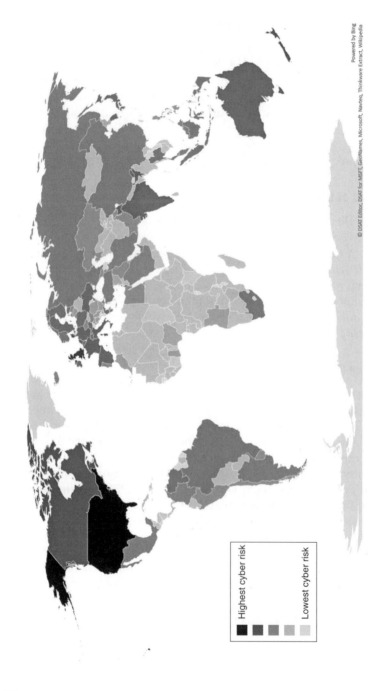

**FIGURE 1.3** Cyber catastrophes, their potential impacts, and their estimated likelihoods.

Highest cyber risk

Lowest cyber risk

Powered by Bing

© DSAT Editor, DSAT for MSFT, GeoNames, Microsoft, Navteq, Thinkware Extract, Wikipedia

estimate that for organizations across the world, the total direct costs of payouts and operational disruption from cyber attacks each year *exceeds $65 billion*. A further *$725 billion is lost in revenues* by enterprises that are impacted so severely that they suffer a significant level of consequential business loss. This affects their trading partners and counterparties, who also suffer as a result, and this adds a further $820 billion of loss to the economy. In total we estimate that cyber losses cost *over $1.5 trillion a year to the global economy*, just under 2% of the global world product.

### 1.6.6   Trends of Future Cyber Risk

The estimates here are based on the current levels of cyber activity. These levels of cyber activity are increasing almost everywhere in the world. In addition to the absolute number of cyber attacks increasing, the average size of cyber loss is increasing: a greater proportion of cyber incidents are large losses, possibly as a result of the increasing professionalization of the cyber hacking community. It is likely that cyber risk in on the increase for the foreseeable future.

### 1.6.7   Risk of Future Cyber Catastrophes

As we have described, the current run rate of losses being experienced from cyber attacks is only part of the risk landscape from cyber threats. Any analysis of the threat of cyber events needs to include the potential for large catastrophic losses to occur that would have major impacts on the economy and on society in general. We cannot assess the likelihood of these occurring with any certainty, but we can make reasonably objective judgments on some order of magnitude of likelihood, based on the rarity of other types of economic shocks and the difficulties of enabling cyber attacks on this scale. Figure 1.2 shows the magnitude of potential economic consequences of cyber catastrophes discussed in Sections 1.1.2 and 1.1.3, with our assessment of the odds of an event as severe as this one occurring within the next year, in any of the advanced markets in the digital economy. We include uncertainty around our estimates. Any analysis of the cost of cyber risk to the economy should include an allowance for the potential for these low-likelihood events with severe consequences. If our economy had to put away funds each year to save up for the costs of these future catastrophes, we would need to put aside around an additional $70 billion to $100 billion each year as catastrophe loading on the economic costs of cyber risk.

### 1.6.8    Working Together to Solve Cyber Risk

Cyber risk presents a clear and present danger to the functioning of our society and the well-being of our economy. The prosperity that information technology has played such a role in creating for the mainstream populations of the developed economies is now under threat. Cyber risk is not just eroding a steady tax of around 2% on our economic output; it also holds the danger of cascading into massive economic shocks of potentially trillions of dollars.

Solving this risk will not be easy. There is no magic bullet to making cyber risk go away. Individual organizations can install expensive security systems to protect themselves, but this does not stop the threat from raging outside their firewalls, seeking any weakness to attack. No individual organization can solve cyber risk on its own. There are many different stakeholders that need to work together to reduce the drivers, motivations, weaknesses, reward systems, and methods of doing business to change the pattern of risk.

Cyber risk is an unprecedented threat. It will need radically new approaches to solving this risk. This book proposes that we need to take a fresh view at cyber risk, and not be afraid of challenging orthodox approaches.

In the coming chapters we explain cyber risk.

Chapter 2, 'Preparing for Cyber Attacks', gives an overview and examples of the five most costly and significant causes of cyber loss, and how the risk of each of them can be measured and assessed. This chapter includes a short management exercise to prepare your organization for the possibility of experiencing these kinds of loss and to take action to reduce their risk.

Chapter 3, 'Cyber Enters the Physical World,' describes cyber risk to industrial control systems and devices that control our physical world. It outlines the growth of the internet of things (IoT) and how these risks can be managed, both by the manufacturers of the devices and by the users of them in systems.

Chapter 4, 'Ghosts in the Code', covers the issues of vulnerabilities in software, and how these are exploited by threat actors. It describes ways to quantify vulnerabilities, and methods to increase the motivations to reduce the frequency of their occurrence and so reduce cyber risk.

Chapter 5, 'Know Your Enemy', describes the seven generic categories of threat actor that are the key malicious perpetrators of cyber attacks, and describes their different motivations, capabilities, and techniques. It outlines 'hackonomics', the representation of cyber risk in terms of the business models of different actors and how to consider the threat from the point of view of the risks and the rewards of the perpetrators.

Chapter 6, 'Measuring the Cyber Threat', provides a structure for analyzing the frequency and severity of cyber attacks, and how past examples can be used to explore the counterfactuals of how major cyber events could have turned out differently, and what they tell us about future risk.

Chapter 7, 'Rules, Regulations, and Law Enforcement', covers the rules and regulations that govern the incentives and penalties for organizations managing cyber risk, the complex legal environment, and the law enforcement processes that are trying to combat cyber risk.

Chapter 8, 'The Cyber Resilient Organization', provides an overview of strategies that organizations can use to manage their cyber risk, the levels of investment being made by typical companies, and techniques for optimizing the resilience of an organization.

Chapter 9, 'Cyber Insurance', describes the growing market for cyber insurance, what protection it provides, and the costs and benefits of different aspects of coverage. It describes the challenges for insurance companies managing portfolios of cyber risk and discusses what it will take for the market to meet the demands for risk transfer from the corporate sector.

Chapter 10, 'Security Economics and Strategies', considers the issues of prioritizing cyber security measures in an organization, and measuring the costs and benefits of different tools and processes. It describes the roles of information security officers and risk management at different levels within the organization. It outlines the issues for society in creating incentives for bug discovery and the game theory principles for managing the constant war between attackers and defenders.

Chapter 11, 'Ten Cyber Problems', articulates some of the key issues that currently face security professionals, policy makers, regulators, and the risk managers of organizations in reducing cyber risk in the future.

Chapter 12, 'Cyber Future', considers how the future of cyber risk could evolve, contrasting a pessimistic future where failure to protect the growing digital economy causes financial dysfunction against an optimistic future where cyber risk is minimized and results in beneficial economic growth. We describe key themes for the future, and make 10 recommendations for solving cyber risk.

This book provides a broad overview of cyber risk – its characteristics, its causes, and its potential impact on different enterprises and business activities. We discuss how best to mitigate and protect yourself and your organization from the threat of cyber risk.

And we propose how we can collectively work together to solve cyber risk.

## ENDNOTES

1. Security Week (2014).
2. McAfee (2014).
3. Shu et al. (2017).
4. McAfee (2014).
5. Shu et al. (2017).
6. Krebs (2014).
7. Perlroth (2014).
8. Target (2013).
9. Griswold (2015).
10. Griswold (2015).
11. *Forbes* (2014).
12. Cisco (2017). Survey of 3,000 security personnel.
13. Ponemon Institute (2017b).
14. Cisco (2017). Survey of 3,000 security personnel.
15. Yahoo's share price dropped 6.5% after it announced the largest-ever data breach of a billion personal records in December 2016. Sherman, Moritz, and Womack (2016).
16. Ponemon Institute (2017b); HelpNetSecurity (2017); Seals (2017).
17. Equifax, a consumer credit rating organization, had its outlook lowered to negative by Standard & Poor's as a result of its data breach in September 2017. Cherney (2017).
18. Nayana, an internet service provider in South Korea, declared bankruptcy after being hit by *Erebus* ransomware that froze its operations in June 2017. BBC (June 2017).
19. Nortel, a Canadian telecommunications company, filed for bankruptcy in January 2009. Analysts cite cyber theft of its IP among reasons for Nortel being outcompeted in the market by Chinese competitors. Reference GW.
20. Equifax faced a class action lawsuit for up to $70 billion brought by law companies Olsen Daines PC and Geragos & Geragos as a result of its data breach in September 2017, at a time when its valuation was $17 billion. Mosendz (2017).
21. Yahoo's acquisition by Verizon was significantly renegotiated after Yahoo's admission of large-scale data breach incidents, taking the original valuation of $4.8 billion down by $300 million. *Financial Times* (2017).
22. CCRS (2014a).
23. We use the definitions of the US Bureau of the Census in categorizing companies by size in terms of their numbers of employees.
24. Reinsurance (2018).
25. Reinsurance News (2017).
26. AIG (2016).
27. *Leakomania* scenario in RMS (2016).
28. *Extortion Spree*, RMS (2016).
29. *Mass DDoS*, RMS (2016).

30. Cloud Compromise, RMS (2016).
31. ICS Attacks, RMS (2017).
32. E-ISAC (2016).
33. *Erebos* ('Business Blackout') scenario, CCRS and Lloyd's (2015).
34. UK Critical Infrastructure Cyber Catastrophe Scenario, CCRS (2016b).
35. *Global Banking & Finance Review* (2017); Lannin (2017); Gurdgiev (2017).
36. World Economic Forum (2016).
37. Reinhart and Rogoff (2011).
38. Taylor (2010).
39. *Sybil Logic Bomb* scenario, in Ruffle et al. (2014).
40. d'Ancona (2017).
41. *The Times* (2017).
42. Reuters Staff (2016).
43. *China-Japan Geopolitical Conflict* scenario, in CCRS (2014).
44. Cyber Loss Experience Database maintained by Risk Management Solutions, Inc., made available to the authors for this publication.

# CHAPTER 2

# Preparing for Cyber Attacks

## 2.1 CYBER LOSS PROCESSES

Organizations suffer losses from a cyber attack, or failure of their information technology (IT) systems, in a number of different ways. Loss might be the disruption to business operations, or costs that the organization might incur as a result of the cyber event. 'Risk' is defined as the likelihood of loss. Assessing cyber risk entails estimating the likelihood of an organization experiencing different levels and types of loss.

These can be broken down into a number of key loss processes, for example:

- Data exfiltration
- Contagious malware attacks
- Denial of service attacks
- Financial transaction theft
- Failures of counterparties or suppliers

This is not an exhaustive list of loss processes. In the next chapter, 'Cyber Enters the Physical World', we consider losses from cyber attacks on physical control systems. There are many other ways that losses could occur, including human error, accidents, and mechanical failures; network failures and disruption to communication protocols; insider threats and malicious acts of sabotage; and others. However, the key loss processes described here are estimated to account for around 90% of the economic losses that businesses suffer as a result of cyber attacks and technology failures.[1] Each of them is a distinctively different loss process with its own implications for cyber risk management and mitigation. We describe each of them in turn.

## 2.2   DATA EXFILTRATION

The highest-profile cyber incidents are data breaches, as in the example in the previous chapter of the attack on Target Corporation: the loss of confidential data from companies that breach the privacy of their customers, employees, clients, or counterparties.

Companies keep thousands of documents and files that may be confidential or highly secret. If these fall into the wrong hands, they may reveal sensitive financial information about the business, intellectual property that provides competitive advantages to rivals, or information that can be publicized to damage the reputation of the company. Leaked email correspondence can be used against individuals and organizations. Failure to protect confidential information has had consequences for businesses that include devaluation of their share prices, downgrades of credit ratings, litigation against them, regulatory fines, resignation of senior executives, loss of customers, cancellation of major contracts with counterparties, and failures of mergers.

Personal confidential data such as identification credentials, payment card information, and healthcare records about individual people that finds its way into the wrong hands can be used for identity theft, to conduct fraudulent transactions, to steal money from bank accounts, to blackmail or demand ransom from the individual, or for other activities that are harmful to the data owner.

The loss of personal confidential data is increasingly regulated across the world, which requires a company to make a timely public notification that these records have been lost, notify the individuals affected, and assist them with managing the consequences of the breach of privacy, including paying financial compensation, and may incur regulatory fines. It is also possible that companies can face litigation, including class actions from the people affected.

### 2.2.1   Protecting Your Data

The types of data that might be at risk of exfiltration are shown in Table 2.1, together with a suggested data classification policy.

Many companies now operate procedures to protect their data, and it is common in larger companies to use a sensitive data management system to identify internal data, track its usage, and control the access to it. First, the data that the company holds is reviewed in a data audit, classifying each type of data by its level of sensitivity and security required, for example, 'Public', 'Sensitive', 'Restricted', and 'Secret'. Second, data in categories requiring

**TABLE 2.1**  Data potentially at risk of exfiltration, with suggested data classification policy.

| Category | Data Type | Description |
|---|---|---|
| *Regulated data* | | |
| | Personally identifiable information (PII) | Credentials such as full name, contact details (address, email, telephone), date of birth, Social Security number, passport number, and driver's license details |
| | Sensitive personal data (SPD) | Regulated sensitive data on personnel, employees, or third parties may include racial or ethnic origin; political affiliation; religious beliefs; membership of a trade union; physical or mental health or condition; sexual orientation; criminal history, convictions, or alleged commissions of offenses; internal disciplinary proceedings or performance censures on record |
| | Payment card and credit card information (PCI) | Financial information such as credit card number, PIN, bank account number and access credentials, credit history or ratings of individuals |
| | Protected health information (PHI) | Medical information such as healthcare records, tests and procedures, insurance plan details, biometric identifiers, medical device identifiers, and serial numbers |
| *Commercially confidential information (CCI)* | | |
| | Customer accounts, passwords, and contact management databases | Information about customers, account information, log-in credentials into online access portals, contact management databases with lists of prospects, contact details, credit checks |
| | Trade secrets and intellectual property | Intellectual property owned by the business; patents held, granted, or filed; pre-patent information; internally written software code; documentation of business processes; research and development; product design; blueprints and business methodology information |
| | Proprietary business information | Trademarks and copyright information; organizational and internal confidential information; market research and competitive landscape information; merger and acquisition analysis |

*(continued)*

**TABLE 2.1**    (*Continued*)

| Category | Data Type | Description |
|---|---|---|
| | Confidential information about counterparties | Customers' and suppliers' contracts and other third-party businesses, invoicing, bids, proposals, credit history, ratings, and applications; contractor performance or payment bonds; competitor information |
| | Operational management and security | Security and safety information, IT vulnerabilities identified, data on health and safety, accidents and responses, complaints and grievance management |
| *Financially sensitive information (FSI)* | | |
| | Payroll | Employee data, salaries, and benefits; bank account information; pay grades; social security; expenses |
| | Accounting and business management information | Revenue, expenditures, tax returns, departmental budgets, sales targets, profitability metrics, subsidiaries |
| | Contract information | Contracts, billing, late payments, credit extended; |
| | Investments | Financial investment assets under management, portfolio performance history, brokerage and investment manager details |
| | Insurance | Insurance policies in place, past and current claims made under policies, intermediary information |
| *Valuation-sensitive information (VSI)* | | |
| | Price-sensitive information | 'Inside information' as defined by the Financial Services Authority, for example information about issuers of qualifying investments that is not generally available, and that would have a significant effect on qualifying or related investments |
| *Sensitive information* | | |
| | Correspondence | Email archives (companies are obliged to retain these for several years); letters |

protection is subject to processes such as restricting the number of people who have access to it, implementing access controls and recording access incidents, prohibiting copies to mobile devices and media, and encrypting data both when it is in transit across a network and at rest. And third, users are educated in the sensitivity of the data that they work with and are trained in their role in keeping it safe.

## 2.2.2 Regulation and Data

Data breach is international, with data exfiltration events being reported in most of the countries of the world where digital business is transacted.

The regulatory requirement for organizations to notify the loss of personal confidential data has been in place longest in the United States, where it has been a requirement in most states since 2002. Since then there have been many thousands of notified events. The number of reported events grew very rapidly after 2009, but peaked in the years 2013 to 2016, and has been at a similar level or less in subsequent years.

In the United States since 2012, on average there have been at least 580 incidents a year of data breach involving more than 1,000 personal records (a P3 or greater) and at least 90 a year of more than 100,000 records (a P5 or greater) (Table 2.2).

## 2.2.3 Causes of Data Exfiltration Loss

Data exfiltration occurs through accidental loss, insider exfiltration, or malicious external action. The relative proportions of events from these causes

**TABLE 2.2**  Data breach loss severity scale for number of personal records (PII, PCI, PHI) in data exfiltration, with statistics for United States, 2012 to mid-2018.

| Data Breach Severity Scale | Range (Min to Max Number of Personal Data Records) | Number of Regulatory Reported Events by US Organizations (Since 2012) | As a Percentage of the Total (%) |
|---|---|---|---|
| P3 | 1,000 to 10,000 | 2,022 | 58 |
| P4 | 10,000 to 100,000 | 918 | 26 |
| P5 | 100,000 to 1 million | 324 | 9 |
| P6 | 1 million to 10 million | 162 | 5 |
| P7 | 10 million to 100 million | 50 | 1.4 |
| P8 | 100 million to 1 billion | 19 | 0.5 |
| P9 | More than 1 billion | 2 | 0.1 |

have changed over time. Before around 2010, two-thirds of incidents where data was compromised was through accidents – typically unsecured laptops or unencrypted data media being lost. Since around 2012 the proportion of events due to accidents has decreased – mainly due to routine encryption of laptops and improved security awareness in employees – but there has been a rapid increase in malicious external attacks to steal data, until it has become the cause of three-quarters of data exfiltration incidents.

Data exfiltration from insiders has been a constant threat throughout the history of reporting, with around 10% of all data losses being attributed to accredited employees selling, giving, or publishing confidential data to an external source. Insider threat – or whistle-blowing – became more common for a few years after 2010, accounting for around 20% of leaks in 2012, but reducing back to around the previous rate of 10% of events from around 2014 onwards. It may be no coincidence that this trend in corporate whistle-blowing coincided with the emerging popularity of WikiLeaks, a site established to publish and popularize government secrets, and that the trend diminished following high-profile warrants, pursuits, and asylum-taking of some of the high-profile promoters of insider action, Julian Assange in 2012 and Edward Snowden in 2013.

### 2.2.4 Costs of Data Exfiltration

When a personal data breach occurs in an organization, the costs and consequences can be severe. The company is required to notify the regulatory authorities rapidly (different jurisdictions require notifications within different periods, ranging from 15 days to a month). The company is required to make a public announcement, and to notify each individual affected – some regulations require a written communication to every person. The company may need to handle large numbers of enquiries from concerned people who want to know if they have been affected. Individuals who have had their personal data compromised are entitled to credit monitoring services for a period of time in case they suffer identity theft. Those who suffer loss will require being compensated. Some may elect to bring a lawsuit against the company. Regulators typically impose fines on the company for its failure in the duty of trust. The organization also faces internal costs from dealing with the breach, including a forensic investigation to identify and rectify any IT system vulnerability that was the cause of the breach, installation of higher levels of security, and disruption to its business practice while it deals with the immediate aftermath of the event.

These direct costs can be significant, potentially hundreds of millions of dollars. Figure 2.1 shows the total reported costs from a collection of data breach events involving the loss of personal data.

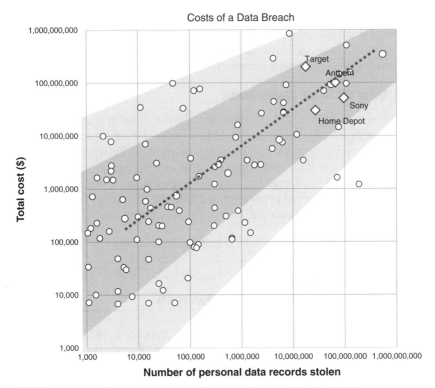

**FIGURE 2.1** Costs of US data breaches by size of breach (2012–2017).

This shows that the costs do not scale exactly with the number of data records stolen, but the larger the data breach event, the higher the costs. Events involving the loss of around 10,000 records average a direct cost of about $30 per record, whereas events of 100 million records average around $1 per record.

Past events have varied widely around these averages, and different factors can change these costs by two orders of magnitude in either direction.

The type of data stolen is important: for a breach of 10,000 records, it will cost a company 1.5 times as much for PCI records than for personally identifiable information (PII), and 5.5 times as much for protected health information (PHI) records. Other factors increasing the costs of a data breach may include delays in discovering or announcing the event, high losses being suffered by the victims, poor media management, and litigation costs.

The average cost per record of a data loss of more than 100,000 records more than doubled from 2010 to 2016.[2] This reflects increasing regulatory fines and procedures, growing costs of compensation, and escalation of legal complexities in dealing with identity loss.

### 2.2.5    Other Costs and Consequences

In Chapter 1, Section 1.2.4, we described how the indirect costs of a data breach can be more severe than the direct costs. The reputational damage causes customer desertion, revenues dip, market share is lost, executives resign, share prices fall, and suppliers and counterparties suffer in turn. Credit ratings are downgraded and the viability of a company can be threatened. The impact of experiencing a data breach can go far beyond the direct costs, and can impact the brand, the reputation, and the viability of the company itself.

---

**MANAGEMENT EXERCISE:
DATA EXFILTRATION CRISIS MANAGEMENT PLAN**

The way that organizations deal with a data breach event can make a major difference to its costs and consequences. Identify the most valuable and sensitive set of data assets held by your organization, using Table 2.1 to prioritize. Now imagine that your organization finds evidence that a copy of this data set has been exfiltrated (ignore your IT security team, who tell you that their advanced protection measures mean that this couldn't possibly happen). Develop a response plan for the next three days and one for the next month, identifying who would be responsible for each task, and the budget implications of each. Ensure that you have:

- a plan for IT investigation and response
- a plan for managing customer communications and enquiries, and providing fair compensation
- a plan for media response, brand promotion, and investor analyst communications. Is it possible to use the crisis as an opportunity to promote the business?

Finally, review your internal security measures in place and scope the budget and organizational changes that would be required to make a material reduction in the likelihood of this event occurring.

## 2.3 CONTAGIOUS MALWARE INFECTION

Malware that can replicate and spread throughout our networks of communication, causing harm to the user community, has been one of the longest-standing cyber threats. Broad categories of malware include 'virus' – computer code inside a host program; 'worm' – a stand-alone piece of compiled software as a program that can replicate itself; and 'Trojan horse' – a program that appears to do one thing but actually does something different.

### 2.3.1 *Melissa*, 1999

One of the earliest damaging examples of malware was the *Melissa* virus, which choked corporate, private, and government email networks in 1999. It was transmitted through email with a Microsoft Word attachment that when opened contained a macro that sent a copy of itself to the top 50 people in the recipient's contact list. The volume of email traffic generated was so large that it caused some companies to discontinue their email service and resulted in the perpetrator, David L. Smith, receiving a 20-month jail sentence.

### 2.3.2 *ILOVEYOU*, 2000

*Melissa* was followed a year later by the *ILOVEYOU* stand-alone worm, which similarly was sent by infected emails and attacked tens of millions of Windows personal computers in 2000, stealing passwords, deleting and replacing files, replicating itself multiple times, and generating more traffic. In contrast to *Melissa*'s limited distribution method of 50 contacts, *ILOVEYOU* sent copies of itself to everyone in the entire Windows Address Book, making it much more prolific. Within 10 days more than 50 million infections had been reported. At its peak, it is estimated that a quarter of the world's entire email traffic was *ILOVEYOU* messages. It apparently emanated from the Philippines, although no one was ever charged. Some estimates put the cleanup and disruption costs at $10 billion to $15 billion.[3]

### 2.3.3 Generations of Malware

Many more generations of self-replicating malware have since seen circulation, each with a different payload and mechanism of spread and infection. Names like *Conficker*, *Code Red*, *Blaster*, *MyDoom*, *SQL Slammer*, *Klez*, *Nimda*, *Storm*, *Shamoon*, and *Netsky* have become notorious as damaging viruses and worms.

Table 2.3 contains examples of contagious malware outbreaks that had global impact over the past 30 years. This is not exhaustive – there have been

**TABLE 2.3** Examples of contagious malware outbreaks ranked by global impact, past 30 years.

| Name | Global Impact | Year | Type | Propagation Vector | Infection Rate | Payload Type | Destructiveness |
|---|---|---|---|---|---|---|---|
| Conficker | 1: Very high | 2008 | Worm | IP block scanning | 1: Very high | Botnet | 1: Very high |
| ILOVEYOU | 1: Very high | 2000 | Worm | Email | 1: Very high | Overwriting files | 1: Very high |
| MyDoom | 1: Very high | 2004 | Worm | Email | 2: High | DDoS | 1: Very high |
| Netsky | 1: Very high | 2004 | Worm | Email | 3: Moderate | Beeping | 1: Very high |
| Sasser | 1: Very high | 2004 | Worm | Buffer overflow | 3: Moderate | DDoS | 1: Very high |
| NotPetya | 2: High | 2017 | Virus | Software update | 3: Moderate | Wiper | 2: High |
| WannaCry | 2: High | 2017 | Worm | Random scanning | 2: High | Ransomware | 2: High |
| Stuxnet | 2: High | 2010 | Worm | Search (Siemens software) | 4: Significant | SCADA control | 1: Very high |
| SQL Slammer | 2: High | 2003 | Worm | Buffer overflow | 1: Very high | DDoS | 2: High |
| Mirai | 2: High | 2016 | Worm | WAN scanning | 1: Very high | Botnet | 3: Moderate |
| Klez | 2: High | 2001 | Worm | Email | 3: Moderate | HTML message | 1: Very high |
| Code Red | 2: High | 2001 | Worm | Buffer overflow | 3: Moderate | Website defacing, DDoS | 2: High |
| Melissa | 2: High | 1999 | Virus | Email | 3: Moderate | Spam generator | 4: Significant |
| Nimda | 2: High | 2001 | Worm | Email + web browser | 4: Significant | Ransomware | 2: High |
| Sality | 3: Moderate | 2003 | Virus | Email | 1: Very high | Keystroke logging | 2: High |
| Chernobyl | 3: Moderate | 1998 | Virus | Pirated software | 2: High | Overwriting files | 3: Moderate |
| Morris | 3: Moderate | 1988 | Worm | Multiplatform (inc. email) | 2: High | Botnet | 5: Material |
| Shamoon | 3: Moderate | 2012 | Virus | Spear phishing | 2: High | Wiper | 2: High |
| Blaster | 3: Moderate | 2003 | Worm | Random scanning | 3: Moderate | Botnet | 2: High |
| Bad Rabbit | 3: Moderate | 2017 | Worm | Corrupted software | 3: Moderate | Ransomware | 2: High |

| | | | | | | | |
|---|---|---|---|---|---|---|---|
| *Neverquest* | 3: Moderate | 2013 | Trojan | Email, web injection | 3: Moderate | Botnet | 3: Moderate |
| *Zeus* | 3: Moderate | 2007 | Trojan | Software download | 3: Moderate | Keyloggers/HTML injectors | 4: Significant |
| *CoinMiner* | 3: Moderate | 2018 | Virus | Random scanning | 3: Moderate | Cryptocurrency miner | 5: Material |
| *Locky* | 3: Moderate | 2016 | Virus | Email | 4: Significant | Ransomware | 3: Moderate |
| *Tiny Banker* | 4: Significant | 2012 | Trojan | Email | 4: Significant | Packet sniffing | 1: Very high |
| *KOVTER* | 4: Significant | 2017 | Virus | Email | 4: Significant | Click fraud | 2: High |
| *ONI/MBR-ONI* | 4: Significant | 2017 | Virus | Email | 4: Significant | Wiper | 2: High |
| *Dukakis* | 4: Significant | 1988 | Virus | Floppy disk | 5: Material | Displays a message | 5: Material |
| *SevenDust* | 4: Significant | 1998 | Virus | Email | 5: Material | Wiper | 2: High |
| *FakeAV* | 5: Material | 2007 | Trojan | Corrupting software, email | 3: Moderate | Scareware | 4: Significant |
| *Storm* | 5: Material | 2007 | Trojan | Email | 3: Moderate | Botnet | 4: Significant |
| *Magic Lantern* | 5: Material | 2001 | Trojan | Email | 5: Material | Keystroke logging | 5: Material |
| *Michelangelo* | 5: Material | 1991 | Trojan | Driver disks | 5: Material | Data destruction | 3: Moderate |

many tens of thousands of pieces of self-replicating malware that have been detected – but includes some of the worst examples of those that succeeded in infecting large numbers of devices and causing widespread disruption to organizations and individuals.

### 2.3.4  WannaCry, 2017

The proof that contagious malware continues to be a potent threat was demonstrated on May 12, 2017 when an aggressive ransomware attack via file-sharing network protocols on computers using outdated Windows XP and v8 OS resulted in 300,000 infections of computers across 150 countries. The *WannaCryptor* used a National Security Agency (NSA) exploit code-named *EternalBlue* (released to the public the previous August by hackers known as the *ShadowBrokers*). It predominantly affected personal users, public-sector organizations, and small and medium-size enterprises, affecting unpatched boxes and equipment on dedicated older operating systems. However, several dozens of large companies also reported disruption and losses from infections of their systems. Of the roughly 400 million actively used Windows computers running version 8 or an earlier operating system, approximately 0.1% were infected. The great majority of the Windows computers running version 8 or earlier were protected by a Microsoft patch MS17-010 issued two months earlier, on March 14, 2017.

The event highlighted the issue of equipment software latency, i.e. that machines and subnetworks within organizations may rely on specific versions of an operating system that render them vulnerable. In these cases, although the majority of systems within organizations ran more up-to-date operating systems, certain departments and activities were maintaining the older versions that contained the vulnerability. Machines such as medical magnetic resonance imaging (MRI) scanners and X-ray machines that were certified only on XP and v8, and maintained on those operating systems, were among those that were crippled by the attack.[4] Businesses reported substantial losses from lockouts of systems around the world, such as manufacturing processes, dispatch and ordering systems, gas pump payment applications, and telephone exchange equipment, as shown in Figure 2.2.

Estimates of the losses caused by *WannaCry* vary substantially, from tens of millions of dollars to $4 billion.[5]

If the *WannaCry* malware was created to generate ransom payments, then it was remarkably unsuccessful. The bitcoin accounts that it requested

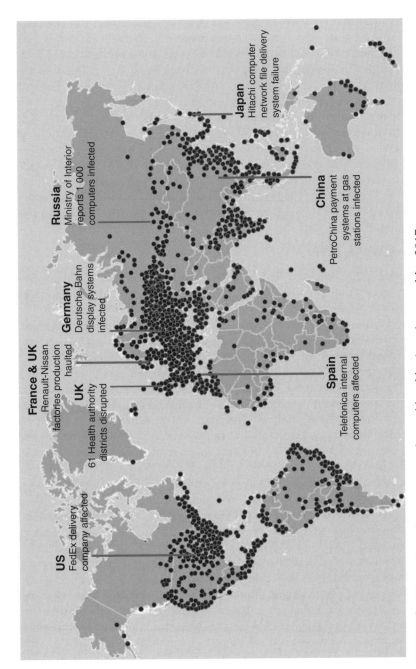

**FIGURE 2.2** *WannaCry* infections across the world and business impacts, May 2017.

payments into received less than $150,000 in payments and may not have been claimed by the criminals. No company that paid a ransom got its data back. The motivation was more likely to sabotage some of the affected companies, rather than generate funds for the hackers. It is possible that the widespread economic disruption was collateral damage to mask a targeted destructive attack on a specific organization.

The propagation of *WannaCry* was stopped after about six and a half hours by a researcher finding a kill switch within the software. Otherwise the infection could have spread to many more machines and had a more severe impact. Our counterfactual analysis suggests that if the kill switch had not been triggered, and if the attack had occurred prior to the issuing of the MS17-010 patch for Windows 8, the infection rates and losses could have been an order of magnitude higher, perhaps reaching $20 billion to $40 billion.[6]

### 2.3.5  *NotPetya*, 2017

On June 27, 2017, a virus that became known as *NotPetya*, to distinguish it from its antecedent versions of the *Petya* virus, infected several hundreds of thousands of devices and penetrated the IT networks of more than 8,000 organizations across 65 countries. Although disguised as ransomware, it was actually a destructive disk wiper. It was hidden in the software update mechanism of M.E.Doc (uk), a Ukrainian tax preparation program that is an industry standard for tax filing in Ukraine. As a result, 80% of the infections occurred in Russia and Ukraine, where more than 80 organizations initially reported being affected, including the National Bank of Ukraine, Kiev's Boryspil International Airport, and the radiation monitoring system at Ukraine's Chernobyl nuclear power plant.[7] Some 9% of the infections occurred in Germany, but they also reached France, Italy, Poland, the United Kingdom, and the United States. *NotPetya* utilized the exploit of *EternalBlue*, similarly to *WannaCry*, but enhanced it with multiple techniques to propagate throughout internal networks, including harvesting passwords and running PSExec code on other local computers. The data encryption payload was irreversible, and the ransom demand was a hoax.

A number of large multinational organizations reported significant costs and losses from business disruption, as shown in Figure 2.3.

Maersk, one of the largest shipping operations, reported that infections of the *NotPetya* virus had caused it to suspend operations in parts of its organization, causing congestion in the 76 ports it operates worldwide, and resulting in business losses of up to $300 million in the initial quarter after the attack. FedEx suspended its share dealings on the New York

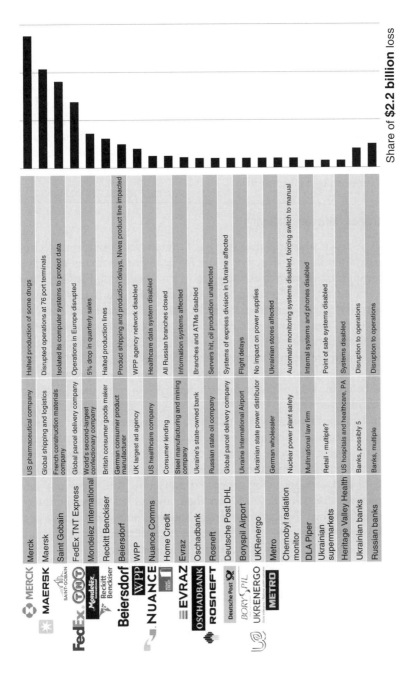

| | | | |
|---|---|---|---|
| MERCK | Merck | US pharmaceutical company | Halted production of some drugs |
| MAERSK | Maersk | Global shipping and logistics | Disrupted operations at 76 port terminals |
| SAINT-GOBAIN | Saint Gobain | French construction materials company | Isolated its computer systems to protect data |
| FedEx TNT | FedEx TNT Express | Global parcel delivery company | Operations in Europe disrupted |
| Mondelēz | Mondelez International | World's second-largest confectionary company | 5% drop in quarterly sales |
| Reckitt Benckiser | Reckitt Benckiser | British consumer goods maker | Halted production lines |
| Beiersdorf | Beiersdorf | German consumer product manufacturer | Product shipping and production delays. Nivea product line impacted |
| WPP | WPP | UK largest ad agency | WPP agency network disabled |
| NUANCE | Nuance Comms | US healthcare company | Healthcare data system disabled |
| HOME CREDIT | Home Credit | Consumer lending | All Russian branches closed |
| EVRAZ | Evraz | Steel manufacturing and mining company | Information systems affected |
| OSCHADBANK | Oschadbank | Ukraine's state-owned bank | Branches and ATMs disabled |
| ROSNEFT | Rosneft | Russian state oil company | Servers hit, oil production unaffected |
| Deutsche Post DHL | Deutsche Post DHL | Global parcel delivery company | Systems of express division in Ukraine affected |
| BORYSPIL | Boryspil Airport | Ukraine International Airport | Flight delays |
| UKRENERGO | UKRenergo | Ukrainian state power distributor | No impact on power supplies |
| METRO | Metro | German wholesaler | Ukrainian stores affected |
| | Chernobyl radiation monitor | Nuclear power plant safety | Automatic monitoring systems disabled, forcing switch to manual |
| | DLA Piper | Multinational law firm | Internal systems and phones disabled |
| | Ukrainian supermarkets | Retail - multiple? | Point of sale systems disabled |
| | Heritage Valley Health | US hospitals and healthcare, PA | Systems disabled |
| | Ukrainian banks | Banks, possibly 5 | Disruption to operations |
| | Russian banks | Banks, multiple | Disruption to operations |

Share of **$2.2 billion** loss

**FIGURE 2.3** Examples of losses caused to businesses by *NotPetya* malware, June 2017.

47

Stock Exchange after reporting $300 million costs from its TNT Express division in lost business and cleanup expenses.[8] Pharmaceutical giant Merck reported losses of $300 million a quarter for two successive quarters, from lost sales resulting from production shutdowns and failure of internal IT systems.[9] French construction materials company Saint Gobain reported a business impact of $393 million from the virus impacting its systems. More than a dozen multinational companies announced losses to quarterly earnings following the attack,[10] and there are reports of disruption to more than 30 international companies and many Ukrainian national organizations. In total, the *NotPetya* malware is estimated to have caused losses of[11] more than $10 billion.

### 2.3.6 Antivirus Software Industry

A multibillion-dollar antivirus industry has grown up to provide protection against these potentially destructive pests. Every major company and most personal computers run antivirus software in the background to catch and cleanse malware from their systems and network traffic. Antivirus software works by identifying malware from virus definitions. It contains a dictionary of templates of known malware characteristics, and compares software that it finds with these definitions. If it finds a match, it stops the code executing, quarantines it, and eradicates it safely. Typically antivirus software will also do 'heuristic checking' or 'anomaly detection' – monitoring programs for unexpected behavior that might indicate a new type of virus that isn't in its library of known malware.

The fundamental requirement is that the antivirus software has access to a dictionary: a library of known malware. Unknown malware escapes detection. Hackers writing malware that they don't want to be detected have to use a new template that is not already included in the antivirus dictionaries. New forms of malware are being generated every day. And every day new forms of malware are being detected, codified, and added to the dictionary of antivirus definitions. Typical commercial antivirus software systems contain dictionaries of thousands of types of malware in current circulation, and they issue new ones to their software at frequent intervals.

It is a constant arms race between the attackers and the antivirus defenders. The speed at which new malware can be identified and added to the antivirus dictionaries – and disseminated to all the users of the antivirus software – is a vital part of defending users. The interval between malware creation and its detection and implementation in the defenses is the opportunity for the attacker. New forms of malware that could potentially evade antivirus detection pose a constant threat to individuals and organizations.

### 2.3.7  Malware Payloads

The main concern with contagious malware is the payload that they can deliver – i.e. the activity that the software carries out when it is activated. Table 2.4 shows examples of different types of payloads of contagious malware.

The types of harm that the payloads can cause to the host system can be broadly classified into categories:

- *Deletion.* The permanent deletion of data and software from devices, for example, using disk- wiper malware or overwriters. Some malware can even find backup data and destroy or encrypt that.
- *Extortion.* The encryption of data on drives with demands for a ransom to be paid to obtain the tools to decrypt the data and regain access to files, from a wide range of ransomware.
- *Theft.* Stealing data from the device or from the infected network by finding it and transferring it out of the organization into the possession of the malware operators, using point-of-sale (PoS) harvesters, packet sniffers, credential stealers, scraper tools, and other types of payloads.
- *Fraud.* Tricking or monitoring personnel to monetize their actions, for example click fraud, keylogging, scareware, and fake security offers.
- *Hijacking.* Malware commandeers computing resources from the infected device to run programs without the user being aware, for example ad traffic generators, botnets, cryptocurrency miners, and spam bots.

This is not an exhaustive list, but it captures the main causes of loss. There are many activities that a payload could potentially do. One of the variants of *Netsky* in 2004 made the infected PC go 'beep' in the mornings. This sounds amusing but it drove users to distraction and made the machine almost impossible to use. There are grades of 'mal' in malware.

### 2.3.8  Risk of Malware Infection

The likelihood that your organization will be hit by future versions of con-tagious malware depends on how often new variants of malware originate that can bypass the protection provided by standard anti-malware security systems, how many companies the malware manages to infect, and whether your organization is among the susceptible population for the vector it uses.

In measuring the infectiousness of a virus, we distinguish between the total number of devices infected (many of which will be less well

**TABLE 2.4** Examples of different types of payloads of contagious malware, ranked by the severity of the consequences it can potentially inflict on the host system.

| Payload | Description | Harm |
|---|---|---|
| Wiper | Wipes the hard drive or permanently encrypts data | Deletion |
| Ransomware | Blocks/encrypts access to data unless a ransom is paid | Extortion |
| Overwriter | Overwrites the entire host file system that it attacks (old-school wiper) | Deletion |
| Point-of-sale harvester | Once in a system, the PoS malware selects data to steal and uploads to a remote server | Theft |
| Credential stealer | Steals private and personal information from infected systems | Theft |
| Packet sniffer/form grabber | A tool that intercepts data flowing in a network | Theft |
| Scraper tools | Screen, web, or memory scraping of information without the consent of the host user | Theft |
| Click fraud | Imitates legitimate software, malware, or advertisements to mislead victim | Fraud |
| Keylogging | Program designed to secretly monitor and log all keystrokes | Fraud |
| Fake security offer | Misleads users to think that they have a virus on their computer and to pay for fake malware removal tools | Fraud |
| Scareware | Programs designed to trick computer users into visiting malware-infected websites | Fraud |
| Ad traffic generator | Automated software imitates the action of users to click on web browser advertisements | Hijack |
| Bot/botnet | Takes control of computers and organizes infected machines into networks of bots that a criminal can remotely manage | Hijack |
| Cryptocurrency mining | Uses computing power to mine for cryptocurrencies without users' knowledge | Hijack |
| Spam bot | Program to assist in the sending of spam through email, forums, Twitter, etc. | Hijack |

*Source:* Smith, Coburn, et al. (2018).

protected personal computers, tablets, or smart phones) and the number of organizations that are infected (have one or more of their devices infected within their protected network). The infectiousness depends on the replication rate, sometimes measured as the doubling time for the number of infections. The spread depends on the vector used for propagation and the size of the susceptible population that could potentially be infected due to the vulnerability being exploited by the malware. Table 2.3 shows that the most successful propagation vectors for high-impact malware have been email and scanning processes. Email uses contact networks to spread the malware. Scanning is a more random process of trial and error, generating internet protocol (IP) addresses and hoping that some of them will be susceptible to penetration by the entry ploy being used by the software.

Maximizing the levels of security on incoming email acceptance are obviously beneficial in reducing the risk of contagious malware. Routinely scanning your own organization's attack surface (i.e. all IP addresses that are externally facing) to identify IP addresses that could be vulnerable to entry ploys will assist with reducing susceptibility to infection.

A large number of malware entry ploys exploit older and unpatched versions of common commercial software. Companies that take longer to update their software systems tend to be more susceptible to malware infection. 'Patching latency' – the average age and versioning of software running in an organization, relative to the latest version available – is a measure of a company's security diligence and susceptibility to malware infection.

The severity of a malware infection once it has penetrated an organization is determined by the number of devices that are ultimately infected and the types and functions of the infected devices. Business operations are clearly more disrupted if large numbers of devices are infected. When Maersk was infected by the *NotPetya* virus, this required the reinstallation of 45,000 machines, more than 50% of the machines on the company's internal network, taking 10 days and inflicting business losses of at least $300 million. Other organizations infected with *NotPetya* were luckier and had only a small number of infected machines. The lateral propagation of malware within an organization determines the likely severity of impact on the business. Lateral propagation is mainly driven by the malware programming and its ability to replicate within a network without detection and prevention by network traffic monitoring systems. The architecture of the IT network can also assist in reducing the impact of a contagious infection. Where it is possible to isolate business-critical systems and essential servers from the main networks, and to segment the IT network into smaller subnetworks with protected gateways between them, this can minimize the business impact of an infection.

Malware can be combated by rapidly publishing its indicators of compromise, so that these can be added to anti-malware detection dictionaries and prevent further spread. The speed at which the exploits used by the malware can be patched by the vendors of the exploited software is important, as is the urgency in installing the patch by the user community, to curtail spread. Some malware may contain a kill switch, typically in the code for its own internal development and testing, which, if found and controlled fast enough, can halt the spread of the virus. The speed and effectiveness of internal IT teams can also mitigate the severity of the business impact when faced with an infection if they are able to isolate infected machines quickly, identify the extent of infection, and develop countermeasures or work-arounds.

Some of the worst impact on an organization can be inflicted by a ransomware infection, and this is one of the most prevalent types of contagious malware in circulation. In the next sections we describe ransomware as one of the more severe types of contagious malware.

### 2.3.9 Ransomware

A particularly pernicious form of malware locks and encrypts files and demands a ransom payment to unlock the data. Ransomware has been a common method of extorting individuals using personal computers and small businesses for some years. There are many examples of ransomware that have been developed since the first generation came into circulation around 2005, from early programs in 1989. The most common type is crypto ransomware that encrypts files, but there is also locker ransomware that disables a computer, server, or other hardware.

Most of these PC ransomware programs operate in a similar way. They usually infect a personal computer through an email that appears to be a legitimate invoice, utility bill, or image, or from the user visiting a website. Once the computer is infected, the hardware and software continue to work while personal files such as documents, pictures, and spreadsheets become encrypted, at which point the user is confronted with a pop-up screen demanding a payment to unlock the data and providing a telephone number or other methods of providing payment. Ransom demands range from $25 to $500, averaging around $300. Only a small proportion of victims pay the ransom (around 3%), but this is enough to generate significant incomes for the perpetrators.

Bitcoin, a digital currency, and other cryptocurrencies, such as Monero, Ethereum, Ripple, and BitCoinCash, have made it easier to monetize cyber attacks semi-anonymously. Prior to cryptocurrencies, hackers used to ask for payment vouchers, such as MoneyPak, PaySafe, or iTunes gift cards, which they could resell. Cryptocurrencies have enabled the rapid growth of the ransomware industry, facilitating the untraceable monetization of the ransom demand.

It is difficult to estimate the extent of ransomware success – how many personal and small businesses are infected and pay up – because these events often go unreported. However, one operation, *CryptoWall*, is reported to have earned $18 million from US citizens between April 2014 and June 2015, suggesting it might have extorted as many as 100,000 victims in a single year. Worldwide, *CryptoWall* is estimated by the Cyber Threat Alliance to have earned almost 20 times that much ($325 million).

## 2.3.10 Cyber Extortion Attacks on Larger Organizations

Cyber extortion has become increasingly more ambitious, targeting organizations that can afford higher payoffs or that are likely to pay for large numbers of devices to be unlocked. Although ransomware that encrypts data and locks computers is the most common type of extortion, companies may also be asked to make payoffs to avert the threat of other cyber attack types, including denial of service attacks, data exfiltration breaches, and sabotage to deny a company internet or cloud services. Table 2.5 provides examples of large organizations that are reported to have made ransom payments in response to cyber attacks, typically involving ransomware. The costs of business disruption are typically much higher than the ransom payment.

Ransomware incidents are reported more commonly in certain industries, namely healthcare, telecommunications, computer system design, and chemical and drug manufacturing sectors, while some sectors, such as manufacturing, food, and agriculture, have reported a comparably low number of incidents. Financial institutions are prime targets for extortion attacks. Small and medium-size companies have seen a higher incidence of customized malware attacks on their businesses.

Public-sector organizations and government departments are not immune: local administrations in Italy are reported to have paid ransoms of about €400 (US$440) to recover corrupted files. Even a US police department in Tewksbury, Massachusetts, near Boston, notoriously paid $750 in bitcoin to prevent its files from being lost.

Perhaps most perniciously, hospitals and healthcare institutions have been repeatedly targeted by cyber extortionists, possibly because hospital managers typically, and understandably, put the well-being of their patients first and have shown a propensity to pay up. Several facilities and clinics in the United States, Germany, and elsewhere have experienced potentially life-threatening failures to their computer systems accompanied by demands for payment to restore IT functionality.[12] Payments in the ranges of thousands of dollars and tens of thousands of dollars have reportedly been made, usually in bitcoin. Examples include the Hollywood Presbyterian Medical Center in California, which paid a $17,000 bitcoin ransom in February 2016 for the decryption key for patient data.[13] Several MedStar

**TABLE 2.5** Examples of ransom payments reported to have been paid by large organizations hit by cyber extortion attacks.

| Organization Affected | Date | Ransom Amount Allegedly Paid | US$ |
|---|---|---|---|
| Nokia | 2014 | 'Several millions' | $?,000,000 |
| Three Greek banks | 2015 | €7 million each | $7,507,500 |
| Two Indian conglomerates | 2015 | $5 million each | $5,000,000 |
| UAE Bank | 2015 | $3 million | $3,000,000 |
| Nayana, ISP provider, South Korea | 2017 | $1 million | $1,000,000 |
| Rubber Estate Nigeria Limited | 2015 | N35 million | $176,000 |
| TalkTalk | 2015 | £80,000 | $117,000 |
| CD Universe | 2000 | $100,000 | $100,000 |
| Domino's Pizza | 2014 | £24,000 | $35,167 |
| VIP Management Services | 2003 | $30,000 | $30,000 |
| Hollywood Presbyterian Medical Center and other US hospitals | 2016 | $17,000 for HPMC; undisclosed amounts from other hospitals | $17,000+ |
| Banque Cantonale de Genève | 2015 | $12,000 | $12,000 |
| ProtonMail | 2015 | $6,000 | $6,000 |
| Three Indian banks | 2015 | At least 15 machines at one bitcoin each | $3,500+ |
| Sony | 2015 | N/A | Unknown |

Health hospitals and clinics in the Baltimore-Washington area were reportedly hit with ransomware in March 2016, leading to patients being turned away.[14]

Not all companies give in to demands. A ransomware attack that froze the payment system of the San Francisco municipal railway system, accompanied by a demand for $73,000 in November 2016, was dealt with by allowing customers to ride for free while the system was rebuilt instead of paying the ransom.[15] The moral hazard of paying ransoms is that it encourages the extortionists to repeat the crime on other victims, and the money paid provides them with the resources to sustain and expand their operations.

### 2.3.11    The Business of Extortion

There is a growing infrastructure, extortion economy, and organization around the criminal industry of cyber extortion. The extortionists have become professional at the process, including setting up call centers in third-party countries to assist the individuals that they are blackmailing with the necessary payment steps and providing technical support for the unlocking of their data, providing decryption codes for the software. Support extends to helping their victims set up bitcoin bank accounts to make untraceable payments. To avoid being traced, the call centers are quickly disbanded after a certain number of payments are extracted.

Essential to sustaining the extortion business model is that the criminals honor their side of the bargain by freeing up the locked data when the payment is made. And, in more cases than not, the users get their data unlocked once they pay up. But there are also counter examples where cyber criminals do not do what they promise. For instance, ProtonMail paid a group called the *Armada Collective* $6000 to end distributed denial of service (DDoS) attacks on its email service, but attacks resumed even after ProtonMail had paid the demanded ransom.

### 2.3.12　Ransomware Attacks on the Rise

Successful extortion of major companies using cyber attacks is still relatively rare, but events are growing in frequency and the scope of their ambition. Generally, cyber extortion attacks seem to be operating in an environment with low risk and high return. Ransomware is common in personal computing and is occasionally seen in attacks on companies. The number of crypto ransomware families on the threat landscape doubled between 2013 and 2015. Extortion claims are tending to become both more frequent and larger in monetary amount over time. The use of ransomware, where particular malware is infiltrated into the networks of a company and disables servers or locks up data until a ransom is paid, has become more of a concern of cyber security specialists. Both *WannaCry* and *NotPetya* appeared to be ransomware when they first infected a system. This demonstrated that with the right vector and ability to exploit a susceptible population, malware can penetrate the defenses of even quite sophisticated and well-protected companies.

Ransomware is becoming easier to generate, with toolkits being made available on the black market, and even 'ransomware as a service' being offered, which is making it easier for people with lower skill levels to carry out ransomware attacks. There are tools such as polymorphic malware generators being more commonly used, enabling large numbers of more sophisticated ransomware to be created to order. Variants of ransomware being offered for sale on the black market can demand ransom payments as high as $1 million.

As regulatory penalties for data breaches become increasingly severe, criminals who steal data may decide that extorting the company against the threat of openly publishing the data is more profitable than selling it on the black market. Companies may be tempted to pay a ransom rather than pay severe regulatory fines.

Ransomware could potentially become a major scourge of organizations.

---

### MANAGEMENT EXERCISE: RESPONDING TO A RANSOM DEMAND

In this exercise, your organization has overnight suffered an infection of malware that has encrypted all the data currently held on many of the servers on your main IT network. It produces a screen that is demanding a payment of several millions of dollars in bitcoin, and a phone number to call or dark web access code to obtain the decryption key to unlock the data. Your IT security team has taken the infected servers offline and isolated them.

Review the options that you might have. List the known data sets and importance and urgency of accessing these data for your operational continuity. Review the alternative ways you could manage without these, and the losses and challenges that your business would face. Check the latest backups and alternative systems that you could use to continue business operations. Develop a media and customer communication strategy for dealing with enquiries while you are responding to the crisis.

Review the ethical issues in paying the ransom, and the pros and cons.

Finally, develop a contingency plan, so that if a future ransomware attack did happen, the contingency plan would minimize the impact on your business, and give you more options for avoiding giving in to extortion.

---

## 2.4   DENIAL OF SERVICE ATTACKS

### 2.4.1   The Threat of DDoS Attacks

Half of all major US companies experience a denial of service attack on their websites each year, and one in eight of those attacks overwhelms their resilience and renders their internet services unavailable.

Distributed denial of service (DDoS) attacks are a common method of disrupting website business activities by bombarding them with traffic. There are different types of DDoS attacks (see next section), but the most common is 'volumetric attacks', which flood a website with traffic. These attacks are unsophisticated and relatively easy to carry out by attackers. They do not need to penetrate the company's defenses; they simply have to generate large volumes of traffic to the company's site. Traffic volumes can be generated by botnets – a network of remotely controlled zombie computers, which are personal computers infected by malicious software that sends out messages without the owner even noticing. Traffic can be amplified through 'reflectors' – other computers that add traffic to a target site – and through 'amplifiers' – computers that will respond with more information as a response to a single stimulus. These types of attacks coordinated from a network of computers are DDoS attacks.

The broad types of denial of service attacks are:

■ *Volumetric attacks* flood a target network with data packets that completely saturate the available network bandwidth. These attacks cause very high volumes of traffic congestion, overloading the targeted network or server and causing extensive service disruption for legitimate users trying to gain access.

■ *Application-based attacks*, also known as 'layer 7' attacks, target the application layer of the operating system (open systems interconnection model). The attack does not use brute force, but is a disguised instruction that forces functions or particular features of a website into overload to disable them. It is sometimes used to distract IT personnel from other potential security breaches. Application-based attacks are reported to constitute around 20% of DDoS attacks.

■ *Protocol-based or Transmission Control Protocol (TCP) connection attacks* involve sending numerous requests for data as synchronized (SYN) packets to the victim server – typically a firewall server – which opens a new session for each SYN packet, overwhelming the control tables of the server. These TCP SYN floods are one of the oldest types of DDoS attack, but are still used successfully.

■ *Fragmentation attacks* use internet protocols for data re-aggregation as an attack vector to overload the processing power of a server. The fragmentation protocol manages the transmission of volumes of data by breaking the data down into smaller packets and then reassembling them at their destination. Sending confusing or conflicting protocols floods the server with incomplete data fragments.

### 2.4.2 How to Protect Against a DDoS Attack

During a DDoS attack a number of things occur:

- Users experience much slower page load times in their browsers.
- Transactions fail.
- Services are unavailable.

Defending against a determined DDoS attacker is time consuming. Defenders have to analyze the traffic samples to determine the patterns of traffic that they need to disrupt. They then try to block, thwart, or redirect the unwanted traffic. It may be difficult to distinguish DDoS traffic from legitimate user traffic. A clever attacker will confuse the two. It may be possible to react to common attacks within 15 minutes, but some defenses can take up to three hours to deploy. The best mitigations have contingency plans in place with upstream providers in readiness so as to avoid impacting customers.

### 2.4.3 Intensity of Attack

The intensity of volumetric DDoS traffic is measured in gigabits per second (Gbps). An attack of 10 Gbps (significant intensity) is likely to overwhelm the capability of a website with the infrastructure to support around one million visitors a month, and cause it to become unavailable, if it does not have specific anti-DDoS measures in place. A website with more infrastructure and capacity is less vulnerable, and it takes more attack intensity – higher Gbps volumes – to take it down.

An intensity scale for DDoS attacks is defined in Table 2.6, together with the approximate thresholds of website vulnerability as a guide. Websites are ranked by their traffic, so the worldwide ranking of a website is also a rough guide to its capacity and vulnerability threshold for DDoS attacks. The actual ability of a website to withstand a DDoS attack also depends on the response of the operator team, the countermeasures they take, and the redundancy and alternative service capability they might deploy.

Attack rates have been seen of more than 1000 Gbps – a terabit per second (Tbps) – although maximum attack intensities are constantly being exceeded. Each year there are thousands of DDoS attacks observed with an intensity of 100 Gbps or more (very high intensity). Analysis suggests that worldwide there are several millions of DDoS attacks of significant intensity or more each year.

**TABLE 2.6** Intensity of distributed denial of service attacks that will disable servers of given volumes, if unprotected.

| Intensity Scale for DDoS Attack | Significant Intensity DDoS | Moderately High Intensity DDoS | High Intensity DDoS | Very High Intensity DDoS | Ultra-High Intensity DDoS |
|---|---|---|---|---|---|
| Volume (gigabits per second) | 1–10 Gbps | 10–50 Gbps | 50–100 Gbps | 100–109 Gbps | ≥1 Tbps |
| Website vulnerability threshold (number of visitors per month) | 1 million | 10 million | 100 million | 1 billion | 10 billion |
| Approximate global website ranking for vulnerability threshold | Top 100,000 | Top 10,000 | Top 1,000 | Top 100 | Top 10 |
| Daily attack rate (worldwide) | 962 | 101 | 3.53 | 0.40 | – |

## 2.4.4 Duration of DDoS Attacks

The duration of attacks and the time that servers can be interrupted is a key component of potential business disruption loss. If an attack is intense enough to degrade or stop a server from functioning, the key issue for managers is the length of time that the attack can be sustained to disrupt business activities. The duration over which a volumetric DDoS attack can be sustained varies significantly. Most attacks are of short duration: half of recorded attacks last for less than two hours and 70% last less than six hours. But some attacks persist: more than 10% of recorded significant intensity DDoS attacks last longer than 12 hours. There are several thousands of high intensity DDoS attacks worldwide each year. The most severe DDoS attack recorded in recent years lasted for a total of three hours at 1,200 Gbps.[16] Long-duration attacks of low intensity and multiple repeat attacks are more common. The potential is evidently growing for high intensity attacks to be sustained for long durations, potentially for days at a time, but this is not yet a common characteristic of DDoS attacks.

## 2.4.5 Repeat Attacks on Targets

Repeat attacks on targets are a common characteristic of DDoS attacks. The average number of DDoS attacks per target is increasing, almost doubling in a single year, 2015–2016.[17] There is a wide variation in number of attacks per target, with some companies reporting many hundreds of repeated attacks.

### 2.4.6 Magnitude of DDoS Attack Activity

The total volume of DDoS activity can be measured in Gbps-hours: the number of attacks combined with their total intensity metric of Gbps and the duration of attacks in hours. This provides an estimate of the magnitude of DDoS attack activity (Table 2.7).

The number of annual DDoS attacks fluctuates significantly, but analysis of recent trends suggests that the overall number of individual attacks may not be increasing substantially. However, attacks are getting more intense, with a greater proportion of attacks being of higher intensity and sustained for longer durations.

With increasing intensities of attack being observed, along with new forms of attack that harvest spare capacity from unprotected devices on the internet, analysts have speculated about the total capacity that could be harnessed for attacks if threat actors tapped the full potential of the internet. Studies of this, surveying the number of unprotected devices that could be unwittingly recruited to participate in a DDoS attack, estimate that today's IPv4 internet is capable of at least 108 Tbps in DDoS capacity.[18] This study concludes that the bandwidth of connection to the target is the most likely constraining factor on the upper limit of intensity of DDoS attacks.

### 2.4.7 Motivation of DDoS Attackers

Very few DDoS attacks are successfully attributed or the attackers identified, caught, or prosecuted, so it is not always possible to identify the motivation of DDoS attacks. A proportion of DDoS attacks are motivated by direct financial gain, with some extortion demands being made to the victim by criminal gangs. However, the large majority of attacks are destructive, with only indirect or no monetary benefit to the perpetrator. Some DDoS attacks mask other criminal activities, such as a simultaneous breach of a network to steal data. Some may even be accidental or collateral damage from attacks

**TABLE 2.7** Increasing magnitude of DDoS activity year on year.

|  | 2014 | 2015 | 2016 | 2017 |
|---|---|---|---|---|
| Magnitude of DDoS activity worldwide (Gbps-hours) | 8 million | 12.8 million | 21.8 million | 32.6 million |

on imprecise targets. There may be commercial competitive dimensions to disabling other organizations' servers. However, most attacks are deliberate attempts to disable the functionality of web systems as acts of sabotage and vandalism.

## 2.4.8 The Big Cannons

Major players include state-sponsored actors. State-sponsored threat actors are discussed in more detail in Chapter 5: 'Know Your Enemy.' DDoS attack capability is seen as a potential weapon for use by nation-states in influencing foreign policy or deterring malicious cyber activities from external agents, or as a method of augmenting military actions in a conflict. A number of countries are known to have military or state-sponsored units with powerful DDoS capability, such as the Chinese 'Great Cannon' and the US National Security Agency QUANTUM internet attack tool. These are predominantly defense and counter-hacking tools, but have the potential to be used against commercial businesses. These 'big cannons', as they are known, are reportedly able to bring to bear ultra-high intensity attacks for long-attacks, capable of shutting down even the most robust servers.

Over a half of all recent attacks are multivectored, making them more difficult to mitigate. Attacks most commonly originate from, or are routed through, servers in China, although attacks are directed via servers in many countries, including the United States, Turkey, Brazil, South Korea, and other territories.

## 2.4.9 Sectoral Preferences in DDoS Targeting

There are significant differences in the types of businesses that experience the highest number of DDoS attacks. Software and technology companies are targeted in a quarter of attacks. Over half of all attacks are directed against gaming companies and their servers. Media and entertainment companies are the next most popular targets, followed by internet and telecom companies.[19] Financial services companies have seen significant reductions in attacks over a period of years – previously they were attacked more than media, entertainment, internet, and telecom companies. Other sectors, such as retail, education, the public sector, business services, and hotel and travel, continue to receive a significant though smaller proportion of all attacks. Targets for DDoS attacks include government, local, or administrative authority sites or military and operational service sites.

A significant number of DDoS attacks are on customer support functions, such as problem reporting, complaints, and bug fixes.

Many DDoS attacks appear to be acts of protest. Some are coordinated protests by so-called hacktivists around ideological issues such as human and animal rights, anticapitalism, climate change, and ecology. The most likely perpetrators of systemic DDoS attacks on commercial businesses are well-organized special interest groups that can orchestrate campaigns of DDoS attacks. DDoS attacks are relatively easy to carry out, and the capacity for generating volumetric attacks is already fairly commoditized. There are black market websites offering botnet capacity for rent at relatively low cost.

Denial of service attacks are a major component of the cyber risk landscape. The number of attacks has increased, with businesses reporting DDoS attacks up by as much as 130% year on year,[20] and the intensity of attacks breaking new records.

### 2.4.10 IoT Being Used for DDoS Attacks

An innovation in the technology of creating DDoS attacks has helped increase the intensity of attacks. The internet of things (IoT) has brought

---

**MANAGEMENT EXERCISE: RESPONDING TO A DDOS ATTACK**

Review the e-commerce activities of your organization and identify the technologies and servers that are most critical to the continuity of your e-revenue and customer servicing.

In this exercise, your servers and counterparties come under a sustained ultra-high intensity DDoS attack that initially is continuous for 12 hours, then returns intermittently for the next 10 days to attack any public IP addresses you use. Estimate the revenue loss to your business and consequences of lost customer satisfaction.

Develop a contingency plan to ensure business continuity so that you suffer less than three hours of lost e-revenue, and less than six hours of customer service capability.

Review options for mitigating future DDoS attacks through improved technology solutions, and estimate the cost and efforts of implementation. Estimate the realistic likelihood (as odds of it occurring in a year) of experiencing an attack of this scale on your business. Discuss with senior management whether the costs of implementing this type of mitigation would be worthwhile for your business.

many devices online with low security levels. An HP Fortify study found that as many as 70% of IoT devices are vulnerable to attacks due to weak passwords, insecure web interfaces, and poor authorizations, and new vulnerabilities are being discovered each year.[21] These can be enslaved fairly easily to create volumes of traffic to fire against a target. The *Dyn* attack in October 2016 utilized freely distributed software to infect IoT online devices to control their use in the attack. Until the security of online devices is improved, these types of attacks can be expected more commonly, likely in greater and greater intensities as the number of online devices proliferates.

## 2.5  FINANCIAL THEFT

### 2.5.1  Networks of Trust

Financial theft is a major source of cyber attacks and cyber-enabled fraud. Financial transaction systems are major targets. If cyber criminals can break into the network of trust of a financial transaction system, they can create fake transactions and syphon funds away. Retail or wholesale financial transaction systems in organizations can include some or all of the following:

- Credit card payment systems in retail outlets, such as point-of-sale card swipers and payment processing through credit and debit card issuers, check-clearing systems, and other channels.
- Online payment systems taking payments for goods and services via secure channels, including via intermediary companies and payment services providers. There are many online e-commerce business models, all of which involve revenue transfer of some sort.
- Bank payment systems, where funds are transferred to accounts with authorization and verification procedures. Interbank payment systems are specific networks used by financial institutions licensed to provide banking services, such as SWIFT, Fedwire, Target2, and similar systems, which are becoming increasingly automated.
- Currency exchanges, providing conversion from one currency to another via networks of payment systems, clearing systems, and trading platforms.
- Investment asset management systems, including the buying and selling of stocks and bonds via brokers or securities bourses.

## 2.5.2    Credit Card Theft

The most common manifestation of cyber financial theft is in retail or consumer finance with credit card misappropriation. Some of the higher-profile
credit card misappropriations have been in retail operations and hotel
chains, with online fraud plaguing the e-commerce, airline, and retail
industries.[22] The previous chapter and the data exfiltration section earlier
in this chapter both describe credit card data losses from major retailers.
Major hotel chains have also been targeted in separate theft campaigns
involving data harvesting from their point-of-sale systems.[23] Point-of-sale
systems remain targets, particularly with legacy systems that are widely
distributed and slow to be updated.

The growing use of chip and PIN commonly used in Europay, Master-
Card, and Visa credit cards, and known as EMV, is reducing theft levels
in many countries. Barclays attributes EMV technology to reducing credit
card–related thefts in the UK by 70% since its introduction in 2003. EMV
now has an 81% adoption rate in Europe and is in use in Australia, Russia, and several other countries. However, EMV uptake in the United States
is slow, resulting in higher credit card misappropriation levels than in countries where this is standard. In 2015, Barclays noted that although the United
States accounts for 24% of total credit card transactions worldwide, it represents 47% of global credit card fraud.[24]

Card companies have carried most of the liability for cyber card fraud,
making good the losses to the users and retailers. This may not be sustainable
if losses continue to escalate. In 2016, EMV credit card companies introduced new rules requiring retailers in Europe to upgrade their point-of-sale
systems to EMV and – importantly – requiring retailers to bear the liability
for fraudulent card transactions if they do not do so. This move could potentially signal a shift of responsibility for data and financial security, placing
more of the cost on the retailer and potentially ultimately on the user.

## 2.5.3    Wholesale and Back-End Financial Systems

There have been high-profile cyber attacks that have succeeded in penetrating the volume wholesale financial transaction systems operated by financial
institutions. Sophisticated threat actors have penetrated the SWIFT banking
system, the Polish financial regulator, and individual bank-to-bank trading
systems. It is difficult to gauge the full extent of these criminal successes
because they are understandably kept confidential by the banks and systems
operators to avoid crises of customer confidence. However, events that are
in the public domain show that individual cyber operations can cause losses
of multiple millions of dollars of loss.

In an operation that lasted from 2013 to 2015, *Carbanak*, an organized cyber crime syndicate profiled in Chapter 5, carried out cyber theft attacks against financial institutions in a number of countries, including Russia, the United States, Germany, China, and Ukraine. The attacks compromised more than 100 financial institutions, with loss estimates as high as $1 billion. The criminals exploited vulnerabilities in Microsoft Office via spear phishing emails (targeted fraudulent emails) to gain access to money processing services, ATMs, financial accounts, and the SWIFT network, giving the cyber criminals a means to move and transfer money. They were also able to get ATMs to dispense money at a specific time for mules to collect.

Another large-scale cyber heist came to light in the United States in 2013. A gang of five were charged with breaking into numerous US financial networks and syphoning off more than 160 million credit card details and more than $300 million from Visa payments of JCPenney, JetBlue Airways, and French retailer Carrefour.

Financial systems can also be vulnerable to market manipulation. The advanced persistent threat (APT) group *FIN4* is notorious for stealing insider information to gain an edge in stock trading.[25]

### 2.5.4 *Lazarus* Attack on SWIFT Banking System

The most notorious cyber theft in recent years has been the attack on the SWIFT interbank financial transaction system by a criminal gang called the *Lazarus Group* using specially crafted software.[26] The software enabled the criminals to gather information on standard practices and send fraudulent requests through the SWIFT system for financial transfers disguised as legitimate transactions, from other software that had been infiltrated into a number of banks with many layers of subterfuge to prevent discovery. The fraud was combined with a complex money-laundering process that obscured the proceeds of the theft from investigators. To break into the trusted SWIFT network, the gang located lower-security banks in many different countries around the world, and found a variety of ways of secretly infiltrating the gang's malicious software onto the SWIFT transaction servers. Banks were reported compromised in Ukraine, Bangladesh, the Philippines, Ecuador, Vietnam, and other Southeast Asian countries.[27] Over a period of months these banks requested other banks, including the US Federal Reserve, to transfer funds via the SWIFT system with fully credentialed authentication protocols. The money was then diverted through laundering operations, including casinos in the Philippines and cover accounts in Sri Lanka and Hong Kong. The full extent of the operation and total amount stolen remain undisclosed, but reports include

$81 million unrecovered from the Bangladesh National Bank, a $10 million loss from a Ukrainian bank, a bank in Ecuador with a $12 million loss, and a dozen more potential losses to Southeast Asian banks.[28] At one point, the gang issued 30 transfer requests totaling $951 million to be withdrawn from the Bangladesh National Bank account with the US Federal Reserve. Security alerts blocked $850 million of the transfers.[29] In 2017, the Far Eastern International Bank in Taiwan suffered a separate attack, with an attempt to fraudulently transfer $60 million to accounts in the United States, Cambodia, and Sri Lanka, and succeeding in stealing $500,000.[30] These multimillion-dollar heists resulted in a radical overhaul of the SWIFT system and new security systems put into place.

We discuss the *Lazarus* SWIFT attack again in Chapter 6: 'Measuring the Cyber Threat'.

Other examples of cyber attacks and thefts from financial services institutions include the following:

- The compromise in 2009 of the US payment processor system responsible for 100 million transactions a month for 250,000 US businesses. Cyber threats have been made to the US Automated Clearing House (ACH) and credit card transaction systems, financial clearing houses, transaction processing systems, private electronic payments networks and currency exchanges, point-of-sale systems, and ATM systems.
- In 2011, Visa, MasterCard, and PayPal suffered denial of service attacks on their systems that resulted in service disruptions and reportedly reduced their capacity to 1000 transactions per second in apparent retaliation for these companies blocking payment to WikiLeaks ('Operation Payback').
- Cyber attacks have been recorded against a number of other companies, including PostFinance, Heartland Payment Systems, Forcht Bank, and the Swedish prosecutor's office.
- In 2014, the Brazilian payment system was attacked by *Bolware*, with cyber criminals infecting about 200,000 computers in Brazil and stealing about $3.75 billion.

### 2.5.5 Security Spending

Banks and financial service companies are fully aware of their susceptibility to attempted hacks and are leaders in the implementation of security systems and measures for preventing cyber theft. Expenditure on cyber security by banks has been high profile and extensive; the banking industry is the single largest sector of cyber security expenditure.[31] Bank of America disclosed that it spent $400 million on cyber security in 2015, and in January 2016 its CEO said that its cyber security budget was "unconstrained".[32] JPMorgan Chase & Co. announced the doubling of its cyber security budget from $250 million in 2015 to $500 million in 2016, and levels of expenditure reported by other banks reached record levels, including Citibank with $300 million and Wells Fargo with $250 million.[33] Following attacks in 2011, Visa and MasterCard significantly strengthened their security, with MasterCard announcing a $20 million security spend and Visa expanding its Visa Token Service, a unifying payment platform with high security standards.

## MANAGEMENT EXERCISE: DEALING WITH A MAJOR CYBER HEIST

Review the financial transaction processes of your organization and identify the systems being used to transfer the largest volumes of payments, with their authorization levels.

In this exercise, your largest financial transaction system is compromised. Someone has obtained credentials to the payment processing authorization, and five payments of the maximum authorization amount have already been paid out to a fake recipient before the fraud was detected and the alarm was raised. The funds are unrecoverable.

Estimate the financial loss to your business, and implications for the business balance sheet or operational continuity. Review your contingency plans for financial fraud to identify how you would go through the procedures of notifications and remediation that would be required.

Review internal operating procedures for carrying out financial transactions. If they are not already in place, consider additional procedures for verification and authorization, including methods that do not use the same transaction system infrastructure, reducing authorization limits, and involving additional personnel sign-off.

Discuss which measures would have the greatest impact in reducing potential loss. What are the downsides of these measures, in terms of operational inefficiencies that they would introduce? How likely do you think a scenario of this type is for your organization?

## 2.6  FAILURES OF COUNTERPARTIES OR SUPPLIERS

### 2.6.1  Risk in the IT Supply Chain

All organizations depend to some extent on third parties to operate their information technology systems. Third-party relationships are very beneficial to leveraging efficiencies and providing business benefits. Different organizations have different approaches and strategies to utilizing third-party suppliers and outsourced operators. Modern system design increasingly integrates software components and outsourced or third-party services into offerings. The benefits that are provided also come with potential issues in giving organizations exposure to cyber losses. The failure of a provider may result in a major loss to the business.

There are many potential counterparties of an organization that could cause the organization a loss. Any counterparty that has access to the company's data, particularly those that may be using, generating, or processing the types of data listed in Table 2.1, could potentially present a risk for an organization. These could include providers of outsourced payroll services, payment systems, data processing, archiving, conversion, and integration.

Vendors of key components that an organization relies on could present risk to the organization if they fail, or if they are unable to maintain or protect their products. A vital piece of third-party software that is integral to the operations of an organization could leave a company exposed if the vendor of that software is unable to provide a patch – perhaps as a result of suffering a cyber attack itself. Companies are increasingly scrutinizing their 'IT supply chain'. In addition to appraising the risk of cyber attacks directly against the organization itself, risk assessment has to include the risk of vital suppliers being attacked or compromised, and the threat that could pose to the organization in turn.

Third-party software products provide their own vulnerabilities and present a risk of triggering a loss to an organization if failures occur. There are many examples of failures in commercial and third-party software that have caused large-scale losses. Examples include flaws in scanning algorithms that randomly alter numbers in the digitization capture of printed documents,[34] banks having to write down large losses resulting from errors in software calculations of interest rates,[35] and errors in software parameters of industrial control systems resulting in substandard product manufacturing and major product recall.[36] Unlike other products, the liability limitations and waivers included in licensing agreements mean that companies that suffer loss through software errors are unable to sue the provider of the software for the full extent of damages that were incurred. Responsibility for software errors is discussed further in Chapter 4: 'Ghosts in the Code'.

The trend towards systems integration from multiple third-party components make these issues of dependency and supply chain risk even more acute. As businesses pull data streams from other people's application programming interfaces (APIs) and apply multiple algorithms from different providers, even diagnosing malfunctions will become highly complex: when two different artificial intelligence algorithms combine and produce unexpected outcomes, whose responsibility is it?

## 2.6.2  The Risk of CSP Failures

Dependency on third-party providers is most marked by the rapid uptake of cloud services. A rapidly growing number of companies make use of a cloud service provider (CSP) by outsourcing to it elements of their data storage, analytics, and information technology functions. The use of CSPs generates major business benefits by allowing businesses to take advantage of scalable resources and save on the capital costs of computing infrastructure. CSPs have remarkably high reliability, but when they occasionally fail, they can do so catastrophically, with many of their customers suffering business losses.

Cloud computing has seen very rapid uptake to become a major driver of the digital economy, with expenditures on public cloud computing having doubled every four years and now being used in some capacity by more than 90% of companies[37] to generate up to $246 billion in revenue worldwide.[38] Large numbers of companies depend on the cloud, particularly in the e-commerce sector, which now accounts for around 10% of total sales in the United States.

There are more than 100 companies that currently provide third-party cloud infrastructure services, but the global market of CSPs is dominated by the 'Big Four': Amazon Web Services (AWS) with 47% of the market, Microsoft Azure at 10%, Google Cloud Platform with 4%, and IBM Softlayer with 3%.[39]

## 2.6.3  Cloud Service Types

Cloud services can be broadly categorized into four application areas:

1. Software as a service (SaaS) is the largest sector of the cloud market, accounting for nearly half of cloud-related business volume. In SaaS,

companies such as Salesforce, Cisco Webex, and Intuit run their businesses as cloud applications.

2. Platform as a service (PaaS) accounts for nearly a quarter of all cloud-related business and provides companies with environments for CSP customers to develop, run, and manage their web applications, with the CSP providing networks, servers, storage, and other services to host the customer's application.

3. Infrastructure as a service (IaaS) constitutes less than 20% of cloud business and provides virtual computing power and resources, such as virtual computing resources, servers, data partitioning, scaling, security, backup, and other services.

4. Enterprise private cloud (EPS) accounts for around 10% of the cloud market. EPSs and virtual private clouds are cloud computing platforms that are implemented within the corporate firewall under the control of the organization's IT department.

Most companies adopt a hybrid strategy that involves several of these approaches.

## 2.6.4  Cloud Adoption and Strategies

Companies are following many different strategies for using cloud services, and are at many different stages of cloud adoption. It is extremely easy for an individual to spin up a cloud account, and surveys show that departments in many organizations have experimented with accessing cloud accounts for part of their activities, without necessarily coordinating this with their central IT departments. Most adoption is currently piecemeal, with many managers concerned about governance of the use of CSPs internally, combating this 'shadow IT culture', and developing an integrated strategy for cloud adoption. Many organizations may be more exposed to cloud outages than they realize.

Experienced managers advocate a structured approach to cloud adoption that follows six stages of putting business activities onto the cloud:

1. Data storage (low value)
2. Delivery of scalable SaaS (non-revenue)
3. Data storage (higher value)
4. Migration of existing apps
5. Building (new) revenue streams
6. Tackling legacy systems and replacing them with cloud equivalents

Industry analysts grade the levels of cloud adoption of organizations into five levels:

1. No plans
2. Cloud watchers (planning for cloud activities)
3. Cloud beginners (carrying out their first cloud projects)
4. Cloud explorers (having apps running in the cloud)
5. Cloud focused (making heavy use of multiple apps)

Surveys suggest that around a third of companies currently may be 'cloud focused' and making heavy use of the cloud. This proportion is higher in small and medium-size businesses (38%) than large enterprises (28%).[40]

For organizations using the cloud, the average cost of an hour's downtime is estimated at around $100,000, with 33% of larger enterprises that are cloud focused reporting that one hour of downtime costs their firms $1 million to $5 million.[41]

## 2.6.5 CSP Outages

There are a number of ways that CSPs could suffer an outage that affects their customers. These include:

- Mechanical failure of equipment, fires, or physical damage of server sites
- Power failure or other essential utility provision, including failure of the backup generators or cooling systems
- Cyber attack by malicious external actors seeking to disrupt services or steal data
- Internal software system failure by accident or from a malicious insider

CSPs have designed their operations to anticipate these threats to their business and have strong security, redundancy in their design, protection measures in place, and contingency plans to minimize their potential for disruption from any of these causes. Data centers, like those used by CSPs to service their availability zones, have high specifications to ensure business continuities:

*"This [data center] can withstand earthquakes and hurricane-force winds of up to 170 mph. A 1.5-million-gallon storage tank cools the system. Diesel generators onsite have enough power, in the event of an outage, to keep the center running for nine days."*[42]

Service-level agreements (SLAs), such as those for the AWS compute service 'EC2' and Microsoft Azure's cloud services, provide a commitment to their customers of 99.95% reliability for each region, expecting less than four and a half hours of outage a year. Annual reliability statistics are monitored carefully and reported by independent observers.

Nevertheless, system failures do occur and customers suffer outages. On February 28, 2017 Amazon's Simple Storage Service (S3) saw 'high error rates' in multiple AWS services in the US eastern region, which escalated to cause a four-hour outage, and quickly cascaded to other regions and services, including CloudWatch, EC2, Storage Gateway, and AWS Web Application Firewall (WAF). The outage was triggered by an AWS S3 team user error, providing incorrect commands while debugging. This outage affected the websites of around 148,000 AWS customers – initially losing graphics and slowing up performance, but cascading to other services and causing complete website failure. Among these customers were 54 of the top 100 internet retailers. Ironically, the Amazon Health dashboard, which reports the working status of services, was taken offline globally by the outage, preventing all clients, regardless of S3 usage, from access to updates about service status and downed regions.

Other notable outages have included:

- In April 2011, AWS's misrouting sent a cluster of elastic block stores into a remirroring storm, taking down much of AWS's US eastern region for **eight hours.**
- In 2009, Microsoft Sidekick suffered a **weeklong** service outage, leaving users without MS services (email, calendars, personal data) and losing their cloud-stored backup data.
- In 2010, during a Gmail outage, 150,000 Google Cloud Gmail users had empty emails for up to **four days** while Google attempted to restore services, eventually resorting to using physical tape backups.
- Microsoft Hotmail suffered a similar outage, also in 2010, when testing scripts deleted 17,000 email accounts, taking **3–6 days** to restore from backups.
- In 2011, Intuit cloud service platform – providing SaaS for TurboTax, Quicken, QuickBooks, and other applications – went offline for **36 hours** following a power failure that triggered routing problems.

Two-thirds of cloud outages are caused by either insecure interfaces and APIs, data loss and leakages, or hardware failure. Cloud Security Alliance lists 12 main threats to cloud computing, ranging from weak access management to shared technology vulnerabilities.[43]

Hypervisors have come under scrutiny as a potential vulnerability that could have the potential for causing significant cloud outages. Hypervisors are software that creates and runs a virtual machine. Virtualizing software is an alternative for physical hardware. Sources of risk for hypervisors include software vulnerabilities, backdoors, and 'race conditions' – a bug that causes continuous reboots, incapacitating a system if it is on the booting procedures of a system. Hypervisors going into race conditions have been cited as potential causes of widespread cloud outages.

Hypervisors are also susceptible to other attack vectors such as through network services and denial of service attacks.

It is rare that a failure causes the entire cloud service to suffer an outage. More typically a failure occurs in a single service or a single geographical region. Because of the interconnected architecture of the CSP services, if the failure cascades, it can affect other applications and spread to other geographical regions.

A typical hierarchy of outages is:

- Individual application failures for users of a particular cloud service in a specific region
- Failure of a specific application across multiple regions
- General service failure (multiple applications) for all customers of a particular region
- General service failure (multiple applications) for all customers of multiple regions

For this reason it is worth understanding the applications architecture and the geographical service regions of the main CSP suppliers.

Cloud service is broadly provided by 'services' and 'regions'. Each CSP has its own naming conventions and branding for these. There are hundreds of individual services (applications) offered by CSPs, but the very large majority of customers use one or more of six primary classes of services. Figure 2.4 shows the six main classes of popular services provided by CSPs and the equivalence for each of the Big Four.

The major CSPs all serve a global market, and each provides regional hubs as large physical operations centers in locations that serve the main market areas of demand. For example, AWS structures its operations around 30 geographical 'availability zones' served by 11 regions, with their primary hubs and several hundreds of individual data centers, including serving the United States with five regions and 13 availability zones. Each CSP has its own geographical structure, and these serve key market areas of demand. Figure 2.5 shows the geographical architecture of each of the Big Four CSPs.

| | | amazon webservices | Microsoft Azure | Google Cloud Platform | IBM Bluemix™ |
|---|---|---|---|---|---|
| 1 | Cloud Computing | Amazon EC2 | Azure Virtual Machine | Compute engine | Virtual |
| 2 | Object Storage | Amazon S3 | Azure Blob Storage | Cloud storage | Object storage |
| 3 | Load Balancer | Elastic Load Balancing | Azure Load Balancer | Cloud load balancing | Local load balancing |
| 4 | Relational Database | Amazon RDS | Azure SQL | Cloud SQL | Dash DB for transactions SQL database |
| 5 | Networking & Content Delivery | Amazon Cloud Front | Azure CDN | Cloud CDN | Content delivery network |
| 6 | Networking | Amazon Route 53 | Azure DNS Azure Traffic Manager | Cloud DNS | Domain name service |

**FIGURE 2.4**  Classes of cloud services – equivalent or similar services being provided by the Big Four cloud service providers.

The provision of cloud services is represented by a matrix of geographical regions combined with provision of services as shown in Figure 2.6. This shows the potential for cascading outages across regions and services, represented by the example of the AWS S3 outage event of February 28, 2017.

Individual companies might find it useful to plot their own intensity of use of cloud services in a matrix like the one in Figure 2.6, to identify their exposure to potential future cloud outages.

## 2.6.6  Duration of Outages

Although there were more than 10,000 outage incidents reported across all the CSPs in 2017, typically involving a single service in an individual region, when they have occurred, most outages experienced by customers have lasted only minutes. The average duration of an outage in recent years has been eight minutes. However, some of the more extreme outages have exceeded four hours, as shown in Figure 2.7, which presents the number of events per year that exceeded a certain number of minutes. In any given year, this suggests that the odds of having a CSP outage of over six hours somewhere in the world are around 1 in 5, and the odds of having an outage that lasts longer than 12 hours are around 1 in 200. Significantly longer-duration outages are possible, with diminishing likelihood.

Businesses using cloud services should consider the potential for experiencing outages of extended duration in the services and regions they use, and their contingency plans for these eventualities. The longer-duration events are typically associated with hardware and connectivity restoration,

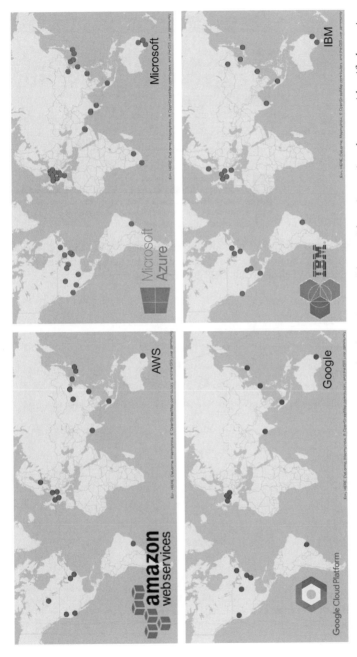

**FIGURE 2.5** Geographical architecture of the Big Four cloud service providers, with major regional centers identified, serving local markets.

| | A | | | B | | | | C | | | D | E | | |
|---|---|---|---|---|---|---|---|---|---|---|---|---|---|---|
| | North America | | | Europe | | | | Asia | | | Australasia | Rest of World | | |
| | East Coast | West Coast | Canada | UK | EU | Scandinavia | Russia | China/Japan | Indian Subcont | SE Asia | Australia | Africa | Middle East | Other |
| 1 Cloud Computing | | | | | | | | | | | | | | |
| 2 Object Storage | | | | | | | | | | | | | | |
| 3 Load Balancer | | | | | | | | | | | | | | |
| 4 Relational Database | | | | | | | | | | | | | | |
| 5 Networking & Content Delivery | | | | | | | | | | | | | | |
| 6 Networking | | | | | | | | | | | | | | |
| 7 Other Services | | | | | | | | | | | | | | |

- 5 hours of outage; all customers
- 3 hours of outage or significantly reduced performance; most customers
- 2 hours of outage or significantly reduced performance; most customers
- 2 hours of reduced response times or intermittent failures
- Some reduction in service performance

**FIGURE 2.6** Regions and services provided by each of the Big Four cloud service providers, identifying the potential for cascading outages across both dimensions. The AWS S3 outage of February 28, 2017 is plotted for reference.

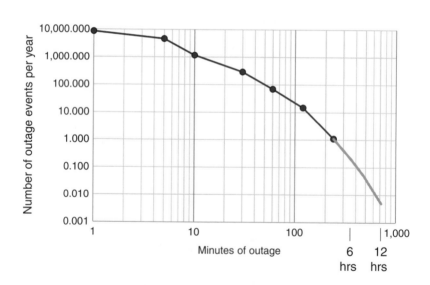

**FIGURE 2.7** Duration of cloud service outages reported in a single year (2017 statistics for 100,000 events) extrapolated for likelihood of longer outage events per year.

although problematical malware infections could also lead to long-duration outages. Once a specific problem has been fixed, some customers are restored quickly while others must wait longer to be reconnected. The type of technical issue that has caused the outage determines the speed and process of restoration, and there are some examples where all of the affected customers are restored at the same time, but this is rare. More typically, customers are restored incrementally, with most customers back online quickly but a minority of customers may take a lot longer. Big customers are prioritized in the restoration process, but sometimes technical issues make this impractical.

## MANAGEMENT EXERCISE: MANAGING THROUGH A CSP OUTAGE

Review the cloud services you use from each of the main CSPs, and which operations in your business depend on the continued operation of which services. Ensure that the review includes cloud-related operations from all of your major departments. If it is helpful, plot your intensity of usage on a matrix of services and regions, similar to Figure 2.5.

In addition, review the main counterparties and suppliers that you do business with, and establish the degree to which they are using the cloud in their business and their dependency on continued cloud provision.

In this exercise, assume that the main services you depend on from your most significant CSP go down for 12 hours, in many regions of the world.

Track how this would affect your business, and estimate the losses that this would cause in terms of lost revenue and business disruption.

Review your contingency plans for operational continuity in an event of this kind.

Identify which of your counterparties and suppliers would also be affected by this or similar events. Review your contingency plans for these suppliers being disrupted.

Review options for reducing the impact of an event like this to your business, including developing alternative deployment strategies for the key services you would need. Estimate the costs of implementing this risk mitigation strategy. Estimate the realistic likelihood of your business suffering a CSP outage event on this scale. Discuss with senior management whether the costs of implementing this type of mitigation would be worthwhile for your business.

Most companies that have a significant portion of their business operations in the cloud have increasingly sophisticated engineering approaches to maintain their own resilience and structuring contingency from individual CSP failures, including having multiple CSP providers and the ability to rapidly redeploy alternatives if critical services fail.

## ENDNOTES

1. CCRS (2018a).
2. Advisen (2017).
3. Landler (2000).
4. National Audit Office (2017).
5. Berr (2017).
6. Woo (2017).
7. Palmer (2017).
8. Thompson (2017).
9. Khandelwal (2017).
10. Cybereason (2017) and O'Conner (2017).
11. Reinsurance (2018).
12. Beazley (2017) and Zetter (2016).
13. *Los Angeles Times* (2016).
14. Cox (2016).
15. The Merkle (2016).
16. York (2016).
17. Akamai (2015).
18. Leverett and Kaplan (2017).
19. Akamai (2016).
20. DigitalTrends (2015).
21. Rawlinson (2014) and Constantin (2016).
22. Europol (2017a, 2017b).
23. *ComputerWeekly* (2015) reports 45 hotels of Mandarin Oriental hotel chain compromised, and *ComputerWeekly* (2016) discusses card data losses from chains such as Hilton and Starwood.
24. Security (2015).
25. Dennesen (2014).
26. Symantec Security Response (2016).
27. Van der Walt (2016).
28. Riley and Katz (2016) and Van der Walt (2016).
29. Zetter (2016).
30. Shevchenko et al. (2017).
31. IDC Report (2016), reported in Forbes Tech (2016).
32. Forbes (2016).
33. Forbes (2015).

34. Kriesel (2013).
35. EYC3 (2013).
36. Duggan et al. (2005).
37. Right Scale (2017).
38. Gartner (2017).
39. Coles (2017).
40. Right Scale *State of the Cloud* (2018).
41. Woodward (2018).
42. *USA Today* (2012).
43. Cloud Security Alliance (2017).

# CHAPTER 3

# Cyber Enters the Physical World

## 3.1 A BRIEF HISTORY OF CYBER-PHYSICAL INTERACTIONS

### 3.1.1 Cyber-Physical Systems

There is a rapidly growing number of physical control systems that can be controlled electronically, connected to networks for remote access. They provide great benefits in automating previously manual control systems but pose a security risk if accessed by unauthorized third parties. These smart devices and 'cyber-physical' systems consist of a wide range of sensors, actuators, valves, switches, mechanical devices, and electronic controls that are generically known as operational technology (OT), to distinguish them from purely digital information technology (IT). In industry, they are sometimes called supervisory control and data acquisition (SCADA) systems and, for major pieces of machinery, industrial control systems (ICSs).[1] Many electronic systems now contain elements of connectivity for diagnostic read-outs, upgrading and programming uploads, data transmission, and signal processing.

The proliferation of devices that are connected to the internet has given rise to the term 'internet of things' (IoT). This is also described as 'the infrastructure of the information society'. It is estimated that there are currently around 28 billion devices connected to the internet, and various projections suggest that the number could reach 50 billion by 2020.[2] The number of devices connected to the internet is currently increasing by 30% year on year.[3] There are many studies that describe the growing potential for the transformative power of IoT, including smart grids, smart homes, intelligent transportation, and smart cities.

The simple truth is that developers of these systems prioritize increasing their functionality over improving their security. This chapter sets out the risks inherent in the increasing usage of cyber-physical systems and argues that we need to redress the balance and improve the safety of these systems.

### 3.1.2 Growing Consciousness of Cyber-Physical Interactions

It has taken a while for the general public to appreciate the full extent of information technology's interaction with the real world. Security professionals have been grappling with this for a long time. Although popular culture has mostly perpetuated the myth of the internet as purely 'virtual', the concept of hacking to gain cyber control of the real world has become a theme in subcultural hacking films: *Wargames* in 1983 explores the risks of hacking and nuclear conflict; *Sneakers* in 1992 notes the vulnerability of power grids and air traffic control systems; *Hackers* in 1997 shows manipulation of sprinkler systems in a school, lights in buildings, and dangerously creating New York traffic jams by hacking traffic signals. Indeed, this is an often-repeated trope from hacking cinema, with the first depiction of automotive traffic manipulation in *The Italian Job* in 1969.

### 3.1.3 The Earliest Hack of a Physical System

It has been possible to remotely 'hack' a system to produce physical consequences since before the history of computing itself. It is recorded in an act of 'scientific hooliganism' performed at the Royal Institution by Nevil Maskelyne during a demonstration of the security of radio used for sending orders to ships at sea in 1903. Maskelyne was hired by the Eastern Telegraphy Company to prove that the radio protocols used by Fleming and Marconi were insecure in what might be considered the world's first electronics penetration test. He successfully used another radio transmitter to overpower a long-distance communication between Marconi and Fleming and send some taunting songs during their demonstration in front of a live audience. Although it would still need to fool a ship's captain into believing the message, it made the public painfully aware of the real-world impacts if ships at sea were to use such a technology to take orders.[4]

The demonstration proved an important principle: it was possible to remotely cause physical impacts from the moment we started sending long distance messages. This lesson continues to be learned by new generations today. In 2015, Neil Moore, a con artist, had himself released from jail simply by forging an email.[5]

## LEARNING IT THE HARD WAY

### Éireann's Introduction to Spoofing Attacks

Éireann Leverett had his first experience of the social disruption that could be caused by spoofed email as a teenager attending a small Midwestern college in 1992.

He was given his first email account, and six months later was learning snippets of computer science as part of the liberal arts education. An older student taught him to spoof emails by telnetting to port 25, and he knew another eight or so others on campus who knew this trick. A few months later the university community was consumed by infighting as a spoofed email on a very divisive issue was sent from the president of the college to all students. It was distressing to know it had been spoofed, to have no idea which of a handful of students had done it, and to watch the community tear itself apart over the issue. The president denied having sent the email, but already trust in email was so high that the students put the burden of proof on the president to prove he hadn't sent it. Thus the victim of hacking becomes burdened with proving his own innocence!

From that day on Éireann realized that hacking almost always had a real-world impact, setting him on his career doing industrial systems assessments in an effort to make such environments safer. Thus began Éireann's campaign to help people understand that hacking can have very real and physical impacts.

## 3.2 HACKING ATTACKS ON CYBER-PHYSICAL SYSTEMS

### 3.2.1 Examples from the Past

Some notable examples of real-world hacks and vulnerabilities include the following case studies.

**3.2.1.1 *Stuxnet* – Sabotaging Nuclear Development** Possibly the most notorious cyber-physical hacking example is the US-Israeli operation known as *Stuxnet*. Books have been written about this single event that set back the Iranian nuclear program.[6] The code targeted programmable logic controllers (PLCs) to damage centrifuges. This delayed atomic energy research, and made staff suspect stupidity or sabotage within the team.

It had a significant psychological effect on the personnel of the Natanz uranium processing plant.[7] It seems that the operation started in 2005, and the code was written years before its effects came to light in 2010, when different malware researchers worked together to reverse engineer and understand the binaries that led to the events.

**3.2.1.2 Scramming Nuclear Power Plants**   On January 25, 2003, Davis-Besse nuclear power plant was infected with the MS SQL Server 2000 worm. The infection caused data overload in the site network, resulting in the inability of the computers to communicate with each other. The slowness in computer processing speed began in the morning and by 4:50 p.m., the Safety Parameter Display System (SPDS) became unavailable and remained unavailable for 4 hours 50 minutes. By 5:13 p.m., the plant process computer was lost and remained unavailable for 6 hours and 9 minutes.[8]

Though this incident did not result in physical damage, it did result in the scram of a reactor. This was a near miss worthy of informing other generator operators about. More importantly, it demonstrates that a worm not even written to affect industrial systems can nevertheless impact critical energy operations in first-world countries.

**3.2.1.3 Burning Out Power Generators**   Researchers in 2007 demonstrated that spoofed control signals on a 2.25 MW electricity generator could cause physical damage to the unit, including making itself inoperable. It was also possible to cause damage to the local grid in the process. The *Aurora* vulnerability, as it became known, has the potential to cause damage to the generator, surrounding buildings, and electrical cabling via rapid fluctuations of electrical load. An attack on the power grid using the *Aurora* vulnerability could cause a lengthy blackout for many customers, because generators are large and costly to replace, with a long lead time to getting a new one operating effectively.[9]

**3.2.1.4 Shutting Down the Ukrainian Power Grid**   An intrusion on Ukraine power companies caused a power outage for thousands of customers for around six hours in December 2015.[10] Thirty substations were affected, and 73 MWh went unsupplied. There was a repetition in December 2016, which also led to smaller power outages. This event demonstrated to the world that critical national infrastructure in countries can and would be targeted in a new age of cyber-physical warfare.

**3.2.1.5 Derailing Trams in Poland**   A 14-year-old schoolboy hacked into tram systems in Lodz, Poland, and derailed four vehicles over a few months.[11]

He used electronics skills to modify a universal remote control. This in turn was used to change the points of the tram's track by sending infrared control signals he recorded and replayed with the modified remote control. We profile the schoolboy of Lodz as an example of an amateur threat actor in Chapter 5: 'Know Your Enemy'.

**3.2.1.6  Damaging a German Steel Mill**  In 2014, a report surfaced of a German steel mill being heavily damaged by an intrusion into its process control system.[12] The furnace was improperly shut down, and the material hardened inside it, creating material damage to the facility and making it inoperable afterwards. The event still has an air of mystery about it today, since the victim has not been publicly named.

**3.2.1.7  Shutting Off the Heating in a Building**  A distributed denial of service attack on an internet-connected building management system (BMS) was responsible for the loss of control of the central heating system in two tower blocks in Lappeenranta, Finland, in 2016. Early reports had the building without heat for a week and some residents having to be relocated, though later the BMS operator denied this.

**3.2.1.8  Remotely Spilling Sewage**  In April 2000 an Australian named Vitek Boden went on a hacking campaign in Maroochy Shire, Australia, that released 800,000 gallons of sewage into parks, rivers, and streams, and in one case sent sewage spilling through a hotel lobby.[13] In revenge for losing his job at the sewage company, Vitek sent radio commands to sewage substations on 46 different occasions. The environmental, political, and social impacts in the community were severe. While this is often discussed as an insider attack, it was done remotely after he no longer worked for the organization involved.

**3.2.1.9  Heart Pacemaker Vulnerabilities**  It is not just large infrastructures that can be hacked – implanted medical devices can also be vulnerable to cyber-physical interference. The first paper to deal with pacemaker security, published in 2008,[14] detailed radio protocol hacking and potential lethal effects. Safety of pacemakers hasn't made a lot of progress over the subsequent years, as demonstrated by Barnaby Jack in 2012,[15] and work done by Dr Marie Moe in collaboration with the authors, presented in her talk *Unpatchable*.[16]

**3.2.1.10  Lessons from Examples**  This small selection of examples of hacking attacks on physical systems shows a wide range of potential consequences and complexities of attack. The ability to shut off a building's heating system with a simple denial of service attack (just bombarding it with data traffic) is at one end of the spectrum, with the *Stuxnet* attack, a complex multimodule piece of malware constructed by a sizeable nation-state team and infiltrated into the control systems of nuclear fuel processing plants, at the other. Simple techniques, as well as complex ones, can cause very significant real-world consequences.

## 3.3  COMPONENTS OF CYBER-PHYSICAL SYSTEMS

### 3.3.1  A Framework for Control Systems

*Cyber-physical systems* is a broad term, defined at the beginning of this chapter, and includes SCADA systems, industrial control systems, vehicle-to-vehicle networks, and even medical devices. These diverse applications, while varying in detail, are built up from similar central computer science principles and components.

A cyber-physical system is typically made up of sensors, actuators, networking equipment, data stores, and deciders. Between these different components, real-time systems take sensor readings, carry them to other devices over a network, store them as data and use them to make decisions, and then use a network to carry a signal to an actuator that produces some desired outcome.

### 3.3.2  Sensors

Sensors are crucial devices to protect, as they are the primary source of decision making throughout cyber-physical systems. A computer program is only as good as its input ('garbage in, garbage out'). This is just as true of distributed systems as it is of any single computer program. The importance of sensors is often underappreciated in cyber risk assessments.

Protecting the sensor data inputs is difficult but vital. For example, thermostat sensors are used in many temperature-sensitive industrial processing systems. When they are remotely connected and fed into a system that controls the heating, their information is critical. If they provide a false reading, the system may continue to heat up with potentially catastrophic results.

In farming systems, agricultural watering of grain fields includes temperature sensors to ensure that irrigation occurs more frequently during hotter weather. A simple spoofing device can include holding a cigarette lighter under the temperature sensor. Unless the reading is verified and cross-checked, a determined adversary armed only with lighters can flood a field.

### 3.3.3 Actuators

Actuators can be robotic arms, lathe axles, dough mixers, electrical switches, or automated vehicles. Actuators are a central part of the machinery or system that makes something happen in the real world. By sending a command to a garage door, for example, we tell it to open, and we think of this command as a control signal. Many of these control signals are unencrypted and unauthenticated, meaning that once a malicious actor understands the protocols (the language the controller speaks to the door), it is simply a matter of replaying them or crafting them by hand to get actuators to do unauthorized things, like opening the garage door to let the hacker in.

### 3.3.4 Data Stores

Data – particularly parameters that feed into algorithms that control cyber-physical systems – are held in a database or data store, typically a hard disk, log file, printer stream, or memory. Interference with data in the store is another way of manipulating the cyber-physical system, and is easily overlooked. Parameter data can be altered or destroyed. A good system design includes backup systems that hold copies of the parameters as a source of veracity. Data store redundancy is good practice in system design, and can be used to restore compromised systems to a verifiable state. Of course, the backup systems also need to be well-protected against hackers.

### 3.3.5 Networking Equipment

Networks within, to, and from the system need to carry data instantly, faithfully, and without error. Every network is itself a system of many components – a 'box'. An industrial ethernet switch is a box, with processors, memory, and sometimes fully programmable gate arrays inside, also made up of configuration files and binaries that can be altered to subvert operations. Every network is actually a computer. We tend to think of them as 'ether', but in reality even a simple system such as domestic Wi-Fi is a little box in the corner of your house that contains important configuration files and details.

Networking devices can be overlooked when thinking about security. Networks can be attacked. Networking protocols are not resistant to tampering. The interplay between network protocols is important. Attackers know that subverting an insecure protocol can be used as a rung on the ladder to later subvert one assumed to be secure.

Data stores and networks are similar in that they both hold data – one is at rest, and one is in transit. Data can be subverted while it is transmitted or stored if it is done so insecurely. To quote the computer science legend Danny Hillis: 'Memory locations are just wires turned sideways in time'.[17]

In short, data at rest and data in motion are subject to the same threats, albeit for different periods of time. So conceptually, we can simplify our thinking to simply 'Can data be manipulated?' at some point in its journey through the network. The network is actually a computer that briefly stores data as it transmits it across the network.

### 3.3.6 Deciders

The decisions in a system are made in the computer itself, the processor, which operates on decision logic: the amount of watering a grain field requires at different temperatures, the routing of a packet in a network switch, the heat of the arc welder from the thickness of the steel, the length of time to bake the bread at which temperature, the lift of the crane based on the weight of the shipping container.

This is where the logic lives. This logic can be complex, often involving feedback systems and nonlinear effects that are not simple 'if ... then' statements. The classic illustration of this is proprioception in a robot picking up an egg. It is a challenge to grip the egg just the right amount: too lightly and it will drop as it is moved, too hard and the shell will crack; so feedback from 'fingertip' sensors helps maintain just the right pressure.

### 3.3.7 Safety Systems

Safety systems are designed to be reliable, predictable, and redundant. They help protect us when things go wrong. They can be either passive or active safety systems, such as the overflow pipe in a bath (passive) or the fire alarm in a building (active). In cyber-physical systems they might prevent over-current in an electric grid, or drain a nuclear reaction vessel.

## 3.4 HOW TO SUBVERT CYBER-PHYSICAL SYSTEMS

### 3.4.1 Designed for Accidents, Not Malicious Attacks

Safety systems are typically designed to protect against accidents, not intelligent malicious attacks. They are designed to prevent the most common fault scenarios, or to warn us when dangerous situations have emerged. Their capabilities are often surpassed when intelligent, capable adversaries attack these systems. It is commonly assumed that the standard safety system will override the activities of any hacker that gets access, but experience shows that adversaries can and do override standard safety systems fairly easily. Some safety engineers will swear: 'That isn't possible, because the safety system would do x, y, z'. To be properly secure, cyber-physical systems have to be designed against malicious attack by intelligent adversaries.

Designers of security systems should design their systems to avoid their exploitation from a number of techniques typically employed by penetration testers. These techniques were commonly used by one of the authors during his career performing penetration tests on industrial systems. To avoid triggering industrial accidents, these were typically carried out as safety simulations, with the experiment being conducted on a test network.

### 3.4.2   Overriding Safety Alerts

Operators can be fooled into ignoring safety alerts. Generating large numbers of fake safety alerts induces operators into 'alert fatigue' so that they ignore real alerts when the attacker triggers one. Combinations of fake alerts can also induce engineers to perform dangerous actions in trying to combat the perceived crisis.

Safety alerts can be spoofed in systems that fail to protect their alert communication protocols – for example, alerts that are sent unencrypted over the internal network. These can easily be spoofed once the attacker understands the format. Safety simulations show that operators are susceptible to manipulation, even to the point of carrying out illogical and potentially dangerous actions, once the attacker has gained control of the alert messaging system.

### 3.4.3   Entering a Secure Facility

Some activities require attackers to gain entrance to secure facilities. Accessing systems that may be isolated from the outside networks is typically easier from within control centers. Gaining access typically requires credentials, but these can be subverted.

A classic example is tripping a fire alarm test, so that the attacker can discretely enter a building during the test period. Attackers can, and do, call up the operators and pretend to be a health and safety engineer from the head office, to schedule a fire alarm test at a time they intend to surreptitiously enter the building. If successful at scheduling, the attackers get to choose the time that they want to gain entry, and if unsuccessful the staff may very well complain that it is not the date of the scheduled test, and blurt out the actual scheduled during the phone call.

Other creative ways of getting through locked doors exist, including unlocking a bank lobby door with a glass of whisky, demonstrated by Deviant Ollam in a YouTube video in 2016.[18]

### 3.4.4   Deactivating Fire Suppression Systems

Preventing safety systems from working in a crisis can cause or exacerbate damage. For example, sprinkler systems can be prevented from putting out a fire. Some BMSs have remote maintenance operations that can be hacked, including draining wet pipe sprinkler systems. This remote functionality is designed to save engineers time and money from driving out to each building, but the result is that the piping system that serves the sprinkler system can be drained and disabled, so that an arson attack could be made much more destructive. However, these sprinkler systems cannot be activated remotely, so the chances of an attacker remotely triggering the sprinklers to go off and cause water damage to the building contents are minimized.

### 3.4.5   Triggering Fake Safety Procedures

There are, however, other types of safety systems that could cause damage by being maliciously triggered. It may be possible to trigger a halon gas suppression system while people are in a data center and lock the door access control system simultaneously.

### 3.4.6   Achieving Malicious Aims by Abusing Security Systems

So now we see that safety systems have three crucial abuse cases:

1. Spoofing safety alerts to induce dangerous decisions
2. Abusing safety systems to bypass security
3. Abusing safety systems to cause harm or damage

These examples are overly simplistic, but they demonstrate a principle: by abusing predictable safety mechanisms, one can achieve malicious aims. There are many more ways to subvert and abuse these systems, and safety and security have been philosophically isolated from each other in computer systems thinking for decades. This distinction is slowly eroding (necessarily), as insecure safety systems are not safe, and unsafe security systems are counterproductive. This rough taxonomy is not exhaustive, and no doubt it will take many more years of research before consensus is reached and social utility becomes optimized in this field.

## 3.5  HOW TO CAUSE DAMAGE REMOTELY

### 3.5.1  Change the File and You Change the World

Everything is a file in a computer or a network somewhere. Change that file, and you change the world.

Astute readers will recognize this philosophy as a Unix development principle: everything is a file descriptor. That file might be plans for a forge and crucible, configuration files for networking equipment in vehicle-to-vehicle communications, or safety settings for shunting electric loads in large electrical systems. All of these things can lead to desirable outcomes for the hacker and maybe neutral outcomes (at best) for the victim, or can lead to destruction of property, wealth, or life (at worst).

For each type of node in a cyber-physical system, file changes lead to different results.

### 3.5.2  Spoof the Sensors

It is possible to spoof sensor values digitally when they aren't protected by encryption (integrity and/or authentication), and deliberately sending the wrong values can lead to dangerous side effects. This approach can work by altering the network traffic, or by compromising the sensor itself (if it is complicated enough to have its own firmware or web server). Even when it doesn't have its own firmware, there are often calibration constants in sensors, to adjust them in firmware or microcode for slight deviations in physical manufacturing. These calibration constant files can be changed to alter the values.

### 3.5.3  Control the Actuators

The actuator control signals can be vulnerable too, in much the same way as the sensors. They can be forged in a variety of ways and in different nodes within the network. So it is a matter of protecting not only the sensor signals, but the controller itself or the machines that send the controller the signal.

For example, consider a simple digital lightbulb that turns on when it receives a 1, and off when it receives a 0. If attackers send the opposite value than is desired by the victim, they can subvert the system. This can be done directly on the network, but it can also be done on both the sender or receiver sides of the connection.

### 3.5.4  Subvert the Logic

It is also possible to change the logic of the devices themselves, wherever that logic may reside within the distributed system. It can be additionally deceptive in changing the timing of the effect. Changing the logic means the malicious effect comes when the operator or system exercises control and gets a very different result than the expected one. This might often be the opposite effect, but a patient and knowledgeable attacker can think about the physics to exacerbate unsafe scenarios, rather than limit them.

For the digital lightbulb, what does it mean to subvert the logic of the firmware? The logic could be reversed, so that the bulb will turn off when it receives a 1, and on when it receives a 0. So when the operator sends the signal, the opposite effect results rather than the one that is wanted. Alternatively, the firmware could be altered to behave randomly, which is much more frustrating to remediate. Why? Because the effects of the actions are not reliably and instantly reversible. A system that doesn't behave the same way every time you use it is a nightmare to control, especially in a crisis.

## 3.6    USING COMPROMISES TO TAKE CONTROL

### 3.6.1    Intent and Compromises

In estimating cyber risk, we can get lost in the weeds if we focus on all the things an attacker could do – physics offers a lot of destructive potential. We should instead focus on quantifying and understanding the ways capable and motivated opponents can get to the point where they can carry out their intentions. We also need to consider what their intentions are. What might they be trying to do, and what would they gain from achieving it? (We consider this more in Chapter 5: 'Know Your Enemy'.) So imagine that the attacker wants to take control of the system. We propose that there is a simplified taxonomy of compromises that could potentially be used. The physical results of those compromises can usually be reduced to their worst-case scenario (for different values of worst: loss of life, economic harm, explosive perimeter, downtime, etc.).

### 3.6.2    Disable the Safety System

Safety systems are logic systems too, but of a specific type. Disabling safety systems is criminal, but it happens. Mario Azar, a former oil and gas contractor, turned off gas leak detection on oil platforms using unauthorized access to the network operations center after the company had declined to give him a permanent job.[19]

This is merely disabling a safety system, but the Triton attack framework systematically worked to subvert an entire safety instrumentation system product line.[20]

By changing the logic of our safety systems, our allies can become enemies. Crucially, they do so when we most need their aid, during a safety critical event. Imagine someone who swaps the water from a sprinkler system for gasoline. The safety team could be forgiven for engaging the sprinkler system in the event of a fire (accidental or arson), never knowing it would make the damage worse instead of limiting it. Our safety systems are designed to put out fires, and yet they can also be abused by smart hackers to pour fuel on the conflagration. Some people just want to see the world burn.

Sufficiently advanced malice is indistinguishable from misfortune, so some of what we previously thought were accidents may turn out to be hacking.

### 3.6.3 Change the Display/Induce Operator Error

Another method for producing dangerous situations is simply to change the display of information, or the visualization of the system state. In technical circles this is known as a loss of view, where the operator (or computer) managing the situation is caused to experience a model of the process that is different from the reality.

So, for the digital lightbulb, this would be a remote indicator saying the light is on, when actually it is off. A more dangerous example would be an indicator saying a valve is closed when it is open.

This is still an alteration of the logic, but the logic of the display system rather than the control or safety logic. This causes operators (or algorithms) to make the wrong decisions, and they can be catastrophic as we have previously emphasized. We include it here simply to capture how flexible an alteration of the logic can be, and how it takes effect not immediately, but later at a time that may be predetermined, or a logic that waits for a particular state to be reached.

Cyber risk is a 'time-shifted' risk, with the specific time shift under at least partial control by the attacker, and often unknown to the defender. The bounds of these delays are critical to the dimensions of the risk posed.

## 3.7 OPERATING COMPROMISED SYSTEMS

### 3.7.1 The Byzantine Generals Problem

In Ross Anderson's seminal work, *Security Engineering*, there is a chapter called 'Distributed Systems.'[21] It begins with a quote by Leslie Lamport: 'You know you have a distributed system when the crash of a computer you've never heard of stops you from getting any work done'. The chapter describes the many problems of building distributed systems, and gives us a useful metaphor for the limits of safe operation in a partially compromised system.

How many nodes can be compromised in a cyber-physical system before we reach catastrophic damage? Ideally, we should not need to care what kind of node it is, whether sensor, actuator, data store, or even network switch.

The same Leslie Lamport wrote a key paper (with Shostak and Pease) called *The Byzantine Generals Problem*.[22]

## DISTRUSTING YOUR SENSOR INFORMATION

### The Byzantine Generals Problem

What do you do if you suspect that some of your sensors are not providing true readings? How much resilience do you need to build into the system to overcome the possibility of mistrusted components?

The Byzantine military considered this problem. The tactical challenge is called the Byzantine Generals Problem. The Byzantine commander has a number of generals, each commanding a division of his army. They are fighting a war. The commander suspects that some of his generals are traitors, but nevertheless they must collectively win the war. Communicating only via messenger, the generals must agree on a common battle plan. How should the commander set up his messaging and pattern of warfare to ensure that the loyal generals will reach agreement and win the war, even with defective generals?

Lamport et al.'s paper restated this centuries-old military problem within the modern context of the reliability of a computer system, subject to the failure of some of its components.

The problem is amenable to mathematical analysis. It shows that a system can be built to resist as many as a third of the nodes being faulty or compromised, provided certain principles are followed.

The paper examines some conditions of building a reliable system as a mathematical problem, and whether such a system can be built, as long as four principles are followed:

1. *All messages by non-faulty processors must be delivered correctly.*
   However, in real systems communication networks do fail for a plethora of reasons. Most cyber-physical systems cannot fulfill this claim.
2. *The process can determine the originator of any message that it receives.*
   This assumes each node identifies itself in a non-spoofable manner such as with cryptographic authentication. Unfortunately, this

assumption does not always hold true, since some industrial system protocols are known to be spoofable (for example Modbus).
3. *The absence of a message must be detectable.*
   This is rarely a property of IoT systems, but does exist in some (exceedingly well-engineered) real-time systems.
4. *The message integrity must be provably verifiable.*
   Once again, this is not a common property in industrial systems, and especially rare in IoT devices.

So if we had algorithms that worked to actively detect compromise and to combine them with these four principles, we could resist the compromise of up to a third of our nodes. Unfortunately, in the systems we build today, we rarely see even two of these principles fulfilled.

This suggests we have a great legacy of 'security debt', as technologists like to refer to it. This debt may take years to clear in society, as the lag time is a function of the technology refresh rate of organizations. That refresh rate in cyber-physical systems tends to be longer than in desktops, in the rough range of 2–10 years.

So we will be living with the poor choices of cyber risk we have made as a society for a long time to come. Another way of saying this is that the technologies we build today will have attacks created against them that may be beyond our current expectations. Illustrative of this inability of the developer to predict, consider the Ukrainian power outage. The initial vector was phishing with macro-enabled documents. Do we imagine that the inventors of Word macros in 1997 could have foreseen that their technology would be abused to cause power outages in the next millennium? Can we blame them for 'not doing enough'?

Bluntly speaking, we should not hope for the developers of today to foresee the attacks of the future, but rather we should develop cyber risk analysis frameworks that are flexible enough to detect and study any future attacks, regardless of their strangeness.

## 3.8 EXPECT THE UNEXPECTED

### 3.8.1 You Can't Change Physics

Cyber attacks cannot make fire more hot, nor alter gravity to make pipes reverse their flow. This might seem obvious, but it is an important fact in our quantification of cyber risk, particularly in cyber-physical systems. Why?

When engineers and industrial architects build factories or power-generation plants, they take great care to minimize the maximum damage that could occur during catastrophic events. The construction of a turbine hall for electricity generation, for example, is no simple task. It is constructed in such a way that damage is limited to the building inside. Often these large turbines have blades that could be flung from the machines when they are spinning at high speed. Employees are not allowed in the turbine hall when they are operational, and the halls themselves are constructed to contain damage under maximum severity.

### 3.8.2 Worst-case Scenarios

When we consider the impacts of cyber attacks, we can similarly design the safety requirements to constrain the most lethal, or costly, or damaging events. This anchors our discussions of severity in cyber-physical events. It means we don't have to rework everything in terms of finding a worst-case scenario; we can crib from the physical world and knowledgeable safety engineers to use it as a starting point for discussions on just how bad things could get in a hacking situation. Engineers use the concept of 'design load scenarios' to incorporate the necessary safety factors into their resilience calculations. Similarly, we need to consider worst-case scenarios, or design situation scenarios, in the design of safe cyber-physical systems.

Talented cyber-physical hackers study the safety cases too, looking for ways to trigger safety states unlikely ever to be seen in nature. They optimize the mayhem they wish to achieve, and they can do so by studying safety diagrams from facilities they have hacked. An early stage of a cyber-physical attack may well often involve a breach that allows attackers to gather data on network architecture and industrial process design. So when we consider these cases, it is best to assume that an attacker knows everything that we know: a sort of cyber-physical corollary of Kerckhoffs's principle of cryptography.

### 3.8.3 Estimate the Consequences

Once we have defined our worst-case scenarios for physical effects, we can usually quantify that catastrophe in some sort of manner: cost of repairing the damage, potential number of lives lost, workers' compensation payouts, liabilities incurred, environmental impact. The discussion can then turn to how this would be accomplished through hacking, using experienced ethical hackers to identify the potential processes through which compromises could occur.

Even with great intentions, most people will consider worst-case scenarios highly implausible. Until there are more examples of catastrophic failures of systems caused by external hackers, it may be difficult to convince managers that safety measures are needed to protect against these eventualities. Safety engineers may (and often do) believe that it is impossible to damage their systems, but tests demonstrate how easy it is to do. Safety tests to identify the vulnerabilities may take a few weeks, so they are often considered an expensive extravagance, but this will save money and time, and greatly enhance the security of a system.

### 3.8.4 Prioritize Mitigation Against Multiple Scenarios

It is often better to rapidly enumerate a variety of risks, and look for mitigations and solutions that help in most of them. Insisting that every

## MANAGEMENT EXERCISE: REHEARSING FOR A CYBER-PHYSICAL ATTACK

Review all the cyber-physical systems of your organization, and for each one produce an inventory of the components of the system, including sensors that the system relies on, actuators being controlled, the control system itself and its core logic or control software, data stores for parameters, safety systems, and alert protocols. Identify the most important cyber-physical system for your organization.

In this exercise, your most important cyber-physical system has been compromised. Hackers have managed to gain control of the key actuators that your systems use to manipulate real-world processes, and the sensors that provide confirmation that they are performing normally.

Develop a scenario for a high-impact act of sabotage that the hackers could achieve with this level of control. Estimate the scale of physical damage they could potentially cause, the number of people whose well-being could be jeopardized, the length of time that the system would be out of commission, and the consequential operational impact on continuity and costs to the revenues of the organization.

Develop a contingency plan to ensure business continuity if such an attack were to happen. Identify precedents of similar, or even remotely similar, kinds of attacks on cyber-physical systems. Estimate the odds of such a scenario occurring in the next five years.

Review options for improving the protection of your cyber-physical systems from external hackers or malicious insiders. Discuss with other senior management whether the costs and efforts of implementing these improvements in security would be worthwhile for your organization.

risk must be demonstrated in depth means necessarily slowing the process of identifying all risks.

It is usually a reasonable assumption that any given system can be hacked, if the hackers have sufficient time and resources. Identifying the individual process by which the attack will occur may be less important than improving security generally. It is a better principle to work across many risks to identify mitigations or detections that assist you against multiple cyber attack scenarios (or indeed safety or fraud or environmental scenarios), rather than wasting energy discussing any one case in great detail.

### 3.8.5  How Likely Is a Cyber-Physical Attack?

The likelihood of a future attack is a key component in any discussion of implementing safety procedures, and in justifying additional expenditure or resource requirements for solving cyber risk.

There are two ways to consider likelihood of attack. One is using historical rates of attack observed against similar organizations and target systems. The other is analysis of vulnerabilities and the potential for an attacker to find a vulnerability in your system and to exploit it.

Historical attack rates vary a lot by type of organization and system. Some organizations, like energy companies, may see hacking attempts daily, while others, such as mining and agricultural systems, might have much lower rates of attempts.

Some individual facilities may never have been hacked before, so they may not consider the possibility as a serious likelihood. This can be compounded by the fact that many of these facilities have been hacked before but did not detect it.

You may also consider the frequency that attacks are being carried out against the general population, against similar organizations to yours, and to the sector in which you operate. This provides an indication of a population view of likelihood of attack. If there is data on the number of attacks per year against half of the population of industrial factories similar to yours, but no data on the other half, then it may be reasonable to assume that the other half experiences a similar rate, or you may adjust the uncertainty according to whether the unknown population is more vulnerable or more of a target than the population sample for which good data exists.

### 3.8.6  Variation in Risk over Time

Any attack rate reflects the number of malicious hackers motivated to mount an attack against that class of target system. If that attacking population were to double, we might expect the number of attacks to double and the likelihood to increase for any target system.

That could happen for a variety of reasons: fiscal motivations shift, or social sentiment and ideological motivations arise, or the hacker groups targeting educational facilities go on a concerted recruitment drive. Both the vulnerable (prey) population and the malicious hacker (predator) population are relevant to assessments of the likelihood of future attacks. We know that the number of potential targets is increasing rapidly; the number of internet-connected devices, for example, is increasing by about a third a year, with forecasts of reaching 22 billion devices by 2020. The dynamics of the attacker community are less easy to estimate, but are considered in further detail in Chapter 5. We should also be considering the change in frequency of attacks, because a rising frequency represents a poorly managed risk.

Historical averages are poor guides to future incident rates. Variations can be large, year on year.

## 3.9 SMART DEVICES AND THE INTERNET OF THINGS

### 3.9.1 The Infrastructure of the Information Society

The IoT has significant vulnerability to malicious manipulation. The increasing ubiquity of connected devices causes concerns for malicious effects in everyday life spilling over into the physical world. Connected and smart devices are a growing part of that world, and cyber security issues have been raised around products varying from household appliances and entertainment systems to industrial process control systems, building heating and ventilation systems, webcams, drones, autonomous cars, and medical devices such as pacemakers.

### 3.9.2 Security Levels in Connected Devices

Many of these systems were originally designed with poor attention to security, and have relatively low levels of anti-tampering protection. This is likely to change over time as manufacturers are held to higher standards of security, but low profit margins and high volumes of products constrain the levels of protection that can be expected. The January 2017 filing by the Federal Trade Commission against the D-Link Corporation[23] for its devices being used in the Dyn DNS attack is the first example of a lawsuit against a manufacturer of IoT devices for poor cyber security, and this may prove influential in improving the security standards of IoT devices in the future.

Improvements in security are unlikely to occur rapidly, so society and managers of businesses may have to accept vulnerabilities in these systems and their potential for use in cyber-physical attacks for some time to come.

### 3.9.3  Making Our Devices Safer

Cyber-physical risk has been possible since before the invention of computers, hacking, and cyber-physical systems. The risk itself is not new, but it is appearing to be actualized with more frequency. That frequency will be driven by awareness of it as a possibility, access to capabilities to make it happen, and motivation to do so. Nation-states will almost always be motivated to sabotage one another, and currently there is very little in the way of diplomacy, policing, international norms, or economics to prevent them from doing so.

Society has undervalued this risk for at least 30 years, with a combination of confirmation bias, recency bias, and inability to price the risk.

We have invested heavily in technical solutions to technical problems, and this is rarely examined from a rational economic perspective. You can get a computer science degree for building a firewall, but which academic institution has evaluated the ever-changing value of firewall deployment from a business risk perspective? Can we scientifically or economically or probabilistically demonstrate their efficacy with respect to some attacks?

### 3.9.4  Why Isn't This Studied More Articulately?

Even the discipline of security economics tends to examine the mis-alignment of incentive, rather than the thorny thicket of cyber-defense economics and technological efficacy. Even where we do evaluate efficacy, we tend to make assumptions that this will be true for all time against all attackers. In reality, the efficacy changes over time, and we continue to assume that all cyber risk can be mitigated in the best manner, and for the lowest cost, through the adoption of more technology that causes the very same risks we are mitigating. Firewalls have vulnerabilities too. There is a heavy bias towards technological risk prevention, rather than detection and cost reduction.

### 3.9.5  Need This Always Be So?

Cyber-physical risk has a unique position amongst our pantheon of cyber risks, because its severity isn't significantly amplified by digital actualization of the risk. We can crib those severities from previous fields of study, and learn much from safety experts if we keep in mind that their protections may become a malicious hacker's recipes for disaster. We can use safety to understand security severity, but we should not imagine that safety systems automatically reduce the frequency or probability of security incidents.

Those who study cyber-physical vulnerability will have a bright and extremely busy future. Study is needed of capabilities to detect more attacks, metrics that explore sudden changes in the frequency of attacks, metrics for sudden growth in the vulnerability or deployment of cyber-physical systems, the cost reduction of effects after attacks, and the growth in capabilities of threat actors.

All of these things are on the threshold of knowability, either intra-organizationally or inter-organizationally. Some are knowable a priori, others a posteriori. Once these elements of cyber risk become more clearly and quantifiably recognized across society, we will see both cyber-physical risk in particular and cyber risk in general for what they are: collective action problems.

What interest will a nation-state have in cyber-physical sabotage of another country's infrastructure when it counts the cost of that country's losses against its own loss in GDP from imports? Communicating this to all stakeholders would have a more powerful effect than 50 years of diplomacy around cyber norms and the escalation in cyber-physical risk that we are currently facing.

## ENDNOTES

1. Loukas (2015).
2. Statista (2017).
3. Gartner (2016) reports 6.4 billion connected devices in 2016, up 30% from 2015.
4. New (2014).
5. Gander (2015).
6. Zetter (2014).
7. Rid (2013)
8. US Nuclear Regulatory Commission (2003).
9. CCRS and Lloyd's (2015).
10. E-ISAC (2016).
11. Baker (2008).
12. BSI (2014).
13. Smith (2001).
14. Halperin et al. (2008).
15. Alexander (2016).

16. Moe and Leverett (2015).
17. George Dyson, in one of his talks on the history of computer science, relays the story of Danny Hillis having this insight while working on the engineering of early computers.
18. Ollam (2016).
19. *United States v. Azar* (2009).
20. Johnson et al. (2017).
21. Anderson (2010).
22. Lamport et al. (1982).
23. FTC (2017).

# CHAPTER 4

# Ghosts in the Code

## 4.1  ALL SOFTWARE HAS ERRORS

Software contains errors. An undetected error typically occurs at least once in every 50 lines of computer code, even in commercial software released after completing quality assurance (QA) processes.[1] It is these errors that are at the heart of cyber risk. An error that causes a malfunction is known as a 'bug', after a 1947 glitch in the Harvard Mark II electromechanical computer was caused by a moth in the machinery.

### 4.1.1  Accidental Malfunction

Even rigorous checks can fail to find the hidden ghosts in the code.

Errors can cause the software to malfunction, even without external intervention, usually in ways that the QA system hasn't anticipated. Some of these can be very costly. On August 2, 2012, investment company Knight Capital ran a test of its new software system, written in-house, for executing automatic rapid electronic trades on the US stock exchange. Unfortunately, an error in the software inverted the conventional wisdom of trading: it bought high and sold low, losing money on every trade, 40 times a second, for 30 minutes. By the time the traders managed to get the rogue system back under control (yes, they tried switching it off and switching it back on again), they had lost $440 million, and nearly bankrupted the company.[2]

Software errors have been blamed for billion-dollar rocket launch failures,[3] deadly helicopter crashes,[4] and malfunctions of medical equipment that have cost lives.[5] A 2002 study by the US Department of Commerce concluded that:

> *Software bugs, or errors, are so prevalent and so detrimental that they cost the US economy an estimated $59 billion annually, or about 0.6 percent of US gross domestic product.*[6]

### 4.1.2 Errors as Exploitable Vulnerabilities

Software errors can also form vulnerabilities. These vulnerabilities – particularly in the software that is at the heart of commercial activity – are hunted down by malicious hackers and exploited to thwart security, to make software do things that it shouldn't, and to cause cyber losses in the many different ways that we have documented in Chapter 2. Errors in software are weapons in the cyber war once they become exploitable vulnerabilities.

It is a race between the defenders (the software developers, security industry, and law enforcement) and the attackers (malicious hackers) to identify software vulnerabilities that can be exploited. When the defenders find a vulnerability, they notify the software developer, who fixes the problem and issues a 'patch' to the users of the software. Once the users have installed the patch, they are generally safe against the software's exploitation by attackers.

If the attackers find the bug first, they can use it for gain. An exploitable bug that is discovered by malicious cyber hackers, but not known by the users of the software, is known as a 'zero day': the first time that the user realizes that the software has a flaw is on day zero when the hacker has already started to exploit it and the damage is done.

The process of reducing error rates in software, and managing the process of finding them and stopping them falling into the wrong hands, is the subject of this chapter.

If vulnerabilities in software can be reduced, this will go a long way to solving cyber risk, yet what is the scope and scale of such a task? Can it be accomplished quickly and easily?

## 4.2 VULNERABILITIES, EXPLOITS, AND ZERO DAYS

### 4.2.1 Arsenals of Exploits

Knowledge of vulnerabilities in commonly-used software confers an advantage to national cyber teams that work to protect the economy and military against the activities of cyber criminals and incursions by national cyber teams from other countries. They invest significant resources in finding these vulnerabilities, and stockpiling them for their own use in carrying out their own cyber operations of offensive actions. They create arsenals of exploits and vulnerabilities as a toolkit to use in their operations.

An insight into how extensive these arsenals are came from the embarrassing public release on August 13, 2016 of a selection of cyber hacking weapons obtained from 'Equation Group', an elite cyber hacking team of the US National Security Agency (NSA), by a group calling itself the *ShadowBrokers*.[7] The released showcase folder contained 15 exploits, 13 implants, and 11 tools, most notably a number of previously unknown 'zero day' exploits to penetrate industry standard firewalls such as Cisco ASA, Fortinet FortiGate, and Juniper SRX, along with other corporate penetration tools.[8] It was an impressive array of technologies and, significantly, revealed that the NSA had kept these vulnerabilities secret, even from the software companies themselves. This gave the NSA team an advantage to carry out their own operations, but raised serious questions about whose interests are best served. The fact that some of the exploits released in this cache were later used in the *WannaCry* and *NotPetya* malware attacks in 2017 added insult to injury. How did we get to such a situation?

## 4.2.2 The Vulnerabilities Equities Process

On November 15, 2017 the US White House offered the world an unprecedented peek into a strategic process of cyber offense and defense trade-off discussions, by publishing its report on the Vulnerabilities Equities Process (VEP). This process had been running since 2008, but was only whispered about by those in the know of US federal government and intelligence circles. The process itself was designed and continually evolved over the next 10 years to balance the keeping of zero days secret for US intelligence operations against the dangers of not informing US companies and federal organizations of the existence of a flaw. The Interagency Review Board meets when an agency discovering a zero day vulnerability summons the others, to deliberate how exploits are used, and how long they are kept secret before they are revealed to the companies that might be able to patch the vulnerability. At the time of writing, the EU is discussing replicating the approach, with much more transparency for civil society groups.

The process is an important one, and the metrics used to make such decisions are precisely the same metrics we should concern ourselves with in this chapter. Though we know only some of the techniques used, we must imagine others, and then reimagine them for use not by intelligence agencies, military, and police, but for society and risk management. We will use this discussion of the utility versus the risk of a given zero day vulnerability or exploit to tackle some of the key research questions of cyber risk. Many of those questions are answered or answerable easily, but many have not yet been tackled by research, and yet we know they are very important.

Some of these questions are timeless ones of computer security, such as how do we know how many vulnerabilities a given body of code has? Is the number limited, verifiable, or even estimable? Does that number grow or shrink in time, and do some vulnerability management strategies work better than others for reducing vulnerabilities in code?

### 4.2.3 Software Is Milk, Not Wine

*Purchase a fine wine, place it in a cellar, and wait a few years. The aging will have resulted in a delightful beverage, a product far better than the original. Purchase a gallon of milk, place it in a cellar, and wait a few years. You will be sorry. We know how the passing of time affects milk and wine, but how does aging affect the security of software?*

This problem statement by Ozment and Schechter neatly sums up what we need to know foundationally about software vulnerabilities.[9] We need to understand the provenance and history of vulnerabilities in a single piece of software, and ultimately audit a similar inventory for the thousands of applications running on a desktop computer, phone, and other devices we use day to day. It would be valuable to be able to know and manage the number of exploitable vulnerabilities present in any given company's tech stack, the code its people have written themselves, and all the code they run to do their basic daily tasks.

This is clearly an aspiration, but is not possible today using current tools and processes. Vulnerabilities in software systems are so plentiful that penetration testing teams (and hackers with a reasonable level of skill and dedication) can usually construct a way in to gain access to their target company. The authors speak from experience, with years spent in penetration testing. There is no shortage of methods by which to compromise and subvert computers, networks, code, and people.

It would be helpful to quantify this, and to count vulnerabilities and catalog their severities. To be more scientific we must deep dive into an entire field of computer security literature: vulnerability management, remediation, and notification.

### 4.2.4 Issuing Security Patches

The target time for a vendor to develop a security patch is within 45 days.[10] If it takes longer, vendors tend not to internalize the cost, and instead push it onto their user base as an externality. The computer emergency response team's coordination center (CERT/CC) of the Software Engineering Institute in Pittsburgh, Pennsylvania, maintains this target time window for issuing patches as part of a process known as 'coordinated disclosure'. This used to be called 'responsible disclosure', which cast ethical aspersions on researchers for publishing vulnerabilities without a patch.

There is a dynamic and potentially a misalignment of incentives between the vendors producing the software, the users who are exposed to any vulnerabilities that the software contains, and bug finders who identify the existence of vulnerabilities in software. Vendors know that managing their vulnerabilities is important, but do not derive revenues directly from patch releases, and can be slow to issue patches to known vulnerabilities. Even the teams who work on vulnerability projects for vendors feel insufficiently resourced and supported by the businesses they serve. The vendors' business models are not well-enough aligned with patching and taking total cost of ownership of the problem.

Addressing this problem will take greater transparency. A key step here would be the Common Numbering Authorities (CNAs) who issue Common Vulnerabilities and Exposures (CVE) identifiers, to record and publicly display the vendor notification time, as well as the patch issue time. This could lead to significant academic research into patching effectiveness. For example, we could see which vendors respond more quickly on average to vulnerability notifications. It may also reveal whether some freelance vulnerability researchers are more effective at getting companies to build effective patches. There is a suspicion that higher-profile researchers may prompt vendors to patch faster to avoid negative publicity. Greater transparency into the process will be possible only if we start to record such time stamps. We will say more later about these CNAs and the challenges they face in standardizing almost everything to do with vulnerabilities.

## 4.2.5 Getting Users to Install Patches

Of course, getting the patch developed is only the first part of a defense.[11] Many users take a long time to install a patch after it is released. 'Patching latency' – the gap of time between a patch being released and it being installed by a company – is one of the key determinants of cyber risk rating for a company. And a patch that isn't installed not only affects the security of that company; it also affects the security of all the other users of that software.

So should we perhaps be more aggressive about notifying users and improving patching speed? A blossoming literature in user notifications of vulnerabilities exists today, suggesting that much more work on usability and nudge theory is desperately needed.[12] Studies show that it is difficult to get more than 15% of users to patch quickly, and that there is also a small hard core of users who will never patch. Some vendors know this already and devote considerable resources into usability studies to help get users to install patches. Improving notification and patching speed metrics would have a significant effect on the VEP too, if you knew reflected distributed denial of service vulnerabilities would never be patched, or if industrial control systems were likely to patch faster.

Users are right to be confused about patches. Some companies 'silently patch', which means they patch for security without explicitly declaring a patch to be a security patch. This can create problems, as security patches can break previously working functionality. In desktops the user might be able to adapt, but in medical products, aircraft, and other high-assurance, life-critical systems this is unacceptable. Other companies announce their patches, but sometimes too the patches don't work for some users using more arcane configurations, and they have to be tested before usage. Still other companies refuse to create security patches because the product has reached the end of its life, and is no longer actively supported. It is often not cost-effective for software vendors to support legacy systems.

### 4.2.6   Lifespan of Software

This raises questions of how governments or other longer life cycle organizations should buy software. After all, a bridge can be maintained by engineers even if the company that built it goes out of business, but some software companies try to assert rights that mean you cannot change their code. In these cases, what shall we do when they go out of business? There's a literature on code escrow too, but it suggests that even when it is performed, the wrong versions of the code get escrowed, or it is otherwise unusable for technical reasons.[13]

## 4.3   COUNTING VULNERABILITIES

### 4.3.1   US NIST National Vulnerability Database

The National Vulnerability Database (NVD) of the US National Institute of Standards and Technology (NIST) tracks reported vulnerabilities in public software, both commercial, by vendor, and open source.[14] Each report is given a score in the Common Vulnerability Scoring System (CVSS), based on several metrics to reflect the characteristics and potential impacts of information technology vulnerabilities. These are commonly used to prioritize vulnerability remediation activities and for estimating the severity of impact of vulnerabilities if discovered in a system. CVSS (v3) scores range from 0 to 10, and are also categorized into Low (0.1–3.9), Medium (4.0–6.9), High (7.0–8.9), and Critical (9.0–10.0).

The NVD has recorded and graded more than 110,000 vulnerabilities since it began in 2009, and averages around 1,000 new vulnerabilities recorded each month. Around 15% of vulnerabilities are graded as 'Critical'.

**4.3.1.1   Standardizing Vulnerability Identifiers**   A common technical definition of a vulnerability might be something that has an assignment from the Common Vulnerabilities and Exposures standard of a CVE number. At one time, these were issued only by the MITRE Corporation and CERT/CC, but in time others were trusted to become a CNA. For example, once Microsoft developed a large operational security team, it became more efficient for them to manage their own CVE numbering program and submit the CVE numbers to MITRE's database later. All CNA programs agree to adhere to MITRE's standard of assignment and de-duplication, which consists of 83 organizations and growing yearly.

Many vulnerabilities pass through the US NVD or CERT/CC and MITRE systems, but others can run through the smaller CNAs. However, there is no necessity for other countries to agree to this format, particularly those that do not trust the United States to handle their vulnerabilities. There is nothing to prevent them setting up their own vulnerability reporting infrastructure, and naming or renaming vulnerabilities as they please. The lack of a unique standardized naming convention makes it difficult to use these statistics systematically to track trends and progress.

This problem statement was put succinctly by the international team of Art Manion, Takayuki Uchiyama, and Masato Terada at the annual conference of the Forum of Incident Response and Security Teams (FIRST) held in Berlin in 2015: 'Vulnerability identification is infrastructure'. Their Vulnerability Reporting and Data eXchange Special Interest Group (VRDX-SIG) identified many problems with globally naming vulnerabilities, many of which they are still working to solve. This represents only the public repositories of vulnerabilities and exploits. It is assumed that governments are maintaining their own additional secret stockpiles of vulnerabilities and exploits, and similar problems will exist within the identification and management of those stockpiles.

**4.3.1.2   Quantifying Vulnerability Identification**   Some 95% of commercial software companies have fewer than 10 CVE numbered vulnerabilities, while the top eight have more than 500.[15] Is this because vulnerability researchers focus on the top brands, or because those brands produce more code? Is the number of vulnerability reports a good or a bad indicator of security? Can we extrapolate these numbers as predictive of future numbers of vulnerabilities, or do things like automated vulnerability identification suddenly skew the numbers?

CERT/CC discovered exactly that when it instigated automated testing of Android apps and their handling of SSL/TLS connections. The automated process discovered 23,000 vulnerabilities within one year of testing. To put that in perspective, other vulnerability databases across all types of vulnerabilities identified 10,000–15,000 in the same year. As we automate vulnerability discovery, our ability to extrapolate vulnerability trends will fail us.

The number of vulnerabilities is likely to increase with the growth in deployed code bases too, for example in websites. They may grow or fall because of incentive changes such as bug bounties (black or white hat, full disclosure or non-disclosure). They could very well fall because of legal challenges to researchers, or rise because of changes in software liability. They may grow simply because we have a surge of computer security graduates.

In conclusion, vulnerability discovery statistics should be thought of as arising from a dynamic system, subject to all the perils of predicting non-linear effects with extrapolation. Beware of such predictions if the bearer does not also give uncertainty bounds. We expect that many cyber risk practitioners will continue to be fooled into thinking that vulnerability discovery follows a linear trend for at least another decade to come.

**4.3.1.3  Quantifying Vulnerability Severity**  The standard of measurement in vulnerability severity is the CVSS, which ranges from 0 to 10. This severity metric is machine focused, which means it rates the severity as it might occur to an *individual computer*. It is already accepted and built into the metrics that they will be different for different deployments, because of network architecture or use of kernel protection mechanisms such as memory address layout randomization. So the base CVSS score can be altered for your individual business through the use of environmental scores to adapt a generic score to be more appropriate to your operating environment.

The scoring system also takes into account temporal elements such as the maturity of the exploit and the quality of the vulnerability reporting. CVSS has evolved over three iterations with the input of many people and organizations and has evolved very well to cope with an individual business's view of machine-level risk.

### 4.3.2  Open Source versus Closed Source Vulnerabilities

The statistics from CVSS scores tell us many things, but, like the vulnerability metrics extrapolation, we should attempt to bring as much context as possible to discussion of CVSS scores. There is a long-running debate about open source versus closed source vulnerabilities.

*The median CVSS scores for closed source vendors are greater than the median scores for open source vendors.*[16]

This statistic seems pretty definitive about the severity of vulnerabilities in closed versus open source software. It could lead you to the conclusion that closed source software is less secure. But let us look a bit deeper at the way these analyses are carried out.

Open source code means researchers can look directly at source code without having to decompile binaries and reverse opaque proprietary protocols. The consequence of this is that they can automate the bug-finding process to find many more low-severity bugs. Making automation easier skews the median score of CVSS severity. Open source and closed source software have not been assessed in the same way.

There are also personal motivation issues for researchers in identifying vulnerabilities. Higher-severity scores are more rewarding and reputation enhancing. Minor severity vulnerabilities are less reported in closed source software, usually because they are discovered in-house, and fixed before release.

Vulnerabilities can also be mistakenly classified by their severity. Many vulnerabilities reported by less experienced bug hunters as a denial of service are actually a buffer overflow, which would be categorized as more severe because it could have been exploited for remote code execution. Vendors may collude with the lower classifications of vulnerability severities to preserve their reputations. Some bug hunters trawl through vulnerability reports knowing they can improve the severity of these misclassified vulnerabilities.

This kind of trading in severity and bundling of vulnerabilities happens because different actors are interested in different statistics. Good vulnerability management teams avoid such short-term thinking to focus on long-term lessons.

### 4.3.3   Vulnerabilities Impacting Populations of Companies

The CVSS is an important tool that serves its intended design purpose very well; however, it is entirely unfit for some cyber risk practices. This should not be misconstrued as a criticism of a useful tool, but rather to identify that we need new tools for new professions.

To illustrate, consider a policy maker or someone who wants to calculate the impact of a new vulnerability on society in general, and on the whole population of organizations or subsections of it. Her concern is not the impact of integrity, availability, or confidentiality of an individual computer, but rather an estimate of the potential costs of the vulnerability to many businesses. She usually wouldn't have visibility into the number and types of computers in any specific organization, and is even less likely to know the proportion of vulnerable versus unaffected computers within the business.

Being the smart researcher she is, she might consider the market share of the specific software in use, or use a tool like Shodan to get an initial estimate of such a proportion on the open internet, but she would know that the variance of such a proportion might differ substantially from one organization to another. At the core of her concern are two factors: prevalence of vulnerability across a population (such as a country, across all IP addresses in an autonomous system number (ASN), companies in the Fortune 1000, or all the devices in an individual business), and a very different kind of severity score: the cost to each population.

In conclusion, we have some good severity taxonomies for engineering and protecting businesses tactically, but strategically we might want to develop better methods for studying the prevalence of a vulnerability across a population, and the severity to the affected group at the organizational level rather than the machine level. Improving both these metrics will enhance future cyber risk management.

### 4.3.4   Estimating Population Impacts

In Chapter 1 we made some estimates of the global costs of cyber attacks to the economy and various populations of businesses. These techniques use approaches based on an attacker's views of the problem in research analyses since 2013.[17] This attempts to quantify the numbers of different organizations of different types in the business and public sector populations, and to use various types of evidence, surveys, and sweeps of the prevalence of software usage and business practice in the target population, combined with models of vulnerability and precedents for costs that have been caused by similar types of cyber attack disruption, to estimate metrics of cost per device.[18]

Other metrics have been proposed to assess how hard it might be for an attacker to find the vulnerable systems to exploit. A Leverett-Wightman (L-W) cost measures the opportunity cost for an attacker to exploit a given vulnerability, based on how common it is in the population.[19] For example, CVE-2017-7269 has an L-W cost of $0.000028 across all IPv4, whereas CVE-2017-5689 has an L-W cost a thousand times higher at $0.027027, meaning that the former is more common across the internet, is easier for attackers to exploit, and represents the greater risk to the community in total. It is of greater concern for incident response teams and businesses because it is much more prevalent.

We urge other researchers to use similar approaches and log their cost per device as a useful metric. Why would this metric be interesting or novel? There are nine reasons:

1. This metric is independent of methodology and technology.
2. As costs for parallelization fall, this is incorporated into the metric.
3. As newer, faster scanners (such as ZMap) are developed, they are also included in the metric.
4. The density of vulnerability across a network space is factored into the metric.
5. Partial scans can still be used for metrics.
6. We understand the cost to attackers of finding opportunistic targets.
7. We understand the low cost to this methodology of defending.
8. We understand the change over time in the life cycle of exposure and vulnerability.
9. It naturally translates a technical problem into an economic one ready for debate and policy discussion.

It is important to enhance vulnerability tracking with metrics that incorporate the size of the populations at risk from the vulnerability. This would make it possible to assess whether one organization is more vulnerable than another and to compare vulnerabilities across networks and across the entire internet. It will provide a metric of 'attacker opportunity effort', and allow us to estimate when the ease of opportunistic hacks falls below $10,000, or $1000, or 1 cent, which will greatly inform our defensive strategies.

We propose that the use of population-based metrics will help CERTs to improve their understanding of their own technical exposure across a constituency as new CVEs come out. Finally, we urge their adoption as a contribution to risk management of vulnerabilities at scale, at least until better metrics of vulnerability distribution across machine populations are created.

## 4.4  VULNERABILITY MANAGEMENT

### 4.4.1  Within a Project or Technology Under Your Control

Adhering to a secure software development life cycle is a well-established methodology for vulnerability management in software products under an organization's stewardship, and there are many useful books written on the topic.[20] These use several metrics, each with its own merits and flaws.

The first metric often encountered in the literature is 'lines of code' (LoC) or 'thousand lines of code' (KLoC). These are typical metrics for counting the vulnerability incidence rate, such as '6 vulnerabilities per KLoC'.

This measurement of ratio per code base is useful, but has drawbacks. LoC was a useful concept during the pre-web era, when code was monolithic, written from scratch each time, and compiled before use. This quantum of software development was fairly atomic and indivisible in nature at that time. In the era of web-based/modular/object-oriented development though, JavaScript, and calling dynamic-link libraries (DLLs), vulnerabilities that occur in the libraries become inherited into the main body. It may or may not call all the LoC of the initial library. A library can be called by a single line of code, and a program will call as many lines as it needs. How should the vulnerability metric of $N$ per LoC for the library translate into the vulnerability assessment of the main program?

The problem of vulnerability inheritance doesn't apply just to programming languages that import libraries or modules; it is also deeply important in web-based languages. Modern JavaScript-based systems call JavaScript functions from other websites, and interact dynamically, with many components and subscripts spread across many sites. Each of these could be created by other developers, and could be being modified, updated, and enhanced by them without the knowledge of the script calling the function. Community software of this type is more difficult to assess in terms of vulnerability prevalence. It would be helpful if each library was transparently assessed with a vulnerability metric.

Standardized comparisons are needed for:

- Comparability of vulnerabilities per LoC in different languages
- Comparability of vulnerabilities per LoC in different applications in the same language
- Comparability of vulnerabilities per LoC over time

Further issues include the fact that measuring vulnerabilities per LoC provides an average, which may vary within key blocks of code – probably higher or lower in the block you are most concerned about – so it would be better practice to quote estimates with their uncertainty bounds, for example: 0.5 vulnerabilities per LoC ± 0.2.

However, of course, all these approaches are a measurement of the vulnerabilities we know about and know how to find. This is fraught with a number of cognitive and quantification biases we should be careful to manage. Estimating the number of remaining vulnerabilities has a different literature, as exemplified by an excellent paper by Dan Geer called 'For Good Measure: The Undiscovered Login'.[21]

### 4.4.2 Supply Chain Due Diligence

It is also important to assess the lurking cyber risk in your supply chain: all the software and hardware that your business relies on every day.

As a consumer of open source code, or of proprietary code that uses a secure software development life cycle, you can use some of the metrics discussed earlier. However, it isn't common for a small to medium-size enterprise to ask Microsoft what its vulns to LoC ratio is, and reasonably expect to receive a reply.

It is worth considering a few indicators of organizational receptiveness to our enquiries, as part of our due diligence on a supplier or software counterparty.

### 4.4.3 Across Different Companies Within Your Supply Chain

Assessing the cyber risk in any given technological supply chain is complex.

Ideally, you would be able to audit companies' software or hardware development practices before you engaged them in contracts. In practice this is difficult for small businesses, or indeed large ones that aren't big enough purchasers to warrant such special treatment. Indeed, because software is a business of scale it is very rare for one customer to make up a substantial purchasing contribution of the user base. So no single software purchasing organization (even one as large as the US government) can regularly expect to audit large software vendors to satisfy their due diligence in supply chain management. If you happen to be one of those organizations large enough to make such demands on your software suppliers successfully, then do your best to protect the rest of us!

A good start is the checklist provided in the inset box.

We much prefer a company that discloses its vulnerabilities transparently. We should be looking for regular and informative vulnerability reports, with accurate CVSS scores that truly depict the impact on the organizations we are protecting. Compare those frequencies with the patch-issuing cycle of the company and see what the potential window of exploitability is, with the company's patch cadence. Does the patch-issuing cadence match the patch-installation cadence of your organization? There is no point in demanding that the vendor issue patches monthly if your organization can only install them yearly.

## DUE DILIGENCE ON YOUR TECHNOLOGY SUPPLY CHAIN

### Checklist for a Software Provider

When examining a vendor of technological systems, we should ask if it has systems for receiving vulnerability notifications from third parties. Indicators of this include:

- An existing email address such as security@vendor.com or perhaps vulnerabilities@vendor.com is a good sign.
- Check that the email address is posted in easily visible form on the vendor's website.
- The same location should include a GNU Privacy Guard (GPG) or Pretty Good Privacy (PGP) key, or other method of cryptographically sharing sensitive vulnerabilities of the vendor's products. This is a requirement of ISO standard ISO/IEC 29147:2014, so most companies should be compliant with at least that. This tells us that the company accepts and analyses external reports of security or privacy vulnerabilities.
- Does the company have an incident response team?
- Is the company a member of either FIRST (https://www.first.org) or the Trans-European Research and Education Networking Association (https://www.terena.org) (two organizations that help manage trust, accreditation, and introduction to the global incident response community)?
- Check how many vulnerability notices the vendor has published – willingness to publish and fix its own flaws is a sign of a healthy cyber risk management culture.
- Check if the company has any known vulnerabilities in vulnerability databases.[22] Review the average or median scores, and the yearly frequency of vulnerabilities. This is relevant if the vendor compares badly with other similar companies; however, you should prefer working with a company that discloses its vulnerabilities transparently, rather than one that has fewer vulnerabilities.
- A company that claims that it 'has no vulnerabilities because our security is so good' should be treated with suspicion.

You also want evidence that the company can do business with you securely. You want to know that the vendor as a business will continue to exist, and that it has a patch cadence on its own infrastructure that matches its cyber risk appetite. You want to check how it manages the security of the products you will come to depend on as your infrastructure, but you also want to know how it manages its relationships with its own vendors on whose products it relies as its own infrastructure. In short, supply chain problems are recursive. Businesses are interconnected in the digital economy, as we represent in Figure 1.1 in Chapter 1. It matters whom your suppliers rely on as their suppliers, just as much as how they satisfy your requirements. Thus you may find that your demands of your supply chain align very well with your suppliers' demands of their supply chains.

Some suppliers are good at protecting their product, and some are good at protecting their business, but you want both. Typically, suppliers have two separate teams tackling these tasks, without much discussion or overlap. A bit of dialog between both missions enables far greater innovation, and is a sign of excelling in supply chain management.

### 4.4.4 Telematics Assessments

Many people now make use of assessments of their suppliers provided by an emerging set of security rating companies that use telematics to scan the *externally facing infrastructure* of different companies and score them. They check a number of attributes that can be detected unintrusively, including patching cadence of their key technologies such as web servers and mail servers; checking that TLS certificates are up to date and carefully managed; network hygiene, including presence of botnets or other indicators of malware; and unauthorized traffic on company networks. Some security score providers monitor breach reports, and check underground forums for stolen credentials.

Telematics companies use these data assessments to provide a security score or rating that purports to correlate to various propensities for having cyber loss.

There is a small industry of telematics-based security scoring companies currently offering such services. Over time these should prove to be predictive of cyber risk for individual companies, based on demonstrable correlation of attributes with rates of cyber event incidences.

### 4.4.5 Specializations in Security Solutions

Some companies specialize in their own unique or bespoke competitive security solutions. This might be innovation in the assessment of the risk using honeypots and honey tokens, for example. When honey tokens in fake documents are accessed, this triggers a notification. They then work very diligently with a talented human resources team to identify the source of the leaks and discover if they were the work of external, internal, or combined threats.

Another company carries out undercover work to find people who are trying to carry out distributed denial-of-service (DDoS) attacks and mitigate this risk before the DDoS attack is made. Some of these innovations in approaches to security assessment are the result of security companies developing specialized expertise.

This kind of innovation may not show up on corporate reports, or security scorecards and metrics agencies. It can be discerned only by having some discussions with companies' security teams (if they trust you, and are willing to share their recipes for success). So while there may be no standardized way of scoring all your suppliers, it is worth taking some security and privacy technologists along to negotiations, and asking that your suppliers bring theirs too, so that it is part of contractual discussions.

## 4.5  INTERNATIONAL CYBER RESPONSE AND DEFENSE

### 4.5.1  National Vulnerability Agencies

When we discuss vulnerabilities and defenses at the national scale, one of the first organizations that should be contacted is the aptly named FIRST. This is a professional incident response and security/privacy organization that is made up primarily of computer security incident response teams (CSIRTs) or CERTs. Many of these function at the national level, so you can meet the Austrian CERT (CERT.at), for example, and discuss what kind of incidents they see, and perhaps their yearly report.

Most countries have their own CERT membership and teams. There are also CERT teams operated by individual large companies, and some product lines have their own CERT teams, focusing on the metrics for their own business and products. There are regular discussions of cyber risk and global metrics of FIRST, and it is worth becoming a member for any serious professional interested in comparing the global causes, management, and mitigation of cyber crime. The organization has many yearly conferences and colloquia, and good blogs and papers.

## 4.5.2 How Many Vulnerabilities Can You Find Easily in a Given Country?

Vulnerabilities can be found in computers online by scanning them. The art and science of scanning is complex, but there is a good set of resources on the subject for the interested researcher, security specialist, or cyber risk statistician. Nmap and ZMap projects are examples with strong development and user bases. Search engines like Shodan can be used for simple levels of scanning operations.

Shodan also provides a database of results, which provides a history of scans of the internet going back 10 years. The results are geo-located, and can give some good perspectives on the machine demographics of the internet. You can answer questions such as 'Which countries use more Linux than Windows?' or 'Which city hosts the most NGINX servers?' You can partition the data in many different ways: by country, by city, by autonomous system number (often more useful if you want to effect change), by operating system, or by port/protocol. Shodan democratized scanning, and made it accessible to a community that wanted the information without having to understand the underlying protocols and art of scanning. Presumably it is for those who don't want to grapple with artisanal packet crafting, and the exaltation of heaps or lexxing UDP length zones (TEH LULZ). There's no accounting for taste.

There are many reports that set out the landscape of cyber threat for the less technical or those who want a strategic view of risks without doing the scanning themselves. The Microsoft *Security Intelligence Report* has some very useful statistics on infections by country. The compilers are even careful to state detections per investigation, which is an often neglected method for admitting that most of our collection methods for incidents show heavy selection bias. In short, we don't detect every malware event in a country, nor are we even sure it is possible to do so in any computer science sense. So it is best to demarcate not just how many infections we found, but also how many times we tried to find them. This allows further analysis of our own uncertainty bounds, so as to build a more realistic view of the problem.

## 4.5.3 Posing a Risk to Others

When we are 'at risk' in a cyber sense it is highly likely we also pose a risk to others, either as a transmission vector of malice or through our neglect. My neglecting to use antivirus software might very well lead me to give you an infected file. Those we exchange files with are just as likely to pass us harm in a computer as every person we shake hands with is likely to give us the flu.

Many DDoS attacks come from unprotected computers, sometimes even from your own computer without your knowledge. Most people view DDoS events as 'something bad that happens to me', not as something 'my company's negligence allows to happen to myself and others'. In other words, rDDoS is a collective action problem. An analysis that made this more apparent to the accidental collaborators, not just the victims, was carried out by Cyber Green, which ranked countries by their rDDoS risk to others, in having unprotected computers in their jurisdiction, rather than concentrating on the victims of DDoS.[23] Information was presented globally, by country, and by ASN. This is a good example of communicating security issues as an externality on a public good, and making data available in a format that is useful to both security engineers and cyber risk researchers.

It would be useful to manage vulnerabilities at the country level, and that seems tantalizingly possible when you can scan whole countries in seconds. However, the issues of financial and organizational incentives make this more complex, as we explore in the next section. That said, there are some wonderful ideas of how economical this might be if pursued with seriousness.[24]

### 4.5.4  Victim Notification

Contacting the owners of servers that have been compromised, or the owners of vulnerable computers on the internet, is commonly done via a CERT. The two processes are slightly different and elicit very different reactions.

In the first case the CERT has been informed or has discovered that a number of computers are compromised in some manner. For example, a number of email addresses and clear text passwords are discovered in a darknet data dump. The CERT might want to inform both the email owners and the company whose emails they belong to that they have been compromised. Most people respond well to such emails, and work to stem the cyber incident they have been informed of. A few of them, though, distrust governments on principle or react badly, thinking they are in some legal trouble rather than being helpfully informed.

In the second case, the number of adverse reactions goes up, because the CERT is simply informing people of the *potential for harm*. Most people don't like having more hard work suddenly added to their day because it might be an issue in the future. This is a particularly well-documented phenomenon, and the reader is referred to literature on the subject.[25]

## 4.5.5   Bug Bounties

In recent years bug bounties such as Hacker One have brought exploit development into the public eye. Previously, vulnerabilities were discovered and needed proof of concept or code to demonstrate the vulnerability. Some vulnerabilities were even thought to be unexploitable, until innovators in the field demonstrated how it could be done. This is white hat exploit development, but the dark markets do exploit development too, and this is a part of cyber risk that goes widely unquantified – needlessly, in our view.

Such bug bounties and penetration testing firms could offer their data for cyber risk analysts. How long do exploits take on average to develop? Are they easier to write in one language than another? How many versions do they go through? How many exploits are probabilistic or deterministic in their success rates? How much does it cost to create them, and then use them at scale? What are the minimum/maximum/average numbers of public-facing computers that different exploits could affect?

These statistics could allow us to quantify threat actors in interesting ways. We could then estimate the number of zero days they could have at their disposal, or how many machines they operate illicitly. To make good decisions on allocating resource priorities for thwarting attacks, it is valuable to know that one threat group can target 10 core switches and another can compromise 100,000 laptops.

About 2.8% of vulnerabilities are discovered because of an exploit already written. In other words, 2.8% of vulnerabilities reported come from situations where they are already being exploited in the wild, and white hat researchers find the exploit and then reverse engineer the vulnerability from the exploit. Now should we assume that unethical hackers have 3% of the vulnerabilities, or that we are terrible at detecting exploitation for zero days?

This is why we should put effort into quantifying the logistical burden of exploit development and stockpiles. The uncertainty is currently unquantified, but not inherently unquantifiable!

## 4.5.6   Lifespans of Exploits

One particular open research question is how long exploits remain operationally useful; what is their half-life? This is a function of defenses, but also the natural life cycles of technology. If you find a vulnerability in a website today and keep it secret, how long will the vulnerability be useful before either it is detected and fixed or the website changes? If we could measure all uses of an exploit globally, what statistical distribution would it follow? Would it follow one distribution in space and another in time?

These are crucial questions of cyber risk that are answerable, but need to be identified and resourced as part of our trans-scientific wish list. They are core questions of cyber risk.

**4.5.6.1  Matching the Vulnerabilities to Losses**  As we conclude this chapter, let's discuss one final piece of the cyber risk puzzle. If we knew how often vulnerabilities could be found, and we knew how long those vulnerabilities were exposed, how widely distributed the vulnerable technology was (it could be software or hardware), and how often exploits were used, we would still be missing the final piece to truly quantify cyber risk. We know that not all breaches are due to vulnerabilities, such as insiders just walking out with data, for example. Yet for those situations where vulnerabilities were used in a compromise, can we quantify losses per exploit, or rather exploit set?

If we could dedicate even 10% of the expected losses to the discovery and prevention of vulnerabilities being exploited, then we might be going quite a long way toward the quantification and solution of cyber risk.

## ENDNOTES

1. Data from 10,000 code inspections in professional software at the end of module development, as presented in Panko (2014).
2. Olds (2012).
3. A software bug in the on-board guidance computer program was blamed for the destruction of the European Space Agency's Ariane 5 rocket, costing over a billion dollars, shortly after launch in 1996. Lions (1996).
4. A software bug in the engine-control computer of a Royal Air Force Chinook helicopter was blamed for its crash in Scotland in 1994, killing 29. Airforce Technology (2010).
5. Patient deaths from radiation overdoses in the 1980s were discovered to be due to errors in the software controlling the Therac-25 radiotherapy machine. Lim (1998).
6. NIST (2002).
7. Greenberg (2016).
8. CERT (2016).
9. Ozment and Schechter (2006).
10. Arora et al. (2004).
11. Lee (2007).
12. Li et al. (2016).
13. Conley and Bryan (1985).
14. NIST National Vulnerability Database (2018a, b).
15. Shahzad et al. (2012).
16. Shahzad et al. (2012).

17. Leverett and Wightman (2013).
18. Example metric code for a Shodan query can be found here: https://github.com/blackswanburst/afistfulofmetrics/blob/master/Leverett-Wightman-cost.py.
19. Leverett and Wightman (2013).
20. Howard and Lipner (2006).
21. Geer (2015).
22. Such as those found in this list from http://FIRST.org https://www.first.org/global/sigs/vrdx/vdb-catalog.
23. Cyber Green (2017).
24. Clayton (2011) and Hofmeyr et al. (2013).
25. Li et al. (2016), Cetin et al. (2017), Stock et al. (2018).

# CHAPTER 5

# Know Your Enemy

## 5.1 HACKERS

### 5.1.1 They Don't Wear Balaclavas

The people who carry out cyber attacks are largely anonymous figures – famously caricatured in thousands of media stock photos as faceless youths in hoodies, wearing 'Anonymous' Guido Fawkes masks or balaclavas, and typing fiendishly at computer keyboards in black burglars' gloves.

The reality is that cyber hacking has progressed from its early stereotype as a hobby for amateur teenagers in their bedrooms to a professionalized, informal but well-organized, international industry with a hierarchy of participants, a set of guilds with niche specializations, its own social networks, cryptocurrencies, trading networks, e-commerce markets, communication systems, and vocabulary. Cyber attackers are commonly referred to as 'threat actors' (by theoreticians), 'hackers' (by us), 'black hats' (by the security community), 'the red team' (by company IT staff), 'perpetrators' (by the law enforcement community), and the 'bad guys' (by everyone else). Cyber attacks are criminal acts, so it is also correct to call them 'cyber criminals'. In general we prefer the term 'hackers', with no disrespect to the many ethical hackers who work on the side of the angels, and are sometimes called 'white hats' or 'the blue team'. We will generally mean criminals when we refer to hackers.

In addition to the threat of external attack, businesses and organizations are vulnerable to cyber compromise from their own employees and internal trustees. Many cyber attacks have occurred from disgruntled insiders, whistle-blowers, rogue traders, and internal saboteurs.

Although hidden and criminalized, the cyber black market behaves like most other sectors of the economy, subject to supply and demand, conscious of cost structures and cash flow, and requiring capital that needs to produce a return on investment. It operates using global and dynamically reconfigurable infrastructure that defies the geographical jurisdictional constraints of conventional law enforcement. The costs, rewards, and business models of hackers are known as hackonomics. We outline here how the understanding of hackonomics helps with devising security strategies and protection measures to reduce cyber risk.

Many companies go through red teaming exercises where they role-play how they would mount a cyber attack on the company, and have to imagine the motivations and priorities of the protagonists they will face in real life. The defending team is usually referred to as the blue team. Let's meet the teams.

### 5.1.2 In the Red Corner …

It is useful to know what we are up against when we are trying to solve cyber risk. Cyber risk is more than cyber security systems and technological superiority. It is about understanding the motivations, the capabilities, and the 'tactics, techniques, procedures' (TTPs) and targets of the protagonists. Hackers are not a homogeneous bunch. We segment the universe of hackers into the following seven types, described further in the next sections:[1]

1. Amateur hackers
2. Hub-structured cyber criminal gangs
3. Hierarchically organized cyber criminal syndicates
4. Mercenary teams
5. Hacktivists
6. Cyber terrorists
7. Nation-state and state-sponsored cyber teams

Although all cyber criminals try hard to be anonymous and undiscovered, we know quite a bit about the activities, motivations, and capabilities of them as groups, even if we may not know their names or exact information. We can piece together profiles about them from the individuals who are arrested by the law enforcement teams, and from the information about the attacks they perpetrate and the fingerprints they leave behind them. We may not have enough evidence to convict in a court of law, but security specialists work on a principle of 'soft attribution': assigning the perpetrator on the balance of probability of the evidence.

There is an increasing interest in cyber criminology, becoming an established discipline of social science, research, and publication, with teaching courses being offered at universities, academic journals, and conferences providing a body of published studies.

## 5.2 TAXONOMY OF THREAT ACTORS

### 5.2.1 Amateur Hackers

Amateur hackers are people who do not earn their living from hacking but have a passion for working with computers, a curiosity for what they can achieve, and a flexible attitude to right and wrong. They are often experimenting or part of a community or social group, alerted to techniques and computer tools they can use through the forums and chat channels they share. They are commonly disparaged as 'script kiddies' (or 'skiddies'): people who use someone else's script or code to hack into computers, as this is easier or they don't have the skills to write their own.

Amateur hackers are individuals who have curiosity and some base levels of skills, and can occasionally pull off some surprising accomplishments by penetrating previously unknown vulnerabilities. As cyber attack tools

## AMATEUR THREAT ACTORS

### Teenage Hackers (and Not So Teenage)

Some of the headlines about cyber crime have been made by the young age of amateur hackers who achieve notoriety, such as Jonathan James, alias '*cOmrade*', who was arrested at the age of 15 for hacking into the US Department of Defense. James went on to be suspected of several other cyber crimes, suffering house arrest, serving jail time as the youngest person to be convicted of violating cyber crime laws, and finally shooting himself while under investigation for a major hack of protected customer data from TJX in 2007.[2]

Youth is a common characteristic of the experimental amateur hackers. A 14-year-old (too young to be named in court) exemplary pupil at his school, who had achieved outstanding grades in electronics, adapted a television remote control to change the points in the tram tracks in his hometown of Lodz in Poland, causing a tram to derail and injure 15 people.[3]

But not all amateur hackers are young. '*Astra*' has never been publicly identified other than as a 58-year-old Greek mathematician working alone and in his spare time, who was arrested for hacking into the Dassault Group and stealing weapons technology information to sell on the black market.[4] His hacking cost Dassault $360 million in damages.

become increasingly commoditized, there is potential for people with relatively low levels of skill and capability to deploy toolkits that have been developed by others and to apply them with increasingly damaging effect. As they graduate from script kiddies to becoming kit kiddies, they become increasingly powerful. The amateur hacker can also graduate by going pro. The pool of amateur hackers acts as the feeder system for the various layers of more sophisticated threat groups.

### 5.2.2 Hub-Structured Cyber Criminal Gangs

An example of an amateur going pro, Albert Gonzalez began as teenage hacker, and graduated to organizing his own international organized cyber crime gang. He was known as *soupnazi* at his South Miami high school, where he enjoyed and played up to his reputation as a computer nerd, becoming notorious at the age of 14 for hacking into NASA networks. He gathered other computer programming enthusiasts into his orbit and by the age of 19, having moved to New Jersey, he helped organize a group calling itself the *ShadowCrew*.

Hub-structured cyber criminal groups are thought to be the most numerous and active in the organized cyber crime economy. They are amorphous and each group may not last long before re-forming as another team. Some estimates put the number of active hub teams at around 6,400, suggesting that more than 100,000 individuals might be active in this sector of the cyber black economy,[5] but everyone acknowledges that it is difficult to quantify. The core gang members maintain a loose affiliation with a wide range of individuals, including specialists in exploit development, botnets, malware, phishing, ransomware, social engineering, and the monetization process of cyber crime. Each hub may have tens of core gang members, and the peripheral criminal fraternity that trades with this core, both providing services to them and buying their outputs from them, may number several thousands.

Unlike other criminal sectors of society, the members of this community are not the disadvantaged, poorly educated, marginalized individuals who constitute the bulk of traditional criminal activity and convictions. The typical profile of individuals convicted related to hub-structured cyber criminal activity is 'aged 14–30, middle class, with high levels of educational achievement, predominantly white'.[6] Geographically, the known and suspected perpetrators are from regions with high levels of graduate unemployment, although not all regions with high levels of graduate unemployment give rise to populations of hub cyber hackers.

## HUB-STRUCTURED CYBER CRIMINAL GANGS

### *ShadowCrew* Cyber Criminal Gang

The *ShadowCrew* group that Albert Gonzalez pulled together from his computer nerd friends had around 20 core members, and was organized to steal credit card credentials, ATM codes, and other stolen identity data, such as Social Security cards, health insurance, and passport information. They set up and ran an auction website for stolen data, which attracted a loose affiliation of around 4000 individuals who bought and sold stolen information. In total they stole data that made them an estimated $4.3 million. They mounted some sizeable hacks of companies to steal protected data, including hacking 5000 credit card credentials from Dave & Buster's corporate network in 2007, and an alleged theft of 45.6 million credit and debit cards from TJX from 2005 to 2007.[7]

The *ShadowCrew* group shared its technology and methods with other related gangs of cyber criminals, including *Carderplanet*, a Ukrainian and Russian group of cyber criminals, and *Darkprofits*, a black market online trading site offering a range of stolen goods. Unlike legitimate businesses that compete with each other, these organizations cooperate with each other and share goods, services, and members in an informal network. Individuals in one group would also work with another, and associates with specialties are shared and recommended across from one team to another. This type of clustering of cyber criminal activity around core teams with leading members and a peripheral set of associate members is classified as 'hub' cyber crime.[8]

Albert Gonzalez's hub of activities spread to groups in a dozen countries in North America, Eastern Europe, Scandinavia, and Western Europe. He was finally arrested following an extensive Secret Service investigation (*Operation FireWall*) and agreed to cooperate with the authorities and provide evidence, which enabled the indictment of at least another 30 individuals, among them several key individuals who the authorities identified as being hubs of key cyber crime organizations in the United States, Turkey, and Russia.

It is estimated that up to 80% of cyber crime is committed by groups with some form of organized activity, either hub-structured or hierarchical.[9]

### 5.2.3 Hierarchically-Organized Cyber Criminal Syndicates

A separate and distinct pattern of organized cyber criminal activity is hierarchical organizations of teams that include hackers.[10] These organizations have formed from traditional organized crime, moving to add cyber crime to their activities, as well as some cyber criminals developing start-up hierarchical structures that mimic organized crime practices but that specialize in cyber activity (sort of 'disruptive' new start-ups to compete with complacent old-crime business models, to use an analogy from the legitimate digital economy).

Hierarchical cyber groups are similar to traditional criminal organizations, with a clear management structure, division of labor, and accretion of proceeds towards the top of the control pyramid. Traditional crime groups have embraced cyber crime as a new vector of profit. Europol estimates that it is dealing with 5000 international criminal organizations operating in the European Union, with a significant number of those operating to some degree in the cyber black economy. It is likely that blocs of similar levels of organized crime exist in North America and in other major regions of the advanced economies.

These hierarchically-organized cyber criminal groups operate with structures that are similar to traditional organized crime, and with characteristics that would not look out of place in any business in the 'white' economy. They have management structures to control expenditure (albeit enforced a bit more brutally than you might find in conventional businesses), track profitability, identify opportunities, invest in research and development, and optimize their return on investment.

Many of these groups invest in physical assets, buying property to house their operations in, and investing in high specifications of IT infrastructure and equipment, and other costs related to running a physical business. There has been evidence of hierarchical organized cyber crime groups having a marketing department, 24/7 customer care lines, ransomware call centers, executive benefit packages, and even a human resources department (maybe even criminals can't get away from performance reviews?). To protect these fixed assets from interdiction by law enforcement, these have to be located in safe areas outside their jurisdiction. Countries with poor law enforcement, with weak extradition laws, or without international cooperation agreements, are favored locations. This has given rise to widely publicized enclaves in countries like Romania: the town of Râmnicu Vâlcea (AKA 'Hackerville') in the foothills of the Transylvanian Alps has become notorious for its population of Mercedes-driving unemployed computer science graduates, and its concentration of IP addresses suspected of being origin points of dubious transactions.[11] Interpol is reported to be investigating criminal extra-jurisdictional hacker centers in many different countries, including Armenia, Azerbaijan, Brazil, Indonesia, Mexico, the Philippines, Russia, Taiwan, Turkey, and Vietnam.[12]

Hierarchical cyber crime groups have more stability than hub-organized crime groups, which enables them to invest capital in their equipment and teams, and so can build up expertise and capability. Some groups have shown a willingness to invest time and money in patient preparation for an attack, developing software and customizing tools for a specific target. They also reinvest some of their profits after a successful operation to improve their abilities and generate more money from their next attacks.

Despite the scale of their robberies, software experts suggest that the *Carbanak* team are far from being the most skillful software engineers. They have typically assembled toolkits and compiled software from multiple sources, repurposing the malware they create from a library of sources, and subcontracting key components of their systems from mercenary coders.

It is clear, however, that the *Carbanak* team and other hierarchically organized syndicates are much more than producers of software. They are business enterprises, albeit operating in a black economy. They have dedicated teams to research and identify their targets, specifically looking for hooks for their spear phishing campaigns. These employ social engineering techniques to find tricks that are most likely to fool a senior executive or an accounting clerk to click on the link in the email that will download the malware into the corporate network. They also invest in building sophisticated money-laundering operations.

These syndicates are motived to maximize their economic profit by choosing targets and attack vectors with the lowest cost. They invest in targeting, but they also operate opportunistically. They maintain lists of the types of companies they would like to gain access to, but also operate 'watering holes' operations where they will set out bogus websites or activities that could attract the kinds of individuals that they are interested in, and will wait to see if they get a bite.

Although there is a lot of variation between different syndicate operations, hierarchically-organized syndicates are generally considered to be more of a threat than hub-structured cyber crime gangs, as they concentrate capital, invest in new crime enterprises, and have greater resources at their disposal.

## HIERARCHICALLY-ORGANIZED CYBER CRIMINAL SYNDICATES

### *Carbanak* Cyber Crime Syndicate

*Carbanak* is a cyber crime syndicate, also known by security analysts as *Fin7*.[13] This group specializes in cyber attacks to steal credit card credentials and financial information that can be used fraudulently to steal money. They have targeted banking, retail, hospitality, and other business sectors. Their attacks have followed a similar process of tactics, techniques, and procedures (TTPs) that investigators have dissected after each of their operations. Most significantly, the group has evolved remote access Trojan (RAT) software that can penetrate a company's defenses and then operate from within their network, each evolution of their software remaining undetected from scanners that have been trained to look for the indicators of compromise published by security analysts who have studied their previous versions. In 2016, the group went on to develop an even more powerful generation of malware, based on the *Cobalt Strike* penetration testing software. *Carbanak*'s name comes from two of their early Trojans, *Carberp* and *Anunak*, used to break into banking networks.

A typical *Carbanak* operation involves handcrafting an entry into a target company, typically involving spear phishing, followed by a rapid scanning of the network to find financial transaction systems, point-of-sales systems, ATM networks, and databases of credentials information. Once they have found these data vaults, they escalate their privilege credentials to gain control of the systems, de-encrypt databases, and begin bulk harvesting and exfiltrating the information in well-disguised data streams. Stolen credit card data is efficiently sold on quickly through carder forums. ATM machines are reprogrammed to spit out cash at prescheduled times ('jackpotting'). One of *Carbanak*'s trademarks is the speed at which they operate once they have gained access.

*Carbanak*-like fingerprints have been found at the scene of more than 250 major financial data exfiltration attacks. One of their most notorious campaigns was against financial institutions in Russia, the United States, Germany, China, and Ukraine lasting at least a year from 2013, siphoning money into laundering accounts through the SWIFT banking system, extracting money through ATMs, and selling on stolen credit card details. Exact details of all the losses have never been made public, but one bank reported a loss of $10 million, and another had $7.3 million stolen from its ATM machines.

Some estimates suggest that *Carbanak* may have got away with as much as a billion dollars.

An international hunt by law enforcement agencies resulted in the Europol arrest in Spain of the leader of *Carbanak* in March 2018.[14]

### 5.2.4 Mercenary Teams

Mercenary teams of software coders and specialists of various types now offer their services on the cyber black markets. These services cover a wide array of tools and techniques, including offering 'for-rent' botnets,

## MERCENARY TEAMS

### *Hidden Lynx* Hacker-for-hire Operation

*Hidden Lynx* is a professional hacker-for-hire operation, based in China, that is contracted by clients to provide information, including industrial secrets and protected data. The group is named after a text string that was observed in their command-and-control server communications.[15]

They steal on demand whatever their clients are interested in, and tackle a wide variety of missions and targets. The group has carried out at least six significant campaigns since 2011. Their ability to mount multiple international campaigns at the same time with high proficiency using different tools and techniques suggests that they have considerable hacking expertise at their disposal, estimated at between 50 and 100 operatives, organized into a number of teams.

They have hit hundreds of organizations worldwide, with widely varying characteristics, including financial, educational, and government sectors, and many of their targets have been in the defense industrial sector of Western countries.

They have gained a reputation of being experts in being able to breach well-protected networks, and have two particular playbooks: mass exploitation using a specially designed Trojan, and pay-to-order targeted attacks, including a zero day implementation, to obtain intellectual property. They have broken into some of the best-protected organizations in the world and are considered one of the most capable independent cyber threat teams outside of nation-state control.

designing malware, trading zero day exploits, and providing professional hackers-for-hire to attack organizations.

Mercenary groups usually consist of small teams of skilled and experienced developers who are hired by organized cyber criminal groups to hack targets or develop malware or exploits that may be beyond the skill level of the personnel of most organized cyber criminal groups. They require sophisticated technology and infrastructure to operate, so skilled individuals who may have no particular criminal alignment originally have joined these mercenary teams to monetize their skills on the black market, within a team that offers specialized challenges and sells these skills through a black market to the highest bidder.

### 5.2.5 Hacktivists

Ideologically motivated cyber attacks have become an increasing threat in the cyber black economy. Hacktivist cyber groups typically represent counterculture or protest movements, and may be offshoots from or aligned with political and social organizations.

Information-age protests include defacing websites, spreading propaganda, providing or combating fake news, organizing hate mail and trolling campaigns, DDoS attacks, and network breaches against targets. They have also escalated into more damaging threats, such as bringing down the internet, to protest global inequality. Hacktivist movements have included anti-capitalism, anarchist anti-government, anti-military, and anti-copyright laws movements; radical ecological movements; political movements such as pro-Palestinian protests; and human rights, animal rights, anti-pornography, anti-terrorism, and other causes.

Hacktivist groups like *Anonymous* tend to operate in a 'swarm', as a large collective movement bound by a common purpose but with no clear leadership and with a minimal command structure. The capability they can bring to bear against their targets depends on the skills of the individuals who are motivated to contribute, and this may depend on the passion generated by the specific cause.

Other hacktivist organizations may be more focused and have a central organization and operational team that have caused damaging cyber attacks on businesses and government organizations that parallel activism, and damaging physical attacks on employees and property.

Hacktivists also encourage whistle-blowing, where insider employees of organizations release confidential information that shows up their employers

# HACKTIVISTS

## Anonymous

*Anonymous* is an international hacktivist group that has carried out direct-action protest campaigns of cyber attacks against authoritarian government, big business, and other targets, such as the Church of Scientology. Campaigns have consisted of distributed denial of service (DDoS) attacks on websites and servers, data breaches, causing localized internet outages and interrupting communications, distributing malware, spoofing control systems, and defacing websites. It also embraces a lighter side of a counterculture approach to in-jokes, pranks, and computer obsessions.

*Anonymous* has no formal membership but uses social media to coordinate and derive consensus for action, and crowdsources volunteers to act on suggestions. It embraces a distinctive brand and encourages its members to remain anonymous, popularizing stylized Guy Fawkes masks.

An *Anonymous* attack on Sony in 2011 compromised 77 million PlayStation Network accounts, causing the company significant commercial loss.

*Anonymous* and similar hacktivist groups took an interest in the 2011 Arab Spring uprising, helping dissidents in Arab countries access government-censored information and attack official websites.

They continued their support for populist uprisings when they helped coordinate the Occupy movement (Occupy Wall Street, Occupy London, etc.) later in 2011, when anti-austerity resentment combined with protests against social and political inequality and instances of corporate malfeasance, under the slogan 'We are the 99%', brought millions of people onto the streets of 950 cities. This was accompanied by 'Operation Global Blackout' – a threat that failed to materialize to cripple global business by sabotaging the internet using a specially-created cannon to carry out a DDoS attack on the root Domain Name System (DNS) servers.[16]

Over the years *Anonymous* has been associated with many campaigns against people and organizations they take issue with. The capability of the group to muster a coherent threat of high capability depends on the collective will and skills of the volunteers who care about the specific issue.

or sheds light on malpractice. One of the most notorious data breaches, the Panama Papers, saw an insider release 11 million confidential tax documents from a commercial law firm, Mossack Finseca, in 2016, to highlight 'income inequality' by disclosing how high-profile individuals hide income and avoid paying taxes.[17] Sites such as WikiLeaks, offering an outlet for the publication of leaked information, have become synonymous with hacktivism.

### 5.2.6 Cyber Terrorists

Terrorist groups seek political change through violence. Terrorism has a long history, with many sudden changes in tactics, as underground terrorist groups seek the element of surprise against the more powerful resources of law enforcement and the established political order.

Terrorist groups commonly use information technology to assist their cause, ranging from spreading propaganda and recruitment, to enabling encrypted communications between members, through to information gathering on counter-terrorism operations against them, raising funds through cyber crime, and providing operational support to physical attacks.[18] A specific convergence of hacking and terrorism is the publication of 'kill lists' of stolen data on military personnel to urge followers to attack them.

Many commentators have speculated on the future next phase of terrorism, ranging from terrorist groups acquiring various types of weapons of mass destruction, through to all-out economic and psychological warfare, or repeated use of insurgency tactics undermining the political tolerance of Western populations. A common area of speculation is that terrorists may seek to carry out spectacular destructive and mass-casualty attacks using cyber hacking techniques.[19]

The US State Department lists 58 organizations as foreign terrorist organizations. Many other Western countries maintain similar watch lists of proscribed international terrorist groups. Terrorist groups range from right-wing survivalists to separatist political movements, extremists of several religions, and groups espousing violence to support specific issues. In the twenty-first century, the leading, but not the only, terrorism threat to Western democracies has become the militant Islamic movements of groups such as Al Qaeda and the Islamic State (IS). The militant Islamic movement has generated cyber divisions, such as *Al Qaeda Electronic, United Cyber Caliphate, Cyber Caliphate Army, Afaaq Electronic Foundation, Syrian Electronic Army, Hezbollah Cyber Group*, and others.

## CYBER TERRORISTS

### United Cyber Caliphate

*United Cyber Caliphate*, also known as *Islamic State Hacking Division* and *CyberCaliphate*, is a disparate group promoting itself as the digital army for Islamic State of Iraq and Levant, effectively the cyber team of the Islamic State terrorist group. It carries out cyber attacks, such as the defacing of websites, the hacking of emails, credit card theft for fund raising, and data exfiltration attacks, for example to post 'kill lists' of the names and addresses of serving Western military personnel to exort followers to attack them physically.

The *CyberCaliphate* is a disparate group of volunteer followers of the violent ideology of the Islamic State, a militant Islamic group. The IS membership is responsible for terrorist acts such as bombings, mass killings, and attacks on military forces in Iraq and Syria. It has claimed responsibility for murderous attacks in Western countries.

The main activities of *CyberCaliphate* are predominantly propaganda and IT support to their cause, posting messages to followers and spreading the ideology to gain volunteer recruits; facilitating communications and enabling encrypted messaging between members to avoid detection; and information gathering, listening, and data gathering on anti-terrorist operations against them.

Originally the leaders of *CyberCaliphate* operated servers and computer networks from buildings located in towns in Iraq and Syria controlled by IS in their self-proclaimed caliphate, but these were consistently located by US and Western alliance military, and targeted and frequently destroyed by drone missile attacks from 2014 to 2017. Several of the known key figures in the *CyberCaliphate* were killed in targeted strikes.

Following the recapture of the geographical territory held by IS in Iraq and Syria by the combined military efforts of Western, Russian, and local forces, IS members have largely dispersed, with many of the foreign volunteers who were fighting for IS returning to their home countries. Abu Bakr al-Baghdadi, the leader of IS, has urged its membership to continue fighting, and has devolved power to the *wiliyets* or local committees, including espousing a 'virtual caliphate' to be conducted online.

*(Continued)*

This is principally taking the form of online propaganda and incitement, the provision of how-to manuals, and fund raising through low-level cyber crime. The threat remains of the *CyberCaliphate* improving their capabilities to provide cyber attack support to amplify the impact of physical terrorist attacks or in the future to achieve their assumed aspirations of spectacular and deadly cyber attacks.

Cyber capability assessments are made by counterterrorism intelligence. These are not made public but are occasionally referenced in official documents or pronouncements. The general consensus of intelligence analysts is that the leading radical Islamic threat groups aspire to carrying out spectacular destructive attacks using cyber techniques, but that the groups' current capabilities fall short of the advanced mastery of cyber-physical controls that would be necessary.[20]

The dispersal of the followers of the Islamic State from the physical territory they had occupied in Syria and Iraq has led to the creation of a 'virtual caliphate' and an increased emphasis on information technology as an enabler to sustain and inspire disparate followers. The dissemination of online propaganda and tactical instruction manuals is a key concern for the authorities, as it incites followers to carry out physical attacks and may improve the effectiveness of terrorist operations. Interventions by the authorities are made to remove hate content and terror-related materials such as recipes for bomb making from websites and social media groups. Terrorist manuals that are available online are commonly doctored by intelligence teams to make them ineffectual or worse. Cyber crime, such as credit card theft, is used by terrorist followers to fund some of their activities, including financing their physical attacks.

Counterterrorism operations are increasingly targeting the cyber capabilities of terrorist groups, deploying offensive cyber attacks that destroy equipment and disrupt networks to systematically degrade their capabilities and to suppress propaganda.[21]

As militant jihadists become more accomplished, it is likely that they will use cyber means to augment and enhance their physical attacks, perhaps providing disinformation or disabling communications to confuse counter-terrorism responders to a terrorist incident. Spectacular and deadly cyber attacks may be an aspiration of these groups, and it is important to monitor any improvements in capability of these threat actors to be prepared for future attacks of this type.

### 5.2.7 Nation-state- and State-sponsored Cyber Teams

There are many nations around the world that now maintain their own teams of cyber specialists. We identify a cyber team as being nation-state or state-sponsored if it can be identified as part of the state apparatus, funded by the government, or part of a national institution. An important distinction from other types of cyber threat actors is that they are ultimately answerable to their national sponsor, and although they can seem to be acting as though they are uncontrolled and may be operating with deniability, they may be restrained by protocols of international convention and fears of retaliation. A minor distinction is sometimes made between nation-state actors effectively acting as official agents of the state, and state-sponsored teams that may receive national support and endorsement but may be more deniable and only distantly related to official bodies.

State-sponsored cyber teams are typically part of a national security unit or intelligence-gathering organization. They are increasingly linked to military capability and commonly regarded as a fifth branch of the armed services. Various divisions of government have interests in cyber operations, ranging from law enforcement to homeland security, foreign policy and trade, diplomatic corps, and counter-terrorism, so that in more advanced countries cyber units may be attached to some or all of these departments. All of these groups may be conducting different types of cyber operations, ranging from passive data gathering and listening, to offensive attacks to damage the computer networks of people in other countries that they regard as posing a threat.

In Figure 5.1 we list a selection of active state-sponsored cyber teams from 14 countries. These are by no means the only state-sponsored cyber teams operating. Almost all advanced countries with armed forces are maintaining some level of a cyber operations team. We have divided them into countries that either are aligned with Western democratic economies or potentially could be adversarial. Countries listed as adversarial have at some point carried out cyber operations against commercial interests of Western businesses, and have been tracked exploring vulnerabilities in military, government, and critical national infrastructure.

State-sponsored teams are well resourced. Where they have high levels of capability, they are referred to as advanced persistent threats (APTs). Many of the Russian and Chinese teams are labeled as APTs. Different commercial

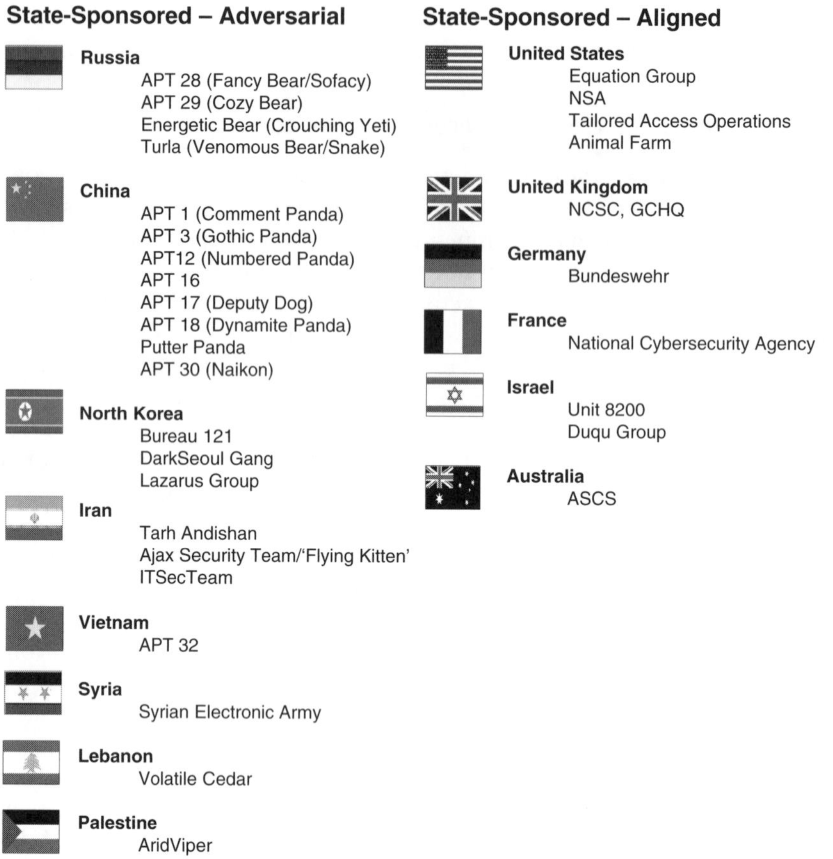

## State-Sponsored – Adversarial

**Russia**
APT 28 (Fancy Bear/Sofacy)
APT 29 (Cozy Bear)
Energetic Bear (Crouching Yeti)
Turla (Venomous Bear/Snake)

**China**
APT 1 (Comment Panda)
APT 3 (Gothic Panda)
APT12 (Numbered Panda)
APT 16
APT 17 (Deputy Dog)
APT 18 (Dynamite Panda)
Putter Panda
APT 30 (Naikon)

**North Korea**
Bureau 121
DarkSeoul Gang
Lazarus Group

**Iran**
Tarh Andishan
Ajax Security Team/'Flying Kitten'
ITSecTeam

**Vietnam**
APT 32

**Syria**
Syrian Electronic Army

**Lebanon**
Volatile Cedar

**Palestine**
AridViper

## State-Sponsored – Aligned

**United States**
Equation Group
NSA
Tailored Access Operations
Animal Farm

**United Kingdom**
NCSC, GCHQ

**Germany**
Bundeswehr

**France**
National Cybersecurity Agency

**Israel**
Unit 8200
Duqu Group

**Australia**
ASCS

**FIGURE 5.1**   State-sponsored cyber teams: a selection.

security teams, such as Kaspersky and Symantec, track the activities of these APTs by their use of infrastructure and reuse of software code, and each is given a pet name, so that the same team may be referred to by multiple names.

Nation-state cyber teams are well resourced and have high capability. Most operate as clandestine cyber-spies, but some mount aggressive campaigns of intrusive attacks that infect and damage machines, disrupt business operations, and steal valuable information.

A few state-sponsored teams are responsible for some of the most severe financial thefts, data exfiltration attacks, and contagious malware attacks. It is alleged that *Lazarus Group* was responsible for the highly

## STATE-SPONSORED CYBER TEAMS

### *Energetic Bear* Russian Advanced Persistent Threat (APT) Team

*Energetic Bear* has been tracked as a Russian APT team since 2010, so named by Kaspersky Lab because of its clear interest in the energy sector, targeting oil and gas companies.[22] Symantec calls it *Dragonfly*. Kaspersky has proposed that the more recent diversification of the group into broader interests in manufacturing, construction, and IT companies merits renaming it *Crouching Yeti*. You can take your pick.

*Energetic Bear* focuses on industrial espionage, stealing intellectual property from Western oil and gas businesses, renewable energy, and regulatory information from international energy bodies.[23] It may also have an interest in potential cyber-sabotage of Western energy infrastructure, and in putting tools in place to influence the global energy market.

*Energetic Bear* is classified as Russian because of build-time stamps in its malware on Moscow standard time, and as state-sponsored because its command-and-control servers operate out of the Federal Security Services (intelligence service) buildings of the Russian Federation.[24] It is assumed to be siphoning Western IP to Russian oil and gas companies.

During the period 2013–2014, *Energetic Bear* ran at least five overlapping campaigns, including spear phishing key individuals, inserting Trojan software into target businesses, running a watering-hole attack to obtain credentials, and creating different types of malware. The group has compromised industrial control system software used in commercial devices, created contagious *Havex* malware that has infected thousands of computers, hacked into more than a hundred organizations, and maintained over 200 command-and-control servers in more than 20 countries. A typical attack infects companies through Windows operating systems, injecting Trojans that connect back to a large network of enslaved websites acting as command and control.

It is estimated that *Energetic Bear* must have at least 350 staff and $1.5 million in capital resources.

damaging 2014 attack on Sony Pictures, attempts to steal nearly a billion dollars from banks via compromising the SWIFT interbanking network in 2016 and 2017, DDoS attacks on South Korean government agencies from

2009 to 2013, the release of the *WannaCry* malware in 2017, and thefts of cryptocurrency. *Lazarus* is so-called because it re-emerges in slightly different manifestations for each campaign but retains characteristic signatures in its malware, of which there are more than 150 known variants.[25] Its operations have involved Chinese middlemen. The attribution of *Lazarus* as a North Korean state-sponsored team is considered highly probable by US government officials, from complex and classified tracing by the US National Security Agency (NSA) of command-and-control signals back to North Korean URLs.[26]

From its operations, *Lazarus* looks more like a cyber criminal organization stealing money and monetizable data assets than following a politically-inspired agenda. The overlap and blurring between what might be a political agenda of destabilizing and punishing organizations that annoy national administrations versus financially motivated campaigns to steal money may be a fine line.

Inflicting cyber loss as punishment or to destabilize opponents or manipulate competitors may be a characteristic of state-sponsored campaigns. The *NotPetya* contagious malware attack in 2017 (described in Chapter 2) was disguised as ransomware but was actually a disk wiper, so was carried out from a motivation of inflicting damage rather than for financial gain, and delivered via a vector in Ukrainian tax reporting software, presumably to target businesses with Ukrainian trading connections. The US, UK, and Australian governments all blamed the Russian military for creating and releasing the malware.[27]

Russian state-sponsored teams *Sofacy* (APT 28) and *Cozy Bear* (APT 29) have been blamed for politically motivated hacks, such as the leaking of the Democratic National Convention's (DNC's) emails in an attempt to influence the 2016 US presidential election.[28] The effectiveness of cyber operations in swaying democratic elections has become a major theme ever since, with a wide variety of allegations of foreign interference, ranging from manipulating social media networks to hacking ballot reporting, in elections all over the democratic world.

Cyber units are used to apply diplomatic pressure and to threaten punitive cyber attacks if intergovernmental relations break down. Following a diplomatic row in 2018 over British allegations that a Russian refugee living in London had been poisoned by Russian agents using nerve gas, fears of a Russian cyber attack as a reprisal prompted an unprecedented public alert from US and UK governments, with instructions on purging suspected Russian malware from IT networks and even domestic routers.[29] There have been fears for some time that Russians have infiltrated dormant and undetected malware into a wide range of IT systems in the West, from commercial business, government, and military systems through to critical national infrastructure, power grids, and utilities, giving the Russians the ability to cripple Western economies at will, in echoes of Cold War paranoia.[30]

Whether foreign state-sponsored cyber agents have already embedded malware in all our systems or not, the Western democracies have become increasingly proactive and aggressive in empowering their state-sponsored cyber teams to go on the offensive and strike back or preemptively. Laws have been passed to enable 'active cyber defense' for teams to conduct cyber attacks against foreign targets where it is deemed necessary to do so. Active cyber defense powers have been granted to US NSA groups, to the UK Government Communications Headquarters (GCHQ) National Cyber Security Centre, and amid some controversy for the German military Bundeswehr cyber command. The UK GCHQ cyber attack mandate was first used in April 2018 when it attacked networks and servers of the Islamic State.[31] Other aligned countries are debating the basis in international law and levels of proof required to sanction offensive attack operations by their cyber units. The capabilities and sophistication of the toolkits that have been amassed by Western nation-state cyber teams became apparent in 2016, when an arsenal of exploits apparently used by Equation Group, an NSA cyber team, was published online by a group calling itself *ShadowBrokers*.

It is clear that state-sponsored cyber teams represent a major force in the cyber risk landscape. Some of the more errant and less controlled teams, like *Lazarus* and *Energetic Bear*, are already causing significant losses to Western organizations and our economy. Others could potentially be unleashed by their political masters to cause even more destructive and disruptive impacts under certain circumstances. There are few, if any, organizations that could withstand a concerted cyber attack by a well-resourced and skillful state-sponsored cyber team if the organization is directly targeted.

## 5.3  THE INSIDER THREAT

### 5.3.1  Accidents Will Happen

It is natural to focus on the threat from external actors. However, a lot of cyber risk also comes from inside an organization. The internal risk is both accidental and malicious. The large majority of privacy breach events where personal data is leaked and companies have had to pay out compensation have been accidental. Individuals have left their unencrypted laptops in taxis or airports, or have lost memory sticks or other mobile media – even paper printouts – with key data sets on them. Even if a criminal doesn't find the lost data set, the incident still has to be reported to the regulator and all the procedures followed and compensations paid. In the decade before 2013, over half of all privacy breach data loss events were from accidental losses. The advent of password-protected laptops and standard practices of encrypting data sets in transit have rapidly cut the incidence of accidental data loss. Now less than 20% of data loss incidents come from accidental causes – two-thirds are from malicious external actors.

### 5.3.2   Human Vulnerability of Your Staff

The personnel of an organization are the unwitting vectors of many of the cyber incidents that occur. An employee clicking on a bogus link in a phishing email or browsing on the wrong website can trigger a new malware infection. The larger an organization with more employees, the more chances there are for one of them to be fooled and enable a cyber loss to occur. When analyzing cyber risk, the strongest characteristic of a company that correlates with likelihood of having a loss is the number of employees it has, for this very reason.

The human vulnerability of an organization is just as important as the technology deployed for IT security. Personnel are recognized as being the human firewall that protects the company.[32] Improving cyber risk awareness of the staff is a growing focus of security measures, and there are various ways of scoring the awareness level of employees, monitoring metrics of improvements over time, and benchmarking against industry sector averages and an organization's peers, that are worth instituting in any business with significant cyber risk.

### 5.3.3   Disaffected Employees

A small proportion of cyber loss incidents to a company results from the deliberate act of an employee. Since records of cause began in 2005, around 10% of regulatory-reported data loss events each year have been attributed to the malicious acts of insiders.

Insiders may be acting for financial gain, or may be acting through motives of whistle-blowing to publicize activities of the organization they disagree with, or acting to punish their employer. There are many examples of employees acting against the best interests of their employers, including theft, fraud, vandalism, and sabotage. This is known as 'workplace deviance', and is heavily under-reported. Insider cyber crime is a growing area of study to understand the root causes, the circumstances, and the characteristics of employees who carry it out. Surveys of workplace deviance acts of cyber crime suggest that most insiders were acting out of revenge, often triggered by perceived insults by or being treated unfairly by their employer, with motivation related to a negative work-related trigger event.[33]

---

## INSIDER THREAT

### The Disaffected IT Engineer

Statistics of unauthorized cyber activities by employees causing harm to organizations suggest that most are caused by motives of revenge arising from perception of being treated unfairly, and are usually triggered by a negative work-related event, such as being reprimanded, demoted, or laid off. Organizational factors may enhance employees being aggrieved, such as job stress, organizational frustration, lack of control over work environment, and weak sanctions for rule violations. Most of them have complained to colleagues openly in the workplace about their grievance prior to their action. Two-thirds of them act after they have resigned, or simultaneously with their termination. Roughly equal numbers resign or are fired.[34]

Eighty-six percent of them are in the IT department or are in technical roles in the organization, and 10% are professional positions elsewhere in the organization. Common actions include compromising computer accounts, creating unauthorized backdoor access paths or fake accounts, taking copies of sensitive data or protected personal information, or using shared accounts in their attacks.

---

## 5.4 THREAT ACTORS AND CYBER RISK

### 5.4.1 Threat Actors and Their Variety Act

We have described some of the main categories of cyber threat actors. There are, no doubt, other types of individuals who can pose a threat. (There may, for example, even be skilled IT teams or individuals in a company's competitors that may not be above carrying out a sneak attack if it gets them a minor advantage, and they think they won't get caught.) Threat actors have a wide range of skill levels and motivations.

These ecosystems of different cyber threat actors interact, feed off each other, and together may represent a population of several millions of individuals around the world who are engaged in criminal activity to cause cyber losses to businesses and society.

If you are concerned about protecting your organization from a cyber attack, then your red teaming exercise needs to consider each of these threat actors. Where would your organization rank in the targeting prioritization of each of these groups? Do you represent a target that holds reams of personal data that would be a prize for the organized crime groups that specialize in data theft? Do you deal in volumes of credit card transactions that would be a key attraction for hub-structured cyber criminal gangs? Do you carry out financial transactions that could be a motivation for hierarchically-organized cyber criminal syndicates to infiltrate? Does your organization carry out practices that could make it a target for a hacktivist? Could your business be the focus of a state-sponsored attacker interested in espionage of industrial secrets or punishing your organization for its business dealings?

## 5.4.2   Cyber Criminology

Criminology is the science of criminal motivation, causes, and control.[35] To solve cyber risk in society, we need to understand the motivations and deterrence of the people carrying out cyber attacks. Cyber crime challenges many of the conventions of other types of crime: cyber criminals are highly educated, middle-class, and do not fit many of the characteristics of deprivation-induced crime and marginal populations, so theoretical bases for cyber criminology are still evolving.[36] Many of the theorists agree on variations of rational choice theory for the underlying understanding of choices and motivations. This suggests that threat actors are driven by rational choice and weigh costs and benefits when deciding whether to commit cyber crime – essentially, they think in economic terms. Cost is expressed in terms of risk to the actor: the likelihood of being caught and punished is the key deterrence.

The burgeoning industry of cyber crime demonstrates that the risks are currently low relative to the benefits that can be gained. Cyber crime is still met with little deterrence – with extremely low conviction rates for perpetrators. Cyber crime statistics show that in the United States less than 1 in 200 reported cases of cyber identity theft resulted in a criminal case being brought, and only 1 in 50,000 resulted in a conviction.[37] In contrast, armed robbery in the United States results in conviction rates as high as 1 in 5.[38] Even if convicted, cyber criminals face short sentences as judges are still struggling to determine whether harm was caused by stealing data, and what a reasonable punishment should be.[39]

Solving cyber risk will entail increasing the likelihood of being caught, making punishments appropriate to the harm, and establishing deterrence that will rebalance the rational choice for threat actors more towards legitimate use of their talents and away from perpetrating crime.

## 5.5   HACKONOMICS

### 5.5.1   Cyber Black Economy

So if the risks of apprehension, conviction, and sentencing for a cyber criminal are so low, how about the rewards? How much do threat actors make from their endeavors, and what levels of effort and skills are required to generate what levels of rewards?

The cyber black economy consists of operations on the internet that generate illegal money flows for commodities and services. This economy is an ecosystem where illegal activity thrives and enables interaction between suppliers and customers for these goods.

### 5.5.2   Dark Web Trading Sites

Online black markets allow cyber criminals to buy cyber attack tools such as malware and botnets, along with illegal firearms and drugs, and stolen credit card and other information, using cryptocurrencies like Bitcoin, Ethereum, Litecoin, and Monero for transactions.[40] Dark web black markets function like other legitimate online markets, with auction sites, e-commerce, and swap activities.

Large exchanges are periodically discovered and taken down by law enforcement, which reduces trading activity until another site takes over. In 2017, *AlphaBay* (once known as the Amazon of the dark web) and *Hansa Market* were closed down by the US Department of Justice in a major international operation. *AlphaBay* was reported to have daily postings of 300,000 listings of stolen credit cards and digital data thefts, along with drugs and other contraband items, generating up to $800,000 a day in revenue.[41] Although other black markets sprang up to take their place (look-alike trading site *Empire Market* was launched only months later),[42] the disruption of revenue streams to cyber criminals has proven highly effective in reducing their capabilities. The closure of the original flagship dark web trading site *Silk Road* in 2013 generated many more sites for drug trafficking and cyber tool sales, including *Black Market Reloaded*, *Sheep Marketplace*, *Atlantis*, *Agora*, and *Silk Road 2.0*, many of which were closed down in turn, or occasionally ceased operations because – guess what – they got conned by the con men running them.

### 5.5.3 Dark Web Prices

Typical prices of products being offered for sale on trading sites on the dark web are shown in Table 5.1. These prices vary according to supply and demand. Analysts watching the prices on these sites can sometimes tell when a large cache of stolen data has hit the market because the prices fall. Avoiding flooding the market with large data sets may be one constraint for cyber criminals in planning large-scale data exfiltration attacks.

An analysis of provision of online 'booter services' websites that offer denial of service attacks for a fee concludes that payment by PayPal is generally possible; however, alternative payment options are usually available, including digital currencies such as Bitcoin. Entry-level pricing allowing 10-minute attacks on one target at a time was typically priced at less than US$5 a month.[43]

### 5.5.4 Logistical Burden of Cyber Attacks

Putting a successful cyber attack together requires resources. It takes skills, time, people, equipment, and some amount of money. Of these, the level of skill and expertise is probably the most critical. Table 5.2 suggests a scaling for the skill levels of operatives that may be involved in a typical attack.

Cyber attacks can be assessed by the level of difficulty, or 'logistical burden', needed to carry them out. This estimates the numbers of people with different levels of skills needed to work together to write the malware code, do reconnaissance on the targets, explore entry points and vulnerabilities, do the social engineering to find someone who will inadvertently provide a way in, implement the attack itself with sufficient proficiency to minimize detection, and fence or money launder the proceeds.

The logistical burden assesses an index for the attack, using notional costings for personnel with different skills needed, for certain durations, and for the costs of utilizing equipment and obtaining technology tools. Estimates of the total logistical burden make it possible to estimate the total effort required for teams to mount campaigns of cyber attacks, monetized into dollars. Many of the attacks that we have analyzed required a logistical burden index value of between $100,000 and $2 million. Some of the more sophisticated financial transfer attacks have index values

**TABLE 5.1** Prices of commodities available on dark web black market sites.

| Item | Details | Price on dark web |
|---|---|---|
| Fullz | Complete sets of personally identifiable information (PII) for an individual, usually including Social Security number | $1–$8 (US citizen); bulk discount available Fullz with credit card, PIN number, and bank account details: $30 (US) |
| Credit card details | Card transaction credentials taken from malware, point-of-sale terminals, or online transactions. Typically includes card number, expiration date, cardholder name. | Individual cards: $2–$20 Dump prices: $5–$100 |
| Bank account details | Online bank account details, including balance and access credentials | Priced according to balance in account, e.g. $100 for details of account with balance of $1,000; $1,000 for details of account with balance of $20,000 |
| Subscriptions | Netflix subscription or PayPal credentials | $0.50 |
| Exploit kits | User-friendly pre-written software, including ransomware, Trojans, and malware | Licensed for $80–$100 a day, $500–$700 a week, and $1400–$2000 a month |
| DoS-for-hire | Denial of service attack botnet networks | From as low as $1 an hour Booter services (DoS on behalf of customer): $5–$30 an hour Attacks on military, government, or bank websites: $100–$150 an hour |
| Remote desktop protocols (RDPs) | Compromised RDP providing a vector for initial entry penetration of a network | Around $10, but varies by type of network |

*Source:* Rowley (2017); Dark Web News (2017).

**TABLE 5.2**   Skill level gradings for cyber hackers.

| Level | Type of Hacker | Experience |
|---|---|---|
| 1 | Amateur or entry-level hacker (ELH) | High school or in higher education |
| 2 | Coder or software engineer (CS) | Science degree, or at least years of amateur coding |
| 3 | Experienced coder (EC) | More than five years of professional experience, possibly with zero day development experience |
| 4 | Highly experienced coder (HEC) | More than 10 years of professional experience, possibly with experience in industrial control systems |
| 5 | Integration engineer and systems architect (SA) | Project design skills and ability to manage software development teams of up to 10 |
| 6 | Senior technical operations lead (STOL) | Large project conceptualization and management, with ability to manage software projects of very large teams |

above $5 million. These logistical burden index values can be thought of as a notional budgeting cost without sunk costs or standing commitments, and at professional charge-out rates – i.e. what it would cost to hire a team to carry out this type of attack. This is done simply to benchmark and compare the effort and skill requirement of one type of cyber attack with another.

This type of analysis identifies the 'hackonomics' of carrying out attacks as a rational actor seeking reward for the investment of resources. Some types of threat actors do not have the 'logistical budget' – skills, capabilities, and resources – to carry out attacks above a certain index value. Some attacks do not provide a good enough return to merit a threat actor investing effort in them.

Overall, we can see that a few hackers must be making a lot of money from cyber crime, but the large majority of hackers seem highly unlikely to be generating earnings from their skills that would be comparable with what they could earn with the legitimate use of their skills in employment. Some of this may be lifestyle and cultural choices, but if we could find ways of helping hackers find legitimate channels for reward from their talents, everyone might win.

### 5.5.5 Hackers Are Rational Game Players

Overall, in designing security systems and considering how best to manage the threat of cyber attacks, it is useful to consider the risks and rewards of the attacks from the hackers' point of view. They may well want to attack you, but they will take a more attractive or easier target if there is such an alternative available. They have finite resources, and they are looking to get a return on the effort they will invest.

By the principles of deterrence, you don't need to make their task impossible. Just to make it not worth their effort. Make the risk-return ratio unworthwhile for them. Most of what we know about hackers leads us to believe that they are rational game players.

To solve cyber risk, we need to play them at their own game.

## ENDNOTES

1. CCRS (2018d, Smith et al).
2. Poulsen (2009).
3. Squatriglia (2008).
4. Carr (2008).
5. CCRS (2018d, Smith et al.).
6. BankInfoSecurity (2006).
7. BankInfoSecurity (2006).
8. Broadhurst et al. (2014) and Kshetri (2010).
9. McGuire (2012).
10. Broadhurst et al. (2014) and Kshetri (2010).
11. Bhattacharjee (2011).
12. Bing (2017); ABC News (2017).
13. RSA (2017).
14. Meyer (2018).
15. Doherty et al. (2013).
16. Danchev (2012).
17. InfoSEC Institute (2016).
18. See chapter 'The New Media' in Hoffmann (2006) and see Weimann (2006).
19. The US National Academy of Sciences first warned of a 'digital Pearl Harbor' as early as 1990; see Weimann (2004).
20. CCRS (2017b).
21. BBC (2018).
22. Kaspersky Lab (2014).
23. Symantec (2014a).
24. Symantec (2014b).

25. Kaspersky Lab (2017).
26. Schwartz (2017).
27. Heller (2018).
28. Khandelwal (2017).
29. Kirkpatrick (2018).
30. Perlroth (2018).
31. BBC (2018).
32. Cyber Risk Aware (2017).
33. *E-Crime Watch Survey* reported in Keeney et al. (2005).
34. CCRS (2018e, Daffron et al.).
35. Treadwell (2013).
36. Jaishankar (2011); and see also the *International Journal of Cyber Criminology*.
37. FBI IC3 (2016).
38. Grimes (2012).
39. Williams (2016).
40. PYMNTS (2017).
41. Greenberg (2017).
42. *Dark Web News* (2018).
43. Hutchings and Clayton (2016).

# CHAPTER 6

# Measuring the Cyber Threat

## 6.1 MEASUREMENT AND MANAGEMENT

### 6.1.1 A Man-Made Threats

Society is exposed to all manner of threats. These may affect the safety of citizens and their well-being, freedom, and livelihoods. Threats may emerge from land, sea, air, space – and cyberspace. The cyber threat involves an attack in cyberspace that recognizes no geographical boundary, nor any political jurisdiction. Mediated by information technology, a cyber attack ultimately is instigated and perpetrated by a human aggressor. Managing an adversarial threat is different from managing an environmental hazard in that there is an intrinsic pervasive behavioral component. This requires the knowledge and skills developed from experience in human conflict situations.

In a conventional war, the government makes military and strategic decisions collectively on behalf of its citizens, taking appropriate action to deal with any threat. Those serving in uniform take up arms to protect the population at home and overseas. Civilians can carry on with their daily lives without having to worry each moment about hostile forces turning up at their door. Now, without any formal declaration of conflict, we, as citizens, are all embroiled in a perpetual guerrilla cyber war on a global scale. A totalitarian state like North Korea can launch cyber attacks anywhere and at any time with little deterrence. By contrast, a physical attack by North Korea using conventional military means against a foreign country would bring rapid and overwhelming military retribution from that country and its allies.

### 6.1.2 Defending Ourselves

For our own cyber security, we cannot rely just on the government to protect us, although national security initiatives are helpful in dealing with the cyber threat. Only a small proportion of criminal hackers are arrested or ever brought to justice. The tough reality is that all of us have to take responsibility for making our own defensive decisions, and take our own initiatives to counter cyber attacks. We are under continuous cyber siege, bombarded with endless salvos of cyber projectiles by cunning, malevolent adversaries ever eager to evade perimeter security and breach our firewalls. Under relentless pressure of cyber attack, the chief information security officer (CISO) of a corporation is effectively the defensive commanding officer responsible for protecting corporate assets and ensuring business continuity, without interruption by attackers who may be of any background and motivation and from any territory. We return to the important role of the CISO in an organization, in Chapter 10, 'Security Economics and Strategies'.

The enlistment of technical expertise in siege defense against persistent powerful external attack has a long history that goes back as far as the Greek polymath Archimedes. At the siege of Syracuse, Sicily, from 214 to 212 BCE, he directed the city's defense, devising an ingenious array of defensive devices to keep the Roman aggressors at bay. In response, the Romans had to create their own technical inventions to maintain the siege. For Archimedes, managing the Roman threat required measuring it. Precision engineered parabolic mirrors focused the hot southern Mediterranean sun onto the sails of the Roman ships, setting them alight. Without detailed measurement, the mirrors would have been ineffective, and the offensive capability of the besieging enemy would not have been substantially diminished. In the third millennium, individual corporations need to have their own specialist Archimedes technical team engaged around the clock to keep the persistent hostile cyber attackers at bay.

### 6.1.3 Measurement to Make Improvements

An article in the *McKinsey Quarterly* in 1997 declared: 'In the world of management gurus, Peter Drucker is the one guru to whom other gurus kowtow'.[1] Even though this Austrian-American management consultant passed away in his mid-90s in 2005, the philosophical and practical foundations of business that he laid are as relevant for the age of the online worker as for the age of the knowledge worker, which is a term he coined. Credited with creating and inventing modern business management, Peter Drucker asserted: 'If you can't measure it, you can't improve it'. Anyone who has tried to lose weight knows how difficult it is to do without actually weighing yourself regularly. Cognitive dissonance over tell-tale signs of weight gain makes it all too easy to fool yourself about your real weight.

If you can't measure something and check the results, it is very hard to make a consistent improvement.

In all important aspects of business management, measures of performance need to be made regularly to determine where improvements are most needed, and where they can best and most effectively be made. If objective measurements are not made, and reliance placed on subjective assessments, managers can easily fool themselves, their colleagues, and investors that everything is on track and under control, when actually corporate mishap and even disaster may be around the corner. According to a *Fortune* survey,[2] many IT decision makers reckon that stopping cyber attacks is ultimately the responsibility of the board of directors. To keep corporate senior leadership well informed, the CISO needs to demonstrate explicit measures of security improvement, not just talk about them in a vague way.

Unwitting self-deception might be more acute amongst managers lacking formal training in a quantitative discipline. There is still a misperception amongst some students of the liberal arts that science is perhaps as much a matter of opinion as is literary criticism. Of course, there are some aspects of corporate culture that are more naturally described qualitatively rather than quantitatively, and hence are not so easy to measure. Measuring the level of staff morale, which is relevant to gauging the severity of the potential insider cyber threat, is one. Assessing employee level of awareness of external cyber threat is another. These do not need sophisticated assessment techniques to gauge, as assessing them with a simple grading (e.g. 1–5) serves as a way to compare and monitor them over time.

The CISO of a corporation should be constantly seeking to improve corporate cyber security, rather than just maintaining the status quo. Since the threat is always advancing, standing still would be effectively going backwards. Because of the rarity of extreme events, complacency can easily take hold if there hasn't been a major cyber attack for a long time, if ever. Improving corporate cyber security requires measurement. This takes time, effort, and budget. The CISO should organize regular penetration test exercises to gauge corporate vulnerability to cyber attack.

### 6.1.4 A Monitoring Checklist

The CISO should then identify a set of key variables to be regularly monitored and measured to keep track of cyber security, and to assess ways in which this might be tightened, without inordinate extra expense.

A number of such key quantitative variables are listed in turn.

**6.1.4.1  Turnaround Time for Implementing Software Patches**  It is crucial that once a software patch is issued, action to implement it is made as rapidly as possible, subject to real-time operational constraints, such as the impact on business continuity. Opportunistic cyber criminals prey on those organizations that are slow to patch their computer systems, or may occasionally make the error of forgetting to patch them altogether. Criminals can make a good living from picking such low-hanging corporate fruit without needing to spend money in the black market for hacking tools. The time taken to implement patches should be logged, so that slippage in this time is recognized immediately by the IT department, including the CISO, and urgent remedial efforts are made to reduce the patch implementation delay. Lessons should be learned from the high-profile cases of failure to implement patches in a timely fashion.

**6.1.4.2  Frequency of Social Engineering Failures**  A weak link in the cyber security chain – arguably the weakest link – is human error. Where a malevolent software engineer may fail to breach security barriers, a psychologist may succeed. The art of manipulating people to give up confidential information is euphemistically termed social engineering. Clever social engineering tricks may entice an unwitting staff member to click on a dangerous attachment or give away a password or other confidential data. The frequency of social engineering failures should be logged so that the need for improved training is assessed, and the remedial effect of enhanced staff cyber education can be gauged.

**6.1.4.3  Time to Detect Intrusion**  In October 2014, the director of the US Federal Bureau of Investigation (FBI) said there are two kinds of big companies in the United States: 'There are those who've been hacked by the Chinese and those who don't know they've been hacked by the Chinese'. The latter should be the more worried. Early detection of intrusion is essential to minimize the damage and loss caused by unauthorized system access, and to deter attackers. The duration of each intrusion should be monitored and checked for corporate progress in dealing with such events.

**6.1.4.4  Frequency of Corporate Cyber Attacks**  Even though it involves time and effort, the daily rolling log of the frequency and characteristics of monitored cyber attacks is a vital management tool. This helps quantify the risk and prioritize future cyber defense expenditure to combat the most prevalent attack modes and to deter hackers. Comparisons with other corporations are also insightful for gauging relative security.

**6.1.4.5 Frequency of Significant Cyber Near Misses** Security, like safety, can benefit from good fortune, but should not depend on luck. A parallel log should be maintained of cyber attacks that might have caused a major loss but fortunately did not. These near misses might arise from internal corporate security mismanagement such as social engineering frailty, insider malevolent action, professional oversight, negligence, and error. Additionally, near-misses might arise from external security environment factors such as late patching of known bugs by software vendors and deficient security of third-party service providers.

**6.1.4.6 Staff Morale and Awareness of Cyber Threat** The human vulnerability of a company may be more significant than the technological. Tracking the risk awareness of employees through simple training and refresher courses, carrying out routine exercises such as phishing tests, and monitoring morale can provide useful indicators of the readiness of staff to deal with cyber threat.

### 6.1.5 Measurement for Better Risk Management

Software manpower and budget resources are finite and need to be allocated efficiently. The principal source of computer system vulnerability is the existence of software bugs. In Chapter 4, 'Ghosts in the Code', we demonstrate that vendor software can never be guaranteed to be free of bugs. For one thing, fixing a bug runs the risk of creating a new bug.[3] So the task of eliminating bugs can cycle on and on in perpetual motion, running down the development budget. Accordingly, software is often shipped with open items – bugs deemed to be acceptable.

Of course, there needs to be a systematic process for software development. In this process, project measurement programs can help project managers identify best practices and supporting tools. Measurement helps identify and correct problems early. With high-quality objective data, managers can track actual measures against a plan, and assess progress towards project objectives.

So measurement helps track and manage the risk of the creation of software bugs. It also helps the CISO to manage the cyber threat.

### 6.1.6 Setting a Cyber Security Budget

Cyber security requires a non-trivial proportion of the overall IT budget; 3% is a benchmark figure. For both physical and cyber attacks, attackers follow the path of least resistance in targeting. Accordingly, expenditure on security needs to be commensurate with the security budgets of other similar corporations to reduce the risk of being specially targeted.

Just how to allocate this budget to maximize cyber security is a challenging question for the CISO. Expenditure on cyber security must be cost-effective. However, demonstration that security is cost-effective encounters the fundamental conundrum that deterrence is rather a slippery parameter to measure. The absence of a major security breach may be attributable to new security systems that have significant deterrent value, or may be just due to the diversion of attackers' focus elsewhere towards softer targets. This applies as much to physical security as to cyber security. The counter-terrorism budget for the US-VISIT program would be hard to justify solely on the number of terrorists arrested at US airports.

Investments in security technologies such as network and desktop forensics have the capability of identifying abnormal behavior in transit and on the host. They are often purchased ex post after a major breach occurs, notably if, embarrassingly, the breach has lain undiscovered for many months. But well in advance of any such loss, the more knowledgeable and risk-aware corporations invest in these advanced technologies that go beyond traditional pattern matching and signatures for known attacks. They have the capability of identifying abnormal behavior in transit and on the host.

## 6.2  CYBER THREAT METRICS

### 6.2.1  Perception of Threat

It is well known that the human perception of a threat may be discordant with reality, and can lead to poor decision-making and misallocation of resources. The most notorious example in the early twenty-first century was the perception that Saddam Hussein had weapons of mass destruction in Iraq. The international consequences of this error of threat perception had long-lasting consequences. The misperception of the scale of risks may not always have such momentous consequences, but it always matters because scarce resources for risk mitigation may be squandered, or not allocated in an effective or efficient manner. Because of the war in Iraq, strategically important military resources were diverted away from efforts against the Taliban in Afghanistan.

So it is vital that an accurate and objective assessment is made of the actual level of cyber threat that an organization faces. This can be categorized as the likelihood of a loss occurring from a cyber incident, and the chances of different severities of loss being suffered by the company.

The frequency of cyber attacks can be extremely high, and the spectrum of threats is very broad. Indeed, cyber threat assessment has become a classic Big Data challenge; cyber threat databases have volumes measured in hundreds of terabytes. However, the focus on the potential for large loss allows the organization to prioritize on the key risks, rather than grapple with the potential threat universe.

Big Data research provides analysts with modern methods to visualize cyber attacks rapidly and simplify the seemingly inexplicable complex patterns. Organizations need to be current with the latest vulnerabilities to prevent known attacks. Big Data and modern analytics allow companies to identify anomalies and advanced attack vectors. The characteristics of suspicious files need to be analyzed regularly, as malware is becoming more evasive. Trends in malware movements need to be better understood, and statistics on the performance of malware detection need to be assessed. Cyber security improvement requires risk management and actionable intelligence that emerge from exploration of Big Data. Furthermore, analysts need to be capable of categorizing dynamic cyber threats on a similar time scale to that of the evolving threat change.

## 6.2.2  Threat Attributes

A defensive coordinator should have basic data on the threat attributes of adversaries. These attributes cover capability, resources, intent, commitment, and targeting. In the future, cyber threat information may be collected and disseminated by government agencies, as they currently do for terrorism. However, until that is the case, each corporation needs to make its own threat assessment. To aid corporate decision making over cyber risk, threat metrics need to be defined and parameterized, and compared with subjective views of risk. These views may be grossly off-track. Surveys suggest that two-thirds of UK small businesses have thought they are not vulnerable to cyber crime, whereas the reality is that half of UK small businesses could be hacked within an hour. Small businesses are in fact more vulnerable targets than larger businesses because of the inferior level of security they have in-house. Small businesses collectively may hold more data than individual larger businesses but they may not implement the higher levels of additional security more typically found in larger businesses to keep their data safe.

A key quantitative threat metric is the number of group members that a cyber threat organization is capable of dedicating to the strengthening and deployment of its technical capability. Amongst the group members are technical personnel with specific knowledge or skills, and those directly involved with the actual production and deployment of the group's cyber weapons. Evidently, a threat with a higher level of technical personnel has a greater potential for innovative design and development, allowing for the possibility of new methods of reaching a goal that may not have been available in the past. In addition, a higher level of technical personnel also expedites the design and development of a threat's plans for attack. Threat metrics associated with such plans could be defined in increasing technical detail down to coding level. The focus here is on a higher level of threat discussion.

### 6.2.3 Threat Matrices and Attack Trees

A common vocabulary is clearly advisable for government agencies and intelligence organizations to categorize threats in a mutually understandable manner, without talking at cross-purposes or communicating in a quasi-foreign language. Two basic terms of this vocabulary, useful for conveying technical threat information in a compact and efficient manner, are threat matrix and attack tree.

The concept of a generic threat matrix is a useful term that allows analysts in the unclassified environment to identify potential attack paths and mitigation steps to thwart attacks.[4] The threat profile is specified in terms of the commitment and resources required by the aggressors. The commitment attribute can be elaborated as covering the three factors of intensity, stealth, and time.

- *Intensity* is the diligence or perseverance of a threat in the pursuit of its objective.
- *Stealth* is the ability of the threat to maintain a necessary level of secrecy.
- *Time* is the period that a threat group is capable of dedicating to planning, developing, and deploying methods to reach an objective.

The resources attribute can similarly be elaborated as covering the three factors of technical personnel, knowledge, and access.

- *Technical personnel* are those group members who may be dedicated to the building and deployment of the technical capability.
- *Knowledge* is the level of proficiency, and the threat group's capability of actually deploying this proficiency in pursuit of its objective.

■ *Access* is the threat group's ability to insert a group member within a restricted system environment.

Associated with the three commitment factors and the three resources factors are corresponding threat levels ranging discretely from grade 1 (least) to grade 8 (greatest) in increasing order of threat capability.

As the grand monuments to successful generals celebrate, making decisions is the most essential and critical action for those engaged in adversarial conflict, which includes cyber attackers. Decision making has a natural branching structure: out of a set of options, one is taken; then a new contingent set of options open up, and one of these is taken; and so on. To capture the sequential repeated branching structure of decisions, the metaphor of a tree comes naturally. Thus, decision analysts speak of decision trees, having multiple branches and leaves.

In the context of cyber risk, the specific decisions made by cyber attackers cover all the characteristics of a cyber attack. Threats can be characterized and analyzed using attack trees, the nodes of which are parameterized by threat matrices. Whether or not a cyber attacker constructs an attack tree during the planning of a cyber attack, it is instructive for cyber security officers to think through the logical process of constructing the component geometry of an attack tree. This helps to organize thinking about threats.

An analyst begins by defining the attacker's overarching objective. This objective serves as the root node in the tree. Subordinate nodes detail the logical relationships among the actions the attacker might undertake to achieve the objective, and the actions themselves. Each unique path through the tree represents an attack scenario. No attack tree of finite size could of course be anywhere near complete. Sets of possible attack modes could be left out through oversight or lack of lateral thinking. Furthermore, an attacker's options are liable to change dynamically according to the resistance encountered. A classic military adage is that no plan survives first contact with the enemy. This holds in cyberspace as in the physical world. An attack tree can be reviewed by iterating the nodes and considering alternative adaptive pathways through the attack tree by which the attacker's objective might be attained. Knowledge of the brief but eventful history of cyber attacks is helpful in this review process. Major security breaches have occurred from the basic failure of security officers to enquire sufficiently diligently how else an attack might happen. The Trojan horse is of the course the iconic example of an attack emanating from an unforeseen direction.

**ILLUSTRATIVE ATTACK TREE FOR SYSTEM INTRUSION INTO A TARGETED ORGANIZATION**

1. Send spear phishing emails to selected target staff.
   (a) Bypass system access control.
      {i} Install malware on the target system.
2. Identify vulnerable contractor for the target.
   (a) Use social engineering to obtain ID authentication for the contractor.
      {i} Install malware onto the contractor's system for infecting the target system.
   (b) Set up a watering hole to trap the contractor.
      {i} Install malware onto the contractor's system to infect the target system.
3. Search for IT job opportunities at the target.
   (a) Apply for job with system access.
      {i} Gain administrator's privileges.
      <1> Install malware on the target system.

## 6.3  MEASURING THE THREAT FOR AN ORGANIZATION

### 6.3.1  Using Scenarios

It is possible to assess the threat of cyber loss by considering scenarios that would cause an organization a severe level of loss. In Chapter 2, we set out five major types of cyber loss process: data exfiltration, contagious malware infection, denial of service attacks, financial transaction theft, and failures of counterparties or suppliers. This is not an exhaustive list of loss types, but represents some of the major drivers of large losses to an organization, and between them they account for an estimated 90% of costs from cyber loss. For each loss process we provided examples of different levels of severity and the magnitudes of costs that these have inflicted on organizations in the past and, in some cases, how often these types of events have occurred. The management exercises were designed to illustrate a scenario of each type of loss process, and invited you to consider the effect that a scenario like that would have on your business.

## MEASURING THE CYBER RISK OF AN ORGANIZATION

### MediaMark's Cyber Risk Profile

MediaMark Inc. is a (fictional) media company, with around a thousand employees and a billion-dollar turnover. The cyber risk assessment for MediaMark begins by assessing how often companies like it suffer cyber losses of different types and severities.

The statistics of data breach suggest that a large US company in the entertainment and media sector might expect to have a breach in which 1,000 or more of its protected records are stolen, with odds of around 1 in 30 each year. A breach of around 5,000 personally identifiable information (PII) records could be expected to cost MediaMark an average of $500,000. The chances of a very large data breach involving more than a million data records are lower: 1 in 225; but if one did occur, it could cost the organization more than $10 million. There are scenarios in which the costs resulting from the data breaches could be an order of magnitude larger – the odds of an exceptionally large cost given the occurrence of a data breach are around 1 in 10. MediaMark benchmarks its cyber security standards against the other 500 large companies in its sector, and finds that its cyber security is below average – in fact it is in the bottom quartile of similar large media businesses. This means that its odds of experiencing a breach are significantly higher than the average for the sector, at around 1 in 13.

In addition to data breach losses, companies of this size and business sector have an estimated chance of around 1 in 100 a year of being penetrated by a piece of contagious malware that disables at least one device on their network. If a company had an infection, the chance that it could have more than a third of its computers disabled is around 1 in 50. If a third of the organization's devices were infected, this would cost the organization around $500 million in lost revenues from downtime and incident response costs.

MediaMark has a sophisticated media management software platform that matches advertisements to customers, and this integrates

*(Continued)*

multiple sources of content and algorithm software from multiple providers, including being hosted on one of the leading cloud service providers, so there is an additional level of risk of counterparty failures causing disruption to MediaMark's revenues.

Other potential cyber loss processes – denial of service attacks, financial transaction thefts, and network failures – pose less risk, but are similarly evaluated in terms of their likelihoods of occurrence and potential loss outcomes. There are a large number of scenarios that represent the different loss possibilities, and if the probability-weighted losses from all of the scenarios are summed up, the average annual loss that might be expected from all cyber causes would be around $5 million – around 0.5% of turnover. This represents the attritional cost that the company faces from cyber risk, but probably as lots of small losses, with the occasional rare but severe one.

The MediaMark board of directors is less concerned by the smaller, more frequent cyber losses, and more concerned about the potential for a large loss from a cyber attack. A loss of above $50 million would mean that the company would have to issue a profits warning, and could possibly trigger a downgrade to its credit rating. The cyber risk assessment for MediaMark identifies a number of scenarios that could cause the company a loss of $50 million or more, shown in Table 6.1.

From the sum of the likelihoods of these scenarios, MediaMark can expect to have a $50 million loss from one cyber cause or another at odds of around 1 in 50 – i.e. a 2% chance each year.

The MediaMark directors decide that this likelihood of a $50 million cyber loss is beyond their risk appetite. They decide to make an investment in cyber security to reduce their risk exposure. They embark on a program of hiring additional IT security personnel, implementing new technologies and procedures, conducting awareness training for staff, and purchasing cyber insurance. These measures collectively reduce the chance of exceeding their risk appetite, by bringing the odds of a cyber loss of $50 million or more down to less than 1 in 100, which the board judges to be an acceptable level of risk.

**TABLE 6.1** Selected examples of scenarios that would cause MediaMark to have a loss of more than $50 million, with the odds of that scenario occurring in a given year.

| Loss Process | Magnitude | Vulnerability | Potential Cause | Odds per Year |
|---|---|---|---|---|
| Contagious malware | Over 1% infection of key servers | Network traffic scanning | Ransomware | 1 in 200 |
| Data exfiltration | Over 10 million PII records | Network intrusion | Malicious external | 1 in 250 |
| Data exfiltration | Over 1 million payment card information (PCI) records | Payment process malware | Malicious external | 1 in 500 |
| Contagious malware | Over 10% infection of general devices | Firewall and AV failure | Disk wiper | 1 in 600 |
| Counterparty failure | Serious bug in MM platform software | Third-party plug-ins | Quality assurance (QA) in supplier | 1 in 750 |
| Financial theft | Multiple multi-million-dollar bank transfers | Bank transfer authentication | Insider or external | 1 in 800 |
| Data exfiltration | Over 100,000 protected health information (PHI) records | Access control failure | Insider | 1 in 900 |
| Contagious malware | Infection of media management platform | Network traffic scanning | Targeted payload | 1 in 1000 |
| Denial of service | Ultra-high intensity DDoS on server, 7 days continuous | Web application firewall | Hacktivist external | 1 in 4000 |
| Denial of service | Very high intensity DDoS on server, 20 days intermittent | Web application firewall | Hacktivist external | 1 in 4800 |
| Counterparty failure | 4+ days cloud outage: object storage; US | Cloud platform continuity | Human error | 1 in 5000 |

Of course there are many potential scenarios that could occur, and it is only possible to consider a manageable range of them, but a cyber threat assessment exercise would typically select a representative set of scenarios – perhaps several levels of severity for each loss process – and assess the impact on the organization if they were to occur. This then has to be set against the likelihood that these scenarios might occur, say in the next year. The threat assessment sets the costs and potential impacts on the organization against the likelihood. The most important threats are those with the most severe impacts and with the highest likelihoods.

Assessment of the likelihood of the occurrence of any particular scenario does not need to be precise and of course is highly uncertain. Especially important are the relative likelihoods, comparing one threat scenario with other and against other threats to the balance sheet of the business. Assessment of the likelihood of scenarios can be anchored on how often attacks of that type have been seen against organizations like yours – for example of your size of business, or in your country, or in your business sector. Assessments can also be developed from the more sophisticated event tree analysis techniques described in the previous section.

Evaluating the likelihoods and severities of different cyber threats establishes the framework for managing cyber risk for your organization.

### 6.3.2  Building Safety and Cyber Security

As pointed out in Chapter 3, 'Cyber Enters the Physical World', security and safety management are closely linked as professional disciplines. Breaches of security can jeopardize safety, and vice versa. Cyber security managers have much to gain from studying building safety issues. A building facilities manager responsible for the physical safety of occupants should know about the building construction. Quite apart from familiarity with the building codes used in the design process, the facilities manager would gain risk awareness by considering the safety perspective of the design civil engineer. What specific perils did the engineer design against? How did the engineer ensure that any building fire would be contained within a specific section of the building? What can go wrong? What should be done about what can go wrong?

These are important practical questions to answer. Often the hardest answers are provided by harsh experience. To concentrate the mind of a building manager, consider a major fire disaster that occurred in West London on June 14, 2017, at a 24-story residential apartment block: Grenfell Tower. Fire started in one apartment, and spread rapidly upwards along the exterior walls, the cladding of which was not fully fire-resistant. There was no sprinkler system, and the fire engulfed the building, killing 80 people in the towering inferno. This mode of fire catastrophe had not been adequately appreciated, modeled, or even anticipated. The tall smoke plume rose as though from an urban volcano. There was no disaster contingency plan scenario for what actually happened.

### 6.3.3   IoT as an Amplifier of Risk

Fire has always been a domestic peril for human habitation. But it is only in the twenty-first century that conflagrations in high-rise buildings might be ignited remotely by cyber-physical attacks that could disable automatic sprinklers and other fire-suppression systems.

The internet of things (IoT) amplifies considerably the cyber fire risk; not everything that can be connected should be connected, especially when elementary default passwords such as 000000 are often left unchanged. Many connected household items could catch fire, even electric kettles, which might be hacked so they fail to switch off. Accordingly, cyber threat modeling not only can protect computer systems, but could also be a life-saving activity.

To gain deeper technical insight into cyber protection, a CISO should benefit from understanding security from the inner perspective of the design software engineer. What strategy was adopted at the design stage to keep hackers from attacking? The software designer needs to model the cyber threat diligently, so as to minimize the systems' vulnerability to cyber attack. Systems should be designed at the outset for security. Yet, as systems grow in size and complexity, this is a goal that is ever harder to achieve, and even hard to contemplate as a potential mode of reality. A systematic approach to tackling this goal involves modeling the threat, and exploring in depth how things could go wrong.[5]

### 6.3.4   Ways Things Can Go Wrong

Economics Nobel laureate Daniel Kahneman has suggested the concept of a *premortem* as a way of overcoming overconfident optimism about corporate disasters.[6] When an organization has almost come to an important decision, a group of those knowledgeable about it should convene, and consider the situation where one year ahead the decision has been implemented and the outcome is a disaster. The task is to write a brief history of the disaster. This would have been very instructive prior to the recladding of Grenfell Tower before the fire, and would be a valuable exercise for any major cyber security decision, because there are so many ways things could go wrong.

Modeling the cyber threat is a means of anticipating future cyber disaster. This logical process starts with identifying the different ways in which the threat manifests itself to confound the best efforts of the software system designer. The implications of outsmarting the system designer are then evaluated, and the consequences for system fragility and failure are assessed.

There are some threats, such as the elevation of privileges and denial of types of service, that have to be aggressively countered in the fundamentals of software design, such as authorization checks for the protection of administrator security. Unfortunately for the software system designer, things can go wrong in numerous ways because the most dangerous adversary is cunning, patient, malevolent, and potentially state-sponsored.

All warfare is based on deception. This basic military adage, expounded by Sun Tzu, applies as much to the virtual world now as to the real world 2500 years ago when he wrote his military masterwork *The Art of War*. China is the most internet-enabled country in the world, and is one of the principal national exporters of cyber attacks such as industrial espionage. Chinese cyber attackers (who study the wisdom of Sun Tzu in their own language) have manifestly adopted his strategic principles in their global cyber attack campaigns.

One of the most celebrated US hackers, Kevin Mitnick, who once was featured on the FBI's most wanted list, even wrote a book focused solely on the art of deception.[7] He testified to Congress on security's weakest link being the human factor, and how he has managed to obtain passwords and other sensitive information from people in a deceptive way using social engineering. Building trust is key to success for a social engineer, whose interaction with a victim is akin to playing a chess game. Enjoyment in chess comes from the challenge of outmaneuvering your opponent – and winning. Social engineers gain similar satisfaction from a large library of devious moves, which may lead to winning results if the right plays are called.

- Baiting an unsuspecting victim with a malware-infected device, such as a USB stick.
- Sending phishing emails that appear to come from reputable sources. Spear phishing targets specific employees within the corporation the hacker is trying to access.
- Vishing for information by telephone by posing as a fellow employee, or asking questions to verify an employee's identity.
- Pretexting a victim by telling a phony story to hook the victim.

- Farming a victim, developing a relationship to string out the period of data extraction.

Pretending to be someone or something else is a classic tactic for gaining military advantage. Sun Tzu would have recognized spoofing, if not the following third-millennium computer variations:

- Spoofing a process on the same machine, such as creating a Trojan and altering the path.
- Spoofing a file such as creating a file in the local directory.
- Spoofing a machine such as internet protocol (IP) redirection.
- Spoofing a person by setting an email display name.
- Spoofing a role through declaration of having a specific role.

Another form of deception that Sun Tzu would have recognized is tampering. Of course, in cyberspace, tampering is undertaken using digital rather than physical objects:

- Tampering with a file.
- Tampering with memory, and modifying code.
- Tampering with a network to redirect or modify data flow.

Claiming not to have done something, or not appearing to be responsible for what happened, is another type of deception well familiar to war historians and strategists. This is called repudiation. Threats of this kind can include claiming not to have received something, claiming to be a fraud victim, or attacking logs to cause confusion.

Leaking information is a classic trick of the espionage trade, as old as spying itself. The various modes of leakage need to be represented in a cyber threat model. There can be information disclosure from a process, such as extracting secrets from error messages if security mechanisms are not used. Furthermore, there can be information disclosure from data stores, such as getting data from logs and temp files. Stealing cryptographic keys is a step towards the launching of further attacks. Another type of information leakage is associated with information disclosure from a data flow, such as inferring secrets from traffic analysis and finding out who is communicating with whom. Social network analysis might reveal substantial volumes of information of espionage value. Traffic might also be redirected directly to the cyber spies, which would be both convenient and conducive to further attacks.

## 6.4    THE LIKELIHOOD OF MAJOR CYBER ATTACKS

### 6.4.1    Not If or When, but How Likely?

In respect of the likelihood of a major cyber attack, like many other public order threats, it is routine for officials to state that it is not a matter of if, but when. For the general public, this statement sends the important security message that continued cyber security vigilance is needed – even if there has yet to be a major societal attack on the scale of the most severe predictions. Of course, from a risk analyst's perspective, the occurrence of almost all hazards is not a matter of if, but when. For example, a major asteroid will strike planet Earth again at some time in the future. So the Hollywood scenario of doomsday impact is not a matter of if, but when.

Beyond establishing whether a major threat event is feasible, risk analysts are interested in estimating the likelihood or annual frequency, or odds, of occurrence. The motivation for wanting to estimate event likelihood stems from the fundamental definition of risk as the product of likelihood, vulnerability, and loss. A risk analyst asks first, what is the probability of a major threat event; second, what is a system's vulnerability to the threat event; and third, what is the resulting loss. Likelihood matters: even if there could be a very large loss from a feared type of disk wiper malware infecting all computers in an organization, investing heavily in protecting against that scenario is not warranted unless the likelihood of that threat is significant.

There are many risk stakeholders who have an interest in the quantification of event likelihood. Civil engineers need frequency estimates for establishing the probabilistic design basis for safe construction. Insurers need frequency estimates to price hazard insurance, and to manage the risk of extreme losses. The latter may require decisions to be made over the purchase of reinsurance.

Corporations need frequency estimates to allocate resources for risk mitigation. There are many risks to which a corporation is exposed. Deciding how much to spend dealing with one particular risk is an individual judgment that can be supported by quantitative risk analysis. Consider, for example, the risk to a corporation from cyber criminals, terrorists, vandals, thieves, and saboteurs. What proportion of resources, expressed in manpower and money, should be spent in addressing each of these diverse threats? With the kind of hindsight that comes readily after a breach has occurred, it is common practice to spend money to remedy a gap in security once it has been exposed. But to justify expenditure in advance of a cyber security breach requires the methods of quantitative risk analysis, balancing the cost of extra security against the corporate value of lost data, weighted by the probability of a successful cyber attack.

### 6.4.2 Measuring Cyber Attack Severity

The study and analysis of cyber crime build upon the foundations of the discipline of criminology, which arose out of the European Enlightenment of the eighteenth century. Before then, harsh punishments kept people in line with strict state authority. A principal motivation for the collection and analysis of crime statistics has been to improve policing to protect potential victims of crime.[8] For example, without statistical analysis of their incidence, crimes of domestic violence might not be given adequate police attention. The geographical and societal differences in crime rates are statistics that shed light on criminal behavior and the root causes of crime. Measuring crime leads to better crime management and more effective policing.

A cyber attack is a crime adapted for the modern age of globalization. To improve the international policing of cyber crime, a European Cybercrime Centre was established by Europol in 2013. There is an important nexus between cyber crime and other forms of organized crime. The use of the dark web for engaging in clandestine criminal activities is one common link. This nexus is recognized by Europol in a joint report on internet organized crime threat assessment.[9] Working with other police agencies as well as private cyber security companies, Europol achieved a major success in December 2016 with the takedown of an extensive online criminal infrastructure *Avalanche*. Criminals had been using the platform since 2009 to mount phishing attacks, distribute malware, and launder money. More than 800,000 domains were seized, blocked, or otherwise disrupted. This is a large number, considering that a typical botnet takedown rate is 1000 domains per day.

Given the attacker's advantage, that it is easier to break into a computer than to protect it, the numbers on the offensive side are much larger still. Indeed, any discussion of cyber attack severity involves getting one's head around some very large numbers, whether expressed in economic loss, computers affected, or records exfiltrated. This is a reflection of the universality of computers in daily life, and the global reach of the internet; more than three billion people use the internet.

The large numbers represented in cyber risk, and their capability to scale up to cause large losses, have similarities with the very large energy-release scaling processes of the natural world. This is fundamentally due to the structure of the natural world being self-similar, i.e. looking the same at different spatial scales.[10] In the social sciences, there is an equivalent universal scale-free power law, known as Zipf's law, which has many internet applications because of the scaling features of social and computer networks.[11] Consistent with Zipf's law, a useful logarithmic measure can be defined for data breach severity.[12] In Chapter 2, 'Preparing for Cyber Attacks', Table 2.2 presented a grading of events on a data breach severity scale, together with the ranges of the numbers of data records.

### 6.4.3 Maximum Severity: Total Data Records Held

Just as the maximum earthquake magnitude varies from one region of the world to another, so the maximum number of records that might be exfiltrated in a data breach varies from one corporation to another. The number of employees provides a general benchmark for the potential maximum scale of data breach experienced by a corporation.

This data breach severity scale is helpful for gauging the likelihood of cyber attacks of increasing severity. As shown in Figure 2.2, in the years from 2012 to 2018, there were many thousands of data exfiltration events in the United States alone, amounting to several billions of confidential records lost. Over the latter half of that particular decade, on average there were around 200 incidents a year of data breach severity P4 and above, and at least 70 incidents of P5 and above. These US occurrence rates have declined slightly in more recent years as preventive measures have reduced the incidence rate.[13]

The statistics on data breach suffer a time lag loss of reliability because of a characteristic feature of cyber crime – stealth. In 2015, the chief security strategist at FireEye, Richard Bejtlich, testified to the US Congress that only for 30% of the time were victims able to identify intrusions on their own.[14] The CISO of Yahoo may have pondered then if Yahoo might have been in the other 70%. A comparative cyber risk assessment would have helped to gauge the likelihood of being hacked unknowingly.

In September 2016, Yahoo disclosed that at least 500 million accounts had been hacked back in 2014. A few months on, in December 2016, Yahoo announced that a billion accounts had been compromised back in August 2013. Then in October 2017, after Yahoo's acquisition by Verizon, it was finally disclosed that all three billion accounts were actually accessed then. Names, email addresses, and passwords were lost in this massive P9 event.

### 6.4.4 Characterizing Extreme Events

As shown by Yahoo, a well-planned targeted cyber attack can cause a massive loss to an individual corporation. Targeted attacks are conducted to steal intellectual property, to damage critical infrastructure, to spy, and to make money. According to an indictment by the US Department of Justice relating to the 2014 Yahoo data breach, the latter two motivated the Federal Security Service (FSB), the Russian espionage agency. Nation-states have the greatest cyber attack resources and technical capability, and the likelihood of extreme events is governed to a large extent by state-sponsored hacking operations.

An untargeted cyber attack would not have the penetration power of one with a specific designated target, but nevertheless can generate extreme losses by affecting multiple computers. Viruses can be transmitted through human action, such as opening a file or executing a program. But far more effective at spreading rapidly to infect thousands or even millions of computers are computer worms. They can spread unassisted and also have the ability to self-replicate, creating multiple copies of themselves to send to other computers. A notorious example, described in Chapter 2, is the *ILOVEYOU* virus that emanated from Manila in May 2000, and infected more than 50 million computers, about 10% of all internet-connected computers at that time. When an email attachment bearing the name of the worm was opened, all image files on the computer were overwritten. Variants of the virus overwrote other types of files. The virus was then sent to all in the user's Windows address book. Some estimates put the cleanup and disruption costs at $10 billion to $15 billion.

If *ILOVEYOU* can be fairly described as the worm that cheated on everyone, *Conficker* is the so-called worm that roared. *Conficker* infected its first computer in November 2008, and within a month had spread to 1.5 million computers around the world. Several months later, it had infected at least eight million home, business, and government computers, creating a massive botnet.[15] The worldwide *Conficker* cleanup costs have exceeded $9 billion, and are still mounting: US police body cameras have been found to be pre-installed with the *Conficker* malware.

### 6.4.5  Challenges of Carrying Out an Extreme Event

A positivist scientific approach to criminology aims to establish general principles for understanding criminal behavior. In this context, real-world crime provides a useful paradigm for understanding cyber crime, in particular major incidents. Imagine real-world criminals planning an ambitious heist on a large bank without resorting to the threat of physical violence. They would need to find a clandestine way of gaining entry into the bank outside of opening hours. Once inside the bank, they would need a security pass to be able to move around freely to access the bank vault. The bank manager's authorization would then be required to remove valuables from the vault. Clearly, this heist could be viable only if security is breached at each stage: entering the bank, acquiring a security pass, and authorizing the exfiltration of money.

A cyber criminal planning a major cyber heist to generate an extreme cyber loss has a comparable sequence of challenges to overcome. A cyber intruder has to gain entry into a target system of high value, then be able to spread across to other network computers, and then upgrade access privileges to administrator status to exfiltrate data. State-of-the-art corporate computer security is configured to prevent any part of this sequence from being realized in practice. However, no computer security is perfect even for the best-resourced IT departments, and such illicit operations can nevertheless be enabled through the deployment of zero day exploits: software bugs that expose hitherto hidden gaps in computer security. These gaps are unknown not only to the software vendors, but also to the antivirus vendors. In the planning of targeted cyber attacks, zero day exploits against unknown vulnerabilities are crucial for making the attacks less easily detectable.[16]

### 6.4.6  Harvesting Bugs

Software bugs may be discovered by a diverse array of bug hunters. There are those who are employed, e.g. by Project Google, specifically to find bugs. Once they find bugs, they report them to the software providers. There are also bounty hunters who spend a considerable amount of effort searching for bugs, which they report on payment of a bounty. They may also auction off their discoveries to the highest bidder, who may well be of malicious intent, or an agent of a nation-state engaged in cyber warfare. Apart from buying zero days, nation-states also spend substantial intellectual resources to harvest software bugs themselves. Many of these may eventually be disclosed to the software providers. However, the most dangerous are likely to be retained within the privacy of cyber war arsenals. To update a classic Roman dictum: 'If you want cyber peace, prepare for cyber war'. Finally, there are the so-called black hat hackers who use their discoveries to launch cyber attacks for commercial gain, or sell malware as a service to less technically capable and more work-averse cyber criminals.

Zero day exploits may be stockpiled for deployment at the optimal strategic moment. But nation-states and others who accumulate such a stockpile would recognize that they have a finite shelf life because of the prospect of discovery by others. Vulnerabilities remain unknown for an average of almost a year. The time between publication and eventual patch can vary from a few days to months.

In order to appreciate how extreme cyber losses can materialize, an elaborate desktop exercise in cyber conflict gaming can be conducted. Desktop war games evolved during the eighteenth and early nineteenth centuries in the German and Austrian courts and military academies to perfect past battles and plan future campaigns.[17] For some war games, large colored boards with more than 1500 squares were used. In the Napoleonic era, table-top war gaming became yet more intricate and realistic. In the twenty-first century, large game boards have been replaced by computer screens, and war games are played out using numerical simulation techniques, whereby a large number of possible scenarios are considered, and their consequences evaluated. A simulation can still be pictured as a board game algorithm, where dice are thrown to move across the board, and a player's actions depend on the square on which the player happens to land. A loss would arise if the square is vulnerable to the attacker. Because of the randomness incorporated, the simulation process outlined in the inset box is called stochastic.

## COMPUTER SIMULATION OF CYBER ATTACKS

A stochastic simulation proceeds via the following basic steps, which are encoded in a computer algorithm and repeated thousands of times.

1. Sample the different potential combinations of zero days available for a cyber attack.
2. Identify optimal vulnerable targets for a cyber attack deploying these specific zero days.
3. Consider alternative strategies for avoiding detection.
4. Account for different defensive countermeasures.
5. Estimate the consequent damage and economic loss to the designated targets.

### 6.4.7 Simulation Process – *Stuxnet* Example

The best-known, most audacious, and most notorious example to illustrate this simulation process is *Stuxnet*, which used three zero days to cause damage to Iranian centrifuges in 2010. Many days and nights of cyber war gaming and computer simulation must have preceded this well-planned and brilliantly executed cyber attack.

First, a Windows shell vulnerability allowed a remote attacker to run code via a malicious file, via an improperly handled icon displayed in Windows Explorer. Second, there was a zero day bug in the Print Spooler Service that made it possible for malicious code to be passed to, and then executed on, a remote machine. Then the malware exploited two different elevation-of-privilege bugs to gain complete control over the system. These zero days facilitated a brazen cyber attack on centrifuges at the Iranian nuclear fuel enrichment plant in Natanz. *Stuxnet* managed to cause many centrifuges to spin out of control. The loss consequence was that about a thousand of the centrifuges disintegrated, and the Iranian nuclear program was set back several years.

With its power and sophistication, *Stuxnet* has been vividly likened to an F16 fighter taking to the skies over the Flanders trenches of the First World War, when aerial reconnaissance was conducted by biplanes flying at the speed of a modern sports car.[18]

### 6.4.8 The Pentagon Cyber Arsenal

As with military jets and *Stuxnet*, the Pentagon has the most extensive resources for weapon development, in collaboration with its allies. Inevitably, the most capable and advanced cyber attack weapons are those developed by nation-states, notably by the US National Security Agency (NSA). The US cyber war offensive arsenal is built up aggressively and purposefully to be as potent as its arsenal of missiles. This capability allows the Pentagon to adopt a forthright cyber strategy whereby a foreign cyber attack on the United States would be considered as much an act of war as dropping bombs on any US city.[19]

For a Pentagon outsider to bypass multiple layers of security clearances to access NSA cyber secrets would be almost unthinkable. But this external mode of breach is not necessary. No less than three times in three years, NSA security has been evaded by one of its very own contract employees. Staff cannot be constantly subject to draconian security measures such as strip-searching; employees have to be trusted to a substantial degree.

In 2013, a Booz Allen Hamilton contractor with the now household name of Edward Snowden managed to exit the NSA facility in Hawaii with thousands of secret document files. NSA security staff who hoped this was just a one-off breach by a well-meaning whistle-blowing young contractor might have been reminded of Mark Twain's remark that history doesn't repeat itself, but it does rhyme. In 2016, another Booz Allen Hamilton contractor for the NSA, Hal Martin, was arrested for taking 50 terabytes out of the agency over a long period of time. Still more cause for internal security concern was the discovery that in 2015 a third contract employee of the NSA had taken home classified materials, including both software code and other information that the agency uses in both its offensive and defensive operations.

### 6.4.9  Insider Theft and the Cyber 'Big One'

The frequency of insider theft at the NSA is a key driver of the likelihood of major cyber attacks that are capable of causing massive loss on a global scale. In earthquake hazard terms, these are the 'Big Ones'. In terrorism terms, these are the weapons of mass destruction. This threat is exemplified by the *WannaCry* ransomware attack on May 12, 2017. It started the previous year, in August 2016, when a group self-styled as the *ShadowBrokers* claimed to have stolen cyber weapons from the elite NSA team: the Equation Group. Hal Martin was arrested by the FBI soon afterwards. Over a period of months, the *ShadowBrokers* leaked more than one gigabyte of their software exploits.

On January 7, 2017, some Windows weapons were put up for auction, but this auction was a flop. Amongst these weapons was the *EternalBlue* exploit. On April 8, this was dumped by the *ShadowBrokers*, enraged at US Tomahawk cruise missiles attacking a Syrian airfield controlled by President Assad, who had crossed a Washington red line in gassing his own people with the nerve agent sarin. A month later, on May 12, 2017, this exploit was incorporated into the *WannaCry* ransomware that encrypted files on approximately 300,000 Windows computers around the world. A decryption ransom demand of $300 in bitcoin was ultimately paid by very few.

Ironically, the president of Microsoft, Brad Smith, likened this criminal theft of an NSA cyber weapon to having Tomahawk missiles stolen – if they had been stolen, the Syrian raid would not have happened. He also criticized the NSA for withholding knowledge of Windows bugs, presumably through the Vulnerabilities Equities Process we discussed in Chapter 4. But for the United States to hand in its best cyber weapons because they backfired would be like handing in its Tomahawk missiles if they caused collateral civilian casualties. One does not have to be a member of the National Rifle Association to know that handing in weapons is just not part of the American heritage. Indeed, the whole story of America can be told through 10 firearms.[20]

From a computer infected by the *WannaCry* ransomware, an internet scanning routine randomly generated IP addresses, scanning them rapidly at a rate of 25 per second. The malware then targeted these IP addresses with attempts to exploit the *EternalBlue* vulnerability. Once a vulnerable machine was found and infected, it became the next stage to infect further machines. The infection cycle continued as the scanning routine discovered more and more unpatched computers. The contagion was fortunately halted by the registration of a bizarre domain name by an English malware expert, Marcus Hutchins, who was actually taking time off. This accidental and fortunate intervention acted as a kill switch.

Predominantly, Windows 7 computers were infected. Of the roughly 400 million actively used Windows 7 computers, approximately 0.1% were infected. The infection of so many Windows 7 computers was bad enough, but it might have been much worse. Indeed, 10 times as many Windows 7 computers might have been infected, and the economic loss might have been correspondingly much greater. Fortunately, when *WannaCry* was launched on May 12, the great majority of vulnerable Windows computers were protected by a Microsoft patch issued on March 14, 2017.

### 6.4.10  Reimagining History

Counterfactually, *EternalBlue* might have been dumped, and *WannaCry* might have been launched, well before a patch became available on March 14. Indeed, a prototype version of *WannaCry* had been used in a small number of targeted attacks in February, March, and April 2017. This earlier version was almost identical to the version used in May 2017, the only difference being the means of propagation. These earlier versions of *WannaCry* used stolen credentials to spread across infected networks, rather than the *EternalBlue* exploit. The authors of *WannaCry*, suspected of being linked with the North Korean *Lazarus* group, might potentially have bid for this exploit in the January 7 *ShadowBrokers* auction, and unleashed their ransomware mayhem soon afterwards.

In estimating the likelihood of extreme hazard events, it is important to recognize that the past is not predetermined or somehow inevitable, but just one realization of what might have happened. Risk insight is gained from exploring how things might have turned for the worse – the so-called downward counterfactuals.[21] (Psychologists contrast downward counterfactuals with upward counterfactuals, where things might have turned out for the better.)

Military historians and strategists have made extensive use of counterfactual analysis. The foremost Prussian military theorist, Carl von Clausewitz, insisted that perfecting the art of warfare entailed knowing not only what had occurred in previous wars, but also everything that could have occurred.[22] So much more can be learned from what might have happened than just what did actually happen. Computerized war gaming can simulate thousands of alternative realizations of past battles, with outcomes that may be quite different from what is recorded in history books. A computerized re-analysis of the 1916 battle of the Dogger Bank in the North Sea, between the British and German navies, has shown that the British navy was fortunate not to have lost this important early naval encounter of the Great War.[23] Similarly, a computerized re-analysis of the release of NSA cyber weapons a century later shows that the United States is fortunate not to have lost an important early encounter with Russian cyber power.

### 6.4.11 Knowing What Could Have Occurred

The art of cyber risk analysis also entails knowing everything that could have occurred. The comparatively brief period of observation tends to stunt the

## CASE STUDY OF THE SWIFT HEIST, FEBRUARY 4, 2016

On February 4, 2016, hackers used a poorly configured network switch to install their malware into the Bank of Bangladesh SWIFT terminal, and used the SWIFT messaging network to steal $81 million. The malware was custom-made, and showed a significant level of knowledge of SWIFT Alliance Access software, as well as good malware coding skills, such as hiding transactions.

The theft might have been almost $1 billion. First, $20 million was sent via Sri Lanka to a bank account in the name of a nonprofit foundation, but the electronic message misspelled it as 'fundation'. This payment was canceled when the Bank of Bangladesh was notified. The Federal Reserve Bank of New York cleared four transactions worth $81 million to false name accounts with Rizal Commercial Banking Corporation (RCBC) in the Philippines. This money was laundered in Manila casinos. Much more significantly, further transactions worth $850 million were blocked by the Fed as suspicious due to a fluke coincidence of names; the recipient bank RCBC's address was on a street named Jupiter, which happened to coincide with the name of a ship on the Iranian sanctions-busting blacklist.

Counterfactually, the money stolen might well have been $951 million – or even more. The *Lazarus* group behind the heist had set its sights on heists targeting other banks in Southeast Asia.

human imagination. Knowledge gained from reimagining history is essential for mapping more extensively the space of possible cyber events and exploring the realm of rare extreme events. It also provides an empirical basis for stochastic simulation of the past. There is a natural human tendency to regard the past as especially significant, rather than being haphazard. But what actually happened may in fact have been rather unlikely. One salient example is given in the inset box.

### 6.4.12 Cyber Events That Could Have Turned Out Differently

By adopting a counterfactual perspective and reimagining how historical events could have unfolded differently, additional insight can be gained into rare extreme losses that might otherwise come as an unwelcome surprise. No driver would wish to be surprised on the freeway with a ransomware demand threatening to prevent the car from braking unless payment was made. In 2015, security researchers Charlie Miller and Chris Valasek demonstrated for a Cherokee Jeep that this remote control of a vehicle was feasible. To the relief of Fiat Chrysler, both were ethical researchers, and 1.4 million vehicles were safely recalled. But had they been of malicious intent, a dangerous accident might have been caused, dealing a serious blow not just to the manufacturer, but to the wider future market for autonomous vehicles.

Regarding data exfiltration extreme events, at Home Depot, around 56 million debit and credit card details were leaked in a breach that lasted from April to September 2014. The cyber thieves broke in using credentials stolen from a third-party vendor, an entry attack mode that should have featured prominently on an attack tree for Home Depot. These credentials did not provide direct access to point of sale devices. A zero day vulnerability in Windows was needed, which gave elevated rights to navigate the Home Depot network. The intruders targeted 7,500 self-checkout lanes because these were clearly referenced as payment terminals. But counterfactually, another 70,000 regular terminals that were identified simply by a number might also have been attacked.

Returning to the massive Yahoo data breach of October 2017, a downward counterfactual thought on the billion data records exfiltrated is why many more confidential records were not taken as well. The simple uncomfortable answer was that there *were* many more taken – in fact, all three billion accounts had been compromised. A lesson from this disclosure ambiguity is that historical data need to be treated with circumspection.

Deception and stealth are central to cyber risk. Those placing high confidence in security technology, and therefore inclined to be skeptical about the likelihood of very large sizes of extreme events, should test themselves on the deception techniques described by Mitnick[24] and Conheady[25] and reflect on the empty assurances about security blogged by Ralph Shrader, the chairman and president of Booz Allen Hamilton, before Edward Snowden's grand deception: 'In all walks of life, our most trusted colleagues and friends have this in common. We can count on them. No matter what the situation or challenge, they will be there for us. Booz Allen Hamilton is trusted that way. You can count on that'.[26]

### 6.4.13  Alternative Versions of the Past 10 Years of Cyber Attacks

According to an old Chinese proverb, prophesying is very difficult – especially about the past. What happened in the past was far from being inevitable. The Roman general and historian Julius Caesar noted that in war, events of importance are often the result of trivial causes. A wise military maxim is that an operation's outcome depends 75% on planning and 25% on luck. The fortuitous random and accidental factors that influence the outcome of human conflict introduce brittleness and fragility to any statistical modeling based too closely on the actual historical record. This applies to all the insured perils of human conflict: war, terrorism, and cyber attacks.

Because what happened historically is just one realization of what might have transpired, we can relive the past in many different ways by simulating large numbers of alternative realizations of it. The decade from 2007 to 2017 was a very active period for cyber attacks, but the losses could have been far worse. Consider, for example, the possibility of a devastating distributed denial of service (DDoS) attack. Over four months from December 2008 to March 2009, *Conficker* assembled the largest botnet in the world. Every compromised host belonged to the botnet, and could have despatched a denial of service attack. The enormous botnet was programmed to call the botmaster and get instructions on April 1, 2009, and nobody knew what would happen then. The *Conficker* botmaster might have issued a command to the millions of botnets to launch a massive DDoS attack that might have taken down the root servers of the internet, and crashed the internet on April 1, 2009. With a bandwidth of up to 2 Tbps, this would have been a record DDoS attack.

Although the botmaster's identity is unknown, his cyber skills were considerable, and it has been speculated that the botmaster was Russian. Given the ruthless Russian DDoS attacks on Estonia in April 2007 and on Georgia in August 2008, there must have been a significant chance of another massive Russian-backed DDoS attack in 2009. Consider the role of the botmaster as DDoS attack commander. Like any battlefield commander, there are a sizeable number $N$ possible decisions he can make. Each is associated with a probability $P$ and a loss consequence $L$. Pursuing a war game approach of simulating a large number of alternative decisions and outcomes, a conditional loss probability distribution can be developed. This can be converted into a loss exceedance frequency distribution by dividing the conditional probabilities by the observational period of 10 years from 2007 to 2017.

## ENDNOTES

1. Micklethwait and Wooldridge (1997).
2. CCRS (2017, 2018d, Smith et al.).
3. Sink (2006).
4. Mateski et al. (2012).
5. Shostack (2014).
6. Kahneman (2011).
7. Mitnick and Simon (2002).
8. Williams (2012).
9. Europol (2017a).
10. Woo (2011).
11. Adamic and Huberman (2002).
12. CCRS (2016c).
13. CCRS (2018a).
14. Bejtlich (2015).
15. Bowden (2011).
16. Sood and Enbody (2014).
17. Gallagher (2018).
18. Zetter (2014).
19. Bowden (2011).
20. Kyle (2013).
21. Woo et al. (2017).
22. Gallagher (2018).
23. MacKay et al. (2016).
24. Mitnick and Simon (2002).
25. Conheady (2014).
26. Harding (2014).

# CHAPTER 7

# Rules, Regulations, and Law Enforcement

## 7.1 CYBER LAWS

Much of the cost of cyber risk is driven by regulatory requirements that govern reporting requirements, penalty payments, and compensation to victims. Countries with the strictest regulations make data breaches most expensive, with costs in heavily regulated countries being more than twice those in countries with limited data regulation. The regulatory landscape is changing rapidly. Figure 7.1 shows that nearly all the major advanced economies with significant cyber risk are now under heavy or robust regulatory regimes, and emerging markets are increasingly regulated.

### 7.1.1 Jurisprudence and Commerce

Regulation of commerce, like the emerging digital economy, has a long history. Drafted under the reign of the French Sun King, Louis XIV, the Great Marine Ordinance of August 1681 was the most complete system of maritime jurisprudence that had ever appeared. A contemporary commentator wrote in awe:

> *'It was so comprehensive in its plan, so excellent in the arrangement of its parts, so just in its decisions, so wise in its general and partic- ular policy, so accurate and clear in its details, that it deserves to be considered as a model of a perfect code of maritime jurisprudence'.*

With the expansion of international shipping trade in the late seventeenth century, such a maritime code shortened the route to economic prosperity. In the twenty-first century, the advent of global online commerce

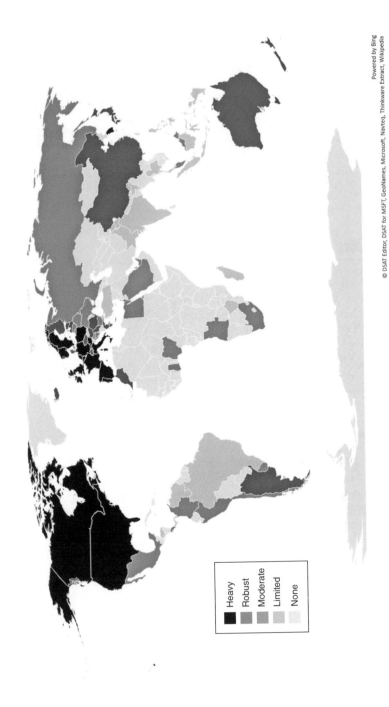

Heavy
Robust
Moderate
Limited
None

**FIGURE 7.1** World map of data privacy regulation.

[1] *Source:* Reproduced by kind permission of DLA Piper.

requires similarly just, wise, accurate, and clear codes for cyberspace jurisprudence. But it would take more than the legal brilliance of the 1681 Great Marine Ordinance to overcome the challenge of drafting international cyber law for a non-terrestrial mode of communication that inherently transcends national borders, cultures, and legal systems. Cyberspace should be part of the international rules-based order, with rights of self-defense in response to damaging attack, especially those that are lethal, and non-interference in the affairs of other states. However, there are major differences in perspectives among permanent members of the United Nations Security Council. The inherent ambiguity in attributing covert attacks may be taken as an opportunity for aggression and risk-taking. The consequent risk of confrontation and miscalculation is rising as a result.[2]

China, one of the foremost global trading nations, espouses the ethos of cyber sovereignty – states should be permitted to govern and monitor their own cyberspace, controlling incoming and outgoing data flows. Accordingly, China has maintained a strict censorship regime, banning access to foreign news outlets, search engines, and social media. Hypocrisy is of course the prerogative of powerful sovereign states. China's tight surveillance over its own cyberspace has been matched by its flagrant but clandestine violation of the cyberspace of others. Sun Tzu would have approved.

China is increasingly focusing on cyber security, and its Cybersecurity Law was adopted by the National People's Congress (NPC) in November 2016 after a year of legislative proceedings. Enshrined in this Cybersecurity Law are a number of features, such as the protection of personal information and critical information infrastructure, which are shared with cyber security laws of Western democracies. So even though cyberspace extends across geopolitical boundaries, some common ground can be found amongst the community of nations in the development of international cyber law.

But China will agree to disagree with democratic states on basic issues of privacy and freedom of expression, in particular where the balance between privacy and security should lie. Clearly, many political hurdles and legal obstacles remain to be surmounted before any consensus emerges among governments on how to develop legal norms that apply to cyberspace. The discussion around cyber security norms centers on a number of general themes.[3]

**7.1.1.1 Avoiding Conflict** Some nations advocate the need to create internationally accepted norms that establish clear boundaries to help prevent and manage conflict in cyberspace. Others are calling for treaties or conventions to address this issue, while still others seek to maintain the status quo. An international legal framework for dispute settlement would help avoid conflict.

**7.1.1.2 Managing Threats and Vulnerabilities** Governments buy data about vulnerabilities in software products for the purpose of exploiting the vulnerabilities to target an entity and advance a national objective. There are no international prohibitions against a free trade in cyber security vulnerabilities.

**7.1.1.3 Building Trust and Transparency** Some discussions about norms include ways to develop and implement confidence-building measures between nation-states. These are activities between states designed to reduce the likelihood of misunderstanding the scope, intent, or consequences of activities such as the deployment of forces about to be or being conducted.

**7.1.1.4 Sharing Threat and Vulnerability Information** Improving incident response and mutual assistance mechanisms among nation-states and key communities such as law enforcement are critical requirements. Sharing threat-based information such as vulnerabilities, hacking trend data, new threat identification, or even unexplained anomalies impacting a product or service can enable the private sector and government to better protect critical systems.

**7.1.1.5 Cyber Security Capacity-Building** Improving global baselines for cyber security capabilities in developing countries, including software development, operations, policy, and risk management, is needed to build capacity to respond to large-scale incidents and to protect critical infrastructure. Also important is the ability to collaborate with other countries, and the development of a security culture amongst the local population.

## 7.2 US CYBER LAWS

### 7.2.1 A Patchwork of Regulation

The United States has led the development of cyber regulation. As a result, it is now a complex patchwork of regulation. State-specific cyber breach regulations have evolved, in many cases quite different regulations one to another, sometimes conflicting. All states require prompt notification, sometimes as soon as 15 days; most states require reporting to government and the media if the data breach involves more than 500 people; and some states set thresholds for the notice requirement, such as reasonable basis to believe the breach will result in harm. Most states establish penalties, and some provide rights of action.[4]

There are also overlapping federal laws. The Health Insurance Portability and Accountability Act (HIPAA) of 1996 regulates the privacy of personal health data, while the Gramm–Leach–Bliley Act (GLBA) regulates the privacy of financial data, with different requirements and powers of penalty.

### 7.2.2 The Origins of US Legislation

The legend of the computer whiz kid is part of hacking folklore, and has also had an influence on the development of US legislation on cyber crime. In the 1983 Hollywood movie *War Games*, a teenage computer-games enthusiast, who does not believe any system is totally secure, breaks into a US military supercomputer programmed to predict possible outcomes of nuclear war, and almost starts a world war. For a kid, this was just playing around; for policy makers on Capitol Hill, this was a crime. This near-disaster scenario was cited the following year in a House Committee Report to a comprehensive crime bill, which ensured that computer crimes did not go unpunished. Emerging from this bill was the 1986 Computer Fraud and Abuse Act, which prohibits unauthorized computer access, interference, and obtaining data. The Electronic Communications Privacy Act of 1986 extended government restrictions on wiretaps from telephone calls to include transmissions of electronic data by computer.

The passage of these two bills in the same year reflects the fundamental duality of cyber risk. Hacking skills can be used for offense as well as defense. A teenager can hack into the Pentagon computer system. Later on, as a mature adult, he could work for the National Security Agency (NSA), hacking on behalf of the US government. Indeed, the opportunity for authorized hacking is one of the attractions in working for the NSA. With all types of espionage, real world and cyber, what is authorized in the tradecraft of spying may not necessarily be fully compliant with US law, let alone the law of the country being spied upon. This explains why espionage is invariably denied, or not commented upon if the evidence is overwhelming.

### 7.2.3 Legitimizing NSA Operations

As with other leading world powers, the United States has an arsenal of potent cyber weapons, which are deployed in a clandestine manner. As an illustration, consider the Windows *EternalBlue* exploit, which found its way into the possession of the *ShadowBrokers* in 2016. Before it was stolen, it had been a highly effective way of secretly accessing computers targeted by the NSA. One staff member likened its use to fishing with dynamite. The fact that covert offensive hacking operations are routinely undertaken by the US government in pursuit of its national interest means that its cyber defense has to be maintained at a very high level. This requires the support of legislation.

The Federal Information Security Management Act (FISMA) of 2002 was put into place to implement a framework for the effectiveness of information security controls for federal information systems, to provide oversight, and to provide for the development of minimum controls for securing these systems. The National Institute of Standards and Technology (NIST) was authorized to develop the standards and guidelines used for implementing and maintaining information security programs for risk management. The Federal Information System Modernization Act of 2014 is an overhaul of FISMA, and is intended to provide a framework for the federal government to assess and ensure its information security controls.

Most computer systems are in the private sector, so there is a strong need for information sharing between and among the public and private sectors. Barriers to the sharing of information on threats, attacks, vulnerabilities, and other aspects of cyber security are a significant hindrance to the effective protection of information systems. Examples have included legal barriers, concerns about liability and misuse, protection of trade secrets and other proprietary business information, and institutional and cultural factors.

### 7.2.4  Cybersecurity Information Sharing Act

The Cybersecurity Information Sharing Act (CISA) of 2015 addresses a universally recognized problem: corporate victims of cyber attacks, while often the best resources for actionable information to prevent future attacks are hesitant to share information that may expose them to civil or criminal liability, embarrassment, loss of trust, or competitive threats. CISA is an attempt to alleviate many of these impediments in hopes of fostering greater cooperation and collaboration to combat cyber threats. CISA authorizes private companies to share cyber security threat information for cyber security purposes with the federal government, and with other private entities.

With its mix of federal and state law, US cyber security legal parameters arise from multiple layers and sources. State law fills gaps in federal law, but can set de facto national standards. Indeed, almost all states have introduced specific cyber breach regulation alongside federal laws. State laws generally require alerts to state regulators and impacted individuals if a breach occurs involving personal data.

### 7.2.5  State-by-State Variations

Alabama, on March 28, 2018, was one of the more recent states to enact data breach notification laws. It is one of the many states that now mandate security controls that require organizations to protect information with reasonable security measures. These include designating someone to coordinate these security measures, tailoring security measures to an appropriate assessment of risk scenarios, and keeping management informed of security measures.

Federal and state regulations may differ and even conflict with one another. In the state of Massachusetts, for example, the attorney general, the director of consumer affairs and business regulation, and the affected Massachusetts resident must all be notified, not only if there is a breach of security giving rise to a substantial risk of identity fraud, but also if personal information about a resident of the commonwealth was acquired or used by an unauthorized person, or used for an unauthorized purpose.

Contrast this with the more permissive state regulations in Alaska. Here, the good-faith acquisition of personal information by an employee or agent of an information collector for a legitimate purpose of the information collector is not a breach of the security of the information system if the employee or agent does not use the personal information for a purpose unrelated to a legitimate purpose of the information collector and does not make further unauthorized disclosure of the personal information.

Whatever the state laws, enforcement is problematic when the suspect is in a state far removed from the victim. With conventional crime, suspects can move across state borders relatively easily. The additional problem with cyber crime is that suspects could be in any geographical location. So personal information about a Boston resident may have been acquired illegally by someone living in Anchorage. Where and how interstate cases would be prosecuted are amongst the complex interstate legal issues that need improved statutes.

## 7.2.6  Regulations for Finance, Healthcare, and Communications

In certain sectors, specific laws impose an additional layer of security duties for certain categories of sensitive personal data. The three categories listed here are financial services, healthcare, and communications. These data areas are key centers of attraction offering substantial rewards for a broad spectrum of attackers, ranging from opportunist criminals to state-sponsored hackers.

For financial services, there is the Gramm-Leach-Bliley Act. Sensitive customer data needs to be safeguarded, and information-sharing practices need to be explained. Customers have the right to opt out of having their data shared with third parties.

For healthcare, there is HIPAA. Prior to HIPAA, there was no generally accepted set of security standards or general requirements for protecting health information. The need for HIPAA was driven by the inevitable transition of the healthcare industry from paperwork to electronic information systems.

For telecommunications carriers, there is the Communications Act. The use of customer proprietary network information (CPNI) was restricted to the limited purpose of providing the telecommunications services from which the CPNI was derived. Consent of the customer was required for any other purpose.

## 7.3    EU GENERAL DATA PROTECTION REGULATION (GDPR)

### 7.3.1    European Citizens' Data Rights

The rate of change in the digital environment, driven by the intellectual curiosity and ingenuity of IT academics and entrepreneurs, will always outpace any attempt at regulating it. After a while, data protection regulations are no longer fit for the purpose. So it is with the 1990s vintage European Union regulations, which were upgraded in the 2018 European General Data Protection Regulation (GDPR). This biggest update of European data protection rules in two decades changes how businesses and public-sector organizations can handle the information of customers. In fact, companies anywhere around the world that hold data about European citizens are subject to GDPR.

GDPR enshrines the rights of individuals in a number of ways: right of access to data held about them, right to data portability to transfer their data from one holder it to another, right to erasure and to ensure that data is no longer held, right to object to data being held (organizations must demonstrate compelling reasons for holding it), and right to transparency.

Companies covered by GDPR will be more accountable for their handling of people's personal information. This can include having data protection policies, conducting data protection impact assessments, and having relevant documents on how data is processed. Under GDPR, the destruction, loss, alteration, or unauthorized disclosure of, or access to, people's data have to be reported to a country's data protection regulator. This can include, but is not limited to, financial loss, confidentiality breaches, damage to reputation, and more.

## 7.3.2 Data Controllers

Major organizations are required to appoint a data controller. Data controllers must notify most data breaches to the Data Protection Authority (DPA). This must be done without undue delay and, where feasible, within 72 hours of awareness. A reasoned justification must be provided if this timeframe is not met. In some cases, the data controller must also notify the affected data subjects without undue delay. Additionally, the UK Information Commissioner's Office expects to be informed about all serious breaches. Notification does not need to be made to the DPA if the breach is unlikely to result in a risk to the rights and freedoms of individuals. The threshold for notification to data subjects is that there is likely to be a high risk to their rights and freedoms. While this may lessen the impact, all companies will have to adopt internal procedures for handling data breaches in any case.

## 7.3.3 Penalties for Breach of GDPR

Penalties for breaching GDPR can reach €20 million or 4% of a company's annual turnover.

Basic economic theory gives an advantage to large organizations that can spread the fixed costs of implementing GDPR over a large user base.[5] However, small and medium-size enterprises (SMEs) face a special challenge in meeting the GDPR requirements. Practical business development priorities for SMEs typically dominate over security issues, and many SMEs do not have a cyber security strategy in place. Implementing business security measures should be as routine as ensuring one's home and vehicle are locked up. But burglars and car thieves are not as resourceful and innovative as cyber criminals. Because technology is dynamic and continually evolving, security is a requirement that should be continually audited and reviewed. Yet, when this was checked, half of the SMEs had not carried out a security audit in the past three months.[6]

## 7.3.4 National Implementation

Each European state has implemented GDPR in accordance with its own national security aspirations and objectives. In its cyber security regulation and incentives review,[7] the UK minister of state has committed to making the United Kingdom the safest place in the world to go online. This would be mere political rhetoric if it were solely the UK government's ambition. The minister emphasized that the responsibility is shared with every business, charity, and institution in the country. The unauthorized gathering of information from these organizations by foreign sources is a common problem, which is recognized by the UK attorney general as a complex sovereignty issue of international law.[8] What level of government response, short of offensive action, would be appropriate and legally justified?

To incentivize better cyber risk management, a number of non-regulatory interventions have been developed. One idea is for the National Cyber Security Centre to send messages to company boards about the importance of understanding cyber risk, and what they can do to improve their cyber risk management. A top-down approach might be particularly effective in organizations where the IT security managers do not always have the attention of the CEO.

Another very practical idea is that of a cyber health check for organizations. This is an independent check to consider whether the security practices in place are appropriate and sufficient to deter attacks, and to provide advice on how an organization can manage its cyber risk more effectively. Especially smaller businesses benefit from having access to trusted and reliable organizations to conduct such cyber health checks. Since 2013, the UK government has undertaken a regular cyber health check survey of the UK's top 350 companies. Decisions about cyber risk are increasingly taken at the executive level, which reflects a significant positive culture shift.

## 7.4 REGULATION OF CYBER INSURANCE

### 7.4.1 Regulating an Emerging Insurance Market

The insurance market is governed by the economic laws of supply and demand. The price of an insurance risk is the annual expected loss augmented by expenses plus a return on the capital at risk. The latter depends on assumptions as to the probable maximum loss. Where there is substantial ambiguity in assessing the annual expected loss and the probable maximum loss, the market price may drift away from an actuarially fair price. In some circumstances, e.g. the US terrorism insurance market after 9/11, angst over the worst-ever property catastrophe loss (~$40 billion) and paranoia about the unknown elevated terrorism insurance rates to stratospheric levels, as the number of insurers willing to write terrorism risk dwindled, and the amount of coverage they were prepared to provide shrank dramatically.

By contrast, in an emerging market where losses have been comparatively light, the supply of cover may expand rapidly, causing insurance rates to fall. Every insurer has its own risk management oversight. But as a collective response to few losses, most insurers may underprice a major risk. Such systemic risk throughout the market is then a practical concern of regulators. To address the issue of systemic risk, in parallel with the book of insurance claims kept by underwriters, another counterfactual book of near-miss claims might be kept to remind underwriters of the element of good fortune in their loss experience.[9]

Regulators have made significant steps to push the insurance industry towards better cyber risk management. Within the London market in 2016, Lloyd's took an active role by adding eight cyber realistic disaster scenarios to the mandatory reporting requirements of its managing agents. The UK financial services regulatory body, the Prudential Regulatory Authority (PRA), has instigated regulatory approaches for insurers to improve their management of cyber risk, with a supervisory statement for consultation highlighting preferred best practices.

### 7.4.2 Role of Rating Agencies

In charting the substantial growth of the cyber insurance market, A.M. Best has acknowledged the business opportunities this coverage presents for the property and casualty industry, but stressed that, due to the uncertainty of this risk, insurers need to be prudent in their underwriting practices and exercise appropriate risk management and mitigation measures.[10] One such measure would be the quantitative analysis of cyber risk. This is an application of catastrophe risk assessment that has been under extensive product development.

Quite apart from the business of underwriting cyber risk, US rating agencies, such as A.M. Best, have added questions about a company's preparedness and disaster plan for responding to cyber attacks as part of assessing an overall enterprise risk management framework. Even if an insurer wrote no explicit stand-alone cyber risk policies, it might suffer serious loss from a large silent exposure to cyber risk, or might be the victim of a carefully targeted cyber attack.

Recognizing that cyber security is more important now than ever, the US National Association of Insurance Commissioners (NAIC) has adopted an Insurance Data Security Model Law, which establishes industry standards for data security that will apply to a broad range of parties, including insurers, agents, and brokers. Organizations are required to have a written information security program for protecting sensitive data, including incident response and data recovery plans to demonstrate their preparedness for cyber events. Companies have to certify compliance annually to their state insurance commissioners and notify commissioners of data breaches within 72 hours of a cyber security event. The American Insurance Association expressed satisfaction that the adopted model law was risk-based and consistent with New York's cyber security law.

## 7.5    A CHANGING LEGAL LANDSCAPE

### 7.5.1    Reactive Legal Developments

The legal landscape relating to cyber risk is still disjointed and uncertain. Lawmakers, regulators, and courts across the world are developing rules and new precedents relating to cyber risk on a reactive basis. This has resulted in a patchwork of laws, regulations, case law, settlement trends, and an environment that makes it difficult to estimate future costs that might result from the cyber losses that are likely to occur.

The outcomes of cases are highly variable and depend heavily on the specific language of each insurance policy, the particular state and federal laws in place, and the facts of the claim, as well as the court's willingness to find coverage.

### 7.5.2    Articulated Damages

The erosion of standards from case law is a concern to lawyers involved in cyber litigation. Historically, data breach suits were dismissed if plaintiffs could not show articulated damages. Recent case law overturned this, allowing a class action to proceed without articulated damages flowing from the breach.[11] This case was settled soon after with monetary awards of $30 per person to individuals whose personal information was stolen but who suffered no articulated damages. The principle was established that it is no longer necessary to demonstrate that the person has suffered damage from a data release, only that the person's data was released.

There are also changing processes in novel pleading strategies being employed by plaintiffs and the willingness of courts to consider new arguments. There appear to be increasing trends in settlement amounts and expansion of the categories of costs being awarded.

A particular area of coverage that is expected to grow in significance in relation to cyber events is liability relating to directors and officers, where the duties of senior management to maintain share price and business viability through adequate security protections and contingency planning may become more onerous with cyber events causing damage to the balance sheet and shareholder returns.

### 7.5.3 Class-Action Lawsuits

Organizations that have the weakest cyber security are likely to be hit with a double-whammy blow. Not only are they more likely to have a cyber loss, but their inferior security will leave them vulnerable to being sued for negligence. The American heavyweight boxer Mike Tyson said that everyone has a plan until they get punched in the mouth. An organization may have a coherent plan for a cyber attack, but if a major cyber loss is followed by a class-action lawsuit, they may need a more extensive plan. With large settlements attracting significant media attention, there is likely to be an increase in litigation in relation to cyber events around the globe, including class-action lawsuits.

The legal landscape relating to cyber risk is currently disjointed and uncertain. A business that suffers a successful cyber attack may be liable to its customers for breach of contract. Businesses can be heavily exposed to claims if, as a result of any attack and the subsequent disruption, they fail to fulfill contractual obligations unrelated to cyber security. It is also possible that, in some businesses, the occurrence of the attack itself may be sufficient to be a breach of an express or implied term that customer data would be stored securely and with due care. Contractual obligations cannot easily be avoided, unless there is an explicit force majeure clause dealing with events happening outside the control of the contracting parties.

### 7.5.4 Cyber Liability Insurance for Law Firms

To illustrate the role of cyber liability insurance in supplementing traditional professional liability cover, consider the situation of law firms.

All organizations have ethical obligations to their customers and clients. The good name and reputation of an organization are at risk if these are not respected. Law firms have an ethical obligation to keep their clients' information confidential and secure. Professional diligence of the very highest level is expected of law firms, so it is especially shocking and disappointing that a record-breaking data breach (2.6 terabytes) occurred at a law firm. Mossack Fonseca is a Panama-based law firm whose services include incorporating companies in offshore jurisdictions. In 2015, 11.5 million confidential files from the Mossack Fonseca database were leaked via an anonymous source to a German newspaper, which shared them with the International Consortium of Investigative Journalists. Panamanian computer forensic examination concluded that there had been a hack of private information from the servers of Mossack Fonseca.

For such a catastrophic exfiltration of extremely sensitive client data to have occurred at one of the world's most secretive law firms should dispel any complacency over cyber security at any law firm. If a massive data breach could happen at Mossack Fonseca, which could have afforded the very best cyber defense protection system available, it could happen almost anywhere. The lack of any data breach over decades is no assurance – let alone guarantee – of future experience; Mossack Fonseca's data breach occurred after 40 years of data integrity.

With their significant investments in network software and their concern over reputational risk, law firms should have been considering the purchase of cyber liability insurance well before the Mossack Fonseca mega-leak. With few exceptions, lawyers' professional liability insurance policies do not contain any specific cyber liability exclusions. Duty of care in the protection of confidential client information is part of the professional legal services provided. However, explicit cyber insurance cover would be appropriate for contingencies such as data loss; network extortion threats; network use in a distributed denial-of-service (DDoS) attack; privacy breaches; regulatory actions, including fines and penalties; and HIPAA fines and penalties. A cyber policy would be primary to a lawyer's professional indemnity policy for claims. Three practical reasons for the purchase of separate cyber insurance are:

1. Many corporations require vendors dealing with sensitive information to have minimum limits of cyber liability insurance.
2. The law firm is subject to an independent assessment by the cyber liability underwriter of its systems and procedures.
3. The response time for meeting cyber claims will generally be much shorter than for lawyers' professional liability policies, where there may be delays over claim evaluation and coverage decisions. A prompt response is desirable, and could mitigate a malpractice claim.

## 7.6 COMPLIANCE AND LAW ENFORCEMENT

### 7.6.1 Cyber Hygiene

The maintenance of high standards of personal human hygiene is vital for limiting the spread of an infectious disease like influenza. Compliance with sanitary measures such as washing hands regularly, and avoiding coughing and sneezing in crowded public places, reduces the likelihood of an infected individual transmitting the disease to others. An infectious disease spreads along human social networks. Those supernodes with many network connections contribute disproportionately to disease spread if their compliance with sanitary measures is poor. In the context of an infectious disease, good hygiene compliance is not just a matter of avoiding personal illness; it also has a broader societal dimension in avoiding making others ill. Furthermore, as and when a vaccine is available, those who are vaccinated protect not only themselves, but also others they might have otherwise infected.

Computer viruses spread from one computer to another. Compliance with high standards of computer security, i.e. cyber hygiene, not only reduces the chance of infection for the compliant user; it also reduces the risk for others. On the other hand, non-compliance increases the chance of infection both to the non-compliant user and to others as well. Compliance with cyber law is therefore in the general interest of all networked computer users.

Consider, for example, the cyber law compliance obligations for third parties. The HIPAA law requires all third-party vendors working with healthcare organizations to have a risk assessment. This is quite an onerous requirement, which can be dodged by all manner of plausible excuses. Maybe the third-party vendor is a small company with limited security resources, or it works for only one healthcare organization and the effort of having a risk assessment seems to be excessive for just one client. A non-compliant third-party vendor implicitly imposes an external cost on the healthcare market, for which no compensation is paid. Economists refer to this as a negative externality.

### 7.6.2  The Weakest Link

The more knowledge one has of past security breaches through third-party vendors, the less plausible or reasonable such excuses become. As with any intelligent enemy aiming to maximize gain for a minimum of effort, a cyber attacker will seek out the weakest link in a cyber defense. Cyber loss history shows that all too often this may be a third-party vendor with lax cyber security, such as an inadequate authentication process of identified users.

One notable example is the exfiltration in 2014 of 53 million email addresses and 56 million credit and debit card details from point-of-sale (PoS) terminals at the home improvement company Home Depot. The stolen payment cards were put up for sale and bought by carders, and the stolen email addresses facilitated large phishing campaigns. Criminals had used a third-party vendor's user name and password to enter the perimeter of Home Depot's network. Home Depot could have had in place measures to prevent the breach from happening and to have been able to detect the breach sooner, minimizing the impact. But Home Depot lacked secure configuration of the software or hardware on the point-of-sale (PoS) terminals. Also lacking were proper monitoring capabilities and the management of third-party vendor identities and access.

### 7.6.3  Damages Provisions

Apart from the statutory penalty for non-compliance, security-negligent third parties may have their contracts terminated for failure to comply with cyber law requirements. Damages provisions may also apply to contracts deemed to be breached through non-compliance. Fear of such negative business consequences may encourage third parties to attend better to cyber security. It clearly is in the public interest for compliance to be as complete as possible.

In order to maximize compliance, increasing sanctions against malfeasants is not the only way; it also helps to take human psychology into account. Compliance with regulations on safety and security is marked by an inherent human behavioral asymmetry; we expect others to comply with all regulations, but can find excuses, such as forgetfulness, for occasional lapses in our own compliance. The vast majority of compliance breaches are actually unintentional – the result of something not being filed quite right, a process being forgotten, or a detail missed. Invoking the influential nudge theory of Thaler and Sunstein, an effective way of creating a culture of compliance is not necessarily having stricter rules, penalties, or even further education. Instead, creating a culture of compliance would make acts of compliance as convenient, simple, and routine as possible for the individual concerned.[12] A good appreciation of compliance management fosters this culture.

### 7.6.4  Compliance Management

Organizations should build a cyber security program that holds its third-party software providers to the same security standards that internal teams are held to. Compliance with cyber regulations cannot be taken for granted; it has to be systematically managed. Audits and reports on internal and regulatory compliance need to be produced for effective compliance management. Such reports provide relevant, actionable, and timely information on inventory, alerts, user authentication events, configuration details, change history, and work flow documentation.

It is important for firms to demonstrate compliance by establishing processes that meet appropriate standards and align with their customers' risk needs and mandates, which includes securing sensitive data. These reports should form part of a comprehensive cyber security and risk compliance management framework. A risk audit for an organization will likely see cyber security as a leading risk, evolving with technology expansion, data growth, online business development, and threat shifting from conventional crime to cyber crime. Compliance management should be an integral part of the overall risk audit.

Compliance with regulations is a legal obligation, but, as with all safety and security measures, compliance with regulations should not be viewed as the end goal of application security. The motivation for cyber regulations is to support companies in better protecting data and systems, so any cyber security initiatives adopted must be continuously applied to ensure ongoing compliance. To achieve ongoing compliance for application security, vulnerability testing must be integrated within the software development life cycle to ensure that software and applications are secure by design. It is also important for organizations to conduct discovery scans of web applications of their entire domain on a regular basis. Identifying forgotten sites enables companies to either continuously monitor them for vulnerabilities or, where possible, shut them down to reduce the attack surface.

For the power, energy, and process industries, risk audits are an essential aspect of prioritizing safety and security. The complex task of securing industrial control systems requires tracking all such systems as well as IT cyber assets. A comprehensive inventory, including configuration data, is needed to achieve a sufficient compliance standard and to mitigate risk. Establishing this inventory is a non-trivial undertaking, which commercial products exist to tackle.[13]

## 7.7 LAW ENFORCEMENT AND CYBER CRIME

### 7.7.1 The Role of Law Enforcement Agencies

Police departments have always been tasked with protecting their communities from local criminals. In the nineteenth century, criminals might have traveled to the scene of their crime by foot or horse; in the twentieth century, they could travel there by rail or automobile. Now, in the twenty-first century, they have no need for travel, but can attack from their computers at home. Protection is thus needed from criminals online anywhere in the world.

During a 10-hour period in 2013, US thefts from ATM machines amounted to $45 million. This was a larger sum than all the losses from

US bank robberies. Willie Sutton, who reportedly said he robbed banks because 'That's where the money is', actually had an adrenalin rush in bank robbery, which made him a chronic repeat offender. 'Sutton's law' of doing the most obvious is an embodiment of the strategic principle of following the path of least resistance. In the twenty-first century, he would be making much more money from online fraud than in bank robbery; he would be enjoying the hacking, and would be spending less time in prison – if any at all.

A criminal hacker's chances of being convicted are generally very slim. Occasionally, police authorities may get lucky, such as when a suspected foreign hacker leaves his national safe haven and travels abroad to a country, oblivious of legal sanctions there against cyber crime. On August 20, 2017, a Chinese computer network security expert, Yu Pingan, was arrested at Los Angeles International Airport en route to attending a conference. He was accused of conspiring with others to use rare hacking tools in a series of cyber attacks against US companies.

For a domestic hacker, the odds of being convicted are higher than for a foreign hacker, but they are low nonetheless. Suppose a young American or European hacker was deliberating over whether to follow a life of cyber crime or pursue a more orthodox career in information technology. The expected financial rewards from criminal hacking might well outweigh the possible risk of being convicted and potentially serving a sentence. Convicted cyber criminals may have little fear of judges struggling to determine reasonable punishments. Sentences tend not to be punitive as long as the goal is just personal financial gain rather than social disruption or damage to critical national infrastructure, such as the power supply or communications network. For the latter cyber crimes, convicted cyber vandals can expect substantial prison sentences, possibly in excess of 10 years. Where a cyber attack leads to serious illness, injury, or even fatality, sentences would be longer still.

### 7.7.2   Low Conviction Rates

Cyber crime for profit is still met with little deterrence, as there are extremely low conviction rates for perpetrators. Whereas armed robbers following in the footsteps of Willie Sutton face formidable conviction rates of 1 in 5, FBI cyber crime statistics show that in 2015 less than 1 in 200 reported cases of cyber identity theft resulted in a criminal case being brought, and only 1 in 50,000 resulted in a conviction. Imagine if the conviction rate for urban parking violations was this low. Few would bother to pay parking charges.

If the cyber theft is small, i.e. under $500–$1000, it is just not worthwhile for the local police to investigate, because of the jurisdictional challenges. Furthermore, federal agencies focus on following up the high-loss cases, leaving local agencies with the smaller cyber crimes. According to the US Police Executive Research Forum, criminal organizations are increasingly turning to cyber crime to finance their operations. In Chicago, for example, drug dealers can make more money by this switch, and with a much reduced chance of arrest. Other street criminals, like robbers, are also making this switch.

### 7.7.3  Cooperation of Private Sector with Law Enforcement

Small businesses are a prime target for many cyber criminals. Indeed, most attacks strike companies with under a thousand employees. As many as 60% of small companies targeted go out of business within six months. Businesses that are hacked are often reluctant to report the crime for fear of undermining consumer confidence. Reimbursement of a victim by the business hacked may be in the business's interest, but it is not in the broader societal interest, because there is no police investigation. Furthermore, it results in a reporting bias in crime statistics. Given that the private sector constitutes about 90% of the internet, the FBI recognizes the need for the cooperation of the private sector in working collaboratively. Police chiefs appreciate that many companies have more cyber crime experience than the law enforcement organizations. Only in cyberspace is the police partnership with the private sector so utterly crucial in cracking down on lawbreakers.

A crucial factor in restricting law enforcement capabilities is the difficulty in hiring, training, and retaining staff adept at investigating cyber crime. Not all police officers are equipped for such positions, which pay less than in the private sector. Increasingly more crime cases have a cyber component, but this poses difficulties for many police officers, who did not sign up originally for such technically demanding work requiring IT knowledge and expertise. Imagine if ordinary sedentary office workers had to chase after and arrest occasional intruders who tried to break in through an open office window or door. They were not trained for this task, and never signed up for this physically demanding and hazardous work.

### 7.7.4  Specialist Police Cyber Crime Units

Tracking cyber criminals is not a routine task for regular police officers, but a task for specialist police cyber crime units that have the requisite training, knowledge, and professional interest. In Britain, the West Midlands police Cyber Regional Organized Crime Unit is a good example. This specialist unit is well aware of the enormous technical challenge of policing cyber crime. In their presentation to the British Computer Society about the work of their cyber crime unit,[14] Q's disparaging remark to James Bond is quoted from *Skyfall*: 'I can do more damage on my laptop sitting in my pyjamas, before my first cup of Earl Grey, than you can do in a year in the field'. To achieve a successful conviction typically requires a lengthy and complex police operation, covering a number of countries. The inset box summarizes one specific case that did lead to a conviction.

## PROFILE OF A CONVICTED YOUNG HACKER

A young man from Liverpool was sentenced to two years in jail on January 18, 2018 for a variety of cyber crimes, to which he pleaded guilty.[15] Creating a botnet of about 9,000 bots, he was responsible for numerous cyber attacks on firms around the world, including Pokemon, Skype, and Google. As well as these cyber attacks, he created malware for sale, allowing others around the world to create DDoS attacks and steal data. At the time of his arrest, his computer held 750 names and passwords from infected computers, as well as two programs for infecting computers and retrieving email, banking, and login details.

This young cyber crime entrepreneur created his own online marketplace on the dark web, and sold malware products developed by himself and others. Amongst these malware products were remote administration tools and programs to bypass antivirus software. His site advertised 9,000 items, had a million visitors, and had made 34,000 sales. Illegal earnings from cyber crime were sufficient for him to be convicted also of money laundering.

### 7.7.5 Interpol and Europol

Law enforcement organizations have always adapted to the changing characteristics of crime. For major organized crimes such as drugs and people smuggling that transcend national borders, an international approach to policing is needed. Because most cyber crimes are transnational, a purely national police response is inadequate and ineffective. Inevitably, Interpol, which is uniquely positioned to combat cyber crime on a global scale, is involved in cyber crime investigation. To facilitate transnational policing, Interpol issues notices of various colors. The three relevant for cyber crime are red, blue, and green. Red is for locating and arresting wanted persons with a view to extradition or similar lawful action. Blue is for collecting additional information about a person's identity, location, or activities in relation to a crime. Green is for providing warnings and intelligence about persons who have committed criminal offenses and are likely to repeat these crimes in other countries.

Interpol's main initiatives focus on operational and investigative support, cyber intelligence and analysis, digital forensics, innovation and research, and capacity building. With its Global Complex for Innovation in Singapore, Interpol leverages global expertise from law enforcement and key private sector partners. The Global Complex aims to give police around the world both the tools and the capabilities to confront the challenges posed by criminals.

Europol established the European Cybercrime Centre in 2013 to strengthen the law enforcement response to cyber crime in the European Union, and to protect European citizens, businesses, and governments from online crime. The European Cybercrime Centre has been involved in many high-profile operations and hundreds of operational support deployments. Close collaboration between Interpol and Europol leverages the international knowledge and experience of each organization in cyber finance, the dark net, and more. Joint initiatives include an annual Cyber Crime Conference, alternating between Interpol's base in Singapore and the Hague, where Europol is headquartered. Cyber crime experts from around the world attend this conference to strengthen cooperation, including with nongovernmental organizations (NGOs), community emergency response teams, and academia. Each year, the European Cybercrime Centre publishes its flagship report on the internet organized crime threat assessment.

## 7.7.6   Cyber Vigilantes

Interpol has a global law enforcement role in dealing with crimes that have a transnational dimension. If criminals flee from the scene of a serious crime and make good their escape to another country, Interpol may be contacted by the police authority in the country where the crime was committed. Interpol can circulate to national police forces all over the world any available information about the suspects, and so help to track them down, wherever they may have fled. Criminals can run anywhere, but they should not be able to hide.

The internet is a global virtual enterprise, and there is no agency charged with protecting it. When the internet comes under threat from a worm that might infect a significant proportion of computers in the world, highly skilled civilians without any specific legal authority may act in a law enforcement capacity to stop the attackers from causing more damage. These individuals might be called cyber vigilantes.

### 7.7.7 Battling *Conficker*

In 2009, the internet came under threat from the dastardly, cunning *Conficker* worm. Countering the spread of the *Conficker* worm required the cooperative effort of a smart band of cyber vigilantes, the so-called *Conficker* Cabal, to fight against the worm in a tough digital battle. When *Conficker*'s controllers became aware that their creation was meeting stiff resistance, they began refining the worm's code to make it harder to trace and more powerful. This adaptive response tested the unity and resolve of the Cabal. As *Conficker* assembled the largest botnet in the world, the US government agencies (NSA, DoD, CIA, FBI, and DHS) that had the legal authority to act were bystanders watching the Cabal of volunteers work late nights fighting the *Conficker* botmaster. One outspoken member of the Cabal summed up the federal government's involvement as 'zero involvement, zero activity, zero knowledge'. To contain the spread of *Conficker*, efforts were made to register the many domain names that infected systems sought out. One of the Cabal, Rick Wesson, ran up large bills on his own credit cards through registering domain names. Every cyber risk analyst owes him lunch – one of the authors honored this obligation at Rick's favorite restaurant in San Francisco.

Eight years later, in May 2017, a British researcher for a cyber security firm, 23-year-old Marcus Hutchins, registered an obscure domain name to halt the spread of the *WannaCry* ransomware. His accidental hero celebrity status was not enough to prevent him from being arrested a few months later in Las Vegas, where he had been attending the world's leading information security event. He was charged with authoring and selling a strain of malware designed to steal online banking credentials. In his mid-teens, he had been one of the computer whiz kids celebrated in cyber folklore.

Had Marcus Hutchins never traveled to the United States, it is unlikely he would ever have been extradited from the United Kingdom. The UK communications agency, the Government Communications Headquarters (GCHQ), actually knew that Hutchins was going to be arrested in the United States but did not tip him off so as to avoid the headache of the 10-year legal extradition battle that was fought over Gary McKinnon, a Scottish systems administrator who had hacked into Pentagon computers in an obsessive search for the truth over UFO evidence. A leading authority on autism, Simon Baron-Cohen, observed that such an obsession is characteristic of Asperger's syndrome. Brain dysfunction is recognized by criminologists as explaining some element of criminality.[16]

### 7.7.8  Ignorance Is No Excuse

To understand the mindset of Marcus Hutchins and Gary McKinnon more deeply, one has to go back in time to the early days of computing in the 1950s and 1960s, and to the campus of the world's most renowned institute of technology: the Massachusetts Institute of Technology. At MIT, a hack is a prank demonstrating an admirable degree of technical capability and ingenuity, qualities for which MIT graduates are justly famous. Richard Feynman, the physics Nobel laureate, was a notorious hacker. The term *hacker* was extended to cover tinkering with computers in a clever, if underhanded, way. For Marcus Hutchins, Gary McKinnon, and hackers of like mind, tinkering with computers may not be perceived as a crime. But however self-righteous they may be, ignorance of the law is no excuse, and ultimately the criminality of their actions is for courts of law to decide.

## ENDNOTES

1. DLA Piper (2018).
2. Osborn (2018).
3. Microsoft (2014).
4. Serfass (2015).
5. Markman (2018).
6. Kennedy (2017).
7. HM Government (2017).
8. Wright (2018).
9. *Economist* (2017).
10. A.M. Best (2017).
11. *Resnick v. AvMed*, 693 F.3d 1317, 1332 (11th Cir. 2012), cited in Serfass (2015).
12. Thaler and Sunstein (2009).
13. PAS (2017).
14. Harris and Sirrell (2016).
15. Sidaway (2018).
16. Williams (2012).

# CHAPTER 8

# The Cyber-Resilient Organization

## 8.1 CHANGING APPROACHES TO RISK MANAGEMENT

### 8.1.1 Identify, Protect, Detect, Respond, Recover

The cyber risk management framework proposed by the National Institute of Standards and Technology (NIST) consists of five functions:[1]

1. *Identify.* Develop an organizational understanding to manage cyber security risk to systems, people, assets, data, and capabilities.
2. *Protect.* Develop and implement appropriate safeguards to ensure delivery of critical services.
3. *Detect.* Develop and implement appropriate activities to identify the occurrence of a cyber security event.
4. *Respond.* Develop and implement appropriate activities to take action regarding a detected cyber security incident.
5. *Recover.* Develop and implement appropriate activities to maintain plans for resilience and to restore any capabilities or services that were impaired due to a cyber security incident.

Cyber security in an organization typically places emphasis on maintaining a secure perimeter, with an emphasis on technology tools for monitoring internal traffic and external communications, and with minimal tolerance of external penetration, malware, or unauthorized software. Cyber security tools include antivirus software, firewalls, network traffic deep-packet inspection, data management systems, email security systems, server gateways, web application firewalls, and many others.

Cyber security system design is a complex and skillful process, matching the specific operations and needs of an organization with the threats it faces, the tools available, and the budget allocated. The values of individual components of security are hard to evaluate independently, because security depends on the weakest link in the chain – if one component is weaker than others, then that is the one that will be exploited by attackers. We discuss this further in Chapter 10, 'Security Economics and Strategies'.

Companies spend on average around 3% of their information technology (IT) capital expenditure budget on cyber security.[2] Cyber security expenditure has grown rapidly, generating a $120 billion industry today. Projections expect the industry to continue to grow rapidly to reach hundreds of billions annually worldwide in a few years.

However, the type of expenditure for typical cyber security budgets is shifting. Traditional purchasing of hardware IT security components, such as servers, networking gear, data centers, and physical infrastructure, is being augmented by broader security solutions, such as personnel training, non-computer platforms, and internet of things (IoT) security.[3]

Key trends include increasing emphasis on incident response, shifting from intrusion prevention to intrusion tolerance, compartmentalization and 'credential silos' with protected endpoints, and risk management in the supply chain. We discuss each of these in this chapter.

### 8.1.2   Threat Analysis

Most cyber security assessments begin with threat analysis. In Chapter 5, 'Know Your Enemy', we provide a profile of the main threat actors and their driving motivations. In Chapter 6, 'Measuring the Cyber Threat', we outline approaches to evaluating how likely different organizations are to suffer attacks. An organization needs to evaluate the likelihood of being the primary target of each of the main threat groups, or being caught in the collateral damage from their activities. Organizations will monitor their cyber events – attempted attacks, malware discovered, suspicious activity – typically in an incident log. Analysis of the incident log provides important insights into the characteristics and frequencies of attempted attacks and the overall threat.

## 8.2   INCIDENT RESPONSE AND CRISIS MANAGEMENT

### 8.2.1   Real-time Crisis Management: How Fighter Pilots Do It

On May 1, 1983, high over the Negev desert of Israel, an F-15 Israeli Air Force jet collided with an A-4 Skyhawk plane. The impact sheared off the right wing of the F-15 jet, which was sent spinning. A second before pressing the ejector button, the pilot pushed the throttle, lit the afterburner, gained speed, and regained control of the plane. At twice the normal speed, he managed to land at an airbase, stopping just 20 feet from the end of the runway. The ability to recover from unexpected precarious and hazardous situations is the essence of resilience. This astonishing feat of resilience was accomplished through a highly effective man-machine partnership. First, the intrinsic aeronautic design of the F-15 meant that it acted like a rocket, with sufficient lift being provided by the large surface area of the stabilizers, fuselage, and what remained of the wings. Second, the enterprising pilot had the presence of mind to light the afterburner and accelerate his way out of a deep crisis.

There is much to learn from this example of surprisingly successful real-time crisis management. Technology should be designed to be robustly adaptive to threats both foreseen and unforeseen. The man-machine interface is crucial. Corporate staff have to be trained and prepared for both the expected and the unexpected. The aim of cyber resilience is to maintain a system's capability to deliver the intended outcome at all times, including times of crisis when regular delivery has failed. A wide range of measures, from backups to full disaster recovery, contribute to cyber resilience, and to maintaining business continuity under the most testing, unusual, and unexpected circumstances.

## 8.2.2   Rapid Adaptation to Changing Conditions

As defined by a Presidential Policy Directive, resilience is the ability to prepare for and adapt to changing conditions and withstand and recover rapidly from disruptions. Cyber resilience analysts assess system deficiencies in disruption response, and develop means of rectifying these weaknesses through cyber security enhancements in prevention, detection, and reaction. Organizations need to be agile in crisis response. Organizations need to prepare, prevent, respond, and recover from any crisis that may emerge.

Cyber resilience requires a coherent strategy encompassing people, processes, and technology. The human dimension is especially important, because people can make imprudent security decisions and take risky actions. On the other hand, under crisis situations, people can rise in an extraordinary way to the challenge of adversity. They can make excellent decisions under intense pressure, coping well with the uncertainty over the trouble they find themselves in and the viability of their emergency response plan.

Corporate decision making starts with the board of directors, who have to drive forward the cyber resilience agenda and involve the whole organization, extending to the supply chain, partners, and customers. To balance risk with opportunity, a corporate risk-based strategy needs to be put in place that manages the vulnerabilities, threats, risks, and impacts. This strategy has to include preparation for and recovery from a cyber attack. At the same time, costs need to be kept under control, user convenience must be taken into account, and business requirements should be satisfied.

### 8.2.3  Cyber Risk Awareness in Staff

Microsoft provides considerations for a cyber resilience program.[4] Amongst the recommendations is that every person with corporate network access, including full-time employees, consultants, and contractors, should be regularly trained to develop a cyber-resilient mindset. This should include not only adhering to IT security policies around identity-based access control, but also alerting IT to suspicious events and infections as soon as possible to help minimize time to remediation.

Training programs specifically geared towards developing a cyber-resilient mindset are particularly productive. Many, corporate training programs exist to help staff to deal safely with social engineering scams. Even the most savvy of staff members may fall victim to one of these scams, which prey upon all manner of psychological, emotional, and cognitive weaknesses. Magicians exploit these weaknesses to fool people with their illusions. In the cognitive science literature, it is established that providing misinformation about past events can reduce memory accuracy and even create false memories. Phishing attacks and social engineering use a wide variety of con tricks, misdirection, and scams to try to get staff to reveal credentials, open toxic attachments, follow false links, and carry out other tasks. Spotting these tricks, questioning their veracity, and identifying the clues to their fakeness are skills that need to be learned and reinforced in staff behavior.

### 8.2.4  Business Continuity Planning and Staff Engagement

All staff members need a good understanding of business continuity issues. Those assigned specialist duties, such as planning testing and incident response, need extra specific training, as all emergency responders do. Middle and senior managers have their own responsibilities, and are required to understand and adopt integrated cyber resilience management best practice and compliance to standards. The key cyber resilience standards that should be adopted are:

- ISO 27001, the international standard describing best practice for an information security management system.
- ISO 22301, the international standard for business continuity.

Successful training can be achieved only with full staff engagement. If the training is perceived as dull, tedious, and boring, the results are likely to be disappointing. No matter how technically expert the training is, eliciting an enthusiastic human response requires addressing an extra dimension: psychology. One way of adding a psychological dimension to cyber resilience training is to reward staff positively for good cyber hygiene. Rewards might be handed out across the whole spectrum of cyber security issues of concern: reporting phishing emails; preventing tailgating; reporting attempted intrusions via social engineering; reporting any USB memory sticks lost or found; keeping desktop software patched and updated; maintaining strong, confidential passwords; attending security seminars and webinars; not leaving laptops unattended; and reporting bugs or vulnerabilities. Such incentivized training achieves measurable and impressive results. In one major corporation, after 18 months participants were 50% less likely to click on a phishing link and 82% more likely to report a phishing email.[5]

### 8.2.5 Gaming and Exercises

One familiar field of human endeavor in which incentivized training is proven to work well is in playing competitive games. The application of gaming principles to business is given the self-explanatory if contrived name 'gamification'. It actually started in marketing, as companies realized they could attract customers more readily by enticing them with a game or competition. Some businesses have been using gamification in the workplace as a way to boost employee morale.[6] The application to adversarial situations like combating cyber risk may be more compelling and relevant than most. Amongst other cyber security firms, Kaspersky Lab has been adopting gamification technology in its security awareness training programs. In 2017, Kaspersky awarded a young talent lab prize to the US-based creators of a gamification app designed to raise information security awareness amongst millennials.

There are four principles to gamification: defining a goal, defining rules for reaching that goal, setting up a feedback mechanism, and making participation voluntary. Gamification usually means awarding points to employees who do the right thing, with various forms of recognition, including badges, prizes, and a leader board listing point totals. Treating cyber security as a competitive game, with scores posted as in a golf tournament, is not inappropriate. Unlike natural hazards resilience, security against cyber attacks is a persistent adversarial game – the attackers are rewarded for their efforts and industry, and so also should the defenders be rewarded. The more points that staff members manage to accrue, the harder it becomes for the adversary to score points by causing major cyber loss and disruption. Adversarial exercises, such as 'Capture the Flag' are good training for security staff and technologists.

### 8.2.6 Nudging Behavior

Another way of using psychology to change staff behavior is through adopting the nudge principle: encouraging good cyber hygiene without having to reward staff accordingly. One of the most famous original examples of nudging, quoted by economics Nobel laureate William Thaler, one of the authors of the nudge principle, is that of hygiene in men's restrooms. Men can be nudged to make less floor mess simply by having a marked target in the center of a urinal. No reward (or penalty) of any kind is needed to encourage better hygiene. In line with the previous golf tournament metaphor, one actual example of a marked target is a golf flag pin. At the Cyber Security Summit and Expo 2017, the chief operating officer at the UK Financial Conduct Authority suggested that staff members may be nudged to talk more about cyber security, and explained that far better cultural outcomes are then seen than with traditional annual mandatory training regimes. She further suggested that the same technique could be used with suppliers, who may be an unsuspecting weak link in overall security. In addition to usual due diligence, a regular conversation with suppliers on security sets a positive nudging tone for a mutually beneficial enhanced cyber security relationship.

## 8.3  RESILIENCE ENGINEERING

### 8.3.1  Safety Management

In traditional safety management, the focus is on identifying and defending against a prescribed set of hazards, using techniques with limited ability to realistically represent the intricacies of human and organizational influences adequately.[7] Also, the search for causal factors of failures is obscured by the social, cultural, and technical characteristics of complex engineered systems. The concepts of resilience engineering address these shortcomings, integrating safety, process, and financial management. Resilience engineering builds on safety engineering, but treats faults and failures in socio-technical systems rather than in purely technical systems. The focus of resilience engineering is on the organization and on the socio-technical system in the presence of accidents, errors, and disasters. In particular, resilience engineering is well suited to systems that are tightly coupled but intractable in the sense that they cannot be completely described or specified.

In general terms, resilience is the ability of an organization to recover to a stable state, allowing it to continue operations during and after a major mishap or in the presence of continuous significant stresses. Both of these contingencies are relevant for cyber resilience. The management challenge of building and leading a resilient organization increases in complexity as more products and services are online and open to cyber disruption by malevolent hackers.

## THE CHALLENGE OF CYBER RESILIENCE: TRUMP HOTELS

Hotels are at high risk of data breach attacks, particularly major chains. Seven of the luxury hotels owned by presidential candidate Donald Trump were infected between May 2014 and June 2015 with malware that stole payment information. This data breach ended up exposing 70,000 credit card numbers and customer records, and was discovered only when multiple banks spotted hundreds of fraudulent transactions on customer accounts where the last legitimate transaction was at Trump Hotels.

Cardholders were unaware of the breach until a notice was posted on the Trump Hotels website four months after the hotel chain had learned of the major data exfiltration. This delay violated New York state laws stipulating timely consumer notifications regarding compromised data. Timeliness of security response is also a requirement of resilience. Trump Hotels duly enhanced security measures, including employee training, comprehensive risk assessments, and regularly scheduled testing of systems – but not before another data breach was discovered in March 2016.

Later that year, hackers broke into the Sabre SynXis Central Reservations System, which facilitates online hotel booking for some of the largest hotel chains. The intrusion remained undetected on the Sabre network for seven months, stealing data between August 2016 and March 2017. This was the third credit card data breach affecting Trump Hotels in three years.[8]

## 8.3.2 Hotel Keycard Failure Example

A simple example is a hotel where room keycards fail after a cyber attack. Black hats have demonstrated how some digital hotel keys can be read with a simple portable device. Even in this dire situation, there has to be a backup plan to allow guests to access their rooms securely. Availability is a vital pillar of resilient cyber security; even after keycard failure, continuity of hotel service must be maintained, and guest rooms have to be available for use. Along with availability, confidentiality and integrity of information are two other vital pillars of cyber security. These also are major issues for the hotel industry because of data breach of the hotel booking and payments system, and the theft of credit card data. Hotels have become popular targets because they have a business hospitality culture of openness. A cyber attack hit 1200 franchised InterContinental hotels in the last quarter of 2016. Hackers have declared open season on the reservation and point-of-sale systems of the hospitality and tourism industry.

President Trump gave a public commitment to keeping America safe in the cyber era.[9] This commitment extended to resilience: building defensible government networks and improving the ability to provide uninterrupted and secure communications and services under all conditions. Although a strident critic of big government, as a victim of data breaches in his hotel chain, Trump may recognize that stronger cyber security regulations may be needed and may need to be better enforced.

## 8.4  ATTRIBUTES OF A CYBER-RESILIENT ORGANIZATION

### 8.4.1  Anticipate, Withstand, Recover, and Evolve

In general, the complexity of a system makes it difficult to classify failure states following a cyber attack, which can impact an organization in innumerable ways. Yet, complexity is a vital system attribute enabling adaptation under external stress. The individual links between people and their environment should adapt under stress in a resilient manner. Because resilience is an emerging property of complex systems, it can be developed through focus on attaining specific goals.

A cyber-resilient organization should aim to anticipate, withstand, recover, and evolve. Given their intrinsic interconnectedness, all four of these goals should be addressed simultaneously. For example, even while withstanding or recovering from a cyber attack, a business manager must anticipate further attacks. Even while anticipating, withstanding, or recovering from attacks, business processes that rely on them are constantly evolving to address changing operational and technical environments. And part of anticipation is withstanding stresses within some bounded range.

Cyber resilience is just one aspect of resilience in general. An organization that aspires to be cyber resilient should aim further to be resilient against all potential stresses. A highly resilient organization will share the six attributes listed in Section 8.4.3.[10] In this list of attributes, which are not cyber-specific, there is a well-merited emphasis on human performance within the organization. This is appropriate since not only are security decision making and preparedness the responsibility of the organization's employees, but the staff members themselves are also a primary source of vulnerability to cyber attack, being susceptible to social engineering deception, as well as the source of human error in undertaking corporate security tasks.

### 8.4.2   Negative Attributes

Case studies of organizations that have suffered major data breaches often highlight missing attributes for a resilient organization. For example, security commentators referred negatively to the security culture at Equifax, which discovered a massive data breach on July 29, 2017, and announced it six weeks later on September 7. In his testimony to a US House of Representatives subcommittee on consumer protection, the Equifax CEO, Rick Smith, justified the delay in communicating the data breach on the grounds of avoiding further attacks and ensuring consumer protection measures could be put in place. A resilient organization would have had detailed contingency plans in place for a data breach, which would have expedited its crisis communication response.

The Equifax CEO also excused the communication delay with reference to Hurricane Irma, which took down two large call centers in September, soon after the breach announcement. This is a classic failure of resilience. Corporate preparedness for natural hazards should include plans to overcome breakdowns in infrastructure. Professional resilience engineers would not have been astonished that some of the 15 million Britons affected by the Equifax data breach were only notified eight months afterwards.

### 8.4.3   Six Positive Attributes for Resilience

For a consumer credit reporting agency, corporate resilience should have been a business priority. The many millions of consumers and businesses whose information was collected by Equifax would have expected the agency to have been a paradigm of resilience. But based on information publicly disclosed after the breach, Equifax may have possessed all too few of the following six attributes of a resilient organization. Indeed, in respect of human performance, the CEO personally blamed a single member of the company's security team, rather than recognize that all errors are the outcome of organizational deficiencies, such as a lack of resilience, for which the CEO is ultimately responsible.

1. *Top-level commitment* to recognizing and valuing human performance concerns, in both word and deed. An organization should provide continuous and extensive follow-through to actions related to human performance.
2. *A just culture* supporting the reporting of issues up through the organization. Without a just culture, the willingness of staff to report problems will be eroded, as will the organization's ability to learn about defensive weaknesses.
3. *A learning culture* benefiting from both good and bad experiences, and not responding to questions about security issues with denial.
4. *Awareness* of the true state of defenses, and their state of degradation. Also, insight into the quality of human performance, and the extent to which it is a problem.
5. *Preparedness* for problems, especially in human performance. The organization should actively anticipate problems and prepare for them.
6. *Flexibility* to adapt that maximizes ability to solve problems without loss of functionality. It requires that important security decisions may be made at lower organizational levels.

These six attributes are qualitative organizational attributes, which have a significant bearing on quantitative resilience metrics: the time and cost to restore operations, the time and cost to restore system configurations, the time and cost to restore functionality and performance, the degree to which the pre-disruption state is restored, the potential disruption circumvented, and successful adaptations within time and cost constraints.

### 8.4.4 Cyber Resilience Objectives

Because the cyber threat is so dynamic, many actions to improve resilience may be effective for only a short duration. However, common to all actions are various general cyber resilience objectives, which are summarized next.

- Adaptive Response
    An adaptive response involves executing and monitoring the effectiveness of actions that best change the attack surface, maintain critical capabilities, and restore functional capabilities.

- **Analytic Monitoring**

  Analytic monitoring involves gathering and analyzing data on an ongoing basis and in a coordinated way to identify potential vulnerabilities, adversary activities, and damage.

- **Coordinated Defense**

  In any conflict situation, having multiple defenses is advantageous, but they have to be carefully coordinated so that they do not interfere negatively with each other, but rather have a maximum positive effect.

- **Deception**

  Sun Tzu's dictum that 'All war is based on deception' applies to cyber warfare as well as older traditional forms of conflict. Deception is an essential weapon of cyber defense, especially against a powerful adversary, such as a state-sponsored threat actor.

- **Privilege Restriction**

  Violation of privilege restriction has facilitated some major cyber attacks. To minimize the impact of criminal action, privileges should be carefully restricted.

- **Random Changes**

  Static security, however strong, is progressively liable to be eroded over time. Frequent randomized security actions that make it more perplexing for an adversary to predict behavior increase the chance of adversary detection.

- **Redundancy**

  The value of redundancy in enhancing system safety is evident from elementary reliability analysis. If the chance of failure of a key component is one in a thousand, then the chance of failure of two such components, assumed to have independent failure rates, is as low as one in a million.

- **Segmentation**

  The attack surface of a system can be reduced if system components can be segmented based on criticality to restrict the damage from exploits. Segmentation often employs either physically distinct entities or virtualization of computing subnetworks to provide the desired separation.

- **Substantiated Integrity**

  It is crucial that critical systems and backups have not been corrupted by an adversary. Their integrity needs to be substantiated and data checked that they are not invalid or out of range.

## 8.5   INCIDENT RESPONSE PLANNING

### 8.5.1   Forensic Investigation

The vast majority of internet crimes are left unreported. A tiny proportion of cyber crimes are successfully prosecuted. Most perpetrators are outside Western jurisdiction, and even if they are within the same jurisdiction as the victim, successful prosecution is difficult to achieve.

However, where a significant corporate cyber crime has been committed, some level of criminal investigation is required for legal reasons, as well as to comply with obligations to shareholders and other corporate stakeholders, and to enhance resilience. This involves computer forensics. As with any forensic investigation, diligence is needed when attending the scene of a crime, to ensure that significant evidence gathered is admissible. In particular, the following four principles must be upheld:[11]

1. No action taken by law enforcement agencies, persons employed within those agencies, or their agents should change data, which may be subsequently relied upon in court.
2. Where a person finds it necessary to access original data, that person must be competent to do so, and be able to give evidence explaining the relevance and the implications of his or her actions.
3. An audit trail or other record of all processes applied to digital evidence should be created and preserved. An independent third party should be able to examine those processes and achieve the same result.
4. The person in charge of the investigation has overall responsibility for ensuring adherence to the law and these principles.

Forensic investigators not only must comply with these principles; they also have to cope with insidious attempts to thwart computer forensic analysis. This may include encryption, the overwriting of data, and the modification of file metadata. And even where no such anti-forensic efforts have been made, a shrewd defense lawyer can query in court the quality of evidence of an intrusion – maybe the log file had been tampered with, or the origination of the internet protocol (IP) address was faked.[12] Thinking through defense arguments is a valuable intellectual exercise in cyber resilience, because it raises technical issues that could lead to ideas for improving the cyber security environment. One argument might be over identifying when exactly a cyber security incident occurred. For example reconciling the timestamp for a connection to a webserver might involve clients in London, a server in Tokyo and various time zones and daylight-saving adjustments.

## 8.5.2 Initial Breach Diagnosis

An initial step in incident response is to assess when security was first breached. This is far from being a straightforward matter, as shown by the 2014 and subsequent 2013 Yahoo breach revelations. The next step is to discover what systems have been compromised, and what data has been exfiltrated or corrupted. An essential aspect of any first response to an unfolding crisis is conducting triage, which consists of classifying incidents, prioritizing them, and assigning incidents to appropriate personnel.[13] Containment of damage and prevention of its spreading are then urgent actions before eradication of the threat and removal of malware from the network. The mark of resilience in incident response is restoration of systems to their normal operation. The main challenges in recovery are in reconnecting networks and confirming that systems have been successfully restored.

Thinking ahead is characteristic of a resilient mindset. Even before, and preferably well before a major incident occurs, plans should be drawn up for investigating incidents, as and when they might occur, and undertaking extensive postincident investigations. Communicating lessons learned to all stakeholders in a transparent and timely manner is a crucial element of a resilient response. Amongst the lessons will be insights into the effectiveness of security measures, and the costs and impacts of cyber incidents. From such lessons the cost-effectiveness of enhanced security measures can be better gauged.

## 8.6 RESILIENT SECURITY SOLUTIONS

### 8.6.1 Resilient Software

Resilient software should have the capacity to withstand a failure in a critical component, such as from a cyber attack, but still recover in an acceptable predefined manner and duration. Factors affecting resilience include complexity, globalization, interdependency, rapid change, level of system integration, and behavioral influences. The complex networked systems prevalent in many organizations make it hard to provide a service platform with consistent levels of resilience. When a critical system fails, the required service may not be readily deliverable, especially when there is high demand. Furthermore, net-centricity can introduce complexities that lead to greater chances of errors.[14] Learning from failure is essential for a resilient organization. When software fails, this is an opportunity for additional resilience features to be introduced.

Security should be fully integrated within the development process, with built-in features such as defense in depth, running with least privilege, and avoidance of security by obscurity. A software development life cycle (SDLC) is a series of phases that provide a framework for developing software and managing it through its entire life cycle. There is no specific technique or single way to develop applications and software components, but there are established methodologies that organizations use and models they follow to address different challenges and goals.

However well written and resilient the software is, and however much the network perimeter defense has been hardened, a determined, highly motivated (perhaps state-sponsored) cyber attacker can eventually manage to find an entry point into any system through some social engineering deception or zero day exploit. Treating a twenty-first-century software system as a medieval fortress with impregnable entry points is itself a counterproductive form of self-deception, and self-denial of reality of the virtual world. This is detrimental to cyber security in general, and to maintaining resilience in particular. It is prudent to accept that system intrusion will occur in the future, and to plan a maximally resilient response. The three pillars of successful response identified by Dr Eric Cole are detection, containment, and control.[15]

### 8.6.2   Detection, Containment, and Control

In biology, a system's capacity to absorb and resist any damage from internal or external mechanisms, and recover quickly, is a measure of its resilience. The universal process of evolution embodies natural selection for resilience. A key criterion for fitness is resilience. In healthcare, a doctor would advise a patient that prevention is always better than cure. Hence those who spend hours in the sun are urged to use sunscreen. Regular use of sunscreen can halve the incidence of melanoma, which is a type of skin cancer. If excessive sun exposure does eventually cause melanoma, the sooner this is detected the better, so that effective treatment can be given. Most importantly, any malignant tumor should be found before it spreads to other parts of the body.

Rapid threat detection lies at the heart of resilient cyber security. Imagine a cyber attack that targets a perceived security weakness in a peripheral device such as a printer. If system security extends to intrusion detection that monitors the device memory for malicious attacks, then threat detection can automatically instigate a reboot from a safe copy of the device's operating system. By restoring the peripheral device without business interruption, cyber resilience is achieved.

### 8.6.3   Minimize Intrusion Dwell Time

A resilient strategy for coping with a cyber attack should minimize the intrusion dwell time, which is the time from initial system compromise

## CASE STUDIES IN GERMAN STEEL RESILIENCE

In February 2016, Southeast Asian hackers exfiltrated technological intellectual property data from Thyssenkrup, one of the world's largest steelmakers. Early detection and timely countermeasures limited the loss from this professional cyber espionage attack, which was discovered, continuously observed, and analyzed by Thyssenkrup's computer emergency response team. This admirably resilient response to a cyber attack contrasts with what happened when a steel mill in an undisclosed location in Germany was targeted for a cyber attack in 2014. (Thyssenkrup denied it was one of its steel mills.) The motive for this apparently senseless act of cyber vandalism remains unknown, but it does provide an instructive contrasting case study in cyber nonresilience.

The attackers used spear phishing emails to access the steel mill office IT network, compromise a multitude of systems, and spread over to the production network. Failures accumulated in individual control components, and a blast furnace was unable to be shut down in a regulated manner, which resulted in extensive damage. This cyber attack came as a shock not just to the steel mill security staff, but to the entire cyber security industry in Germany and beyond. Surprise is the enemy of resilience.

It would not have been feasible for an outside vandal to have physically gained access to the steel mill and sabotaged a blast furnace. Basic site security would have detected the unauthorized intrusion and prevented this kind of criminal damage. The cyber attack was not detected because it was an advanced persistent threat (APT), executed carefully in stages in a slow and stealthy way, keeping a low profile to make detection difficult.[16] Apart from remaining undetected, the attack was neither contained nor controlled.

A more resilient cyber defense strategy would have had a network intrusion detection system (NIDS) deployed. This strategy should also have maintained a strict separation between business and production networks to contain the attack, preventing it from spreading from the entry point to the key industrial target.

to the time the malware ceases to be effective. Controlling dwell time means early detection with an appropriate effective response. Just as with malignant cancer, the lateral spread of intrusion should also be contained and controlled, so as to minimize the number and extent of compromised systems.

Dwell times can be measured in months rather than days or weeks because attackers are often ingeniously adaptive to new security systems, and may change their threat signatures from those detected by threat intelligence service providers. Spotting anomalous behavior is a crucial aspect of resilient cyber security. A network behavior anomaly detection (NBAD) program tracks critical network characteristics in real time and generates an alarm if an anomaly or unusual trend is detected that might signal a threat. Examples of such characteristics include increased traffic volume, bandwidth, and protocol use. Such a program can also monitor the behavior of individual network subscribers.

For NBAD to be optimally effective, a baseline of normal network or user behavior must be established over a period of time. A large volume of network data can enable even a comparatively modest anomaly to be tracked and flagged up. Inevitably, as in any anomaly detection system, there may be false positives, such as when an employee decides to back up the contents of a hard drive on a Saturday evening before going away on vacation the following morning. The flip side of anomaly detection, when dealing with an intelligent adversary striving to keep illicit activities hidden within the noise, is the possibility of false negatives. The international prize for smart detection avoidance might be awarded to the Soviets who violated nuclear test ban treaties by automatically timing the detonation of nuclear test explosions to coincide with the occurrence of regional earthquakes. The seismic signal of a nuclear explosion (the observational basis for nuclear test forensics) would be hidden within the tail of the earthquake signal. This kind of subtle trickery to evade detection ended with the Cold War, but the ingenious cunning of the Russian chess mind in the age of state-sponsored cyber attacks should not be underestimated.

### 8.6.4  Anomaly Detection Algorithms

Anomaly detection algorithms use state-of-the-art artificial intelligence methods, incorporating sophisticated Bayesian techniques of statistical inference. These probabilistic tools for searching for discrepancies have been refined using ideas developed for Big Data analysis. Faster, cheaper, simpler – but less powerful – are signature-based detection methods. Rather like a police biometric database of fingerprints or DNA samples, these methods rely on a database of signatures carried by packets known to be sources of malicious activities. Signature-based methods check for automated procedures supplied by well-known hacker tools. These tend to have the same traffic signatures every time, because computer programs repeat over and over again the same instructions.

Both anomaly and signature-based detection approaches should be incorporated within an overall NIDS. As anyone who lives in a gated community knows, reliance on the detection of an intruder is far from being a resilient strategy for mitigating the risk of burglary. The probability of detection can never be very close to certainty, because the price of false alarms would be unacceptable. Each house needs its own security system to contain and control the criminal action of an intruder. Defense in depth is a cornerstone of resilient security. Recognition of lateral movements of a cyber attacker requires continuous monitoring of the internal network, and a visual interface that provides the right metrics for security analysts to gain situation awareness of any intrusion. With these metrics, an intrusion can begin to be contained and controlled.

Containment of the adverse impacts of security breaches will help avoid an escalation of loss and blunt the force of a cyber attack, so as to make incident response more effective. Containment might be achieved through network segmentation, and redundancy measures such as having logical and physical duplication. Another containment approach that increases resilience is designing systems so that they continue to function and perform their tasks even when connectivity to external systems is lost. With any security initiative, there is also an intrinsic human component that needs to be considered. Dealing with an intrusion effectively requires a degree of security staff preparedness that merits training and rehearsal of an emergency response plan.

## 8.6.5 Penetration Testing

In cyberspace, it is essential to understand the interrelationship between vulnerability assessment and risk analysis.[17] Much more effort is directed towards the former than the latter. But measuring work on vulnerability assessment is not measuring risk reduction. For example, a vulnerability scanner might determine that a server is missing critical operating system patches by detecting an outdated version of the operating system during a network probe. This vulnerability might be remedied simply by a software update and a reboot. Assessing the corresponding cyber risk reduction is not so straightforward. This would involve explicitly devising an exploit to show that the missing patch would allow an attacker to gain access to the server. This might be a difficult task, not necessarily cost-effective for a work-averse hacker.

A penetration test (pen test to its friends) is the process of conducting simulated attacks to discover how successful cyber attacks might occur. Conducting a pen test to prove that a missing patch is a security issue typically raises the cost of testing, and runs the expensive risk of potential system downtime. Not all pen testing is expensive; the simplest type of pen testing involves a handful of social engineering tricks, or taking advantage of an easily guessable password. Some IoT gadgets such as a kitchen kettle leave the factory with a basic default password, which may not be changed by the forgetful or ignorant purchaser. Like all professional occupations, pen testers come with a wide range of knowledge, ability, and experience. The best pen testers have deep knowledge of operating systems, networking, scripting languages, and the like, and use a clever combination of manual and automated tools to simulate attacks with the same complexity as might be conceived by a black hat.

Pen test results are typically reported on severity, exploitability, and associated remediation actions. The information obtained from pen testing can be used to plug security gaps, improve attack response, and enhance cyber resilience. Controlling network entry and exit points and reducing the overall attack surface will make it easier to respond to an attack, and enable functionality to be restored more quickly. This therefore increases an organization's resilience against cyber attacks.

### 8.6.6 The Risk-return Trade-off

Whereas junior security personnel may work obsessively to reduce vulnerability where they find it, cost-conscious senior management and their accountants are particularly interested in the risk-return trade-off. The actual level of risk reduction achieved may in fact be lower than is optimistically perceived, given the large security budget. For example, within days of a pen test, network changes may create new security challenges.

Pen testing is commonly used to address the problem of cyber risk mitigation, instead of more empirical and scientific practices. Although pen testers know what to charge for their professional services, most pen testers cannot put a price on their success or failure. Pen testers can make recommendations on how to close security gaps, and how to prioritize the necessary tasks. But no two pen testers go about their assignment in the same way, and pen testing is usually done on a limited set of targets. Accordingly, pen testing is not strictly a risk management exercise.

To provide another perspective on security risk management, consider the pen testing analog of red-teaming in counterterrorism studies. Ever since 9/11, security consultancies with extensive military expertise have undertaken vulnerability assessments for specific locations and events that might be targeted for a terrorist attack. Red-teaming exercises are particularly valuable in identifying gaps in security that would make a location or event a comparatively soft target relative to other alternative targets. By hardening any one potential target, e.g. deploying additional perimeter security guards and installing CCTV, the risk may be transferred to another soft target, in a process that terrorism risk analysts recognize as target substitution.[18] This tactic should extend to cyber risk as well. Hackers (like terrorists) follow the path of least resistance in their targeting, and if an attractive designated target for a cyber attack has been hardened, others lacking the benefit of pen testing or red-teaming knowledge may become more likely to be attacked.

## 8.7 FINANCIAL RESILIENCE

### 8.7.1 Financial Consequences of a Cyber Attack

A major cyber attack on a corporation can impact it in numerous adverse ways. Intellectual property and other confidential information may be stolen; important computer system files may be corrupted or encrypted; denial of service may bring systems down; physical damage to corporate facilities and property may be inflicted; psychological and bodily harm may be caused to staff and customers; reputational damage may be incurred, and liability lawsuits may be filed. Whatever the impact, business will be disrupted to an extent that depends on the resilience of the organization. We describe many of these consequences and illustrate some of these costs in the first two chapters: Chapter 1, 'Counting the Costs of Cyber Attacks', and Chapter 2, 'Preparing for Cyber Attacks'.

The bottom line for any commercial organization is the ultimate financial cost. Each of the adverse impacts results in a financial loss to the corporation. For publicly listed corporations, the stock price is a resilience measure. For those publicly listed corporations for which cyber security is paramount for customer confidence, the impact of a severe cyber attack on stock price can be devastating. As fallout from a massive identity theft data breach, the stock price of Equifax fell precipitously by about one-third in one week, before a new CEO was appointed in late September 2017 and started to turn the consumer credit reporting agency around. But with further revelations that the data breach was worse than previously thought, the stock price in mid-February 2018 was still lower by 20% than it had been before the breach disclosure.

### 8.7.2   Financial Risk Assessment

Companies have to make assessments of their risk and build resilience into their balance sheet to withstand the types of shock that might be foreseeable. In the United States public companies are expected to file annual 10-K submissions to the Securities and Exchange Commission that identify the key risks to their business and to notify their shareholders and counterparties of those risks. The UK equivalent is the Long Term Viability Statement (LTVS) reporting to the Financial Reporting Council on liquidity. Cyber risk is one of the most commonly reported risks by companies, declared in their 10-K and LTVS filings.

A cyber attack can cause sufficient loss to cause damage to a company's balance sheet, even for fairly sizeable organizations. Examples include companies having to issue profit warnings, suffer credit downgrades, make emergency loan provisions, and see reduction in stock price, and ultimately the loss could be severe enough to force the organization to cease trading. The likelihood of cyber attacks causing a loss sufficient to trigger each of these thresholds depends on the type of risk analysis we have described, defining the odds of experiencing a cyber loss of these levels of severity, combined with the financial structure of the organization, its liquidity, its access to capital reserves, and analysts' interpretation of the event in terms of how it might affect the future business model and position relative to its competitors.

Balance sheet resilience for the levels of financial shock that might be inflicted by a cyber event can be achieved by having all of the standard financial engineering processes to minimize earnings volatility, including having sufficient liquidity margins, reducing debt ratios, having access to emergency loan provisions, being able to cut costs to meet earnings targets, and having cyber insurance to provide a level of financial indemnity against the loss.

### 8.7.3   Reverse Stress Testing

For any specified cyber attack scenario designed as a financial stress test, the implications for a corporation can be evaluated, taking account of the myriad ways that it might affect business. For a particularly severe scenario, a corporation's credit rating might be downgraded. The implications of cyber attacks could start taking a higher priority in credit analysis. Moody's

Investors Service views material cyber threats in a similar vein as other extraordinary event risks, such as those arising from natural disasters, with any subsequent credit impact depending on the duration and severity of the event.[19] While Moody's does not explicitly incorporate cyber risk as a principal credit factor, its fundamental credit analysis incorporates numerous stress-testing scenarios, and a cyber event could be the trigger for one of those stress scenarios. In a 2015 report, Moody's identified several key factors to examine when determining a credit impact associated with a cyber event, including the nature and scope of the targeted assets or businesses, the duration of potential service disruptions, and the expected time to restore operations.

Both the disruption duration and the operational restoration time are basic defining characteristics of resilience. A cyber-resilient organization should know just how bad a cyber attack would need to be to threaten its viability, or to have its credit rating downgraded. This is called reverse stress testing. Through systematic reverse stress testing, measures can be developed to protect a corporation against such unacceptable outcomes.

For insurance companies in the context of Solvency II, the concept of reverse stress testing for an insurer's own risk and solvency assessment (ORSA) is endorsed by the European Insurance and Occupational Pensions Authority.[20] A number of practical cyber reverse stress tests have been developed; see the examples of stress tests in Table 9.2 in Chapter 9, 'Cyber Insurance'.[21] They have been used as management desktop exercises to identify operational weaknesses and areas that need attention.

### 8.7.4 Defense in Depth

The principles of engineering resilience go a long way in cyber resilience. Defense in depth is a crucial objective in building in system resilience. Even if one system fails, overlapping system design will mean there is no single point of failure. This contrasts markedly with a standard check-box approach to security, which sanctions systems with a minimum level of redundancy as having sufficient security. If this standard check-box approach were routine in the passenger airline industry, there would be just a single pilot in the cockpit, rather than two or three.

The Equifax CEO singled out one of the company's 250 security personnel as responsible for allowing the data breach: 'We now know that the vulnerable version of Apache Struts within Equifax was not identified or patched. The human error was that the individual who's responsible for communicating in the organization to apply the patch, did not'.[22] Cyber security should not be reliant on the error-free human action of any individual, just as airline safety should not be reliant on the perfect, impeccable job performance of any one pilot. No computer user can presume that computer software is bug-free, and no CEO can presume that the successful management of such bugs can be achieved without some occasional human error.

Having extra personnel available for patching provides defense in depth. Operational redundancy of course costs money – this is the price of resilience. Deciding on how much defense in depth a corporation should have depends partly on regulation, and partly on corporate risk appetite. The irony of the Equifax data breach is that the CEO might well have stipulated a tight limit to the cyber risk to which Equifax should have been exposed. Given the extreme sensitivity of the identity data retained by Equifax, customers would have been dismayed by any other cyber security policy. However, there was a disconnect between CEO instruction and actual operation. The implementation of this policy lacked the resilience required to ensure its practical effectiveness in a perpetually hostile cyber threat environment.

### 8.7.5 Enterprise Risk Management

Enterprise risk management (ERM) envisages an organizational process applied in developing strategy across the enterprise. It is designed to identify events that might affect the organization, and to help manage risk to within its risk appetite. The degree of cyber resilience sought by an organization should be commensurate with its risk appetite. Traditional ERM measures of cyber risk typically do not quantify severity of financial loss in the event of a cyber incident. As the importance of cyber risk increases amongst organizations worldwide, ERM studies will help to specify optimal levels of cyber resilience investment. Too often, when a large corporation suffers a massive cyber attack loss, the CEO is unable to explain whether the negative outcome was consistent with its risk appetite or resilience objectives. It is easier to attribute blame to staff error.

### 8.7.6 Cyber Value at Risk

Cyber value at risk (VaR) is based on the general notion of VaR, widely used in the financial services industry. In finance, VaR is a risk measure for a given portfolio and time horizon, defined as a threshold loss value. Specifically, given a low designated probability value $X$, e.g. 0.05, VaR expresses the threshold loss value such that the probability of the loss exceeding the VaR value is the low number $X$. As with other types of risks, the concern is not only with expected losses from cyber threats, but should incorporate an understanding of potentially more significant losses that could occur with a small but finite probability. Cyber VaR can be perceived as the value exposed given both common and significant attack risks. Technically, financial value at risk is defined as the maximum loss for a given confidence interval (say, with 95% certainty) on a given time horizon, e.g. one year.

Traditionally, the confidence levels have been estimated under the simplifying hypothesis that the underlying loss variability can be represented by a bell-shaped normal distribution. This is very convenient for mathematical analysis, because the sum of any number of normal distributions is still normal. However, the normal approximation is invalid for open-ended risks like cyber risks, which recognize no bounds of geography and can increase in severity scale by orders of magnitude. A problem faced by cyber risk analysts is the brief observational period of historical data, which may not represent accurately the tail of the loss distribution, which could have a much fatter shape than any bell.

### 8.7.7 Re-Simulations of Historical Events

The historical record of cyber attacks is just a couple of decades long. By conducting stochastic simulations of past cyber attacks within this time window, cyber risk analysts can look beyond the near horizon of history and scan the far horizon, gaining insight into how large cyber losses might potentially have been. For example, suppose that a major bug (such as *Heartbleed*) had been discovered by a black hat rather than by a white hat; what might the cyber loss have been? Even though *Heartbleed* was found first in 2014 by the Google security team, the alarming potential for data exfiltration was demonstrated by Chinese hackers who, after the bug was disclosed, stole the personal data of about 4.5 million patients of hospital group Community Health Systems Inc. The hackers used stolen credentials to log into the network posing as employees. Once in, they hacked their way into a database and stole millions of records. If this bug had not been found by white hats and patched, many criminal hacking groups might have followed this basic modus operandi of using the *Heartbleed* bug to steal credentials, which would then be a gateway of opportunity to exfiltrate very large volumes of valuable data. With a complete medical record selling on the dark web for high prices, the economic loss from tens of millions of medical records alone might have been many billions of dollars.

The sensitivity of corporate vulnerability to cloud failure might also be assessed by revisiting the most severe historical cloud outages involving a cloud service provider, and contemplating some downward counterfactuals where the situation, which was bad already, turned for the worse because of poor resilience of the cloud service provider. In 2015, a notable bug, *XSA-148*, was found in the Xen hypervisor software by the cloud platform security team at the Chinese multinational Alibaba.[23] This bug would have allowed malicious code to be written into a hypervisor's memory space. This vulnerability was probably the worst ever seen affecting Xen, which is a free software project. It is claimed that Xen has fewer critical bugs than other hypervisors, but this would be little consolation to an organization that suffered loss through a Xen bug.

### 8.7.8 Counterfactual Analysis

Counterfactual analysis can also quantify the benefit from past security enhancements, such as regular penetration testing, as well as from the introduction of resilience measures to mitigate the loss from cyber attacks. For example, measures to streamline the process of restoring backup systems in the event of a ransomware attack might be assessed retrospectively for the *WannaCry* attack of May 2017. Suppose that the kill switch had not been found early on by Marcus Hutchins, and that *WannaCry* had spread widely within the United States. How much worse might the corporate cyber loss have been if an improved backup restoration process had not been implemented? Due consideration of past near misses such as this would encourage improved future preparedness for, and resilience against, another ransomware attack.

This kind of counterfactual analysis would also help decide on the cost-effectiveness of additional cyber resilience measures. Suppose that an additional resilience technology had been introduced several years ago. How much would the cyber losses over this period have been reduced? A positive answer would then lead to a quantitative assessment of whether the substantial expenditure on this resilience enhancement is warranted by prescribed corporate limits on its cyber risk appetite. Resilient organizations are less prone to strategic surprise.

### 8.7.9 Building Back Better

In the depth of the financial crisis in November 2008, President-elect Obama's chief of staff, Rahm Emanuel, looked forward optimistically: 'You never let a serious crisis go to waste. And what I mean by that – it's an opportunity to do things you could not do before'.[24] In earthquake engineering, there is an extended resilience concept that reconstruction after an earthquake should not merely aim to restore a building to its pre-earthquake state, which was evidently seismically vulnerable, but to make it more earthquake-resistant in the future. This is called building back better. The same concept applies to reconfiguring a computer system after a major cyber attack. Merely restoring previous functionality with its exposed security vulnerabilities is a poor short-term option; far superior is building in more robust, enhanced security from the outset. For example, if overall system failure can be traced back to a single item failure, which could have either a technological or human source, then introducing some extra redundancy could mitigate this source of cyber risk in the future.

After Target suffered a massive data breach in 2013, details of which are given in Chapter 1, the task of building back better started with Target doing something it had never done before – appoint a chief information security officer (CISO). An experienced CISO was hired from General Motors to lead the post-breach response. Upgrading payment terminals was clearly essential, and $100 million was spent to support chip-and-PIN credit and debit cards, which had been introduced in Europe some years before. Whether it was the cost of hiring a top CISO or upgrading payment terminals, even a simplified VaR analysis would have demonstrated these to be cost-effective security enhancements, considering that customer confidence decline would have sharply limited its corporate cyber risk appetite.

## 8.7.10 Events Drive Change

Cyber criminals learn from each other, and so do their victims. Organizations can build back better, not just when they themselves have suffered loss, but when others have had this misfortune. The Target breach was a wake-up call not just for the retailer's own management, but for management right across corporate America. A survey conducted of 20,000 IT practitioners in the United States by the Ponemon Institute found that respondents' security budgets increased by an average of 34% in the year following the Target breach, with most of those funds used for security information and event management (50%), end point security (48%), and intrusion detection and prevention (44%).[25] Some 60% of respondents also said they made changes to their operations and compliance processes in response to recent well-publicized data breaches: 56% created an incident response team, 50% conducted training and awareness activities, 48% added new policies and procedures, 48% began using data security effectiveness metrics, 47% added specialized education for the IT security staff, and 41% added monitoring and enforcement activities.

From such substantial remedial security measures, organizations show they can be fast learners in cyberspace, and the cyber security market is seen to be highly adaptive, swift, and responsive to new commercial opportunity. Indeed, the digital revolution would not have happened so rapidly had it not been for the spirit of technical enterprise and ingenuity that digital pioneers have abundantly displayed in overcoming enormous challenges. Back in 1996, the Clinton-Gore vision of having the internet in every American school seemed blighted by the proliferation of carcinogenic asbestos in buildings, which made it prohibitively expensive and risky to run internet cables through old school walls. Wi-Fi was the innovative and resilient answer to a seemingly formidable obstacle. In a most timely fashion, Wi-Fi was invented and first released for consumers the year afterwards, 1997.

Transcending the physical barriers of old building construction, this seminal advance in educational opportunity has been crucial in making internet access a basic right of a US citizen. Wi-Fi has also been a major opportunity for cyber criminals, especially public Wi-Fi. Data over this type of open connection is often unencrypted and unsecured, and consequently vulnerable to man-in-the-middle attacks whereby sensitive data can be intercepted. To keep at least one step ahead of cyber criminals, a continuous investment increase in security education will be essential.

### 8.7.11 Education for Cyber Resilience

The universal availability to US schoolchildren of Wi-Fi is now crucial for filling the looming cyber security skills gap. Demand for cyber security professionals is growing faster than the overall IT job market. Many more of the millennial cohort are needed to train and work as cyber security professionals. The increasing demand for young cyber security staff should serve a valuable societal purpose in providing gainful employment for hackers of rather modest IT skill and knowledge, who might struggle to get a well-paying job in a tight IT labor market.

Such average hackers might otherwise drift into a life of petty cyber crime, purchasing from better-skilled cyber criminals off-the-shelf exploit toolkits that they could use to make money illegally in cyberspace. With demand for talented cyber security professionals outstripping supply now and into the foreseeable future, a life of cyber crime makes little sense for a highly able cyber security professional, unless he or she has a penchant for illegal hacking, in which case legitimate and fulfilling government employment at the National Security Agency (NSA) or Government Communications Headquarters (GCHQ) beckons. Collectively, NSA and GCHQ may have the best offensive cyber attack capability, which in itself is an employment draw.

Aviation resilience in the skies ultimately depends on the skill, training, and experience of airline pilots. The safety of airlines varies quite significantly, even though their fleets of Boeing and Airbus aircraft may be quite similar. The cyber security of corporations also varies quite significantly, even though their Microsoft and Apple computer systems may also be quite similar. Cyberspace resilience ultimately depends on the skill, training, and experience of smart cyber security professionals who have the knowledge, capability, and motivation to defend their organization effectively against a continuous barrage of targeted and random cyber attacks, some of which are masterminded by elite state-sponsored hacking teams.

## 8.7.12  Improving the Cyber Profession

In any professional adversarial contest, the outcome depends heavily on the quality of the best players. Nobody appreciates this as much as the North Koreans, Chinese, and Russians, with their prestigious and highly competitive cyber academies. To match such training centers of cyber excellence, the UK National Cyber Security Centre has offered bursaries, specialist training, and paid work placements to a thousand young British students. This training initiative has had the support of major international defense contractors, as well as the City of London Police.

More ambitiously, with additional US expenditure on national security programs, the Pentagon could establish a US National Cyber Academy to defend the nation in cyberspace. This academy would be rather like the existing sea, land, and air academies at Annapolis, West Point, and Colorado Springs. The underlying rationale for this investment is the realization that winning in cyberspace is fundamentally a matter of cyber security skill and expertise.

Beyond the government, recruiting and retaining the best cyber security staff should be a priority of every cyber-resilient organization. In 2018, 70% of CISOs reckoned that lack of competent in-house staff was their top security threat. Other than being targeted by a cyber attack, the resilience of a corporation may be severely tested if one or more of its leading cyber security team were to leave. From the CISO downwards, robust backup plans need to be prepared for this contingency. Management consultants highlight the importance of both CISO succession planning and developing others to represent the CISO. The sooner that individuals are trained and prepared for this role, the more resilient a corporation will be.

## ENDNOTES

1. NIST (2018a), Cybersecurity Framework v1.1.
2. Pacific Crest analyst Rob Owens, quoted in *Investor's Business Daily* News, 10 June 2016.
3. Cybersecurity Ventures, Cybersecurity Market Report Q4 2016.
4. Johnson (2017).
5. Wood (2014).
6. Penenberg (2013).
7. Wreathall (2006).
8. Seals (2017).
9. Trump (2017).
10. Wreathall (2006).
11. ACPO (2012).
12. Grimes (2016).
13. CREST (2013).
14. Murray et al. (2017).
15. Cole (2015).
16. Bartman and Kraft (2016).
17. George (2016).
18. Woo (2011).
19. Moody's Investors Service (2015).
20. EIOPA (2017).
21. See References for list of publications by CCRS.
22. Harmer (2017).
23. Luan (2016).
24. Selb (2008).
25. Ponemon Institute (2015).

# CHAPTER 9

# Cyber Insurance

## 9.1  BUYING CYBER INSURANCE

### 9.1.1  Types of Cyber Insurance

Many companies choose to protect themselves against damaging cyber losses by buying cyber insurance. At least a third of all large companies in the United States buy specific cyber insurance. In many other countries the number of companies that have cyber insurance is lower, but increasing rapidly.

Insurance for cyber losses is one of the fastest-growing lines of insurance business, and is rapidly becoming a standard component of companies' risk management strategy to protect themselves against cyber loss.

There are various types of insurance available to cover cyber losses:

- *Stand-alone commercial cyber insurance* (also known as 'affirmative' cyber insurance) typically to reimburse a company for the costs it would incur as a result of a cyber attack such as a data breach or network compromise.
- *Errors and omissions (E&O) insurance* to cover a company's liability to a third party, for example if the third party suffers a privacy loss from the company having a data breach. E&O liability insurance is one of the oldest forms of cyber insurance.
- *Commercial property all-risks insurance* to cover physical damage and the business interruption that the physical damage causes if the damage results from a cyber attack. However, insurers are increasingly making cyber an explicit exclusion for commercial property insurance, and instead offering it as an extension for an additional premium payment. Be sure to clarify with the insurer whether a commercial property insurance policy covers cyber loss.

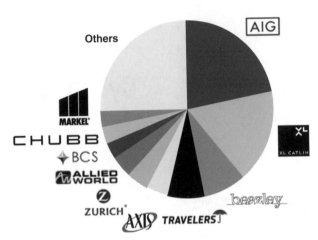

**FIGURE 9.1** Leading cyber insurance companies by market share (admitted market US 2017). Source: S&P Global Market Intelligence; SNL.

- *Personal lines insurance*: some homeowner policies or contents insurance products now include coverage for a cyber attack on home computers, or compensation for family members having personal or financial data compromised. This is more common for personal lines insurance products aimed at high-net-worth individuals.

The stand-alone cyber insurance market is growing very rapidly; there are more than 150 insurance companies that offer a cyber insurance product, although the market is dominated by 10 or so large insurers that write three-quarters of cyber insurance policies, as shown in Figure 9.1.

### 9.1.2 Choosing a Cyber Insurance Product

Choosing an insurance product to protect your company against potential cyber losses means deciding what coverage you want, and then the amount of cover, i.e. the upper limit of reimbursement that you will get from the insurer if an event occurs. Each insurance company offers one or more standardized products – a fixed set of coverages within a policy. Products vary significantly across the market. Table 9.1 shows the different types of coverage that are available in the market, and how commonly that coverage is included in the standardized products that are offered across the market.

Which coverages you think you need will depend on your own risk assessment, and the financial protection that you would want for the operations in your business that could suffer losses from a cyber attack.

Coverages are either for 'first party' – i.e. for losses or costs that are incurred directly by your company (such as the cost of responding to an incident or replacing damaged equipment), or for 'third party' – i.e. the compensation that you might have to provide to another individual or organization as a result of your company suffering a cyber incident (such as providing credit monitoring and compensation to people whose personal data could be leaked from your safekeeping).

Insurance brokers typically provide advice on which products are being offered across the market that best suit your needs, and will arrange and purchase the insurance product on your behalf, for a brokerage fee.

The standard cyber insurance policy is a one-year fixed term. The insurer is likely to offer a renewal at the end of the year, but this is not guaranteed. The policyholder may also shop around for a new policy from an alternative insurer. Typical churn rates of insurance policyholders not renewing with their insurer, for whatever reason, are less than 10%.

### 9.1.3   How Much Cover Should I Buy?

Insurance products are priced according to the amount of coverage being provided; prices will vary significantly from one insurance company to another, and will also be rated according to the risk that the insurer estimates that your company represents. On average across the market, an annual premium payment of somewhere around $120,000 buys around $10 million of limit[1] – the limit means the maximum that the insurer will pay out under any claim. Limits of $50 million or more are proportionately more expensive: somewhere over a million dollars of annual premium. Small and medium-size companies may buy a modest amount of cover, such as $1 million of limit, and spend a few thousand dollars in annual premium for this cover.

Often the purchase of cyber insurance is a requirement of the board or senior management of a company, as a governance or risk management best practice. Cyber insurance can be part of an integrated strategy for protection against potential cyber loss, alongside security spending, staff training, and other components. Deciding how much insurance protection to buy should come from an analysis of how much financial contribution would offset the loss from the range of potential cyber losses that the company could realistically expect.

**TABLE 9.1** Coverages available in cyber insurance products, and how common they are in products being offered across the market.

| Cyber Loss Coverage | Party | What is Included in the Coverage | Percentage of Products |
|---|---|---|---|
| Breach of privacy direct costs | First | The cost of responding to a data breach event, including IT forensics, external services and specialists that might be employed, internal response costs, legal costs, and restoring systems to preexisting condition. | 92% |
| Breach of privacy liability | Third | The cost of dealing with and compensating third-party individuals whose information is or may have been compromised by a data breach event, including notification, compensation, providing credit-watch services, and other third-party liabilities to affected data subjects. | 92% |
| Data and software loss | First | The cost of reconstituting data or software that have been deleted or corrupted. | 81% |
| Incident response costs | First | Direct costs incurred to investigate and close the incident to minimize post-incident losses. | 81% |
| Cyber extortion | First | The cost of expert handling for an extortion incident, combined with the amount of the ransom payment, if required. | 73% |
| Business interruption | First | Lost profits or extra expenses incurred due to the unavailability of IT systems or data as a result of cyber attacks or non-malicious IT failures. | 69% |
| Multimedia liabilities (defamation and disparagement) | First and third | Cost for investigation, defense cost, and civil damages arising from defamation, libel, slander, copyright/trademark infringement, negligence in publication of any content in electronic or print media, as well as infringement of the intellectual property of a third party. | 65% |
| Regulatory and defense | First | Covers the legal, technical, or forensic services necessary to assist the policyholder in responding to governmental enquiries relating to a cyber attack, and provides coverage for fines, penalties, defense costs, investigations, or other regulatory actions where in violation of privacy law, and other costs of compliance with regulators and industry associations. Insurance recoveries are provided where it is legally permissible to do so. | 62% |
| Reputational damage | First | Loss of revenues arising from an increase in customer churn or reduced transaction volumes that can be directly attributed to the publication of a defined security breach event. | 46% |

| | | | |
|---|---|---|---|
| Network service failure liabilities | Third | Third-party liabilities arising from security events occurring within the organization's IT network or passing through it in order to attack a third party. | 42% |
| Contingent business interruption | First | Costs of business interruption to the insured resulting from the IT failure of a third party, such as a supplier, critical vendor, utility, or external IT services provider. | 33% |
| Liability – technology errors and omissions | Third | Coverage for third-party claims relating to failure to provide adequate technical service or technical products and software, including legal costs and expenses of allegations resulting from a cyber attack, error, or IT failure. | 27% |
| Liability – professional services errors and omissions | Third | Coverage for third-party claims relating to failure to provide adequate professional services or products (excluding technical services and products), including legal costs and expenses of allegations resulting from a cyber attack, error, or IT failure. | 23% |
| Financial theft and fraud | First | The direct financial loss suffered by an organization arising from the use of computers to commit fraud or theft of money, securities, or other property. | 23% |
| Intellectual property (IP) theft | First | Loss of value of an IP asset, expressed in terms of loss of revenue as a result of reduced market share. | 23% |
| Physical asset damage | First | First-party loss due to the destruction of physical property resulting from cyber attacks. | 19% |
| Death and bodily injury | Third | Third-party liability for deaths and bodily injuries resulting from cyber attacks. | 15% |
| Liability – directors and officers | First | Costs of compensation claims made against the individual officers of the business, including for breach of trust or breach of duty resulting from cyber-related incidents; and can result from alleged misconduct or failure to act in the best interests of the company, its employees, and its shareholders. | 13% |
| Cyber terrorism | First | Physical damage, such as fire and/or explosion, caused as a result of a cyber attack that is designated an act of terrorism by the appropriate government agency. | 12% |
| Liability – products and operations | Third | Third-party liabilities arising in relation to defects in products or operations provided by the insured, such as software and services. | 8% |
| Environmental damage/pollution cover | 1st | Cover for costs of cleanup, recovery, and liabilities associated with a cyber-induced environmental spill, pollution, or release of hazardous materials. | 4% |

*Source:* CCRS (2016c).

Insurance rates vary every year as a result of the previous year's claims costs to the insurer and how competitive the market is, so the amount of coverage that can be purchased for a given budget of insurance spend varies over time. As the insurance market grows and attracts more insurance companies to offer products, the rates soften and decrease. When a bad year occurs with many costly insurance claims, the rates increase. A cyber catastrophe, where thousands of companies file insurance claims from the same underlying event, causes a particularly large hike in cyber insurance rates, as it causes increases in reinsurance costs and costs of capital (the interest rates that are paid on the reserves held) to the insurer.

In addition to the limit, insurers also impose a deductible or retention where the policyholder pays the first amount of cost of a claim. Retentions are typically a proportion of the limit – between 5% and 10% – so on a policy for $1 million coverage, the insured may have to pay the first $50,000 or more of any claim. Retentions can also be for a period of time for coverages such as business interruption, where the policyholder may have to absorb the losses from, for example, the first eight hours of an outage of an information technology (IT) system, before the insurer compensates for the losses that are occurred from that amount upwards. This retention eliminates losses to the insurer from the occurrence of the more minor losses (which also occur more frequently), which reduces the insurer's cost and ensures that the policy provides protection for the more severe losses where coverage is most needed.

In more complex insurance products, individual components of coverage can be subject to additional sublimits and deductibles. There is a lot of variation in the policy wordings, and the terms and conditions offered by different insurance companies. Be sure to review the policy details and small print and ensure that these cover the types of incidents that your company needs to protect itself against.

### 9.1.4 Isn't Cyber Loss Already Covered in My General Liability Insurance?

Well, probably not actually. Insurance companies are increasingly careful about including cyber liabilities in their traditional policies for other types of coverages. Older policy wordings of commercial general liability (CGL) insurance may offer coverage language that could be interpreted as including cyber liabilities, but over time, more insurance companies have amended the wordings to exclude the potential for having to pay for cyber liabilities under a CGL product. Insurance companies are increasingly trying to provide 'affirmative' cyber insurance as a separate product that companies will need to buy (and that the insurance company can assess and manage appropriately) in preference to including it within general insurance products where the possibility for cyber events to trigger a payout is either implied under an all-risks umbrella description or ambiguous in not mentioning it or excluding it.

Senior managers may think that their company is insured for a cyber loss when in fact it isn't. Surveys in some locations suggest that over half of CEOs or CIOs of large organizations believe that they have insurance that would pay out in the event of a data breach, when in fact only a small fraction of firms actually do.[2] This misunderstanding of what insurance a company may have in place, and what coverage it provides, could be costly.

### 9.1.5   Cyber Insurance Against Property Damage

Most companies insure their buildings, facilities, and machinery against accidental damage from whatever cause, particularly where these are valuable assets or critical to the business operations. Cyber attacks can potentially trigger damage and disruption to the functioning of these facilities, and it is natural for business risk managers to want to include this threat in their protection. However, this is not straightforward in the current state of the insurance market, and may leave business managers more exposed than they realize. Insurance policies for property damage either have a schedule of perils (such as fire, explosion, wind storms, etc.) that are covered or have a more general coverage statement of covering 'all risks' with a separate list of exclusions. Cyber loss is increasingly being explicitly excluded from property insurance, and companies are instead being offered separate 'cyber physical' insurance policies or 'write-back' covers where for an additional premium, cyber is reinserted as a covered peril. A commercial property insurance policy that contains a CL 380, an LMA 3030, or an NMA 2912 clause is excluding a loss that can be shown to have been caused by a malicious cyber attack or, in some cases, IT-related malfunctions.[3] These exclusion clauses may not yet have been fully tested in courts, and some insurance commentators suggest that the difficulties in attributing cyber attacks and assessing the exact chain of events to determine proximate cause for a damaging event could cause insurers and insureds to dispute payouts, and leave insurance policyholders exposed to delays in settlement or denial of claims. It is possible to envision an explosion at an insured industrial plant where there might be suspicion that it was triggered by a failure of a remote-accessed industrial control system, and a cyber exclusion in the policy is cited as a reason not to pay out for the claim.

## HOW CYBER INSURANCE WORKS

MediaMark Inc. is a (fictional) media business with a billion dollars of annual revenue. The business places online advertising for customers, and manages sensitive consumer data on several millions of individuals. Its 10-K annual report, Section 1A on risk factors to the business, identifies potential cyber attacks and disruption to MediaMark's online advertising infrastructure as a material threat. The board decides that the company should obtain $10 million to $20 million of cyber insurance to cover potential shocks it could face in its quarterly results if it were to suffer a cyber attack. This is part of the board's strategy to reduce the likelihood of a financial shock from cyber risk. The board has decided to reduce the likelihood of a shock of $50 million or more to the balance sheet.

MediaMark calls its insurance broker and describes its needs, and the broker recommends an insurance product 'CyberSecure', offered by Eagle, a leading (equally fictional) insurance company. This offers coverage for first- and third-party losses from a data breach event and for business interruption from a number of types of cyber incidents. MediaMark fills out the Eagle CyberSecure underwriting questionnaire: a 12-page form providing information about the company and its security processes. The Eagle cyber insurance underwriter also obtains a third-party telematics report on MediaMark with scorings for network integrity that suggests a security rating of above average for the entertainment and media sector. The rating tariff for companies of this type guides the underwriter to propose that for an annual premium of $100,000, the insurer will offer $10 million of limit, with a deductible of $1 million (MediaMark will have to pay the first million dollars of any loss). The underwriter also proposes that the policy will have a sublimit of $5 million for business interruption losses. MediaMark takes the policy and reports back to the board that it has insurance in place if it suffers a cyber loss.

Some months later, during a peak period of advertising demand, the MediaMark software platform is hit by malware. This software platform matches advertisements from MediaMark's customers with online channels, but, because of the malfunction, it cannot place ads. It takes several days to repair and restore services, but this means lost earnings from advertising of $6 million. The maximum amount of business interruption loss that can be claimed under the policy is

$5 million, and MediaMark has to pay the first million as a deductible, so, after verification of the claim, Eagle makes a claim settlement of $4 million to MediaMark. MediaMark is able to show that its quarterly earnings are reduced by only 4%, rather than the 12% that would otherwise have been the case without insurance.

Cyber attacks can also cause disruption, operational failure, and business interruption by jamming or interfering with the functioning of physical systems – examples range from failures of signaling equipment through to failures of gas station pumps. If the property asset has not suffered physical 'damage', then the holder of a standard property insurance policy cannot claim for this business interruption.

Insurers are increasingly separating out the cyber coverage from other causes of loss in major classes of insurance, ranging from property insurance of offshore and onshore energy to marine, aviation, auto, and other specialized lines. In the longer run, standard insurance coverage for these classes of insurance will probably have cyber coverage folded back in at some time in the future; but in the short term, purchasers of these insurance products should not assume that they have protection against cyber threats, and need to be careful to check what their coverage includes, in order not be left exposed.

### 9.1.6 Are There Alternatives to Buying Cyber Insurance?

Of course a company's first line of defense is to minimize the risk of having a cyber loss by ensuring that security systems are state of the art, that employees behave safely, and vulnerabilities are minimized. However, even the most highly secured companies still suffer successful cyber attacks despite the best efforts of defense. Companies need to have contingency plans for managing this financial impact of a cyber attack on their balance sheets.

The main alternatives to buying cyber insurance are for a company to self-insure or to form an insurance captive. Self-insurance means not buying an insurance product but managing the likelihood of suffering a financial loss through managing the balance sheet – i.e. budgeting reserves and investing for the potential for future shocks. An insurance captive is a subsidiary company owned by a large parent company that puts risk capital into the captive instead of paying premiums to commercial insurance companies. Captives are increasingly incorporating cyber risk, typically existing captives extending their coverage into cyber, but also new captives being formed to manage the cyber risk that a major company wants to insure.[4] Mutual groups and risk swaps can be arranged between one or more companies that want to pool their risks or protect each other's balance sheets.

The limitation of finding sufficient cyber coverage from a capacity-constrained insurance industry has led to alternative cyber risk transfer solutions being developed, including mutuals and captive programs,[5] and discussion of cyber risk securitization instruments and insurance-linked securities where capital markets investors take a risk on principal in exchange for coupon payments against a risk index with a well-defined parametric trigger.[6]

## 9.2  THE CYBER INSURANCE MARKET

### 9.2.1  The Growth of the Cyber Insurance Market

The first insurance products for cyber loss appeared in the 1980s. It became a niche area of specialized insurance for liability from IT errors and omissions throughout the 1990s, boosted towards the end of the decade by fears of Y2K computer failures: the suspicion that date counters in computer software systems would not be able to cope with the date change from 1999 to 2000. The New Year's Eve street parties that year were full of people watching to see if traffic lights would fail or aircraft crash out of the skies, among them quite a few distinctly nervous underwriters and the occasional disappointed lawyer.

The first decade of the 2000s saw the launch of innovative cyber insurance products to cover the third-party liabilities from data breaches, but initially these did not offer coverage for first-party losses, and excluded anything resulting from rogue employees, and costs for fines, penalties, or regulatory actions. In the middle of the decade, coverage was added for first-party losses – for cyber business interruption, network asset damage, and cyber extortion. The US Health Insurance Portability and Accountability Act (HIPAA) set new security standards for the protection of health information about individuals, together with regulatory penalties and reporting requirements for any data that was leaked. This spurred healthcare companies to take out cyber insurance, and insurers to introduce special sublimits for this coverage.

In 2003 California became the first US state to pass a law requiring companies to notify state residents and regulators if personal information they held about them was accessed by an unauthorized person. The other US states have followed suit over subsequent years, each passing its own individual versions of similar laws, with additional federal laws creating a patchwork regulatory framework for data protection. This wave of regulation sparked the formalization of data protection management in US companies and drove the growth of demand for insurance to cover data-related liabilities.

In the 2010s, as a result both of the increase of data exfiltration cyber attacks and of regulations requiring them to be reported publicly, the number of data breaches hitting the headlines increased significantly. Publicly reported data breach events increased from just over 1800 in 2009 to 6700 in 2013.[7] Demand for cyber data breach insurance followed, with premiums paid growing to more than a billion dollars by 2015. The traditional cyber insurers were the main beneficiaries of this, but it also generated experimentation by specialist carriers, offering insurance products for cyber property damage to energy companies, for example.

Premiums from affirmative cyber insurance products continued to grow rapidly, to over $4 billion by 2017, contrasting with nearly static premium growth from other lines of insurance during a soft market for insurance products in general. As the cyber market expanded, it attracted other mainstream insurers to add cyber products to their lines of business. In 2015 fewer than 50 insurance companies were offering cyber insurance, but by 2018 more than 150 companies had affirmative cyber products available.

### 9.2.2 Cyber Insurance Is Profitable (Until It Isn't)

Those that have written significant amounts of cyber insurance have generally found it profitable, with a direct loss ratio across the industry of 48% in 2016 – i.e. less than half of the premiums was spent in paying claims – which is a lot higher margin than many other lines of insurance. But of course the insurance industry is cautious: perhaps the loss ratio seen over a few years isn't indicative of the long-term profitability of this class of insurance – a cyber catastrophe that cost the insurance industry multiple billions of dollars would wipe out many years of surplus.

More than 80% of the cyber insurance market has been from US companies, but markets outside the United States are increasingly becoming significant, with companies in other jurisdictions buying cyber insurance coverage. Regulation is a major driver of cyber insurance uptake, with data protection laws having being passed in 35 countries since 2010.[8] The European Union General Data Protection Regulation, implemented in May 2018, is the latest and most stringent example of regulation that is driving more companies internationally to manage cyber risk carefully, and to buy cyber insurance.

An increasing trend is that insurance companies are partnering with cyber security specialists to provide services that combine insurance with loss prevention and crisis management, offering pre-insurance cyber security audits and, if the insured suffers a cyber attack, providing post-event incidence response management services.

Reinsurance companies provide additional capacity by supplying reinsurance to the primary insurers, allowing risks to be diversified even further across the international markets. The cyber reinsurance market has followed the fortunes of the primary market, initially through offering quota share participation in cyber risks (paying an agreed slice of every claim), but increasingly offering excess of loss capacity – providing coverage for sudden surges in claims above an agreed threshold.

Cyber insurance has also been expanded to cover insurable losses that might be caused by terrorists. The US Terrorism Risk Insurance Act was broadened in December 2016 to include stand-alone cyber insurance policies. In April 2018 Pool Re, the UK terrorism reinsurance pool, extended its cover to include material damage and direct business interruption caused by acts of terrorism using a cyber trigger.[9]

### 9.2.3 Expectations and Reality for the Cyber Insurance Market

A global market of affirmative cyber insurance of around $6 billion in premium is a sizeable industry but is a relatively minor line of insurance business. The total premium from the whole of the property and casualty (P&C) insurance industry, also known as 'non-life', is more than $2 trillion.[10] The mainstream P&C insurance market comes from corporate entities and individuals protecting their physical assets, such as the factories, offices, and equipment used to generate a company's revenues. Many analysts see cyber insurance as a natural parallel to property insurance. As the economy becomes increasingly digital, the need to protect the information infrastructure and digital assets that corporations rely on is expected to become a major part of the insurance industry. In the future, the argument goes, there won't be a specialist class of insurance called 'cyber' (strange name anyway); instead, all insurance will essentially be a flavor of cyber, or contain cyber as one of the many perils that is included in standard coverage, as companies protect their digital assets and technological means of revenue generation; physical assets will be a smaller proportion of what needs to be protected.

Projections for future growth of the cyber insurance markets range from the aggressive to the stratospheric.[11] But past projections for how the cyber insurance industry would grow, dating back a decade or more, have been consistently disappointed. Early estimates expecting very high sustained growth rates have been sobered by a reality of steady 20% annual increases – still healthy and rewarding, but underwhelming compared with the explosive transformation that some expected.

### 9.2.4  Cautious Insurers

The reality has been that insurance companies have been cautious in entering the cyber market. Cyber risk has been difficult to price and to underwrite, and it has not been easy to manage a portfolio of policies. Unlike other lines of insurance, cyber has only a short history of experience, and actuarial analysis is made more complicated by rapid changes in the threat and loss patterns from year to year. Instead, insurance companies have sold policies that represent relatively limited exposure to themselves, chiefly through constraining the level of limit that they provide.

An estimated half of all cyber insurance policies sold are for limits of less than $1 million – i.e. the total amount that insurers are prepared to pay out from any cyber event is capped at $1 million. Limits of over $10 million are rare (less than 10% of policies written), and for a company to obtain cyber insurance coverage of $100 million or more requires the construction of complex 'towers' of coverage involving many different insurance companies, each taking a small slice. Limits are increasing over time as insurers gain confidence, but the protection being offered is not what is being requested by the market.

As we have shown, the losses to a company from a cyber attack can be many hundreds of millions of dollars. The insurer is providing some financial assistance to its policyholders in the event that they suffer an attack, but is by no means indemnifying their losses as insurers do in other lines of insurance. Companies are left to fund most of the big losses themselves. In general we estimate that insurers bear less than 10% of the losses that occur each year. If there were to be a major cyber catastrophe where large numbers of companies were hit by substantial losses, the insurance industry would probably bear 15–20% of the total loss experienced by the economy. The insurers are maintaining their profitability levels, averaging around half of the annual premium generated being paid out in claims, through tightly managed limits and deductibles representing good, safe risk management. The technique of writing a diversified portfolio of relatively small limits across large numbers of customers is standard practice for spreading the risk. In an emerging market like cyber risk, where the true nature of the risk is not yet well understood, the insurers are 'buying loss experience' – building up a database of claims year on year that will help them understand the risk and its characteristics.

### 9.2.5   Expanding Capacity for Cyber Insurance

Expenditure of around $6 billion by companies on buying cyber insurance each year contrasts with expenditure of more than $120 billion annually on cyber security.[12] It is logical that spending on loss prevention (security) would be higher priority than buying loss compensation (insurance), but in other areas of corporate risk, such as fire protection in factories, the two areas of expenditure (loss control through fire prevention engineering vs fire insurance purchasing) are more evenly balanced.

Analysts suggest that, over time, insurance should grow to become a larger share of the amount that organizations spend on cyber risk management.

If companies cannot protect against more than 10% of their potential future losses because they can only obtain policies with small limits, then insurance will stay as a limited component of their risk management strategy. For cyber insurance to become a significant-sized market, companies need to be offered limits that are meaningful against the losses that they face. For insurance companies to offer larger limits, they have to increase the capacity that they make available to cyber risk. Capacity allocation depends on insurance companies feeling confident that they have adequately assessed, and priced in, the risk of cyber catastrophe.

## 9.3   CYBER CATASTROPHE RISK

### 9.3.1   How Much Risk Capital Is Needed for Cyber Claims?

Capacity for any line of insurance depends on the risk capital needed to support it. Insurance works by insurance companies holding sufficient financial reserves (their risk capital) to pay the claims when they are needed. Day-to-day claims are less critical than the occasional surge in claims that might occur randomly or through some systemic event at rare intervals (known as 'tail risk' or 'catastrophe events').

Insurers charge an organization a premium and in exchange they promise to pay up to a limit that might be 50–100 times the premium amount if that organization has a large cyber loss, which could happen the day after it pays the premium. The economics of this for the insurer requires a very careful balance of risk estimation: how often it will expect to pay claims to policyholders, and how many organizations it can collect premiums from.

The most critical analysis for the insurer is 'correlation' – how often might a large number of policyholders have a cyber claim at the same time?

An insurer that has a premium income of $100 million has taken on an exposure (total of all limits) of perhaps half a billion to a billion dollars. Clearly, if all the companies it insures were to have a claim to their full limit in the next year, this could exceed the amount that the insurer has in reserves, and could bankrupt the insurer, or mean that it cannot pay the claims.

It is of course highly unlikely that every policyholder would be hit at the same time. Most cyber claims are individual occurrences affecting one organization, and the law of large numbers means that an insurance company that writes a large, diversified portfolio will suffer manageable rates of claims. The insurer can adjust the pricing and reserves to meet the claims demands of an average year, and as insurers build up experience over a few years they can see how much variation occurs from one year to another and build in safety margins for the fluctuations (volatility) of the claims experience.

However, the phenomenon of cyber risk means that occasionally a cyber catastrophe can occur, defined as something that triggers claims from large numbers of policyholders from the same underlying cause or event. Perhaps a much worse version of the 2017 *NotPetya* malware could be released that, instead of causing multi-million-dollar losses to several dozen corporations, hits thousands of companies, triggering full-limit claims from a sizeable proportion of the insurer's portfolio. The insurer could have run a cyber insurance business for a decade profitably, achieving low loss ratios, and then have a single year in which all the reserves it has built up – or more – are wiped out. The frequency and the severity of these multiple-claim catastrophes determine the long-term profitability and viability of cyber risk as a line of insurance business.

Regulators require insurers to hold reserves that can meet the extreme levels of claims that could potentially occur with a low probability each year, for example, with odds of 1 in 200 (a 0.5% probability) that they could occur in the next 12 months.

Assessing the probability of tail risk cyber catastrophe is critical to the viability of an insurance company maintaining a significant cyber insurance underwriting division.

## 9.3.2 Allocation of Capacity

The capacity that an insurer can make available to providing cyber insurance has to compete for capital with other lines of insurance. Large multi-line insurers provide insurance for several lines of business, including commercial property, homeowners' property, property and liabilities for energy companies, marine insurance, litigation insurance (known as 'casualty'), and a large number of other insurance classes. In these other lines of business, the tail risk assessment is more assured – there is a longer period of claims experience, and the actuarial and catastrophe models of extreme loss probabilities are more mature, so that insurers have higher levels of confidence in them.

Insurers remain reluctant to allocate big lines of capacity to cyber insurance until they can assess cyber tail risk with more confidence. The provision of cyber insurance can grow to meet the demand for it only when insurers are comfortable in assessing the tail risk and adequately including the catastrophe loading into their pricing. In principle, cyber insurance should be an attractive line to add to a property insurance business because it is not correlated with weather events or natural catastrophes so will diversify the risk capital required for the combined exposures.

### 9.3.3 Uninsurability of Cyber Risk

Warren Buffett has warned of the dangers of writing cyber insurance.[13] Some insurance professionals have gone on record saying that cyber risk is uninsurable.[14] They believe that the danger of the tail risk is too great, and it cannot function as a private market solution. In other types of risks, such as flood risk or terrorism, where the risk appears unmanageable, undiversifiable, or too costly against the willingness of the market to pay the high premiums that would be needed, government programs have been developed to either take on the risk completely or to share, pool the risk, or provide a backstop to insurers. So far, cyber risk has not needed a government partnership to enable the private insurance market to grow, but if tail risk were to become more threatening, or emerged as chiefly a geopolitical risk between military cyber warriors, then the issue of government participation would become more pressing. For now, insurers are growing their capacity in the expectation that cyber risk will be predominantly a private market solution.

### 9.3.4 Growing Confidence in the Management of Cyber Tail Risk

Insurance companies are becoming more familiar with cyber risk as a line of insurance; they are building up multiple years' worth of claims experience and underwriting practice, and improving their expertise in cyber as a risk. Analytics are improving and methods are being developed to estimate the potential for future large systemic cyber events to cause widespread patterns of large losses. Many insurers and reinsurers have built their own internal models of cyber risk, including estimates of tail risk and costs of risk capital. Insurance companies can also license models that provide independent views of cyber risk, with several modeling companies offering commercial products.[15] As insurers gain confidence in estimating their tail risk, we can expect them to allocate more capacity to cyber insurance, and to enable the cyber insurance market to attain its full potential.

## 9.4 MANAGING PORTFOLIOS OF CYBER INSURANCE

### 9.4.1 Insurance Market Segmentation

Statistics on cyber attacks show that rates of cyber loss vary very significantly for businesses of different sizes, and also between different business sectors. The demand for cyber insurance, driven by the risk and, more importantly, by the perception of the risk, is similarly varied.

A key segmentation is between the insurance market for small and medium-size enterprises (SMEs) and the market for big individual accounts, the large and premier companies. SMEs are a more volume market, with standardized policies and lower premium payments, but tend to have lower cyber security standards. Big accounts require more customized insurance terms and individual careful (and expensive) underwriting, and are likely to be more targeted by cyber attackers. The very largest companies (Forbes Global 2000 companies, for example) tend to self-insure, so the big account insurance market is dominated by large second-tier corporations.

Demand for cyber insurance is higher in some sectors than others, particularly those at higher risk. Over half of the demand for cyber insurance comes from companies in the IT, financial services, retail, and healthcare sectors, so it is natural for insurers to end up with concentrations of these in their portfolios.

Some insurance companies tend to specialize in or gravitate towards certain types of cyber insurance. As underwriting teams gain expertise in the cyber risk of certain types of companies – banking for example – they become better at assessing the risk, more profitable, and likely to receive more submissions of this type from the market. The market process tends to encourage insurer specialization and concentration, but this needs to be controlled to manage accumulations.

### 9.4.2 Accumulation Management

Portfolios of risk should be balanced and diversified. Accumulation management tries to avoid concentration risk in a portfolio. Insurers monitor accounts by size and business sector to ensure that the portfolio does not have a disproportionate over-representation in any one category. If, for example, an insurance company insures an unusually large number of retail businesses, then a cyber event that hits retail operations would cause it disproportionately higher levels of loss.

Portfolio management requires good information to be held by the accumulation management team about each of the accounts. Detailed data about the insured company and its cyber security posture is provided to the underwriters during the original submission assessment process, but it is not usual practice for all this information to be passed on into the internal portfolio management system. Standardizing to minimum cyber exposure data requirements is becoming more common, aided by published open-source data standards,[16] but is still a key challenge for many insurance companies.

The insurer's exposure managers may set a maximum for the key accumulation categories for the amount of exposure they think is healthy in any one sector or size of market. Frequent analysis of the exposure they have in each accumulation category shows if any of them have reached the maximum, and if so, they will tell their underwriters not to accept any more business in that category.

### 9.4.3 Probable Maximum Loss Scenarios

Insurers assess the potential for cyber catastrophes through a process of organizing and standardizing their exposure data and estimating potential probable maximum loss (PML) scenarios in their portfolios. They define their risk appetite – the amount that the insurance company is able or willing to lose safely from these events – and routinely run the PML scenario analysis. If they approach their risk appetite limit, they may set constraints on their underwriters accepting any more business from accounts that would contribute further losses to this scenario.

The term *probable maximum loss* is a bit of a misnomer. PML scenarios that insurance companies typically apply are not literally the probable maximum that could be experienced. They represent a severe but plausible stress test for the portfolio. Insurers know that in principle, large loss levels have an exceedance probability distribution – larger losses are diminishingly less likely, out to infinitesimally small likelihoods of cataclysmic loss; but with less well understood risks like cyber, the loss probability relationship is very difficult to define. Instead they choose an illustrative example of a hypothetical large loss that they estimate would be somewhere in this distribution, usually many multiples of the typical loss levels seen each year, and analyze this as a PML.

Most cyber insurance companies have developed or use several PML scenarios. They typically include a scenario of a surge of high volumes of data exfiltration claims from their policyholders, possibly a scenario for a widespread and lengthy outage of a market-leading cloud service provider, compromise of a supplier or subcontractor that many insureds might be relying on, a widespread campaign of malicious malware or ransomware, and scenarios that would be detrimental to the specializations and concentrations in their own portfolios, such as medical malpractice litigation for healthcare cyber insurance writers.

There are also a wide range of published cyber catastrophe scenarios, with some examples provided in Table 9.2, produced as studies and thought-leadership analyses, from practitioners, academic groups, consultants, regulators, brokers, and vendors. Some scenarios have been made available as commercial products for licensing, and others have been adopted by regulators in requiring the insurance companies they regulate to report their losses to these specified 'realistic disaster scenarios'.

Proprietary or commercial cyber accumulation management systems have become a standard approach to quantifying a company's cyber PML and managing to a strategically defined risk appetite for this class of insurance.

### 9.4.4  Probabilities of Extreme Cyber Losses

PML scenario analysis is a useful tool for assessing future loss severity, but it is more useful to insurers if they can assess how likely – or unlikely – these levels of claims payout are to occur. They need to assign probabilities to the extreme loss levels in order to allocate risk capital to cyber insurance, relative to the other lines of insurance that they manage. Risk analysts refer to this as assigning 'return periods' to losses, but this simply means the odds of this occurring in the next year (not how many years it will be before this occurs). Loss levels that might be exceeded with odds around 1 in 100 are a relatively standard benchmark (although some regulators require 1 in 200, and individual companies vary in their risk capital probability levels).

Insurers are applying a number of methods to improve their confidence in assessing tail risk. Many are reviewing the statistics of past cyber claims, which are steadily lengthening as a historical record, dating back now for around 12 years (albeit with more confidence in recent years), and extrapolating the observed variation. Over the past decade the like-for-like variation in cyber loss incidence shows that the worst year (1 in 10) was nearly 50% higher than the annual average. However, extrapolating this level of variation out to long return periods of, say, 1 in 100 suggests that losses would be around 2.25 times the average annual loss (the 1 in 100 would be 1.5 times that of the 1 in 10), which probably would not capture the full potential

**TABLE 9.2** Examples of published scenarios of probable maximum loss: hypothetical stress test scenarios used by insurance companies to assess potential cyber catastrophes that would cause large numbers of their policy holders to make insurance claims.

| PML scenario | Description | Variants | Source |
|---|---|---|---|
| *Sybil Logic Bomb* | Software bug introduced into industry standard database produces algorithmic failures for many users. | 3 variants | CCRS (2014a) |
| *Erebos* US power grid outage | Cyber attack damages US power grid generators to cause lengthy power failures. | 3 variants | CCRS/Lloyd's (2015) |
| UK power grid distribution failure | Regional rolling power outage in UK caused by hardware attack. | 3 variants | CCRS/Lockheed (2016c) |
| *Leakomania* | Data exfiltration of protected data from thousands of companies using zero day vulnerabilities. | 3 variants | CCRS/RMS (2016b) |
| Cloud compromise | Lengthy outage of regions from market-leading cloud service provider, from technical error. | 3 variants | CCRS/RMS (2016b) |
| Extortion spree | Ransomware introduced into many corporate networks demanding high payments. | 3 variants | CCRS/RMS (2016b) |
| Financial transaction interference | Multi-million-dollar heists from many banks by compromising payment transfer networks. | 3 variants | CCRS/RMS (2016b) |
| Mass DDoS | Intense and lengthy denial of service attacks directed at many e-commerce servers by hacktivists. | 3 variants | CCRS/RMS (2016) |
| Cloud service provider breach | Cloud service provider failure with variable durations for analysis of loss caused to insurer's exposure. | SQL programmable script | AIR (2016) |
| Payment processor disruption | Loss of protected credit card payment data through hack of outsourced payment provider. | SQL programmable script | AIR (2016) |

| Scenario | Description | Specification | Source |
|---|---|---|---|
| Accidental data breach scenario | Loss of protected personal data from insured businesses through accidental data breaches. | SQL programmable script | AIR (2016) |
| Domain Name System (DNS) provider outage scenario | Business interruption to insured companies through outage of variable duration to DNS provider. | SQL programmable script | AIR (2016) |
| Data theft from an aggregator | Outsourced payroll company suffers data breach by criminal hackers, losing protected data. | Scenario spec for regulatory reporting | Lloyd's (2016) |
| Cloud computing service provider | Lengthy outage of regions from market-leading cloud service provider, from malware infection. | Scenario spec for regulatory reporting | Lloyd's (2016) |
| Offshore energy – MODU DP attack | Attack on control systems of multiple mobile offshore drilling units causes damage and oil spillage. | Scenario spec for regulatory reporting | Lloyd's (2016) |
| Aviation – navigation control attack | Malware causes two large, fully laden passenger aircraft to crash at different airports. | Scenario spec for regulatory reporting | Lloyd's (2016) |
| Marine – ballast control system attack | Large ships are disabled and founder from malware introduced into their ballast control systems. | Scenario spec for regulatory reporting | Lloyd's (2016) |
| Cloud service provider hack | Multiple cloud service providers have lengthy outages resulting from hypervisor hack by hacktivists. | 2 variants plus confidence intervals | Lloyd's/Cyence (2017) |

**TABLE 9.2** (*Continued*)

| PML scenario | Description | Variants | Source |
|---|---|---|---|
| Mass vulnerability attack | Data exfiltration attacks on many companies by multiple malicious actors with access to zero day vulnerability in market-leading operating system. | 2 variants plus confidence intervals | Lloyd's/Cyence (2017) |
| Cyber-induced fires in commercial office buildings | Multiple fire ignitions in commercial property resulting from laptop fires induced by battery hack. | 3 variants | CCRS/RMS (2017) |
| ICS-triggered fires in industrial processing plants | Fires induced in factories using flammable materials through remote hack of industrial control systems (ICSs). | 3 variants | CCRS/RMS (2017) |
| PCS-triggered explosions on oil rigs | Oil rig explosions and oil leakage resulting from malicious insider access of network operations centers. | 3 variants | CCRS/RMS (2017) |
| Cyber-enabled cargo theft from port | Criminals steal cargo from multiple ports by spoofing port management systems. | 3 variants | CCRS/RMS (2017) |
| Lloyd's RDS cyber – major data security breach | Multiple attacks on large multinational organizations in one industrial sector include loss of customer data. | Scenario spec for regulatory reporting | Lloyd's (2018) |
| Cloud down | Multiple methods of causing lengthy outages of a cloud service provider. | 3 variants | Lloyd's/AIR (2018) |

for unexpected future shocks that have not been seen in the past 10 years of data.

Instead, another technique is to draw parallels from the tail risk characteristics of other classes of insurance that are better understood: comparing how cyber loss might scale with fire risk, liability insurance, or natural catastrophe. It is well understood that losses from natural catastrophes (and other man-made and natural phenomena) scale according to power laws.[17] US hurricane insurance loss at odds of 1 in 100 is around five times the loss at odds of 1 in 10, comparing like-for-like. Earthquake insurance loss in California would scale even more – the rare events are even more severe than small, more frequent occurrences, so that the 1 in 100 is eight times that of the 1 in 10.

Expert judgments from experienced practitioners can also be used to estimate how the tail risk might scale. The median estimate from a survey of 145 practitioners asked to estimate the 1 in 100 insurance industry payout was around five times that of the 1 in 10 payout.[18]

These estimate calibrations can be anchored through counterfactual analysis, such as how much loss could have occurred if the *WannaCry* malware event had played out differently.

Different cyber loss processes can be expected to scale differently. Data exfiltration losses depend on the number of population records (credit card, health, Social Security, etc.) available to be exfiltrated from organizations of different sizes. This itself should follow a scaling process, such as Zipf's law (see Chapter 6, 'Measuring the Cyber Threat'). In addition, the tail exfiltration loss frequency could potentially be boosted beyond a power law by the possibility of super-bugs that can overcome most cyber defenses. For contagious malware, the distribution of infections is governed by the mathematics of branching processes. Because of the chain-reaction characteristic of contagion spreading, the frequency of a large number of infections could be higher than a power law. For cloud outage, scaling of the loss potential emerges from the expansion in the number of organizations adopting cloud computer solutions and using cloud storage facilities, and from the size distribution of corporations. Extreme outages due to external hazards are likely to follow a power law, in accordance with the fractal geometry of nature.

Probabilistic stochastic models of cyber risk provide better estimation of how the loss process can be expected to scale. These assess the full range of variables that determine how severe a cyber loss can be, and how it might scale in terms of the numbers of companies that could make claims, and the severity of the claims costs that could ensue. These depend on the estimation of the probabilities that are assigned to each variable in the event tree, but are useful tools to explore uncertainty and potential scaling of loss.

Large numbers of simulations are generated of different scenarios of outcome for a particular loss process, and stochastic models provide a rich data set of potential outcomes, with their associated probability of exceedance of a given level of loss.

These models help insurers gain confidence in the likelihood of tail risk extreme losses, and improve the risk capital decisions they make.

## 9.5 CYBER INSURANCE UNDERWRITING

### 9.5.1 Rating and Risk Selection

Each insurance company has its own pricing tariff for the companies it sells cyber insurance to. Insurers categorize companies by various attributes, such as the jurisdictions they operate in, the company sizes, and their activities, to reflect their risk profiles and the pricing the insurer would want for covering that risk.

Insurance companies try to minimize their exposure to having a major claim, and to control the volatility of their loss ratio, by selecting companies with the lowest risk through their underwriting process. The primary objective is to avoid experiencing a large loss, particularly a 'limit loss' – a loss that will exhaust one of the large limits offered on a major account. Many insurers have low tolerance for having a large loss in one of their major accounts.

### 9.5.2 Cyber Loss Ratio Variation

The direct loss ratio of a portfolio measures the claims paid out relative to the premium income. Direct loss ratios for affirmative cyber insurance from 2013 to 2017 averaged around 50%, but loss ratios vary significantly between companies and from year to year. The top 10 companies by market share of cyber insurance had direct incurred loss ratios in 2016 that ranged from 6% to 81%.[19] Their loss ratios also vary significantly from one year to the next. These are companies with sizeable portfolios, from at least 3% to 22% share of the cyber insurance market. This variability in loss ratio between leading insurance companies is considerably more than in lines of insurance that are more mature and where the risk is better understood.

Loss ratio variation between insurers is a result of different coverages and limits, approaches made to compensating claimants for losses, and the types of companies that they have in their portfolios. But a major reason for the differences in loss ratios between insurance companies is their risk selection and underwriting.

Each insurance company has a system for selecting the companies that it insures from the applications that it receives. Insurers apply criteria to identify the companies that they believe will be least at risk from future cyber losses. This is a complex assessment. There is no unified approach for risk selection, and there are widely different techniques being used. Most companies rely on the personal expertise of knowledgeable and specialized underwriters. Most companies augment the personal skills of their underwriting teams with cyber risk rating systems and external information sources on the companies they review. The skill levels required, and the due diligence processes that experienced underwriters undertake, make cyber insurance business acquisition an expensive process.

### 9.5.3 Causes of a Large Loss

A large loss could be a claim above, say, a million dollars. Limits currently being offered in the market are gradually increasing, but less than half of affirmative policies are estimated to have limits above $1 million, and around 10% have limits above $10 million. Limits of $100 million or more are rare, but are being offered by some insurers.[20] The focus of specialist underwriting attention is on the larger companies that are purchasing these high limits.

A loss of over $1 million could be inflicted on a company by having a data exfiltration attack that compromised the protected personal data of more than 100,000 people (a P5 event). A loss of $10 million could be expected from the loss of personal data of five million people (a P6 event). Losses could be very much higher if certain types of sensitive data are lost (for example, credit card, bank account credentials, or medical data), and if companies mishandle the data breach or suffer punitive litigation. Around 10% of data breach claims involving over 20,000 records have cost their companies more than $10 million. There have been a number of highly publicized data breaches costing companies hundreds of millions of dollars, for example Target Corporation in 2013 and Anthem in 2015.

Data breaches are the most common types of large cyber losses, but losses costing multiple millions of dollars have also been inflicted on companies by the infestation of malware, denial of service attacks, financial transaction interference, and business interruption from failures of networks, server functionality, and counterparties.

The principle of insurance means that these losses need to be covered by the insurance industry, and each insurer accepts that it will pay out its fair share of losses, but in practice each insurer would prefer not to be the single company holding the individual policy that has the rare and very large loss.

## 9.5.4  Shaping Portfolios by Underwriting

A cyber insurance policy typically binds for a year and cannot be canceled. The underwriter is essentially making an estimate of the risk for the year following the contract. Insurers can reshape their portfolios as contracts come up for renewal by deciding not to renew. In reality, however, insurance tends to be a relationship business where long-term, multi-year relationships are common between insurer and policyholder. Acquisition of new accounts is a resource-intensive process, so churn rates of policies in an insurer's portfolio tend to be relatively low. A major claim would not necessarily result in an insurer deciding not to renew a policy.

When an underwriter accepts an application and adds a new policy to the portfolio, this changes the risk profile of its total exposure. In more sophisticated underwriting the company assesses the marginal difference of adding each major new risk into its portfolio. Adding a new risk typically adds to the total risk capital required to support the portfolio, but may not be completely additive. Some risks diversify the portfolio and so improve the efficiency of the use of the available risk capital.

## 9.5.5  The Underwriting Questionnaire

Insurers typically underwrite by gathering and assessing information about the applicant. The information collected is used to assess the level of risk represented by the applicant organization. Applicants for large limits are commonly categorized as a highly protected risk (HPR). The value of HPR accounts justifies a more resource-intensive assessment of their cyber vulnerability and may involve in-depth assessments by third-party security consultants.[21] For the large majority of applications representing smaller premium income, an underwriter can rarely justify the resources or time to carry out an in-depth vulnerability assessment in the way that a cyber security consultant may be able to. Instead, underwriters collect information on the basis of a questionnaire. Every company has its own underwriting questionnaire listing the factors that it requests, and has its own confidential process for using this information in its risk rating.

Information requested on cyber insurance underwriting questionnaires varies significantly from one company to another. Table 9.3 presents a collation of the types of information requested in different cyber insurance application questionnaires across the market. Examples of variation between different insurance companies include the way they assess data security and governance. For example, some insurers focus on the volumes of data being stored, while others are more interested in assessing data

**TABLE 9.3**  Company-specific cyber risk rating variables collected on cyber insurance underwriting questionnaires. Compilation from 32 questionnaires collected 2017.

**1. Company activities and profile**

- Business sector and activities
- Company financials
- Subsidiaries
- Executive team profiles
- Size of company (revenue)
- Legal jurisdictions
- Number of employees
- Historical experience of cyber events
- Criticality of the information systems
- List of website addresses
- Estimated monthly unique visitors
- Online trading volume
- Enterprise transacts with general public

**2. Risk management and information security culture**

- Enterprise risk management philosophy
- Business continuity/crisis incident response plan
- Chief information/chief privacy officer present
- In-house and outsourced IT services
- Number of IT staff
- Employee or contractor background checks
- IT security annual expenditure
- IT capital improvement plan
- Security awareness training for all staff
- Regulatory, PII, PCI DSS, HIPAA, and/or cyber essentials compliance
- Information security/privacy policy
- Procedures for employee termination

**3. Confidential records and data management**

- Types of records and confidential data held:
  - PII – personally identifiable information
  - PCI – payment card information
  - PHI – personal health information
  - CCI – commercially confidential information, trade data, and secrets
  - IP – intellectual property
- Volumes of records and data stored and/or processed, including average and maximum
- Data shared with third party or cloud provider
- Data governance policy
- Encryption practices of confidential data
- Data retention and destruction policy
- Backup processes and recovery

**4. IT network configuration**

- Structure, size, and configuration of network
- Operating systems and main systems
- Network security system software and provider
- Security standards – such as NIST, PCI DSS, CIS Top 20 critical security controls and ISO 27001 quality standards
- List of all major technology providers, software vendors, system components, or other service providers
- Cloud/on-demand service provider(s)

**TABLE 9.3**   *(Continued)*

- Vendor management practices
- Firewall: type, configuration, updating, and testing
- Sizing of firewalled separate data storage compartment
- Antivirus systems and suppliers
- Network intrusion detection systems
- Remote access procedures
- Change management control policy
- Telephone system settings

5. **Cyber security controls**
- Cyber incident response plan
- Maintenance of internal software white list
- Hardware life cycle assessments
- Mobile device security, tablets, smartphones
- Cyber security testing procedures and audits

- External security audit or penetration tests
- Processes for patching vulnerabilities
- USB controls
- Password cryptography management processes
- Email protocols and email security system
- Laptop encryption and security
- Incidents logs

6. **Other underwriting procedures**
- Supply chain vulnerabilities
- Operational technology (OT) security
- Wide range of other questions and assessments

*Source:* CCRS (2018g).

on-site versus being held or processed off-site by a third party. Other comparative studies of insurance application forms have identified that underwriting questionnaires do not align well with cyber security industry standards in, for example, failing to address questions concerning inventories of authorized or unauthorized devices or software.[22]

### 9.5.6   Predictive Power of Company Attributes

Insurance companies calibrate the information from their questionnaires against their past cyber claims data to see how well these attributes correlate with past companies that have had cyber losses. They use data science to assess how well combinations of attributes predict the likelihood of that company having a future cyber loss. Unlike other types of insurance, the fact that a company has had a cyber loss in the recent past is not very predictive of its likelihood to have another loss in the short term future, presumably because companies react to make successful changes to their cyber security standards following a successful cyber attack. The company size, and the company's area of business activity, are important determinants of how likely they are to have a future cyber loss. Many other attributes add to the statistically predictive power of company characteristics in cyber risk ratings.

Insurers are increasingly making use of telematics data to assist with company-specific cyber risk ratings. These are non-intrusive detection techniques for scanning a company's external attack surface and deriving information on the vulnerabilities of the company, and its security posture. A number of third party companies provide telematics cyber security scoring services to insurance companies. Attributes that can be detected remotely using telematics, such as the presence of unauthorized botnet traffic on a company's network, unprotected access ports on external servers, and failures to update software with the latest security features ('patching cadence'), can be shown to have correlation with cyber loss incidence.

As data science and claims experience grows, insurers are becoming increasing precise about calibrating cyber risk for rating and pricing of individual accounts.

## 9.6 CYBER INSURANCE AND RISK MANAGEMENT

### 9.6.1 Protecting the Balance Sheet

Cyber insurance should play a significant role in a company's risk management strategy for dealing with cyber threats.

A company will naturally invest in cyber security and in measures to minimize the possibility of a having a cyber loss, and having insurance is a corollary to this. Even the companies with the best IT security and highest expenditure on cyber protection still suffer successful cyber attacks. Companies need to have contingency plans for managing the financial impact on their balance sheet of a potential large loss from a cyber attack. Cyber attacks have been responsible for many missed quarterly earnings reports, which have been punished by shareholders, credit providers, and business counterparties. It is more expensive in terms of the interest rates charged to access funds through borrowing after the event has occurred, particularly if credit ratings have been impaired as a result. Insurance premium payments smooth out cash flows and protect the balance sheets from shocks, with insurance receivables compensating for unexpected payouts. If cyber insurance were available on the scale that it is needed, then this would be a major benefit to the efficient risk management of an organization.

The fundamental principles of insurance are that each company at risk pays a premium contribution into a mutual pool of similar stakeholders, which spreads the risk and enables each to be compensated when it needs to be. This principle, from fire insurance in the seventeenth century onwards, has proven to be a more efficient use of capital than each company building its own financial reserves against unexpected loss shocks of this type. The modern private sector insurance industry has become an efficient, well-regulated, and secure pool of capital, with sophisticated mechanisms for syndicating, reinsuring, and accessing investment markets to provide cost-effective risk transfer products. This financial services expertise needs to be fully applied to the management of cyber risk, at scale and integrally incorporated into the economic activities of the digital economy. It is far from that today.

### 9.6.2    Creating a Cyber Insurance Industry to Meet Corporate Needs

The insurance industry has been slow to make meaningful capacity available. Insurance managers have approached cyber risk cautiously, with good reason, as insurers could lose very large multiples of the income they generate if they assess the risk incorrectly. They fear that the risk may not be insurable. If state-sponsored cyber warriors from another country were to carry out widespread attacks on commerce, private capital could potentially be insufficient or unable to deal with an attack that is effectively an act of war. It may require government backstops or risk sharing to enable a fully functioning cyber insurance market at the scale that is required.

If the insurers are too slow in developing their market to provide a service that will meet the needs of the companies that hold that risk, then companies will find alternative means of dealing with it. The insurance industry is in danger of becoming irrelevant as a solution for holders of cyber risk. It is important that the industry grasps the opportunity and expands capacity to play a full part in making our society safer against cyber attacks.

### ENDNOTES

1. Advisen (2015).
2. HM Government and Marsh (2015); 52% of CEOs or CIOs in large organizations in the UK in 2015 believed they had cyber insurance data breach cover, when only 10% of them actually did.
3. Marsh & McLennan Companies (2014).
4. Business Insurance (2017); Aon (2016); Marsh (2016).
5. Aon (2017).
6. Artemis (2017).

7. RMS Cyber Loss Experience Database.
8. DLA Piper (2018).
9. Pool Re (2017); CCRS (2017b).
10. Swiss Re (2018).
11. Allied Market Research (November 2016), cyber insurance market report; Security Week (Lennon 2016).
12. Cybersecurity Ventures (2017).
13. Kim (2018).
14. FTSE Global Markets (2016).
15. RMS (2018).
16. CCRS (2016a).
17. Woo (2011).
18. CCRS (2018b).
19. SNL (2017), US admitted market only.
20. RMS Cyber Insurance Industry Exposure Model, derived from market studies and client data.
21. Gnatek and Miller (2016).
22. Woods et al. (2017).

# CHAPTER 10

# Security Economics and Strategies

## 10.1 COST-EFFECTIVENESS OF SECURITY ENHANCEMENTS

### 10.1.1 Impact of Security on Cyber Loss Likelihood

Everyone who attends a major information security convention is confronted with a bewildering range of vendors offering products to enhance cyber security. How can you choose between security products? How can you evaluate the effectiveness of the protection they promise? How can you integrate a suite of solutions and components into an integrated information security solution?

It is not our intention in this chapter to provide a buyers' guide to products, or to recommend one set of solutions over another. There is no universal answer to the security solution for all companies. Each company has different needs, and the solutions, components, and strategies that work best are unique to each organization.

Instead we believe this is best evaluated within the framework of solving cyber risk. We have set out the principle that risk is assessed by evaluating the likelihood of losses of different levels of severity occurring within a given time period. We have proposed that this is built up from considering a wide range of scenarios of different cyber loss processes, including those described in Chapter 2 and adding others that might be important for your organization. Each scenario is evaluated for the loss that would occur, and the likelihood of it happening in the next year. Ranking scenarios from the highest loss downwards and summing the likelihoods cumulatively provides the likelihood of the organization having a loss of that amount or worse from a cyber event, and defines the cyber loss profile.

## 10.1.2    How Security Enhancements Change the Scenarios

The value of security enhancements can be assessed by the difference they would make to the likelihood of loss. A piece of security may reduce the frequency with which losses might occur – for example trapping a larger number of incoming contagious malware indicators of compromise than is achieved without it. Or it may reduce the size of a loss – curtailing the number of internal machines that might be infected if a piece of malware were to propagate within the organization's network. The security enhancement should be assessed for all of the scenarios in the risk evaluation to see if it makes the scenario less likely, and by how much, or if it reduces how much loss would result. The security enhancement may not impact all scenarios. Most security elements are likely to reduce both the frequency and the severity of loss, but it is worth trying to evaluate the specifics of what the element offers.

To be rigorous, the evaluation should take the 'before' baseline risk profile of the organization – the curve that defines the likelihood of each level of loss from minimal to the largest conceivable – without the security enhancement, and then an 'after' analysis with the security enhancement in place. The difference between the two is the risk-reduction benefit provided by the security enhancement.

If possible, this evaluation should be as evidence-based as possible. There are various sources of information that may feed into the assessment. The vendor of the enhancement is likely to have various claims for the efficacy of the product or service. An experienced security manager may be able to make his or her own assessment. There is usually a spectrum of security performance within a population of organizations, ranging from best to worst, and it may be possible to estimate by how much the product or service being considered would change the organization's position within this spectrum.

## 10.1.3    Cost-Effectiveness Surveys

Security costs money, and requires important investment decisions. The problem with asking cyber security vendors for their insight is that they each have their own perspective, and may make exaggerated claims to sell their product. Fortunately, help in making these decisions is provided by objective general studies undertaken by organizations such as the Ponemon Institute, which conducts independent research on information security policy. Ponemon researchers analyzed nine security technologies to assess both the percentage spending level between them and their value in terms of cost-savings to the business.[1] The findings are notable for indicating that many organizations may be spending too much on the wrong technologies. This is worrying for a conscientious chief information security officer (CISO) who wants to achieve an optimum level of corporate cyber security for a given budget, and wants to avoid being duped by a cyber security vendor over-exaggerating the effectiveness of its technologies.

### 10.1.4 Cost-Effective Technologies

The Ponemon Institute published an anonymized survey of a sample of 1254 large organizations spread across a broad range of 15 industries.[2] Information was gathered on corporate expenditure on cyber security technologies, as well as the costs of cyber crime. These are the costs to detect, recover, investigate, and manage the incident response. Also covered were the costs that result in clean-up activities and efforts to reduce business disruption and the loss of customers. From this survey, the following five technologies emerged as the most cost-effective. In order of decreasing return on investment they are listed as follows:

1. *Security intelligence systems* make use of approved white lists and blacklists, provide a baseline of the known and authorized applications and processes on the network and their attributes, support work flow and remediation, and report when unauthorized systems are detected.
2. *Advanced identity and access governance* help protect access to applications and resources, enabling additional levels of validation such as multi-factor authentication and conditional access policies. Monitoring suspicious activity through advanced security reporting, auditing, and alerting helps mitigate potential security problems.
3. *Automation, orchestration, and machine learning* enable users to gain efficiencies across their hybrid environments and provide operators and analysts with intelligent decision support, further increasing productivity.
4. *Extensive use of cyber analytics and user behavior analytics* facilitates the tracking, collecting, and assessing of user data and activities using monitoring systems. They analyze historical data logs to identify patterns of traffic caused by user behaviors, both normal and malicious, and provide security teams with actionable insights.
5. *Advanced perimeter controls* are desirable because the perimeter is becoming fuzzy. Any sort of computing device may become part of the perimeter itself, and many of these devices are mobile. The network perimeter has become a dynamic, changing barrier. The systems that interact with the network perimeter make this network dynamic.

Apart from these five technologies, lesser returns on investment are obtained from:

6. The extensive deployment of encryption technologies
7. The extensive use of data loss prevention
8. Enterprise deployment of governance, risk, and compliance
9. Automated policy management

These rankings by return on investment may be compared with rankings by actual corporate expenditure.

The technology rankings by actual expenditure are:[3]

1. Advanced perimeter controls
2. Advanced identity and access governance
3. The extensive use of data loss prevention
4. The extensive deployment of encryption technologies
5. Enterprise deployment of governance, risk, and compliance
6. Automation, orchestration, and machine learning
7. Security intelligence systems
8. Automated policy management
9. Extensive use of cyber analytics and user behavior analytics

The results may surprise many of those who make cyber security investment decisions. It turns out that there are significant differences in rankings. Most money was spent on advanced perimeter controls, which are ranked fifth in terms of cost-effectiveness. Most cost-effective were security intelligence systems, which are seventh in expenditure.

## 10.1.5 Making Smarter Investment Decisions

Five of the nine security technologies had a negative value gap where the percentage spending level is higher than the relative value to the business. One was neutral: advanced identity and access governance. The following three had a significant positive value gap: security intelligence systems; automation, orchestration, and machine learning; and extensive use of cyber analytics and user behavior analytics. Expertise in these three technologies might well be rather limited in corporate IT departments, which would partially explain the comparatively modest investment in them.

To improve the cost-effectiveness of cyber security, consideration should be given to evaluate potential over-spending in technological areas that have a negative value gap and to rebalance these funds by investing in the breakthrough cyber security technologies that should yield positive value. As part of the latter investment, it would be advantageous to hire cyber security professionals with expertise in the developing fields of security intelligence, machine learning, and cyber analytics.

Making smarter investment decisions on security technologies is a key task for a CISO, who needs to engage in strategic risk-informed discussions with the corporate CFO and CEO about cyber security policy. They will all be pleased to see evidence of a rapid return on investment in damage limitation, threat prevention, and blocking. However, if such evidence is slow to emerge, the CISO, and the budget under his or her management, may be under pressure. But it should not take a catastrophic failure of cyber security for the budget to be raised substantially.

## 10.2 CYBER SECURITY BUDGETS

### 10.2.1 How Much Should an Organization Spend on Cyber Security?

On November 8, 2017, the two former CEOs of Yahoo and Equifax, Marissa Mayer and Richard Smith, testified to the US Congress, apologizing for the billions of records lost in massive data breaches earlier that year. Contrite, and eager to demonstrate improvement in their cyber security culture, Yahoo had doubled its security team. Equifax said its budget for security had increased fourfold since its breach.

These triple-digit percentage increases in post-disaster cyber security budgets beg the question of what an appropriate budget should be – and has been. For the Bank of America CEO, Brian Moynihan, cyber security was the one function within the company with 'no budget constraints'. Realistically, there has to be some finite constraint. Just how much an organization invests in cyber security is linked with a range of criteria. Organizations that are consumer facing and that have a large attack surface, a recognized brand, highly guarded intellectual property, and compliance requirements to industry regulations and government legislation tend to outspend their peers. All of these criteria applied to both Yahoo and Equifax, which should have outspent their peers.

CISOs have to think strategically in security planning. The amount spent by an organization doesn't just affect the security for itself. It has a material impact on the security of the whole sector and its peer group. The worse your security is with respect to your peers, the greater the likelihood that you will be targeted. So it really matters what your peers are spending on cyber security. For this reason, industry reviews of cyber security expenditure, as a percentage of IT budget, are very instructive.

## 10.2.2   What Is Your Security Attitude?

Equifax Canada did not suffer a data breach, although some 8000 Canadians with dealings in the United States did have their personal credit information exfiltrated. Canadian expenditure on national cyber security is far less than across the border (as it is for all aspects of national security). But it is interesting to review cyber security budgets for Canadian organizations. The International Data Corporation (IDC) of Canada, the leading Canadian provider of intelligence for the information technology market, studied the budgets, recent breaches, maturity levels, and several other key criteria of more than 200 Canadian organizations.[4] Relevant to cyber security in other countries, IDC categorized organizations according to four distinct security profiles: defeatists, denialists, realists, and egoists.

1. *Defeatists.* This group of organizations suffers from poorly funded IT security. Underfunding and sub-par planning have caused more damage by making them more vulnerable to security breaches. They are defeatists because IT/security stakeholders and professionals tend to stop lobbying their executives for support. Manufacturing and primary industries lead this profile.
2. *Denialists.* These organizations have moderately funded IT security, but have poor security practices. Their real challenge is that they often fail to recognize how bad the situation is. They are more likely than average to suffer data breaches, yet they retain a high degree of confidence in their security prowess. One tangible problem is excessive focus on buying the right technology and not enough focus on security skills, training, and processes for better risk management. The public sector and telecoms are among organizations in this profile.
3. *Realists.* These organizations are doing a fairly good job at IT security. They may, in fact, be overspending on some items and wouldn't know it. They don't spend enough time working through a formal risk management process to properly assess and measure their ongoing performance for a given amount of investment. Retailers lead this profile.
4. *Egoists.* These are the security elites. They have spending in line with risk, suffer fewer breaches, focus on recruiting and retaining top-notch security professionals, and have achieved a high degree of maturity

across people, process, and technology. The Canadian banking and financial sector leads this profile. There are examples of public sector and service provider organizations within this profile.

The percentage of Canadian organization IT budgets spent on cyber security averages 6%, 8%, 14%, and 12%, respectively, for the four security profiles: defeatists, denialists, realists, and egoists. The defeatists are underspending, and the realists may be overspending. As a comparative reference, a predominantly US survey by the SANS Institute showed a very wide spread of security budget percentages, with significant numbers of corporations both at the low end (0–3%) and the high end (21–25%). Extra names would need to be coined for these tail categories of corporate security.[5]

### 10.2.3  Risk-Informed Security Enhancement

To avoid overspending or underspending, ideally the expected benefits of an investment in information security should be equal to the reduction in expected loss attributable to the additional security.[6] Mathematically, the optimal level of cyber security for an organization lies at the point where the expected marginal investment costs equal the expected marginal benefits derived from the investment. One approach for deriving the optimal level of investment is the Gordon-Loeb model.

The Gordon-Loeb model formulates risk assessment specifically for cyber security, and formally takes into account the potential losses from a cyber security breach, the probability of a security breach, and the different ways in which cyber security investments reduce this probability. One important model finding is that the optimal level of cyber security investment does not always increase with the level of vulnerability. It may be preferable to spend more on protecting information with a medium level of vulnerability than one with a high level of vulnerability.

From a regulatory perspective, the National Institute of Standards and Technology (NIST) has developed a risk framework for improving critical infrastructure cyber security.[7] To manage risk, organizations should understand the likelihood that an event will occur, and the resulting impact. With this information, organizations can determine the acceptable level of risk for delivery of services and can express this as their risk tolerance. With an understanding of risk tolerance, organizations can prioritize cyber security activities, enabling them to make informed decisions about cyber security expenditures.

### 10.2.4  Gauging Your Security Spend to Expected Loss

Most organizations adopt the NIST Cyber Security Framework or ISO 27001, even though practical implementation is a challenge. Loss estimation, for example, is complicated by the need to quantify the loss impact of business interruption, reputational damage, loss of intellectual property, and litigation. The probability of a security breach should take account of the various breach points on an organization's attack surface. It is a daunting task to enumerate these security failure modes and to estimate their frequency of occurrence.

---

### COST-EFFECTIVENESS OF SECURITY IMPROVEMENT

#### MediaMark's Business Case for Investing in Security Updates

MediaMark Inc., a (fictional) media company, has assessed the likelihood and severity of a wide range of cyber loss scenarios and has evaluated its overall expected loss and the odds of it having a large loss that will exceed its risk appetite. This is described in Chapter 6, 'Measuring the Cyber Threat'.

The board of directors of MediaMark decides that they will invest in additional cyber security. They recognize that they have previously been 'denialists', spending only 8% of their IT budget on security, and are prepared to become 'realists', increasing their security budget, to 14%.

They want to ensure that they spend wisely, and request a business case for their investment, with an estimation of the effectiveness that this new spend might be expected to produce, in terms of reducing their risk from cyber attack. The board considers that the potential for extreme loss – the chance of a cyber event costing the organization $50 million or more – is the highest priority to reduce. Lower losses can be absorbed, but the likelihood of this business-crippling level of loss has to be reduced.

The cyber risk analysis is built up using many hundreds of potential scenarios. Each scenario is graded by the loss it would cause and the odds of it occurring in the next year. Examples of scenarios that generate losses beyond the acceptability threshold were presented in Table 6.1. They include loss of large data sets, extensive infection by contagious malware delivering a destructive payload, and any lengthy disruption of the company's media management software platform.

This selection of scenarios has a number of causal processes that could be addressed through certain candidate security systems and changes in management processes, which will reduce the potential for these scenarios in future. They include an advanced identity and access governance system, a security intelligence system, a team to speed up patching implementation and reduce latency, and a program of staff training to improve cyber risk awareness. It is also decided to buy a cyber insurance policy to mitigate some of the loss if it were to happen. Their insurance program is described in Chapter 9.

The effects that these new systems and organizational changes will have on all the scenarios in the evaluation event set are estimated. By improving access governance, the likelihood of large data breaches is greatly reduced. Improving patching latency makes reductions in several of the scenarios where intrusion could be possible through vulnerabilities in standard vendor software. Staff training reduces the potential scale of loss and changes the likelihood of attacks using social engineering.

The assessment shows that these systems and changes in business practice will collectively reduce the odds of having a $50 million cyber event from around 1 in 50 to 1 in 100. These collective actions also reduce the losses and likelihoods from many more of the more frequent and lower-impact scenarios than the ones identified as of most concern. The security improvements are estimated to reduce the annual expected loss (all the losses averaged over time) from $5 million to $3 million.

This business case is taken to the board. The return on investment for this project, as distinct from other capital projects, is in reduced risk rather than improved earnings. This is reflected in terms of reduced cost of capital on the balance sheet. The board adopts the proposal and authorizes the expenditure, suggesting that the performance of the new steps be monitored in use, and a report of the effectiveness be brought back to the board after six months.

Notwithstanding the complexities, ambiguities, and labor of cyber risk evaluation, the technical exercise of risk analysis is inherently valuable in itself. The original Gordon-Loeb model found that cyber security budgets should not exceed a moderate proportion (37%) of total expected losses.

This is because the security offered by a cyber security budget yields diminishing returns with increased spending. The question then is how large the total expected losses might be. These could be enormous, especially if a corporation is deliberately targeted by a nation-state, like China, conducting industrial espionage. In this situation, the probability of a security breach is very high unless there is excellent security, and the loss of intellectual property could threaten the very existence of the corporation.

In January 2009, the 114-year-old Canadian-headquartered telecom Nortel filed for bankruptcy, the largest in Canadian history. Nortel's downfall coincided with the meteoric rise of Chinese rival Huawei, which today is a major global networking and telecommunications equipment and services company. Nortel had invested too little in cyber security, even though it could well afford to do so. At its height, Nortel accounted for more than a third of the total valuation of all the companies listed on the Toronto Stock Exchange. But within the IDC classification of Canadian organizations, it had been a denialist.

## 10.3    SECURITY STRATEGIES FOR SOCIETY

### 10.3.1    Finding Bugs Before the Bad Guys Do

When a dangerous weapon is lost, it had better not be discovered by a potential attacker. In 1950, an American B-36 bomber crashed near British Columbia on its way to Carswell Air Force Base in Texas. The plane was on a secret mission to simulate a nuclear strike and had a nuclear bomb on board. Several hours into its flight, its engines caught fire and the crew had to parachute to safety. The bomb was dumped in the ocean. The Cold War fear was that it would be discovered by the Russians.

The twenty-first-century fear is that the Russians might discover dangerous weapons, not in the sea, but in cyberspace. The discovery of potent zero days provides opportunist cyber surprise attack capability for an adversary. This applies not just to the Russians, but also to the Chinese, North Koreans, Iranians, and other states with a track record of cyber attacks against the United States and its Western allies, aimed at gaining military, industrial, or economic advantage.

Complete technological reliability is an engineering fantasy. The aviation industry has advanced enormously since 1950, but despite the most rigorous testing and simulation, engine fire can still happen, as it did on October 1, 2017, when an A380 engine of an Air France flight over Canada exploded. A similar accident had occurred on a Qantas

A380 flight in 2010. The accident record of an aircraft typically follows a progressive learning curve, whereby reliability increases over time as bugs in the engineering design and manufacture are gradually discovered and rectified. No matter how meticulous, diligent, and smart engineers are, a finite amount of testing and simulation cannot explore the entire parameter space of environmental conditions and system behavior.

## 10.3.2 The Odds Are Not on Our Side

The same kind of progressive learning curve applies to software reliability. Typically, the time to achieve a given level of software reliability is inversely proportional to the failure frequency level. If a software vendor aims for a very low bug frequency, there will be a substantial cost in terms of prolonged development and testing time. This is a reflection of the Pareto Principle or 80/20 rule: the main software development of a new program feature might be done on a Monday, but it may well take the rest of the week to sort out the snags.[8] Quality assurance is a painstaking and resource-intensive process.

Ross Anderson, the pioneer of security economics, conceived the following hypothetical case study to show that quality assurance is an uphill task against the second law of thermodynamics.[9] Consider a large, complex product such as a version of Windows that has a million bugs. A hacker wants to break into a military computer. He has a day job, but can spend 1000 hours for testing a year. The military quality assurance officer trying to prevent the break-in. has the full Windows source code and ancillary resources to spend 10 million hours a year for testing. After a year, the hacker has found just one bug, while the QA officer has found 100,000. However, the probability that the hacker's bug has been found is only 10%. And after 10 years, this bug may well be found, but by then the hacker might have found nine more, not all of which may be known.

Just as there will always be aircraft failures, there will always be software bugs. Indeed, the possibility of in-flight control systems being hacked is an increasing aviation concern for the future, as Wi-Fi becomes a standard passenger service. Safety and security are closely interlinked; a failure of cyber security can compromise safety. A worrying aspect of zero days is that because their weapon effectiveness is unknown and comes as a surprise, there is large uncertainty over their possible exploitation, which may result in all manner of crimes, from theft, extortion, and vandalism, to murder. The process by which zero days are found, and kept away from those with malign intent, is a crucial issue requiring strategic solutions for mitigating cyber risk.

### 10.3.3  Bug Economic Valuation

Leaving aside white hat hackers ethically motivated to provide notification of any discovered new bugs, the hunt for zero days is a lucrative international race involving the participation of diverse groups of stakeholders, as keen to win as any sports competitor. There are nation-states, both friend and foe; there are black hat hackers who might weaponize zero day exploits to target vulnerable organizations or sell as a service to cyber criminals; and there are bounty hunters who would sell directly or auction off the zero days to the highest bidder. As an example of the latter, Vupen Security, founded in 2004, was a French information security company based in Montpellier, with a US branch in Annapolis. Its specialty was discovery of zero day vulnerabilities in software from major vendors. Its mission was to sell them to law enforcement and intelligence agencies, which could then use them for both defensive and offensive cyber operations.

The only sure route for de-weaponizing zero days is if they are promptly reported once discovered. Auction outcomes are uncontrollable; the highest bid may come from a cyber criminal or an unfriendly nation-state. Also, as shown by the *ShadowBrokers*, even if zero days are found first by the National Security Agency (NSA), the possibility always exists that they may end up in criminal hands if they are stolen or even lost through negligence. Cyber risk could be mitigated if the market for zero days encouraged the rapid open reporting of software bugs. Given the economic damage that a zero day could generate, it makes economic sense if rewards for bug discovery are raised generously. But how should these rewards be valued?

Software vendors typically have a backlog of bugs to fix. Like many commercial customer services, it is not cost-effective to hire many more staff to deal with problems quickly; instead, issues are prioritized with attention paid sequentially to those that are most urgent. This explains the tradition for software vendors to remunerate only rather modestly and sometimes reluctantly those who report bugs. Irritation at an apparent lack of urgency in fixing bugs has led some bug discoverers to shame the vendor by disclosing them. Regardless of the length of its backlog of bugs, a software vendor needs to take an initiative to find additional dangerous bugs, which might be exploited to highly damaging effect by cyber criminals.

This objective might be achieved through a bug bounty program. Through crowdsourcing of bug hunters, those who run a private bug bounty program this way can engage with hundreds of top-performing security researchers, who can be incentivized by paying them adequate financial rewards. Quite apart from the bounty itself, public credit for discovering bugs is important for many bounty hunters for peer respect. Listing on a bug bounty hall of fame is an accolade that is widely appreciated. Conversely, a strict legal confidentiality requirement may be a turn-off.

In general, it would be advantageous to incentivize software vendors to fix more vulnerabilities, either through reward (higher-priced software for higher quality assurance) or penalties (for example, making software vendors liable for the losses that defects in their software cost their users).

Unlike quality assurance staff employed by a software vendor to find bugs, bounty hunters have no access to the underlying source code, unless it is open access. For them, the code is a black box. Bounty hunters can probe this black box with an array of unusual inputs and check for weird responses. Because it is impossible to check software for all possible inputs, bugs are found through such occasional weird responses. Within software black boxes are also algorithms used for decision-making that require auditing for bias as well as bugs.[10] Establishment of an algorithmic bug bounty will bring forward an era of crowd-based auditing of important algorithms to hold decision makers to account.

## PROFILE OF A BUG BOUNTY HUNTER

*Uranium238* is the alias of a prolific bug bounty hunter. Like many of his colleagues, he started as a teenager, collecting $10,000 for finding a bug in Uber's internal email system at the age of 17.[11] He is driven by curiosity and a sense of duty to report problems rather than put user security at risk. His day job is employment as a security analyst. Most bug bounty hunters go hunting as a hobby or part-time work. There is an element of good fortune and randomness in discovery of a bug paying out a six-figure bounty. Rather like big game hunting on the savannah, bug bounty hunting is rarely a full-time occupation.

*Uranium238* has no interest in picking low-hanging fruit, but enjoys the challenge of thinking outside the box to find critical bugs. The monetary reward and the sense of professional pride are also more satisfying. He tries to find at least one or two critical bugs in a program that he is hacking.

Creative thinking and imagination are the hallmarks of a successful bounty hunter, who must think beyond the code horizon of the original developers. Bug bounty hunters are constantly reevaluating the assumptions they have made about the software they are searching for critical bugs.

**TABLE 10.1** Bug vulnerability classification.

| Priority | Business Impact | Vulnerability Types |
|---|---|---|
| Critical | Vulnerabilities that cause a privilege escalation | Remote code execution; vertical authentication bypass |
| High | Vulnerabilities that affect the security of the platform | Lateral authentication bypass; direct object reference |
| Medium | Vulnerabilities that affect multiple users | URL redirect; cross-site request forgery |
| Low | Vulnerabilities that affect single users | SSL misconfigurations; sender policy framework issues |
| Acceptable | Vulnerabilities deemed an acceptable business risk | Code obfuscation; debug information |

*Source:* Bugcrowd (2017).

A survey of bug bounty programs shows that organizational security maturity is the crucial basis for determining how to reward a vulnerability.[12] An organization having a more mature security program has a culture with security-focused processes in place, and with the CISO reporting to the CEO and communicating with the board. For such a cyber-security-conscious organization, vulnerabilities will require more time, effort, and skill to find, because the organization already is committed to minimizing their occurrence.

Another determinant of the time, effort, and skill is the importance of the vulnerability discovered in terms of the consequent technical and business impact. This importance can be graded qualitatively in terms of a priority index: critical, high, medium, low, or acceptable. Examples of types of vulnerability that would be assigned these priority indexes are shown in Table 10.1. The payout will depend on both the priority assigned to the bug and the security maturity of the organization.

The lowest payout may be only $100 for a low-priority bug found in an organization that has only basic cyber security and a corporate ethos that security is a necessary evil. However, for a critical priority bug found in an organization with a deeply embedded sense of cyber security, the payout may be in excess of $15,000. Organizations tend to start out with lower reward ranges and increase them over time. Lower reward ranges can bring initial success; however, increasing the reward range allows organizations to compete for talent within the market.

For a given piece of software, the number of remaining undiscovered bugs diminishes over time. Correspondingly, the chance of discovering a bug decreases over time. If searching for bugs in this software is to remain a worthwhile enterprise for a professional bug hunter, then the reward for bug discovery needs to be raised progressively. With the likelihood of making a discovery declining and the reward rising, a bug hunter making a decision on resource allocation encounters the classic eighteenth-century St Petersburg Paradox.[13] Associated with the Bernoulli family of mathematical genius, this paradox considers how much a gambler would pay to play a game with progressively smaller chances of winning an ever-greater jackpot. Doubtless, Russian hackers would be familiar with this paradox, named after the former Russian capital, and would focus on the fresher opportunities for finding zero days. As one example of the lure of the new, the issuance of a software patch can spur the bug hunting community into a frenzy of working around the clock to find any new bugs introduced inadvertently.

### 10.3.4 *Heartbleed* – A Hidden Vulnerability

At the other end of the bug age spectrum, some extremely dangerous vulnerabilities have been found in mature software after lying hidden for a number of years. One of these was the critical *Heartbleed* vulnerability in the Open SSL Cryptography library. The problem dated back to a programming error introduced by an individual German developer, Dr Robin Seggelmann, near midnight on New Year's Eve 2011, and opened a door for cyber criminals to extract sensitive data directly from a server's memory without leaving any traces. The curious origin of the *Heartbleed* bug encouraged the conspiracy theory that it may have been planted by a government security agency. In the wake of the Edward Snowden revelations, Dr Seggelmann stated it was entirely possible that intelligence agencies had been using the bug over the past two years.

Anderson and Moore pointed out that, as in a medieval siege, carelessness by the weakest link can compromise security.[14] Program correctness can depend on minimum effort (the most careless programmer introducing a vulnerability), whereas software validation and vulnerability testing might depend on the sum of everyone's efforts.

Generally speaking, obscure bugs are very difficult to discover, and it takes the most capable of bug hunters to have a reasonable chance of finding them. *Heartbleed* was discovered independently by Neel Mehta of Google's security team, who collected a $15,000 bounty, and Codenomicon, a Finnish cyber security company. After finding a number of flaws in software used by many end users while researching other problems, such as *Heartbleed*, Google established in July 2014 a full-time Project Zero team of clever cyber bug specialists dedicated to finding such vulnerabilities, not just in Google software but in any software used by its users.

### 10.3.5   Bug-Hunting Businesses

With the changing competitive market for bug discovery, in the following year the French information security firm Vupen, stigmatized as a modern-day merchant of death, metamorphosed into a new company, Zerodium. Recognizing the market need for the discoverers of the worst bugs to be best remunerated, Zerodium has paid premium bounties and rewards to security researchers to acquire their original and previously unreported zero day research affecting major operating systems, software, and devices. Zerodium has focused on high-risk vulnerabilities with fully functional exploits, and has paid the highest rewards on the market. The amounts paid by Zerodium to researchers to acquire their original zero day exploits have depended on the popularity and security strength of the affected software, as well as the quality of the exploit.

High prices of a million dollars or more are, on the one hand, an encouraging reflection of the prevailing strength of security, which is reassuring for cyber security officers. On the other hand, there is cause for concern about the very existence of zero days that might pose a serious threat to particular vulnerable targets. To mitigate such concern, Zerodium sells on the expensively acquired zero days to major corporations in defense, technology, and finance, which are prepared to pay the substantial costs of advanced zero day protection. In addition, the highly selective clients of this Washington-based corporation include government organizations searching clandestinely for specific tailored cyber security capabilities. Cyber security agencies within the Western alliance would be obvious clients for the subscription service provided by Zerodium.

### 10.3.6   Zero Day Brokers

In contrast with commercial clients, government clients may not have a fixed budget limit for the purchase of those cyber weapons that are such a threat to national security that they absolutely dare not allow their adversaries to acquire them. Like international arms dealers, zero day brokers can extract higher prices from governments by comparing them with the high prices that rogue states might be willing to pay. Nor may there be any practical restrictions on the intended purpose of the weapons. The mission statement of a zero day broker might be long on profitability but short on ethical commitment: some government usage of these expensive zero days may be of questionable democratic morality, e.g. spying on dissidents and journalists. For example there are suspicions that Amnesty International members may have had spyware planted on their phones by Israeli intelligence.[15]

## 10.3.7  Risk Implications of the Market for Zero Days

It is the task of a cyber risk analyst to assess the risk implications of the evolving zero day market. The price escalation of bug bounties should have a beneficial risk mitigation effect in that the additional financial rewards should result in enhanced bug discovery. The question then is what happens to a bug that is found. If found by ethical bug hunters, all would be well and good; in due course, a patch would be produced. If found within the context of a private bug bounty program, again all is well; the software vendor running the program would pay the reward and patch the bug. But if found by a black hat criminal hacker, the zero day might be used for cyber crime. However, a very high reward offered by Zerodium might be greater than the expected gain to be made elsewhere. Indeed, the reward might be sufficient to entice the discoverer to cash in with Zerodium.

A study of zero days by the RAND Corporation using a confidential data set showed that, for a given stockpile of zero days, after a year approximately 5.7% had been discovered and disclosed by others.[16] With such a comparatively low obsolescence rate, global cyber security does depend on cyber weapon arsenals remaining secure.

## 10.4  STRATEGIES OF CYBER ATTACK

### 10.4.1  Cyber Attacks and Game Theory

Anyone who has watched an unfamiliar professional game knows that mere knowledge of the rules of the game doesn't take you very far in appreciation or relief from boredom. At an amateur level, ball games are largely contests of physical strength, stamina, endurance, and skill. But at higher professional levels, ball games increasingly become contests of the mind as well as the body. A great professional coach can train a team of average physical ability to defeat a superior, more talented team. Everyone will have one's own favorite examples. The difference lies in strategy – calling the right plays. To appreciate a professional game, a spectator needs to understand the strategic aspects.

From the perspective of an organization under cyber threat, insight into the strategic thinking of hostile threat actors is essential for organizing and implementing an effective response. The defender always moves first, with the attacker adapting strategy accordingly. Strategic thinking leads to the recognition of universal principles of cyber attack. One of the most important is the principle of least action: attackers following the path of least resistance in their operations.

The principle of least action is actually a fundamental law of nature, the scientific discourse of which dates back to the French savant Pierre de Maupertuis in the eighteenth century. Not only does this law explain water flow elegantly, but it frames cyber game theory as well. It explains the key modus operandi of cyber attackers, their choice of technology and targets. In respect of targeting, the principle of least action explains the phenomenon of target substitution: given two targets of equivalent value, a cyber attacker will strike the target with inferior security. This is essentially an extension into the realm of cyber crime of the brutal law of the jungle, expressing the evolutionary concept of survival of the fittest: the weakest animal in a herd becomes prey for a carnivore higher in the food chain.

Another food metaphor used by security professionals is the so-called low-hanging fruit, which dates back to an age before orchards were populated by dwarf trees, when only a modest proportion of fruit on trees could be easily picked. There are massive differences in corporate cyber security, reflecting underappreciation of the threat, substantial misallocations of expenditure, and poor design. Given the potential for cyber loss, there are corporations that spend too little on cyber security relative to their peers, and hence are perceived by attackers as low-hanging fruit. In the language of financial trading, these would be viewed as arbitrage opportunities; for cyber criminals, there are all too many free lunches.

### 10.4.2  Choice of Cyber Attack Technology

Apart from targeting, the principle of least action also helps explain the choice of attack technology in cyberspace. Consider the situation where there are multiple vulnerabilities in the wild that are available for an attacker to exploit. Finite resource constraints of the attacker fundamentally limit the exploitation strategy. The principle of least action is embodied succinctly within the work-averse attacker model of Allodi and Massacci.[17] Economic constraints have the consequence that attackers do not need to, and should not, work harder than necessary to achieve their criminal objectives. Accordingly, the great majority of attacks per software version may be driven by just a single vulnerability. Even if other vulnerabilities exist, an exploit kit may focus on just one of them. As further strategic adherence to the principle of least action, vulnerabilities with low attack complexity will be preferred, and new vulnerabilities are likely to be slowly introduced into a hacker's arsenal, especially since bugs in modern browsers are being increasingly fixed through bug bounty programs.

### 10.4.3   Hacker Motivations

It was Sun Tzu, in *The Art of War*, who wrote that if you know your enemy and know yourself, you need not fear the result of a hundred battles. Organizations face hundreds if not thousands of battles in cyberspace, so they had better know their enemy. In Chapter 5, 'Know Your Enemy', we profile several of the main hacker adversaries. Threat assessment from different adversaries is especially challenging for cyber security staff, because the enemy in cyberspace is amorphous and can appear in so many different guises.

On the battlefield, your enemy is in military uniform, and is above some minimum age. In cyberspace, your enemy could well be an unidentifiable young teenager. One of the most notorious child hackers, James Kosta, was just 13 when he and his accomplices hacked corporate and military computers, including major banks, General Electric, and IBM. He was duly convicted of 45 counts of technical burglary and sentenced to 45 years in prison. But in cyberspace, as in the real world, your enemy can become your friend: at the age of 18, Kosta joined the US Navy as an intelligence analyst, and at age 20 he joined the CIA. After 9/11, as an expert on video games, he simulated a dirty bomb attack on Las Vegas, and how rescuers could lock down the city. He might have been reminded of Einstein's aphorism: 'To punish me for my contempt of authority, Fate has made me an authority myself'.

Kosta was an amateur threat actor, as we characterized in Chapter 5, 'Know Your Enemy', a teenage hacker, but with technical capabilities far exceeding those of an ordinary script kiddie (an attacker who uses scripts developed by more sophisticated hackers). For juveniles, hacking carries the youthful thrill and excitement of making a real impact on the adult world, which would otherwise be an impossible dream. As hackers leave school, their daytime thoughts would turn to the serious adult task of earning a living. Part of knowing your enemy is to understand why someone with hacking skills should wish to make money illegally as a cyber criminal, rather than pursue a legitimate career as a penetration tester, a bug bounty hunter, a government cyber warrior – or a wealthy entrepreneur. James Kosta made millions from selling his dot-com businesses.

### 10.4.4   Turning Hackers Legitimate

This important question of security economics has been addressed by Allodi et al. within the framework of game theory, which is the formal mathematical approach to modeling adversarial conflict involving rational players. These Italian security economists consider two alternatives for a hacker: (1) making money by selling an exploit kit comprising various vulnerabilities, and (2) selling the vulnerabilities to legitimate vendors through bug bounty programs, or exposing them at a black hat conference so as to be hired as a penetration tester or defender. The prospects of the first alternative being successful depend on the likelihood of the exploit kit not being detected and disabled. The prospects of the second alternative being successful depend on the hacker's education and previous job experience.[18]

When the maximum benefit from criminal activities exceeds that from legitimate activities, a hacker would be inclined to follow a criminal path. But such an unfavorable decision for society can be countered by raising the benefits from the second alternative. The progressive rise in the rewards from bug bounty programs is an important step in this direction. Combined with the good salaries that very able professional programmers can command in the international employment market for cyber talent, there is little economic incentive for the most skilled hackers to resort to cyber crime. However, crime may well pay for an average hacker, who has only a very slim chance of winning a bug bounty, and a similarly poor chance of earning a reasonable income as a cyber security professional. Increasing employment opportunities for average hackers in Western countries would thus be a step forward to keeping them from a life of cyber crime. However, this does not address the threat posed by average hackers in other countries, living outside the jurisdiction of the Western alliance. These foreign hackers constitute a persistent threat, along with their more able compatriots who may find employment in the elite and domestically prestigious state cyber warfare teams.

### 10.4.5   Functioning Black Markets

Cyber criminals learning their trade will start to navigate their way around the burgeoning black markets. For those with no experience in black market functioning, a visit to a Middle Eastern bazaar would offer some basic training. A visitor interested in buying some local silverware would not be sure that the silverware was genuine; conversely, the seller might worry that the visitor's credit card was counterfeit. Without trust established between the parties, neither could accept the other's word. The more dubious the visitor is about the quality of the product for sale, the less the visitor would be prepared to pay for it. Similarly, the more suspicious the bazaar trader is of the good faith of the prospective buyer, the more the trader would want to charge the stranger. Under these circumstances of mutual mistrust, there can be no fixed price for any purchase: haggling has to take place.

Less exotic than a bazaar, but as interesting a laboratory of human nature, is a used car salesroom. Asymmetry of information between the prospective buyer and seller gives rise to a 'market for lemons'.[19] In this classic context, a lemon is a vehicle that is misrepresented as reliable. If customers cannot properly check for defects, they will tend to make cheap offers. But this would eventually force out good sellers, and the market for used cars would fail. As a last resort, a customer who has bought a lemon could seek legal redress, but this is not an option for illegal trading on the black market.

The fact that cyber black market traders are outside trading law might encourage the hope amongst law-abiding citizens that these markets would become highly inefficient, which would benefit those at risk of attack. However, it turns out that the black market design adopted by cyber criminals is similar to legitimate online forum markets such as eBay.[20] Elaborate reputation mechanisms are established to prevent scammers, known as 'rippers', from ruining a black market by making it dysfunctional. Thus some of these markets are accessible only with an invitation and require a buy-in, which could involve money or goods, like some recently stolen credit cards. Other markets are run on private chat rooms and have quite rigorous vetting procedures for new users. In these more regulated closed markets there is a greater level of trust, which facilitates higher trade volume and lower prices.

In the absence of legal oversight, the quality of stolen goods may always be open to doubt, as some sellers try to sell old data or resell the same data multiple times. To counter such dishonest market behavior, additional service may be offered to verify that the seller's accounts are still active and that credit cards have not yet been blocked. Underground marketplaces may even provide a guarantee for the data's freshness and replace useless blocked credit cards. The principle of least action to achieve their objectives is a powerful force to guide cyber criminals along the unfamiliar path of honesty in market trading.

## 10.4.6  National Conflict Strategies

Many nation-states have substantial arsenals of cyber weapons that could be deployed in cyber attacks against other nation-states. There are also non-state actors who have substantial cyber attack capability, so the attribution of a cyber attack to a nation-state is fraught with ambiguity, especially since attackers typically deny responsibility. This is in marked contrast with a major terrorist attack. Terrorist organizations are keen to accept responsibility for attacks, since they generate 24/7 media publicity for their political agenda, and boost recruitment. Terrorism is the language of being noticed.

Consider the massive distributed denial of service (DDoS) attack against Estonia in 2007, which was the first time that a botnet had threatened the security of an entire country. This happened not long after a bronze soldier Soviet war memorial in the center of the capital, Tallinn, had been relocated. This action would have affronted President Putin, whose soldier father was betrayed by the Estonians to the Nazis during the Second World War. Notwithstanding this personal motive, and its persistent political interest in a former outpost of the Soviet Union, Russia denied responsibility. Estonia, however, was quick to blame the overwhelming DDoS attack on Russia.

Such a blame response does not always follow so quickly, if at all. After the *Stuxnet* attack on Iranian centrifuges in 2010, Iran did not immediately blame the attackers, Israel and the United States, publicly. Where the victim of a cyber attack lacks a suitable response, public blaming of the attacker without backing it up makes the victim look weak. Tolerating an attack rather than risk escalation is part of the blame game. There is an underlying logic to the blame game, which has been analyzed appropriately within a game theory framework by Edwards et al.[21] Their strategic model of cyber attack attribution and blame addresses important political questions such as the conditions under which no attacks or reciprocal attacks take place, and when a non-state actor might undermine the cyber peace between two nation-states.

### 10.4.7  Improving Attribution

For many cyber risk stakeholders, greater clarity over attribution of nation-state cyber attacks would be very desirable, but it is a forlorn hope. Many of the known attribution methods for cyber attacks can be spoofed: digital records can be created and deleted. Furthermore, there are usually compelling strategic reasons for attribution issues to remain obscured. Just as there is a special coded language of diplomacy to express relations between nation-states, there is also a special coded language for the attribution and blame associated with a cyber attack perpetrated by, or on behalf of, a nation-state.

## 10.4.8  Strategies of State-sponsored Cyber Teams

Given the potential damaging impact of a state-sponsored cyber attack, corporations need to understand this language and the underlying cyber strategy. To further such understanding, the basic elements for playing the blame game are summarized.[22] There are two nation-state players, A (the attacker) and B (the victim). If player A attacks player B, player A may or may not be vulnerable to B's blame. Vulnerability arises if geopolitically A would be embarrassed by disclosure from B. If A is vulnerable and B blames A, then A suffers a loss and B makes a gain. But if A is not vulnerable to blame and is not susceptible to a similar cyber counterattack, then A gets away with suffering no loss.

As an illustration, in its cyber-industrial espionage forays amongst US corporations, China (player A) has not been susceptible to retaliatory industrial espionage from the United States (player B), since US technology has been more advanced than that of China. Furthermore, China, with its tight media control, is not embarrassed by any US disclosure of cyber espionage, which is routinely denied. So China has not been vulnerable to US blame. Replacing player A by North Korea, the very limited internet usage in that country limits the effectiveness of any US retaliation by cyber attack. In November 2014, Sony was coerced by terrorist threat into not screening a comedy movie about a plot to assassinate North Korean leader Kim Jong-un. Blamed by the US administration, North Korea denied all responsibility.

## 10.5  STRATEGIES OF NATIONAL CYBER DEFENSE

### 10.5.1  Preparing for Cyber Conflict

The annals of world history are full of accounts of military victories following audacious and brilliant attack strategies. After all, as Winston Churchill said, 'History is written by victors'. The bravery and skill of elite forces such as the US Navy SEALs and the British Special Air Service are well documented and passed down as legends to future military generations. In cyberspace, the attacks of elite hacking outfits such as *PLA 61398* of the Chinese People's Liberation Army have also become notorious, if not the stuff of hacker legend. By comparison, defenders tend to be more anonymous, and their resolute, brave, and often ingenious defensive strategies are less lauded and remembered. Until the 2017 Hollywood movie *Dunkirk*, who knew the name of the pier-master who oversaw the safe evacuation of 240,000 stranded Allied troops in 1940?

As is evident from the nation-state blame game, defending against cyber attacks from another country is an aggravating, frustrating, and even humiliating experience. In some circumstances, it is counterproductive to assign blame. And even if another country is blamed, the culprit may be perfectly happy to tell a diplomatic falsehood in the name of Machiavelli, and deny all knowledge. Both the attacker and the victim know very well that deception is an intrinsic art of war.

### 10.5.2  Theft of Intellectual Property

Each nation-state would wish to retain its arsenals of cyber weapons to prepare for cyber war, but there is room for negotiation over refraining from hacking for commercial gain. For the United States, the principal victim of commercial cyber espionage, striking a deal has been a business necessity: to paraphrase Winston Churchill, never before has so much been taken from so many by so few. Thus, in September 2015, the United States and China agreed that neither government would support or conduct cyber-enabled theft of intellectual property. For the victim, an imperfect pact is better than none. Hard evidence of any violation of this agreement is difficult to procure, but Chinese state-sponsored hackers are suspected of continued targeting of major high-tech US corporations like Google, Microsoft, and Intel.

### 10.5.3  Bringing Cyber Criminals to Justice

Offering bounties for the discovery of bugs is one thing; offering bounties for information leading to the conviction of cyber criminals is quite another. Given that there is no international regulation of cyberspace, financial incentives for bringing cyber criminals to justice would appear to be a sound idea, conjuring up images of the Wild West and Billy the Kid, who had a $500 bounty on his head. This was eventually collected by a sheriff who tracked him down in 1880, at considerable risk to himself. Microsoft might hope that, in the third millennium, public-spirited law-abiding folks would come forward to help convict cyber criminals, and to receive a substantial reward for their effort and the risk they take.

Such hope was fulfilled in the case of another young criminal, just a couple of years younger than Billy the Kid, who generated the *Sasser* worm. This spread to new hosts over the Internet by targeting the known MS04-011 (LSASS) vulnerability, caused by a buffer overrun in the Local Security Authority Subsystem Service. Within 48 hours of the *Sasser* worm being released on April 29, 2004, 1.3 million PCs running Windows 2000 and XP were infected. In July 2005, Sven Jaschan was convicted by a German court for writing and distributing *Sasser*. As a teenager, he received a modest sentence of 21 months of probation and 30 hours of community service. Some of Jaschan's school friends had tipped off Microsoft, who then informed the German authorities. The Microsoft deputy general counsel expressed Microsoft's gladness to provide a monetary reward of $250,000 to the two individuals who provided credible information helping the German police to apprehend the wunderkind.

## 10.5.4  Putting Bounties on Their Heads

A few years later, in February 2009, Microsoft offered the same reward of $250,000 to anyone who could provide information helping to arrest the creator of the *Conficker* worm. Microsoft stated that this worm was a criminal attack, and that citizens from any country were eligible to receive the bounty. Given that this bounty was but a very small fraction of the $9 billion economic damage inflicted, perhaps it should have been more generous to corner the mysterious and highly adaptive botmaster.

The enormous economic harm that botnets can cause was manifest soon after with the *Rustock* botnet. In 2010 the *Rustock* botnet sent about a third of all the spam in the world. It made its criminal operators about $3.5 million, whereas fighting spam cost about $1 billion globally, a third of it on *Rustock* that year.[23] The societal price exacted was a hundred times larger than the gains that criminals made.

A passive defensive strategy of blocking spam is thus an extremely costly option, except for sellers of antivirus products. Recognizing the significant problems caused to its customers, Microsoft opted for a proactive defense. Acting together with its security partners, Microsoft succeeded in dismantling *Rustock*, and offered in July 2011 a bounty of $250,000 for information to bring the *Rustock* gang to justice. The reward was successful in generating 20–50 tips a day of varying quality when it was first issued. Encouragingly, some came from sources engaged in similar botnet activities from Eastern Europe.

An active defensive strategy of going after the criminals, shutting down their operations, and bringing them to justice represents a modest but welcome shift in security onus from users back to the vendors. However, the perverse incentives associated with the principles of security economics do not favor a greater shift, with vendors delaying major shipping deadlines to fix more bugs.

## 10.5.5  The Importance of the CISO

Each corporation needs to take responsibility for its own defensive security strategy, and increasingly organizations are appointing senior managers with the responsibility of protecting against data theft and cyber attack. There is an increasing trend to appoint a CISO or similarly titled person who has to meet this challenge.

Defense strategy is enigmatic because defense is just plain harder than attack. Defending a modern information system takes a CISO back to the Wild West: the men in black hats can strike anywhere, while the men in white hats have to defend everywhere. News that software vendors are hunting down cyber criminals will please every CEO. But it doesn't help a CISO if the CEO is using an inappropriate mental model to assess how much investment is necessary and where to invest.[24] Cyber security is a continuous, ongoing process rather than a finite task like constructing an impregnable medieval fortification. Suppose that there has been no significant corporate breach reported over the past year. The CEO may conclude that the cyber fortress is doing what the earlier large security budget has already paid for, and there is no need for increasing investment in cyber security. In reality, the company may just have been very lucky. Target substitution is a common criminal attack tactic; had it not been for maintenance of the existing security budget, the corporation might have been targeted by hackers in the past year.

A good business rapport between CISO and CEO is essential to ensure that cyber security has a high corporate priority and a budget to match. It is unfortunate therefore that, according to the Ponemon Institute, the average tenure of CISOs has been only several years.[25] CISOs are frequently head-hunted by other firms, because executives with the right skills are hard to find. It takes many years to gain experience in security technology, as well as in governance, compliance, and risk. In August 2013, there was no permanent CISO at Yahoo when it suffered a data breach of a billion user accounts. The company had struggled to retain top cyber security executives, and the search for a permanent CISO had lasted for about a year when the breach occurred. This misfortune highlights the delicate trade-off between finding the best person to appoint as CISO and the heightened corporate vulnerability whilst the post remains vacant. Solving cyber risk involves solving the problem of hiring the right CISO.

The job specification for a CISO is very demanding. The CISO must be technically adept, with an intuitive understanding of a company's systems, how hackers might penetrate them, and how to defend against attacks. The CISO must also understand technically how to detect and handle attacks.[26] Beyond technical skill, the CISO must be technically curious about the future, and critical of past performance. The best CISOs are always scanning the horizon: they assess mistakes they may be making and learn from the mistakes that other CISOs make. In particular, trusting one vendor will never solve all problems. The CISO also needs to be politically astute and organizationally savvy so as to build in security as a core feature from the earliest stage of product development.

Drinkwater has likened the CISO role to a unicorn: technical, but with people skills; executive-level, but with project management capabilities; laser-focused prioritization but with broad overview knowledge and understanding.[27] A knowledge of security economics would also be an advantage. Pliny the Elder, the Roman author of the first encyclopedia, described the fabled unicorn as having the body of a horse, the head of a stag, the feet of an elephant, the tail of a boar, and a single black horn three feet long in the middle of its forehead. Clearly, the appointment of a well-qualified and capable CISO is amongst the most difficult, yet most crucial, security decisions a corporation can make.

## PERSONAL PROFILE OF A CISO

Just as only a few sports professionals ever make it as successful team managers, so only a small proportion of cyber security professionals would have the necessary personal, communication, and project management skills to become a successful CISO. Technical qualifications, knowledge, and experience are prerequisites, but other personal qualities are essential as well.

Changing the cyber security culture within an organization takes more than the best security assessment; it takes patience and persuasive communication skills, especially in board discussions.

To prioritize and execute risk-based security improvements that impact diverse corporate interest groups, a CISO needs to have the listening skills and openness of a professional counselor.

To minimize corporate vulnerability to the pervasive threat posed by social engineering, a CISO needs to have the level of insight into human behavioral psychology that hackers so often exploit to their criminal advantage.

Finally, as with all senior leadership roles for organizations under persistent external hostile attack, the job of CISO is highly stressful. It takes an exceptional person to deal with such constant stress in a calm and composed manner, without suffering post-traumatic stress disorder.

## ENDNOTES

1. Ponemon Institute (2017a).
2. Ibid.
3. Ibid.
4. IDC (2015).
5. Filkins (2016).
6. Gordon and Loeb (2002).
7. NIST (2014).
8. Beattie (2016).
9. Anderson (2001).
10. Bar On (2018).
11. Martindale (2017).
12. Bugcrowd (2017).
13. Maillart et al. (2017).
14. Anderson and Moore (2006).
15. The Citizen Lab (2018).
16. Ablon and Bogart (2017).
17. Allodi and Massacci (2015).
18. Allodi et al. (2012).
19. Akerlof (1970),
20. Allodi et al. (2016).
21. Edwards et al. (2017).
22. Ibid.
23. Anderson (2012).
24. Blau (2017).
25. Ponemon Institute (2014).
26. Schlein (2015).
27. Drinkwater (2016).

# CHAPTER 11

# Ten Cyber Problems

## 11.1 SETTING PROBLEMS

### 11.1.1 The Hilbert Problem Set

The setting of problems is one of the most effective ways of concentrating minds on technical challenges that merit more thought and intensive research. At the 1900 International Congress of Mathematicians in Paris, one of the greatest German mathematicians, David Hilbert, presented a list of ten important problems. A more complete list of 23 problems was published later. These problems were designed to serve as examples for the kinds of problems whose solutions would lead to the furthering of disciplines in mathematics. As such, some were broad areas for investigation. These problems have served their purpose in advancing different branches of mathematics, as the process of attempting to solve them has led to important discoveries and fresh insights. Thirty years after the Morris worm was unleashed from MIT, infecting about 10% of computers connected to the internet, cyber security is more important than ever. The grand global challenge of solving cyber risk has to be constantly renewed. In all hazard areas, both natural and man-made, scientific progress plays a crucial part in risk mitigation. For cyber security, the burden of responsibility and expectation falls on the community of computer scientists. Given that computers are built from Boolean circuits, there is an intrinsic conceptual link between computer science and mathematical logic. The most familiar human face of this link is Alan Turing, who introduced a formal definition of a computing machine, as well as pioneered computer development.

### 11.1.2 Ten Problems for Solving Cyber Risk

Analogous to a set of 10 mathematical problems, the following list of 10 motivating problems in risk and computer security has been compiled as a horizon-scanning exercise to encourage further path-breaking research in cyber risk. Practical challenges in computer science are a spur to technology development, even if the time horizon may be decades away. A classic example is the Turing Test. To address the question of whether a machine can think, Alan Turing conceived the idea of an imitation game, where a computer imitates a human being. Can a computer be programmed with enough artificial intelligence (AI) to fool people into believing that the computer is human?[1] On June 7, 2014, the 60th anniversary of his untimely death at the age of 41, the Turing Test was passed by a computer program written by three Russians masquerading as a 13-year-old Ukrainian boy. During a demanding typed conversation, held at the Royal Society in London under very rigorous conditions, this program managed to fool enough of the 30 judges to pass the Turing Test.[2]

This milestone is significant not just for AI, but for cyber risk as well. Two decades earlier in 1994, a French hacker conned the FBI office in Washington D.C., into believing he was an FBI representative at the US embassy in Paris. Through passing the Turing Test, future cyber criminals may become adept at automated impersonation. This would take social engineering to a new level of deception – where human beings are conned by computers pretending to be human beings.

The problem of making critical decisions in an environment where some messages may have been altered or fabricated by cyber criminals is the essence of the first problem in this list. For simplicity, this is set in the particular context of canal operational security, but there are numerous commercial, civil, and military applications requiring an answer as to how one should make optimal safety decisions in a sub-optimal security environment. Uncertainty is always sub-optimal. Regrettably, all too few people are trained to deal with uncertainty. This requires familiarity with the language of risk. Most people have a subjective feeling of risk without knowing the basic grammar of risk, which is expressed in the mathematics of chance.[3]

### 11.1.3 Security as Well as Functionality

The traditional practise of software developers has been to prioritize enhancements in software functionality and features over security. Cyber risk analysis and risk-informed decision making have been relegated as lower priorities. The direct tangible reward of achieving improved capability through utilizing some additional software outweighs the risk of bugs lurking in this extra software. But introducing missing, erroneous, or malicious code can lead to dangerous and unwitting software dependency. The second problem discussed is that of tackling the software dependency challenge of identifying all the code that depends on any piece of software.

This leads on to the third problem, which is the vulnerability inheritance problem. If vulnerable code is imported, what determines whether the vulnerability remains exploitable? Vulnerabilities are inherited from one software development to another, so this is a rather unfashionable legacy problem. Instead of looking back in anguish at hidden oversights from past projects, most software engineers would rather look ahead to new enterprising software projects.

Programming is a very precise logical discipline, but programmers may have a subjective and biased feeling about the presence of bugs in their own code. To comprehend the bug-generation process better, further multidisciplinary research is needed, integrating cognitive science, software psychology, and software engineering.[4] The assessment of bugs tends to be expressed in qualitative instead of quantitative terms. But obtaining an accurate count of vulnerabilities is important for managing efforts at controlling cyber risk, and is the fourth problem. Related to this is the fifth problem of devising metrics for the overlap of different malware infecting a system. If a system is found to be infected by malware originating from one country, attention will inevitably be focused on this intrusion, and vigilance may be relaxed against stealthy intrusion by malware from another country.

### 11.1.4 Rethinking the Design Time Horizon

The sixth problem is estimating the vulnerability of a computer over its entire operating life. This latter problem is safety-critical for computers with healthcare functions. Medical devices are amongst the rapidly expanding internet of things, and may have numerous vulnerabilities in their code, and have primitive weak security measures. In August 2017, the US Food and Drug Administration recalled 465,000 pacemakers that were vulnerable to hacking. A better appreciation of long-term vulnerability would inform the security economics debate over the desirability of less vulnerable and more fault-tolerant software.

In any criminological field, forensic science plays a key role in understanding criminal modus operandi, detecting crime, and identifying the perpetrators. DNA matching, which was first used in a criminal investigation in 1986, has been a breakthrough technology, vital for bringing criminals to justice even years after a crime was committed. The seventh problem addresses the comparable task in digital forensics of quantifying the similarity between binary machine code files. This is a task that expedites hacker attribution analysis in common situations where there is a blanket denial of culpability. Just as DNA matching acts as a deterrent against serious crime, because criminals know that evidence left at the scene of the crime may allow them to be tracked and convicted, so the similarity matching of binaries may deter nation-states and affiliated hacking organizations from launching aggressive cyber attacks. The underlying calculus of such attacks changes dramatically if the attribution ambiguity can be reduced to an extremely low level. Just how low this threshold needs to be is illustrated by the implacable Russian government denials over its involvement in the Novichok nerve agent poisoning of double agent Sergei Skripal and his daughter Yulia in Salisbury, England, on March 4, 2018.

### 11.1.5  Managing an Evolving Threat

The eighth problem concerns the daunting challenge of detecting computer viruses that are modified constantly. Such computer chameleons are elusive and hard to catch, and are a formidable adversary for antivirus providers. Real-life chameleons have evolved an effective symbiotic relationship with trees, against which they are camouflaged. Whether or not to form a symbiotic cyber relationship with a government is part of the cyber criminal's dilemma. Better understanding of cyber criminal payoffs, choice of targeting, and attack capacity is needed to refine cyber risk quantification. This is the ninth problem.

Given the technical capability and malevolence of state-sponsored hackers, all too many IT managers may have only a vague and optimistic notion of the residual cyber risk to their computer systems after all their painstaking and costly security measures have been taken. Security verification is the tenth and final problem. This fundamental, grandly ambitious problem is open-ended, and therefore addressed to all stakeholders, including regulators and insurers.

### 1.  THE CANAL SAFETY DECISION PROBLEM

How should one make optimal safety decisions with a computer system in a sub-optimal security environment?

Imagine a network of canals, in which there are water level sensors and locks to control the flow of water. You are the lock keeper, and manage these flows while small boats come and go through the canals. You know that half of your water level sensors and gate open/close sensors do not use cryptography to ensure that their messages reach you unaltered. But half of them do use cryptography to ensure the end-to-end integrity of their measurements to your control room. Thankfully, you do know which sensors are secure and which are not.

During a heavy storm with the likelihood of flooding, there is a risk of boats being damaged, so you need to close the locks and confirm that flooding is not occurring. You have to make rapid decisions about which data are reliable and which signals might be hacked. This storm test could be conducted either in the presence of an attacker or without an attacker but in fear of one. Regardless, the problem is the same.

This is a crucial question that is posed to all stakeholders who find themselves in the role of crisis decision makers. Not to belittle the lock keeper's worries, but battlefield soldiers are in dire straits if their satellite communications are insecure.[5] Vital tactical decisions may be compromised. There is no room for complacency; US satellite communications have been hacked. On June 15, 2014, a 25-year-old hacker, Sean Caffrey, accessed and stole the ranks, user names, and email addresses of more than 800 users of a satellite communications system, as well as of about 30,000 satellite phones.[6] He was arrested after intelligence showed that the hack originated from his internet address. The danger that US soldiers might face with insecure communications is starkly illustrated by the hacker's threatening text message:

> *ISIS WARRIORS UNVEIL: We smite the Lizards, Lizard Squad your time is near. We're in your bases, we control your satellites. The missiles shall rein upon they who claim alliance, watch your heads. STOP THE AIR STRIKES, OR WE WILL DO AS YOUDO.*

Caffrey's sentence of 18 months was suspended due to recommendations in his medical report. He was the cyber equivalent of a terrorist lone wolf. Nobody was aware of how he was spending his many hours on the internet, or the potential consequences of his hacking.

## 2.　THE SOFTWARE DEPENDENCY PROBLEM

How can you trace all the component parts of a software system to verify the code libraries and subpackages on which it depends?

Software development is a time-consuming and time-constrained process, which can be more protracted and costly if a software wheel is reinvented. This can be avoided if use is made of other people's software, such as code libraries and packages. However, this introduces a dependency problem if the code being used is changed so that it stops working with your software, or if it is removed altogether.

Imagine you are climbing a mountain in a team. You need to know on whom your safety depends – and also whose safety depends on you. Dependency knowledge matters in software. However, software dependency mapping is easier one way than the other. You may know what your code depends on, but you do not usually know what code depends on it. In the interests of others, a defensive approach to minimize negative aspects of software dependency might be adopted. But allowance has to be made for human factors.

In 2016, a 28-year-old contributor to open-source web development software, who was self-taught through the open source community, became embroiled in an argument over the name of a JavaScript package he had written. Threatened with legal action, he decided to delete a tiny 11-line piece of code he had written (see inset). The result was highly disruptive, and caused malfunctions of large numbers of other pieces of software that had incorporated his eleven lines of code. In his view, he had the right to delete it. Code is written by human beings, who may be more stubborn and inflexible than machines. Even though anybody could have written this nominally insignificant code fragment, it was like a rivet keeping a structure from failing. This petulant gesture of code removal had no malicious intent but nevertheless had the disruptive impact of a little logic bomb on web development worldwide.

This unanticipated outcome is symptomatic of a major problem: it is not possible to identify all the code that depends on any given piece of software, however small. This problem has serious implications for the impact of vulnerability inheritance.

## ELEVEN-LINE CODE THAT WAS DELETED WITH GLOBAL DISRUPTIVE IMPACT

```
module.exports=leftpad;
function leftpad (str, len, ch) {
    str = String(str);
    var i = -1;
    if (!ch && ch  ! = = 0) ch = ` `;
    len = len  -  str.length;
    while (++i  < len)  {
    str = ch  +  str
    }
    return str;
}
```

## 3.   THE VULNERABILITY INHERITANCE PROBLEM

If you import vulnerable code into your code, what determines whether or not the vulnerability remains exploitable?

Many commercial software organizations import previously written code when writing new code, but may not have the capacity to identify which of their applications are affected by a particular component bug. Amongst the downloads from one of the largest public repositories of open-source Java components, as much as 7.5% of these components had known vulnerabilities.[7] In how many places are such vulnerabilities inherited? Poor inventory information makes this question hard to answer.

To what degree are vulnerabilities inherited, versus newly generated? Mapping back from your code to others is fairly tractable, but what about all the code that those projects use? There is an inherent recursive element of dependency that leaves many awkward questions about how vulnerabilities are inherited from one project to another. Many components have third-party subcomponents that have their own bugs. And once a vulnerability ends up in an application, it may remain there for a very long time. Concern over this legacy problem should encourage a diligence check on those libraries that are most often imported, and motivate the conduct of further research into their vulnerabilities.

The vulnerability inheritance problem is safety-critical. Vulnerable open source software has been found in remotely connected parts of automobiles. In the manufacturing industry, product components are typically sourced from elsewhere, but efficient supply chain practices are used to keep proper track of them. Similar supply chain monitoring procedures have been introduced to create bills of materials for software that can restrict which components developers can use, and from which suppliers.[8] In industrial risk analysis, the fragility of complex supply chains is a practical problem that has stimulated extensive research to make these chains more robust. In cyber risk analysis, a comparable research effort is required to tackle the vulnerability inheritance problem.

## 4.  THE VULNERABILITY COUNT PROBLEM

How can we objectively measure the vulnerability of a piece of software?

Anybody who has tried to control a pest infestation would keep an approximate tally of the number of pests removed, hoping unrealistically that there may not be too many more, and discounting their high reproduction rate. Bugs are a universal software hazard. No code is ever guaranteed to be bug-free, and it is good practice to keep a count of bugs discovered. Being realistic rather than optimistic, how many more vulnerabilities might still be lurking in the code? Cognitive dissonance tends to lead to underestimation.

Vulnerabilities per line of code used to be a good metric. It helped us understand how to do quality assurance, and estimate the numbers of vulnerabilities to expect in software we purchased. This worked well when code was written monolithically and ran on the operating system without pulling in external libraries such as dynamic-link libraries (DLLs). The internet of things sees an extension of this philosophy where everything runs as a service. Furthermore, the software used for the internet of things has the same vulnerability inheritance issues as the software for commercial applications.

The problem for bug hunters is to devise a modern metric to make an accurate estimate of the number of code vulnerabilities introduced regularly into products and services. This problem is compounded by the lack of globally standardized vulnerability naming, as discussed in Chapter 4, Section 4.3.1.1. Addressing this and other aspects of the vulnerability count problem would be a valuable contribution to quantitative cyber risk analysis.

## 5. THE MALWARE OVERLAP PROBLEM

How much currently undetected malware resides in a given computer system?

Virologists recognize that influenza strains tend to displace each other, so that there is just one dominant strain circulating at any given time. This is taken into account in the standard type of quantitative epidemiological model for analyzing the spread of influenza infection. By contrast, a computer can be infected more than once by the same malware, and simultaneously by different types of malware. One infection can lie dormant and undetected for many months, during which time a new infection can take hold through a social engineering trick.

Ask any incident response team about penetrations and persistent attackers, and they will probably crack a joke about computers compromised by more than one nation-state simultaneously. Everyone knows the usual suspects. In any emerging international political crisis, each aggrieved country might launch its own reprisal cyber attacks.

Can metrics be formed about the dwell time of attackers, and how likely they are to overlap at different spread rates? A metric or study such as this would make clear to all computer users what patient hackers already know: most computers are vulnerable to something most of the time, and often more than one thing at the same time.

## 6. THE VULNERABILITY LIFESPAN PROBLEM

How many remotely exploitable vulnerabilities remain exposed in a given computer system?

Cyber security begins with risk awareness. Much of this may be qualitative information. But cyber risk analysis requires numerical data, such as a quantitative answer for this question. As a function over time, how many remotely exploitable vulnerabilities are exposed on the average computer? An assessment would benefit from knowing the zero day window for each vulnerability, i.e. the time until the patch is produced, because that yields the minimum time span of vulnerability of the computer.

There are some statistics on how long machines go unpatched for a given vulnerability. However, what we are focusing on here is not the window of vulnerability for a bug, but rather for the entire operating life of the computer, which might be up to five years for desktop computers or 20 years for remote terminal units. This is a special concern for computers operating safety-critical medical equipment and devices.

The medical industry has used a range of older legacy technologies for its software driving X-ray, magnetic resonance imaging (MRI), and other devices. Computers controlling such devices have been targeted by a hacker group, *Orangeworm*, who are especially interested in legacy Windows XP systems. Their attacks have attempted to keep infections active for long periods of time on these devices.[9] Their malware's functionality was extended by downloading and executing additional modules. This type of strategy thrives on ignorance and apathy over vulnerability lifespan, and the lack of adequate attention paid to tackling the vulnerability lifespan problem.

## 7. THE BINARY SIMILARITY PROBLEM

How can we uniquely identify attack binaries?

In computer forensics, one of the principal criteria for gauging similarity between two files is binary similarity. Checking for binary similarity has applications in the attribution of cyber attacks, protection of intellectual property, and malware lineage construction. In the latter respect, tracking the evolution of malware code is obstructed by the tactic of malware developers to repackage their malicious code to avoid detection.

To quantify binary similarity, it is helpful to use the concept of edit distance, which is the minimum number of deletions, insertions, or substitutions required to transform one string of characters into another.[10] For example, the binary string '010011' can be transformed to '0000111' by changing the second digit from 1 to 0, and appending 1 at the end. More generally, we can define an edit distance between two binaries or, more usefully, an edit distance in code, transformed by compilation. This allows us to identify binaries that are similar because they either import the same code or are variants of the same code.

This helps substantially in reverse engineering, where quickly identifying patterns in compiled code saves reverse engineering functions more than once. To illustrate, keep in mind that even viruses are made of mostly standard and useful function calls that have nothing to do with exploits. In other words, they access files, open network sockets, and take screenshots, just like other consensually behaving code. Being able to identify all the standard function calls quickly and home in on the malicious part aids reverse engineering, and also helps solve attribution problems.

Just as a criminal can frame another person by leaving traces of that individual's DNA on a crime weapon, so in cyberspace hackers can frame others with their carefully contrived source code. Days before the opening ceremony of the 2018 Winter Olympics in Pyeongchang, South Korea, the event's IT infrastructure was struck a paralysing blow. The source code looked like that used by the North Korean *Lazarus* group, but US intelligence has concluded that this was a false-flag operation, perpetrated on behalf of Russia. Flying a false flag was originally a deception deployed by pirates, who would have felt at home roaming cyberspace. A North Korean team participated in the Olympics, but Russia was excluded because of previous doping violations. Motivation and tactics are factors that need to be taken into account in computer forensics, along with enhanced methods of binary similarity analysis.

## 8. THE VIRUS MODIFICATION PROBLEM

How can we track and map all the evolutionary variants of modern malware?

In human virology, the development of vaccines can be thwarted by the genetic adaptation of the virus. Multiple pandemic waves may be caused by such adaptations of the influenza virus. In biology, polymorphism is the occurrence of several different forms of a species, resulting from evolutionary processes. In the virtual world, a polymorphic virus is one that contains an engine that modifies the virus endlessly to foil signature-based security systems and evade detection. This makes virus detection very much harder.

An example of a polymorphic virus is the *Beebone* botnet, which controlled at least 12,000 infected computers in many countries. Once a computer has been infected, the botnet operators could instruct it to download more malware, such as banking Trojans, password stealers, spyware, or ransomware.[11] Eventually it took Europol's European Cybercrime Centre to bring down this botnet in 2015. *Beebone* changed very frequently, for example by modifying destination files as it was copied across a network. Simple changes of file name were able to circumvent rudimentary malware-checking systems that relied on a list of files recognized as bad.[12] The rapid changes of *Beebone* generated millions of variations.

For a general polymorphic virus, even if we can never hope to detect all of its modifications, we know we should be capable of detecting many of them. The core question here is this: Given a polymorphic engine, could we catch some portion of its generated binaries by characterizing a signature for similar binaries? What if we have a large number of binaries – could we classify them into clusters guessing they were constructed by the same polymorphic approach? This would be an extension of heuristic scanning that looks for common components of the threat virus, so increasing the chances of detecting novel variations.

## 9. THE CYBER CRIMINAL'S DILEMMA PROBLEM

How can we anticipate the targeting and capability development of cyber attackers?

For cyber criminals, the dilemma of which targets to choose to attack is of crucial operational importance for cyber security.

The attacker's benefit function usually does not match the victim's loss function. In particular, for some cyber-physical attacks, the loss inflicted can be very much higher than the attack cost. The attack leverage, which is the ratio of loss to cost, is typically very high for attacks by resource-constrained hackers, and is particularly high for terrorism and vandalism. A salient reference leverage value is 100,000, which was achieved by Al Qaeda on 9/11.

Using apt biological metaphors, we must study more parasitic and symbiotic relationship structures to understand some variants of serious cyber crime. For example, there is a symbiotic relationship between cyber criminals and the Russian government, with hackers allowed to attack foreign targets with impunity in return for cooperating with the Main Intelligence Directorate (formerly GRU), Foreign Intelligence Service, and other shadowy Russian security services.

Given such license, what is the maximum capability of a state-sponsored attacker? In the estimation of the UK National Cyber Security Centre, Russia is the most capable hostile adversary in cyberspace. According to Western analysts of the Kremlin, malicious Russian actors will use Big Data and technological advances in AI to engage in a new era of political warfare.[13] A challenge for the NATO alliance is to appreciate that such warfare is both inexpensive as well as highly impactful, making it highly leveraged, and therefore intrinsically attractive to Russian hackers.

## 10.  THE SECURITY VERIFICATION PROBLEM

As a society, how do we produce software that is error-free and safe to use?

In software engineering, verification processes check to see if the software meets its specifications. Static verification involves basic tasks such as analyzing code to ensure that coding conventions are followed. Dynamic verification includes typical quality assurance tasks such as unit and functionality testing. Automated tools can cover more code than a human code reviewer, but there remains a significant software security problem.

The cyber security community is still poor at communicating to the public how serious this software security problem is, now and in the future, and how reasonably to resolve it. The time and technical knowledge to verify the security and privacy of any given device are outside the realm of possibility and competence for most consumers. A large army of testers would be needed to fulfill this verification task at the societal level.

This raises some major societal questions. How will the cyber security community communicate the severity of vulnerabilities in a more useful way to the public? What is the future role of regulation, certification, insurance, and privatization in promoting improved safety and integrity? How will society solve the problem of having enough testers to verify the public safety and integrity of computing devices in the everyday world? If there is perceived to be inadequate industry effort to verify, software providers should not be surprised if the public is less willing to trust.

## ENDNOTES

1. Turing (1950).
2. Reading University (2014).
3. Slovic (2010).
4. Huang and Liu (2017).
5. Vab Rassen (2018).
6. NCA (2017).
7. Schelmetic (2015).
8. Constantin (2015).
9. Fox-Brewster (2018).
10. Levenshtein (1966).
11. Sophos (2015).
12. Ibid.
13. Polyakova and Boyer (2018).

# CHAPTER 12

# Cyber Future

## 12.1 CYBERGEDDON

### 12.1.1 Choosing Our Tomorrow

An old proverb says that there are 10,000 tomorrows and that we should choose the tomorrow we want. How might the many futures of cyber risk play out? And which future should we choose?

We can't peek too far into the future, because technology and human change are inherently unpredictable (we really wish those 1950s forecasts of nuclear-powered vacuum cleaners had worked out) but let's say 5 to 10 years from now.

We will begin with Cybergeddon and later we'll consider Cybertopia.

The key trends that drive the Cybergeddon vision of the future are predominantly the negative ones: the growing numbers of cyber attacks, the increasing populations of cyber threat actors, the growing power of computing to inflict ever more severe attacks, and the escalating costs of reparations for breaching someone's data privacy, combined with the sheer scale of the growth of new software being produced with poor quality assurance (QA) levels.

### 12.1.2 Hacker Hordes Rise

We run the risk of the cyber attack community overwhelming society's ability to combat it. The various communities of threat actors, described in Chapter 5, are growing year by year. They reinvest their profits in developing new capabilities, and at present seem to be winning the arms race with the information technology (IT) security industry and law enforcement. There is a generation of highly educated graduates and technically proficient students in many different countries, who are only too easily enticed into illegal hacking. The rewards are high, their chances of being apprehended by law enforcement are minimal, and their alternatives may be limited. As rational choice theory suggests, cyber crime might be the best career option for an enthusiastic young coder living somewhere like Romania.

It is easily conceivable that the global population of criminal hackers could double over the next decade.

### 12.1.3   More Powerful Attack Technologies Are Deployed

Cyber criminals are scaling up their capabilities through technology and commoditizing components. The costs, difficulties, and 'logistical burden' of carrying out powerful attacks are reducing, making criminal tools accessible to more people. A piece of ransomware that might previously have needed the skills of a grade 4 operative (highly experienced coder) might now be able to be assembled from kits by a grade 2 operative. This skill deflation makes attack technology more accessible and increases the number of people who can use it.

## CYBERGEDDON[1]

It was a bright, cold day in April and the clocks were striking thirteen. Julia hurried through the revolving doors into the lobby of Victory Media. As she passed through the electronic device scanner, the receptionists smiled in welcome to one of their most senior executives. As Head of Digital Security, Julia ran an organization whose budget consumed 20% of the running costs of the advertising corporation. She glanced at the wallcast playing the latest news feed from the war, a roll call of the latest casualties. Looks like the *Crazy Bear* team had a busy night. Familiar names, but they were some of the smaller businesses that were still trying to operate outside of the Citadel network, on the old internet. As Julia made her way to her office, the lights flickered. Another power outage, but Victory Media's own power system had kicked in seamlessly.

At the Digital Security control center Julia was met by her entire team of five, and they reviewed the dashboards. 'Problems?' said Julia to her second in command. 'It's the Creatives team', replied Winston. 'Still messaging their non-secure friends using company communications channels'. Julia shook her head. 'What can you expect? It's the last department we haven't been able to replace with algorithmics. Shut down their social media channels! Human activities are still our weakest link'.

The daily security metrics seemed within normal ranges. The internal network traffic, data management, and abnormality readouts within Victory Media's systems seemed fine. Outside their fortress perimeter, however, it was chaos, as usual. Thousands of cyber attacks a second rained down on them, looking for vulnerabilities and ways in. More important than their external scans were their scans of their own security scanning software, monitoring several billions of lines of software code for bugs and vulnerabilities. They had written this software themselves at great expense to ensure they could achieve the quality standards they required. Commercial software from vendors was cheaper, but too bug-ridden to use, and vendors' insistence on sheltering behind liability waivers in their licensing agreements had meant that businesses with mission-critical systems had to build the software themselves. Nobody trusted business counterparties these days. Everything had to happen in-house.

Victory Media had harvested several zettabytes of data about its target market's activities during the previous day, much of it meeting the new global regulation standards of 'HyperPersonal', so the company would be crippled by the litigation costs if any of it were leaked. This data had to be quantum encrypted and held securely while the analysis engines ran through it. It was becoming uneconomic to hold the data for long, as the risk of it leaking almost outweighed the benefits of analyzing it. Julia sighed at the thought of what might have been. She'd joined the company nearly a decade ago among all the hype of the Fourth Industrial revolution, full of promise for commercial and social advances, improved productivity, and wealth generation by using machine learning to interpret all the volumes of free data that were available back then. Sadly, it hadn't turned out as she'd imagined. Data hadn't been free for long. It had become very expensive – all the penalties, the regulatory red tape, the costs of keeping it secure, and the compensation to the people who generated it.

Julia felt secure behind the company's electronic walls. It was a shame that the general public had lost confidence in e-commerce – not that you could blame them, when most of their online transactions were compromised.

But it was all right. She had won the victory over herself. She loved Big Data.

The attack technology itself is also improving. Examples of criminal syndicates reinvesting in developing more capable tools show that they are highly motivated to outwit the security defenses that companies have installed. It is a penetration-testing truism that, given sufficient time and resources, any corporate organization can be breached by a determined attacker. Security technology is a major area of expenditure by organizations (now a $120 billion industry – significantly larger than the revenues of cyber criminals), and considerable amounts are invested each year in new developments by the security industry, but this is an asymmetrical arms race. The attacker only has to win once, through one weakness. The defender has to win every time, plugging every vulnerability.

Future developments could well see the attackers outstripping the capabilities of the defenders. Cyber hackers could use artificial intelligence (AI) to improve their ability to detect every software vulnerability that exists and to automate the probing for weaknesses in the defenses of the organizations they target. A future where companies are routinely penetrated by hackers would lead to a very different behavior by organizations.

### 12.1.4   No Data Is Safe

As companies are routinely penetrated and haemorrhage their protected data, people will lose their confidence in the organizations that hold private information about them. They will demand reparations and withdraw their permissions for big companies to hold data about them. Their political representatives will pass increasingly punitive laws to regulate data loss. Protection of digital assets is likely to become uneconomic. Or at least it could radically change the economics of the Big Data revolution. Companies will protect themselves by reducing the data they hold. They could regard data as toxic – data could turn out not to be 'the new oil'; it might just turn out to be 'the new asbestos' where everyone who deals in it becomes sucked into a chain of litigation and liability.

### 12.1.5   Splinternet

Intercompany trading will still be highly beneficial, but as companies suffer losses they will become increasingly distrustful of counterparties. Companies they share data with, or allow to connect to their networks, will become potential vectors of risk. Businesses will reduce their risk exposure to counterparties by bringing outsourced operations back in-house. The economic gains that have been made by the outsourcing phenomenon of the past decade will be reversed, with more costly business operations required to ensure security. Where trading and electronic data exchange are essential, this will increasingly be carried out through private commercial intranets that operate in secure isolation. The internet will fragment and become two tiers – the 'splinternet' scenario. It will no doubt persist as an open public network, but people will use it knowing that it is insecure, and use it mainly as a chat channel for sharing kitten photos and the like. Businesses will retreat into their expensive technology fortresses and super-secure private networks.

### 12.1.6  Consumer e-Commerce Dies

If cyber heists on bank accounts reach levels that banks can no longer absorb, they will at some point have to change their policy of indemnifying their customers and pass the losses back to the account holders. It will certainly happen very gradually, and banks will be reluctant to publicize it, but individual cases of customer liability for cyber losses will increase. At some point customers will lose faith in online banking, and either retreat to older methods of banking or pay a lot more for an elite system of protecting digital and financial assets in a less connected, more isolated and protected network of trust.

This collapse of confidence in the ability of organizations to keep data safe will affect consumer use of the internet, reduce e-commerce transactions, and cause a slowdown or reversal of the effect of the internet as a booster of productivity to the global economy.

It is no exaggeration to say that global economic growth will be slower in a world where cyber risk is a lot higher than it is today.

### 12.1.7  Cyber War

But perhaps the most profound change will come from the escalation of cyber attacks between nations as a routine instrument of foreign policy. Cyber attacks are occurring every day on civilian and commercial targets that we believe, with high levels of confidence, are being carried out by cyber teams funded and authorized by foreign governments. The frequency of these attacks and the levels of belligerence are increasing.

In retaliation, we now allow our own cyber warriors to conduct 'active cyber defense' offensive operations against organizations in other countries that operate under the jurisdictions of other governments. These low-level, state-sponsored cyber skirmishes and tit-for-tat exchanges have the potential to escalate into all-out cyber wars, and possibly even a real war.

Nation-state cyber teams are currently constrained by their political masters in what they are permitted to do. The superpowers of the United States, China, and Russia are still cautious in what they allow their cyber teams to do in each other's territories, as part of the détente between them. But there are also advanced persistent threat (APT) teams on each side that are operating with some levels of state endorsement and are less constrained by political sensitivities and more deniable, which are carrying out damaging operations against each other's interests. There are, in addition, a number of second- and third-tier countries conducting their own independent operations, some of them quite aggressively. This shadowboxing is made possible because of the difficulties of attribution of activities in cyber operations. International law is not yet adapted to ruling on the legality of these kinds of operations interfering in the affairs of sovereign powers.

This trend of state-sponsored cyber teams continuously probing and pushing the boundaries of what they can get away with will eventually provoke retaliation, or will accommodate to a new understanding of what is permissible between nations. It is easy to envision a pessimistic scenario of state-on-state cyber operations that provoke retaliation, escalation, and a political decision to unleash the full power of the capabilities of their cyber warriors.

In 2017 NATO alliance members agreed that a major cyber attack would trigger Article 5 of their mutual defense clause: an attack on any NATO member will bring all members to its defense. Cyber operations are now considered to be a fifth service of a country's armed forces (army, navy, air force, and marines being the other four). Most military strategists believe that any future armed conflict will have a heavy contribution of cyber activity to attack armed forces infrastructure, disable weapons systems, and disrupt communications. Others go further and suggest that the nature of conflict itself could shift, to focus on the disruption – or complete dismantling – of the economy of an antagonist through cyber attacks, without using conventional military force at all. If this were to occur, private-sector companies would become primary targets, along with critical national infrastructure and government organizations. It is likely that cyber war would be very damaging to the economy, and would be fought against targets, like the power generation and distribution companies, that have not had time, resources, or support from their regulators to build the cyber resistance that would be required against this type of attacker.

Cyber war will shelter behind the difficulties of attribution of attacks, with misdirection and false flags, so that the element of doubt makes the attacked country less likely to retaliate directly.

If a country that suffers severe economic damage can identify its attacker with sufficient confidence, then it may well retaliate with a conventional military response. The histories of conflict show that minor skirmishes, distrust, and misunderstandings can rapidly spiral into full mobilization. State-sponsored cyber operations may lower the threshold at which countries go to war. The 'long peace' between superpowers that has lasted since 1945 could finally erupt into a major militarized conflict as a result of state-sponsored cyber operations.

## 12.2 CYBERTOPIA

On the other hand, there is reason for quite a bit of optimism. There are other cyber risk trends that could make the future a safer and more prosperous one. The key trends that drive the Cybertopia vision of the future are all the positive ones. Security technology that reduces cyber losses is becoming affordable to many more organizations, rather than the protected elite. The software industry is producing higher-quality and less exploit-prone products, which will be improved when we finally lift the protectionism that has sheltered commercial vendors for too long. Threat actors will be deterred by increasing their chances of being convicted and changing the entire calculus of their risks and rewards. And organizations are building the costs of protection and education of their staff into a new safety culture and business model of cyber resilience. We could face a future where cyber threats become as anachronistic as gun-toting bank robbers in the Wild West.

### 12.2.1 Exorcism of Ghosts in the Code

Despite the explosive growth in volumes of software being used by organizations today, and the high occurrence of vulnerabilities that form the 'ghosts in the code' (Chapter 4) and provide the vectors for hackers to operate, there is reason to be optimistic that error rates in this code base can be greatly reduced. Software defect prevention and quality assurance processes are radically transforming software engineering. Automated testing is becoming significantly more powerful and will become greatly aided by AI techniques. Bug bounty reward systems are improving the number of vulnerabilities being reported to the vendors before the hackers exploit them maliciously. Rafts of new codes of practice and regulation are tightening up security in the code in our everyday software products, internet of things devices, medical equipment, and components.

And most importantly, the commercial software companies themselves are being held to increasingly higher standards of care. The software liability waiver (UCC Section 2-719) limiting the remedy for a purchaser in case of defective software to the cost paid for the program is unsustainable and will eventually be replaced by obligations for software producers to be responsible for the losses their defective products cause in the same way that producers of other products are held responsible.

We expect consumers to increasingly differentiate between commercial software vendors on the basis of the quality and safety of their products. Organizations might prefer not to license software products that could provide an entry point for a cyber criminal to carry out a multimillion-dollar loss on their business. Grading software more visibly by its propensity for vulnerabilities will aid consumer choice.

The inevitable consequence of being realistic about the economics of having safe code is that the cost of producing software will rise, and so organizations will have to pay more for their software, both from vendors and developed in-house. Better quality software will cost more and take longer to produce. The economic value of software will become better reflected in the operational costs of a business, but this inevitably means that there will be a period of disruption as we shift from a low-cost, error-prone business model of how we value software to one of higher investment cost but with greatly reduced risks of catastrophic failures. Almost every dangerous product has gone through this cycle: steam boiler manufacturing in the eighteenth century; flying machines, automobiles, and nuclear power plants in the twentieth cenury; and so on.

Will the lifting of protectionism for software vendors cause innovation to stall? No. Innovation will be boosted by higher-value software, and software companies will be incentivized to innovate in their quality control as well as business productivity.

We expect the rate of known vulnerabilities to be reduced by an order of magnitude within a few years of the repeal of the software liability waiver, and by another order of magnitude every few years.

Software in Cybertopia is bug-free, and people shake their heads to recall that it was ever such an amateur and fault-tolerant industry to base a new economy on.

### 12.2.2 Twenty-First-Century Law Enforcement

The indictment and conviction rates for cyber criminals are increasing. The past few years has seen heroic efforts by the US Department of Justice to bring to book some of the worst cyber criminals, to close down dark web trading platforms, and to send a strong message to the hacker industry that cyber crime has its penalties. Ultimately, the reduction of cyber crime will come about only when the perpetrators have a significant likelihood of being caught and punished. The calculus of cyber crime – 'hackonomics' (Chapter 5) – is too heavily weighted towards easy reward, with very little chance of penalty. When the consequences of a hacker carrying out a cyber attack are similar to those for other crimes of the same financial value and emotional distress, we can drain the swamp of the hacker underworld.

Improvement of law enforcement to raise the likelihood of being caught and punished has been impressively successful for many forms of crime. Rates for non-violent crime of all types have reduced quite dramatically in most of the advanced economies over the past generation, in some cases falling as much as 80% since peaks in the late 1980s, owing to increased deterrence, improvements in policing resourcing and methods, and reduced social tolerance of offenders. Cyber crime rates have trended the opposite way, but there is hope that they could similarly plummet in future years with similar emphasis on improving law enforcement and apprehension rates for offenders.

This will not be easy. Cyber crime is complex and highly technical, requiring police investigators to have highly specialized skills. It is difficult to attract people with those skills to come to work for the police force rather than for IT security companies (not least because of the current pay grade differential). It is difficult to attribute and build a criminal case with evidence to obtain a conviction. Courts currently struggle to interpret cyber crime in terms of traditional criminal law: 'Prove that you have been harmed by the theft of your personal data'. Sentencing is mild, because crime punishment codes are baselined against physical violence and personal injury. Cyber crime is often trans-jurisdictional, being carried out by people in foreign locations where the authority to investigate and make arrests is the responsibility of a different country.

To raise the law enforcement game to meet the cyber crime challenge requires a reinvention of the law enforcement apparatus and inevitably more resources devoted to combating cyber crime: increasing the number and quality of specialist detectives, and revising the judicial code to include interpretation of harm, appropriate sentencing guidelines, and possibly a more powerful Interpol or changes to international law to allow the hot pursuit of cyber criminals across (nation-)state lines.

With sufficient political will, these changes will be put into place. It may take a catastrophic cyber event to force this to the top of the political agenda. The general public and corporate business will demand better protection from their elected representatives. It will be realized that it makes more sense to solve cyber risk by putting public resources into law enforcement than for every company in the world to invest in its own increasingly expensive IT security. Making law enforcement fit for purpose against twenty-first century crime will become a political cause. Creating prestigious and well-paid cyber police divisions will become a platform for a new generation of law-and-order politicians, as it has in the past. It will take a long, hard process of reorganizing and resourcing law enforcement forces almost globally, but it will be necessary and worthwhile for the protection it provides and the prosperity it generates. In Cybertopia the cyber cops are the heroes.

### 12.2.3    Geneva Convention for Cyber Operations

In the optimistic view of future cyber risk, in addition to improvements in software quality and law enforcement, the initial wave of cyber hacking that accompanied the fourth industrial revolution has been moderated by continuous advances in security and investment in countermeasures.

Improvements in bandwidth, computing power, and technology advances have been boosted by this renewed confidence in the safety of the digital environment. Encryption technologies and personalization have improved trust and accountability of transactions online. The world enters its fifth industrial revolution, where economy productivity receives a further boost from secure and confident total digital connectivity.

The economic dimension of cyber security is coupled with advances in international relations that reduce the incidence of state-sponsored operations in another country's activities. An additional treaty to the Geneva Convention is agreed that governs cyber operations. Countries with advanced national cyber capabilities agree that it is to their mutual benefit to prohibit cyber operations that interfere in each other's military forces, government agencies, political and democratic processes, business activities, and critical national infrastructure. They establish the Organization for the Prohibition of International Interference in Digital Systems (OPIIDS), modeled on the intergovernmental organizations that oversee the implementation of other treaties, such as those regarding chemical weapons and nuclear disarmament. Signatories agree to procedures for verification, sanctions against offenders, and reporting protocols. Difficulties in attribution of cyber activity are tackled head-on by establishing a process for allegation and investigation by OPIIDS.

This digital 'Geneva Convention' goes a long way to de-legitimizing the activities of nation-state cyber teams in interfering with any other country's assets. It reduces the likelihood of countries triggering an international crisis through cyber trespassing, and it reduces the incidence of businesses being penetrated by the nation-state cyber units of another country.

With this mutual understanding in place, the international communities work together to tackle the multi-jurisdictional aspects of cyber crime. Many international treaties will be required to allow multilateral operations to be carried out against gangs and their server equipment and cyber activities in lawless areas of the world.

In Cybertopia, the prospect of cyber war between countries has been replaced by a coordinated international effort of mutual cyber policing and protection of global business activity.

## CYBERTOPIA[2]

A merry little surge of electricity piped by automatic alarm from the mood organ beside her bed awakened Julia. She scanned through her morning briefing as Head of Digital Security at Victory Media. The news was shocking: a break-in at Rosen Association. There hadn't been a cyber attack on a major organization now for four years. Business had never been better.

Julia joined the incident response meeting of the other heads of digital security of all the major corporations of the world. The indicators of compromise and the diagnostics of the incident were being streamed through. The attackers had gained entry using an exploit in the Securetec software running multilayered authentication protocols for the communications channels. The remedial patch had been available and installed to all users within 15 seconds. Pattern recognition analytics were now being run across all comparable software code to reassess whether this class of vulnerability could be replicated anywhere else. Securetec was already working with Rosen Association to provide full compensation for the damage to its business under the terms of its licensing agreement. It was not for nothing that Securetec was the most prestigious – and expensive – software vendor.

*Stand by for a briefing from the investigating officer.* Rick Deckard of CyberPol was clear and succinct: 'We haven't seen an attack this sophisticated for a long time, but it has the coding signatures of the

*(Continued)*

old *Tardigrade* gang. Looks like they're out of hibernation for one last job'.

There was a buzz of conversation around the meeting. How could this be happening? Cyber crime was less than a tenth of the levels it had been in the crazy days of the late teens. The public outcry that had followed the crippling *BlakDeth* malware attack had triggered the reforms that had restructured the police forces around the world and seen new laws passed to tackle cyber crime properly. Many convictions had followed, deterring further attacks. Improving economic conditions had also helped. The technology boom had pulled many of the gray-hat hackers away from crime and into well-paid mainstream jobs. Safe technology had turned out to be the key to a new wave of economic prosperity. But it looked like there were still some hard-core hackers stuck in their old ways.

As the meeting ended, Deckard asked Julia to stay online. 'Victory Media uses Securetec communications systems, right? Can you help me reverse engineer the attack routing? I need to trace backwards through the false flag trail. I think the *Tardigrade* gang are in Cairo'. Julia smiled and asked: 'What do you need, Rick?'

Julia and Rick worked for most of the morning. Their personalized security protocols ensured that their communications channel was private and secure. Digital data was the most precious resource in modern business, and highly personalized. All individuals now legally owned their own data and any information they generated, receiving royalty streams from the companies they authorized to have access to it. Keeping this data safe from prying eyes, thieves, and unauthorized users had driven Julia's career. She had developed the systems that had turned Victory Media into the powerhouse of protected personalized information provision that it was today. No lousy old-school hacker was going to steal the lifeblood data of her company. Not on her watch.

'I think we are in', whispered Deckard, 'and here's the evidence we're looking for'. Julia scanned the display data. 'Yes, that's the source code of the entrybot, all right. Will this stand up in court?' Deckard gave a big grin: 'Section 93. No problem: possession, compiling history, keystroke log. We'll convince a jury. I'm calling in the Cairo unit of CyberPol to pull them in. We got them'.

Julia gave him a thumbs-up, disconnected the meeting, and, feeling better, fixed herself at last a cup of black, hot coffee.

## 12.3  FUTURE TECHNOLOGY TRENDS

The fundamental twin sciences of mathematics and physics have guided us to where we are in cyberspace technology. There are a number of key future technology trends that are likely to be highly influential in the way that cyber threats and risks of cyber loss for society play out, either negatively in the direction of Cybergeddon or positively towards Cybertopia. Which path is taken may be strongly influenced by the next generation of mathematicians and physicists, following in the footsteps of Alan Turing and Tim Berners-Lee.

### 12.3.1  Security and Cryptography

Since the combination lock was developed in 1878 for Tiffany's jewelers' safe in New York, high security has been found in random numbers. Unlike a standard mechanical lock, there is no need to carry around a key, but recalling the combination can be a memory challenge, like any complicated password. It is not always possible to find a catchy mnemonic such as 'One ate for free, oh, none for tea', which Sherlock Holmes figured out to be the combination 18430040.[3]

Cyber risk is intrinsically dependent on the science of cryptography, and the generation of random numbers is essential to cryptography; strong cryptographic algorithms must foil hacking attempts at pattern analysis. Future technical advances in random number generation are thus important for all cyber risk stakeholders. Encryption techniques make plentiful use of random numbers. Many security protocols also require random bits. Suppose you log in to a website and are assigned a unique ID for the session. The ID is typically a string of random characters, which are very hard to guess. However, someone who had managed to figure out aspects of the random number generation process might then more easily guess your string and impersonate you. In most cryptographic systems, the inferior quality of the random number generator contributes to system vulnerability to cyber attack. Heninger et al. found many thousands of servers vulnerable because of the use of poor quality random number generators.[4]

There are many ways of generating random numbers that differ in their degree of actual randomness. There are two classes of random number generator: deterministic pseudo-random number generators (PRNGs) and non-deterministic true random number generators (TRNGs). However cleverly constructed from a specific mathematical algorithm, the output of a PRNG is determined, and therefore predictable, once its initial state is known. But the output sequences do not have recognizable patterns, and they cannot be readily distinguished from sequences generated by a TRNG, which uses some physical source of randomness. However, a TRNG is harder to construct than a PRNG, and a TRNG may be susceptible to bias, noise, and potential interference by an attacker.

Thankfully, a significant conceptual step forward in producing truly random numbers has been made by Bierhorst et al.[5] They have shown that it is possible to create a provably secure random number generator for which the user has no knowledge about the internal generation mechanism whereas the adversary has a detailed description.[6] This TRNG satisfies Kerckhoff's principle: a cryptosystem should be secure even if everything about the system, except the key, is public knowledge. This new random number generation technique involves a novel process based on the fundamental laws of quantum mechanics. Increasingly, the classical world of computer science is expanding into the mysterious but fascinating quantum domain. Not only is quantum computing on the horizon, but cryptography will be turning in this direction for quantum key distribution. This is reviewed in Section 12.3.9.

### 12.3.2  The Future of Passwords

It would be rather peculiar for individuals to rely on a variety of different combination locks to secure all their baggage, storage lockers, safes, and entrances. Yet, managing a personal collection of passwords is a universal chore in the twenty-first century, and is the bane of every computer user. Not only should every individual password be as different from any dictionary word as possible, but they should not be the same or similar to each other. Furthermore, organizations that keep large numbers of passwords relating to their employees, clients, and customers need to adhere to strict protocols on password management. As with any regulation or recommendation, compliance is enhanced by understanding of the underlying technical rationale. Regrettably, it is all too obvious from the massive theft rate of passwords that the following brief review of this technical rationale is all too necessary.

A password should never be stored as is, but rather as a more or less unreadable string of characters almost impossible to convert back to the original. The conversion of a password into such a string is done through a process called hashing. A hash is designed to act as a one-way function: a mathematical operation that is easy to perform, but very difficult to reverse. Indeed, hashing is intended not to be reversible. A hacker might try to invert a hash by computing many images and storing them in a table. To thwart such a foreseeable hostile act, hashes have a large output with many bits.

For example, the password 'Andrew1Eireann2Gordon3' might be hashed as: f47ad315942dabc1d62xwc152dac37kd8qhs8yt7s.

There is no defined operation that transforms f47ad315942dabc1d62xw c152dac37kd8qhs8yt7s back to Andrew1Eireann2Gordon3. Rather, when a password is entered once again, it is hashed, and a check is made that it is the same as the original. Even though hackers cannot reverse a hashed password, there is nothing to prevent them from trying – and they do. They can simply guess passwords and run them through a secure hash algorithm (SHA), published by the National Institute of Standards and Technology (NIST). A hash-cracking program working on a large database of hashes can guess many millions of possible passwords and automatically compare the results with an entire collection of stolen hashed passwords to find matches.

### 12.3.3 Passwords Should Have High Entropy

Serious hash-crackers have constructed so-called rainbow tables, long lists of precomputed hashes for every plausible password. For example, under the simple hashing function SHA-1, the naive password 'password1' hashes as: e38ad214943daad1d64c102faec29de4afe9da3d. Password crackers do not merely guess passwords at random, but use dictionary attacks to cycle through words, collections of known common passwords from past breaches, and use statistical analyses of those passwords to spot patterns that speed up the guessing of new passwords. Clearly, a password should aspire to have high entropy, i.e. be as long as reasonably practical (e.g. 10 characters), and have a good mix of not just mixed-case alphanumeric symbols, but all characters. Camejo estimated that the cracking time for such a high-entropy password is about 75 million times slower than for a minimal-entropy six-character password with just lowercase letters.[7] If only this were widely known: data from five million leaked passwords from users in North America and western Europe showed that the first and second most used passwords in 2017 were '123456' and 'password'.[8]

Some hashing schemes are significantly harder to reverse than others. A hash can be spiced up by adding a random string of characters, called a 'salt', to the beginning or end of the password before hashing it. A different salt can be used for each password. In 2012, a collection of 177 million stolen LinkedIn accounts went up for sale on a dark web market after the hashing scheme had been reversed. But the company had used only the simple hashing function SHA-1 without salting, allowing almost all the hashed passwords to be cracked. As a result, hackers were able not only to access the passwords, but also to try them on other websites.

Nobody familiar with the insidious techniques of hash-cracking can remain complacent over setting their own passwords. Unsurprisingly, security professionals envisage a terminal decline in the usage of passwords. Passwords alone are totally inadequate to provide sufficient protection. Multi-layer authentication will progressively augment passwords, and the use of behavioral biometrics may emerge as a publicly acceptable method for preventing password-protected accounts from being hijacked. This smart but comparatively expensive technology works by recognizing users based on their behavior patterns, such as keystrokes, mouse dynamics, and screen interactions. It then uses these patterns to spot anomalies between approved users and would-be hackers.

Non-password authentication is a subject of intensive computer security research. There is a regular international passwords conference, with a goal to gather researchers and password crackers from around the world to better understand the challenges surrounding the methods of personal authentication and passwords. One idea for a passwordless future promoted by Frank Stajano is based on each individual having a small hardware token, called a Pico, which might be as unobtrusive as a wristwatch, car key fob, or necklace.[9] Hardware tokens provide a viable improvement in personal security, Carrying hardware tokens is not burdensome, but these themselves could be accidentally lost or become a target for criminals.

### 12.3.4 The Security of Data Encryption

Anyone who has seen the 2014 movie *The Imitation Game* knows that the British mathematician Alan Turing had to improvise a computer to crack the German Enigma code during World War II. Before then, while a Fellow of King's College, Cambridge, he started developing his pioneering ideas on universal computing machines, which established his claim to be the father of modern computer science.

Cryptography is the study of techniques for securing communications from prying eyes. As the most prominent stakeholders, intelligence agencies have been at the forefront of developments in cryptography. In the United States, the National Security Agency (NSA), and in the United Kingdom, the Government Communications Headquarters (GCHQ) have a tradition of hiring bright mathematicians to work in cryptography. One of these was another King's College, Cambridge, alumnus, Clifford Cocks. His arrival at GCHQ as a 22-year-old in 1973 has gone down in employment legend. Imagine starting your first job and solving a problem that would be a major achievement in an entire career. In a matter of hours rather than months or years, he discovered an algorithm that would be named the RSA algorithm for the initials of Rivest, Shamir, and Adleman, who, at MIT four years later in 1977, first publicized this core foundation of public key cryptography.[10]

Why should the introduction of a public key into cryptography be such a great idea? It sounds stupid. Ideas that seem counter-intuitive are often the smartest. Consider cryptography in its basic symmetric form only involving a secret key. This has been the standard means of securing information since ancient times. The Spartans, famous for their physical prowess in battle, had an ingenious cipher system. The problem arises when the secret key or code is intercepted. In a file transfer environment, where there are many users distributed over the world, distributing a secret key in a secure manner is a huge challenge.

This security problem goes away when the only key transmitted is public. Then it does not matter if it is intercepted. Obviously, there has to be more to public key cryptography than a public key. Indeed, there is a private key as well. The public key can be shared with everyone, whereas the private key must be kept secret. The public and private keys are connected via some very elegant mathematical theorems, which provide the intellectual framework for public key cryptography. Through mathematical magic mind-boggling to most of humanity – and which Rivest, Shamir, and Adleman had originally thought impossible – both the public and the private keys can encrypt a message; the opposite key from the one used to encrypt a message is used to decrypt it.

### 12.3.5  Asymmetric Cryptography

In asymmetric cryptography, everyone has one's own encryption and decryption keys. These keys need to be devised so that the decryption key is not easily deduced from the public encryption key. This requires a kind of mathematical trapdoor that allows an encrypted message to be decrypted easily with a private key, but it is extremely hard to do so without access to the private key. It turns out that such a trapdoor can be constructed using the arcane but beautiful mathematics of prime numbers. Multiplying prime numbers is very much easier than identifying the prime number factors of a large number.

To use asymmetric encryption, there must be a way for people to discover other public keys. The typical technique is to use digital certificates. A digital certificate is a package of information that identifies a user or a server, and contains information such as the organization's name, the organization that issued the certificate, the user's email address and country, and the user's public key. When a server and client require a secure encrypted communication, they send a query over the network to the other party, which sends back a copy of the digital certificate. The other party's public key can be extracted from the digital certificate.

The security of the RSA algorithm relies on the high computational difficulty of finding prime factors of large integers. However, two developments are progressively eroding this difficulty. One is the inexorable rise in computer power; the other is the ability of the mathematical community to find clever and efficient factoring methods. As computing power increases and more efficient factoring algorithms are discovered, the ability to factor ever larger numbers increases. Encryption strength is directly tied to key size, so doubling key length from 1024 to 2048 bits delivers an exponential increase in strength, although it does impair performance.

### 12.3.6 Elliptic Curve Cryptography

There is much more in the mathematicians' cryptographic armory than number theory. Another esoteric branch of mathematics that has been researched for trapdoor functions involves the algebraic study of elliptic curves. A topsy-turvy outcome that would have appealed to the mathematical mind of Lewis Carroll, the author of *Alice in Wonderland*, is that the less progress that mathematicians make in analyzing these curves, the more useful they are for cyber security. The sheer complexity of these curves makes for better trapdoors that are harder to break than those based on number theory. Elliptic curve cryptography is thus gaining favor with many security experts as an alternative to RSA for implementing public key cryptography. It can create faster, smaller, and more efficient cryptographic keys. Elliptic curve cryptography is thus likely to expand in applicability relative to RSA cryptography, as it can deliver equivalent security with lower computing power and battery usage, making it especially suitable for mobile apps.

As indicated earlier, public key encryption algorithms are mathematically more complex than shared key encryption algorithms. Consequently, public key encryption is significantly slower than shared key encryption. Accordingly, the most secure and widely used methods to protect data transmission are based on symmetric cryptography, such as the Advanced Encryption Standard. However, the distribution of shared keys is generally accomplished using public key encryption methods.

### 12.3.7 The Quantum Computing Horizon

Faster computing poses a persistent challenge to the security of public key distribution. Increasingly larger asymmetric keys are needed to distribute symmetric keys securely, which has negative time and cost implications. Worrying as this is, the disruptive technological threat on the horizon is the emergence of high-performance quantum computing. Quantum supremacy over classical computing is achieved when a formal computational task is performed with an existing quantum device that cannot be performed in a reasonable amount of time using any known algorithm running on an existing classical supercomputer.[11]

In classical computing, the basic computational unit is a bit, which takes a binary value of 0 or 1. In quantum computing, the basic computational unit is a *qubit*. The significance of a qubit lies in the wonders of quantum mechanics, which have enthralled physicists and baffled the public for a century. In the classical world, a system has to be in one physical state or another; in the quantum world, a system is in a superposition of states, with probability amplitudes associated with each state. Crucially, for an $n$-qubit system, to represent the overall state of the system, it takes 2 to the power $n$ numbers. For $n = 72$, this is an astonishing five billion trillion.

For high values of $n$, there is clearly potential for information processing on an unprecedented scale. A 72-qubit machine lies at the watershed of computing power. It is still within reach of a classical computer simulation, which could validate the accuracy of the output of the quantum computer. Beyond this point, quantum computers could be constructed to have values of $n$ extending into the hundreds, thousands, millions, and the distant horizon.

### 12.3.8 Quantum Computing as a Security Risk

With Google's quantum AI Lab research vision extending well past the quantum supremacy barrier, quantum computing will become a path-breaking, game-changing commercial technology. Scientists and engineers who use supercomputers for advanced numerical analysis, e.g. meteorologists, cannot wait for this to happen. On the other hand, cyber security analysts are fearful. As long ago as 1994, Peter Shor constructed a fast quantum computer algorithm for factorizing integers into prime numbers. A large qubit quantum computer could crack the private keys used in asymmetric cryptography. Even now, quantum computing poses a security risk: present encrypted data might be stored maliciously for future decryption by quantum computers. Of course, much data stored has a practical utility that decays with time. But some encrypted data needs to be kept confidential for more than a few decades, and this cannot be guaranteed in the future era of quantum computing.

Fortunately, there is an answer to the key distribution problem in a quantum computing environment. Fighting fire with fire, this is quantum key distribution. The viability of the RSA algorithm for distributing keys depends crucially on the excessively long time it would take for an eavesdropper to crack the mathematical code by brute force. Quantum computing renders this task tractable, and the distribution of keys insecure. Stepping up to the computer security plate to take over from the mathematicians are their scientific cousins, the theoretical physicists. In the twenty-first century, the most famous of these has been Stephen Hawking, who had a strong interest in quantum computing, although he never lived to witness its commercial development.

### 12.3.9  Quantum Key Distribution

In the ordinary classical world, if a message is sent between two people, it is possible for it to be intercepted without either of them having any knowledge of this. The bits in a computer text can be read without the reader altering any of the zeros or ones. However, in the quantum domain, an eavesdropper's attempt to intercept a quantum exchange leaves detectable traces. This is an inevitable consequence of Heisenberg's celebrated Uncertainty Principle of 1927. The act of observing a quantum state changes it. This would have astonished even a professional magician such as Nevil Maskelyne, who hacked Marconi's demonstration of wireless telegraphy in 1903 – which brings us back to the beginning of Chapter 3. That was the first breach of purportedly secure and private communication. The magic of quantum mechanics provides light at the end of the security tunnel, and hope for a brighter cyber future.

Encouragingly, the concept of quantum key distribution (QKD) has moved forward from academic analysis to technological development. Sufficient progress has been made for advocates of QKD to suggest that this technology be adopted for key distribution even in advance of the coming age of high-performance quantum computing, when it will become necessary.

## 12.4  GETTING THE CYBER RISK FUTURE WE WANT

### 12.4.1  Multi-pronged Approach

In this book, and particularly in this final chapter, we have set out the principal drivers of cyber risk – the technologies, the economics, the people behind it, and their motivations – and the trends that will influence the risk in the future.

We have argued that there are positive trends that give cause for optimism that cyber risk could be greatly reduced from current levels, and that this would generate productivity gains and a secure, safer, and more prosperous future (Cybertopia).

We have also set out the negative trends that make us quite pessimistic, and suggest that we could face a future where the frequency and the severity of cyber losses grow significantly, cause a constant burden of cost, and threaten to force a retreat into highly protected enclaves of activity that will constrain social freedom and hinder economic growth (Cybergeddon).

Of course the future won't be either one of these two extremes, neither Cybergeddon nor Cybertopia. It will be somewhere in between. We suggest that it is up to all of us to choose the future that we want, and to put our efforts into making this version of the future come about.

Reducing cyber risk levels will require a number of coordinated activities in a multi-pronged approach. It will mean each organization and each individual taking their own responsibilities for maximizing their cyber protection. Everyone needs to be aware of the threat environment, to understand the types of social engineering tricks that are used on them, and to play their part in our collective security. It will require change – changes in our legal system, changes in international relations and protocols, and changes to the way we make and utilize technology.

## 12.4.2    Increased Cost of Cyber Safety

Many of the improvements in cyber safety can be achieved with changes in awareness and habits and at very little cost. But many of the more important components of solving cyber risk will require major changes and will mean tolerating greater expenditure. By this we don't necessarily mean paying for even more security technology, although this may well be required. We mean that costs of increased security will be reflected in higher-cost everyday software (spending more on QA to reduce exploitable vulnerabilities), more expenditure on police forces (building new units of specialized, skilled cops to catch cyber criminals), and costs of hardening infrastructure (to keep the lights on in case they are attacked by foreign powers). The benefits of these costs will be reflected in reduced risk, and in the improved prosperity that this will ensure.

### 12.4.3 Ten Recommendations for Our Cyber Future

Here is a summary of some of our more important recommendations for solving cyber risk:

1. *Improve cyber safety culture* in organizations and in the general public. Awareness of cyber risk is the human firewall that keeps our society safe.
2. *Ensure high compliance with cyber security good practice*, including increasingly secure password protection, adoption of high-entropy encryption technology, and behavioral and biometric alternatives to password authentication.
3. *Make our critical national infrastructure resilient to cyber attack.* It is evidently a key target for state-sponsored cyber operations. Regulatory constraints on power grid operators (among others) currently disincentivize them from investing in cyber security, whereas this investment should be encouraged, and arguably subsidized, by national governments.
4. *End the software liability waiver* (UCC 2-719), which shelters software companies from taking full responsibility for the damages resulting from their faulty and vulnerability-ridden products. This will force software vendors to invest in improving code quality. Allow and expect the costs of software to increase as a result.
5. *Grade software products by security.* Establish an independent grading by a standards institution to publish ratings of commonly used software, and products containing software, on their security and propensity for containing vulnerabilities. Enable consumers to differentiate products by the safety they provide, and regulate minimum standards for devices being connected online.
6. *Invest in law enforcement to combat cyber crime.* Make our police forces fit for purpose for tackling twenty-first-century cyber crime and obtaining convictions of key perpetrators. Greatly increase the number of skilled computer specialists to work as cyber detectives and be able to compile evidence and build a legal case.
7. *Overhaul criminal law to update it for the cyber age.* Support the law enforcement effort by updating the legal framework of police operations, including court processes and sentencing guidelines, to ensure that deterrence is equivalent to that for other crimes of the same financial value and emotional distress.
8. *Build an international CyberPol capability.* Put into place international capabilities and cross-border agreements that enable cyber prosecution to follow criminals across jurisdictional boundaries.

9. *Create a 'Marshall Plan' for economic alternatives.* Generate alternatives to cyber crime as a career for individuals in the hacker communities, providing legitimate employment and economic opportunities for educated graduates in emerging market economies.
10. *Propose a Geneva Convention for cyber operations.* Develop international consensus amongst countries with advanced national cyber capabilities to prohibit cyber operations that interfere in one another's' military, governmental, political, and business activities, and critical national infrastructure.

These changes will require significant political will, cooperation, cost, and disruption. But continued inaction is worse. Cyber risk is a blight, and at some point public opinion will demand action. These changes are needed to make cyber risk manageable across society. They are self-evident and important to achieve.

In the past, major changes in safety and security have come about only in the aftermath of a catastrophe. We hope that it will not take a major cyber catastrophe for these changes to occur in solving cyber risk. If and when a major cyber catastrophe does occur, we hope this book will provide a blueprint for making us safer against the next one.

Together, and only together, we can solve cyber risk.

## ENDNOTES

1. With apologies to George Orwell.
2. With apologies to Philip K. Dick.
3. Mower (2017).
4. Heninger et al. (2012).
5. Bierhorst et al. (2018).
6. Pironio (2018).
7. Camejo (2017).
8. Grossman (2017).
9. Stajano (2011).
10. Cocks (1973).
11. Boixo et al. (2017).

# References

A.M. Best; 2017; *Cyber line expected to be one of the leading P/C growth areas.* Best's special report; June 22, 2017.

ABC News; 2017; *The 7 Top Hacking Countries*; https://abcnews.go.com/Technology /photos/top-hacking-countries-19844818/image-19845214

ABC; 2017; *'Runaway algorithms' and the cyber risks facing the global financial system*; Sue Lannin; March 20, 2017. http://www.abc.net.au/news/2017-03-20/ a-cyber-attack-could-cause-the-next-global-financial-crisis/8370860

Ablon L., Bogart A.; 2017; *Zero-days, thousands of nights.* RAND Corporation report; 2017.

ACPO; 2012; *Good practice guide for digital evidence.* Association of Chief Police Officers.

Adamic L.A., Huberman B.A.; 2002; *Zipf's Law and the internet.* Glottometrics, 3, 143-150.

Advisen; 2015; *The Cyber Insurance Market*; Cyber Risks Insights Conference, New York, Oct 20, 2015. http://www.advisenltd.com/wp-content/uploads/2015/02/ cyber-risk-insights-conference-slides-2015-10-20.pdf

Advisen, (2017), 2017 Survey of Cyber Insurance Market Trends, October 2017. https://www.advisenltd.com/2017/10/25/2017-survey-cyber-insurance-market-trends/

AIG; 2016; *Is Cyber Risk Systemic?* https://www.aig.com/content/dam/aig/america-canada/us/documents/business/cyber/aig-cyber-risk-systemic-final.pdf

Air Force Technology; 2010; *Software Hitch Could Have Caused 1994 RAF Chinook Crash*; 4 January 2010. https://www.airforce-technology.com/news/news73503-html/

AIR, 2016; *AIR Analytics of Risks from Cyber*: Open Source Downloadable Scenarios; http://w3.air-worldwide.com/Cyber-Scenario-Subscription

Akamai (2015), Quarterly Security Reports, Q3 2015. https://www.akamai.com/uk/ en/multimedia/documents/state-of-the-internet/2015-q4-cloud-security-report. pdf

Akamai (2016), Quarterly Security Reports, Q3 2016. https://www.akamai.com/ uk/en/our-thinking/state-of-the-internet-report/global-state-of-the-internet-security-ddos-attack-reports.jsp

Akerlof G.A. (1970); *'The market for lemons': quality uncertainty and the market mechanism.* Quart. J. Econ., Vol. 84, No. 3,; 1970.

Alexander, William; 2013; *"Barnaby Jack Could Hack Your Pacemaker and Make Your Heart Explode"*, VICE;

Allied Market Research (2016). *Global Cyber Insurance Market: Global Opportunity Analysis and Industry Forecasts, 2014-2022*; November. https://www.allied marketresearch.com/cyber-insurance-market

Allodi L., Corradin M., Massacci F.; 2016; *Then and now: on the maturity of the cybercrime markets*; IEEE Transactions on emerging topics in Computing; Vol. 4, No. 1; 2016.

Allodi L., Massacci F., Shim W.H.; 2012; *Crime pays if you are just an average hacker*. Int. Conf. Cyber Security, Alexandria Va.; December 2012.

Allodi L., Massacci F.; 2015; *The work-averse attacker model*. Proceedings of the 2015 European Conference on Information Systems.

Anderson R. Moore T.; 2006; *The economics of information security*. Science, Vol. 314; 2006.

Anderson R.J.; 2001; *Why economic security is hard - an economic perspective*. Proc. Annual Computer Security Applications Conf., Washington D.C.

Anderson R.J.; 2012; *Security economics – a personal perspective*. Proc. Annual Computer Security Applications Security Conf,; Orlando, Florida.

Anderson, R.J.; 2010. *Security engineering: a guide to building dependable distributed systems*. John Wiley & Sons. 2010.

Antonucci, Domenic; 2017; *The Cyber Risk Handbook: Creating and Measuring Effective Cybersecurity Capabilities*; Wiley Finance; John Wiley & Sons. ISBN 978-1-119-30880-5.

Aon, 2016, *Cyber–the fast moving target: Benchmarking views and attitudes by industry*; http://www.aon.com/attachments/risk-services/cyber/2016-Captive-Cyber-Survey-Interactive.pdf

Aon (2017), *Aon announces an alternative cyber risk transfer approach*; Aon Global Risk Consulting. http://aon.mediaroom.com/news-releases?item=137537

Aon (2017b), *Global Cyber Market Overview: Uncovering the Hidden Opportunities*; Aon Inpoint; June 2017. http://www.aon.com/inpoint/bin/pdfs/white-papers/Cyber.pdf

Arora, A., Telang, R. and Xu, H.; 2004, '*Optimal policy for software vulnerability disclosure*'; Management Science; vol. 54; INFORMS

Artemis, 2017; *Cyber cat bonds will be a reality within two years: Jean-Louis Monnier, Swiss Re*; October 4, 2017; http://www.artemis.bm/blog/2017/10/04/cyber-cat-bonds-will-be-a-reality-within-two-years-jean-louis-monnier-swiss-re/

Baker, Graeme; 2008; "*Schoolboy hacks into city's tram system*"; News Article; The Telegraph; 11 January 2008. http://www.telegraph.co.uk/news/worldnews/1575293/Schoolboy-hacks-into-citys-tram-system.html

Bank Info Security; 2006; *Case Analysis: ShadowCrew Carding Gang*; https://www.bankinfosecurity.com/case-analysis-shadowcrew-carding-gang-a-136

Bank Info Security; 2017; *DOJ Sees Bangladesh Heist Tie to North Korea*; Mathew J. Schwartz; March 24, 2017. https://www.bankinfosecurity.com/blogs/report-doj-sees-bangladesh-heist-tie-to-north-korea-p-2429

Bar On A.E.; 2018; *We need bug bounties for bad algorithms*. Motherboard, May 3, 2018. http:/motherboard.vice.com/en_us/article/8xkyj3/we-need-bug-bounties-for-bad-algorithms/

Bartlett, Jamie; 2015; *The Dark Net*; Windmill Books.

Bartman T., Kraft J.; 2016; *An introduction to applying network intrusion detection for industrial control systems*. AISTech2016, Pittsburgh, Pennsylvania, May 16-19, 2016.

BBC, 2017; *South Korean firm's 'record' ransom payment*; 20 June 2017; Technology. http://www.bbc.co.uk/news/technology-40340820

BBC; 2018; *UK launched cyber-attack on Islamic State*; April 12, 2018. http://www.bbc.co.uk/news/technology-43738953

Beattie D.; 2016; *The physics of software*. http://opentranscripts.org/transcript/amdahl-to-zipf-physics-of-software/http://opentranscripts.org/transcript/amdahl-to-zipf-physics-of-software/ ; October 6, 2016.

Bejtlich R.; 2015; The evolving nature of cyber threats facing the private sector. Statement for the U.S. House of Representatives Committee on Information Security; March 18, 2015

Bierhorst P. et al.; *Experimentally generated randomness certified by the impossibility of superluminal signals*. Nature, Vol. 556. 223-226, 2018.

Blau A.; 2017; *The behavioral economics of why executives underinvest in cyber security*. Harvard Business Review; June 7, 2017.

Boixo S. et al.; 2017; *Characterizing quantum supremacy in near-term devices*. Arxiv.org> quant-ph.

Bowden M.; 2011; *Worm: the first digital world war*. Atlantic Monthly Press, New York.

Broadhurst, Roderick, Peter Grabosky, Mamoun Alazab, and Steve Chon. (2014) Organizations and Cyber Crime: *An analysis of the Nature of Groups engaged in Cyber Crime*. International Journal of Cyber Criminology, Vol 8 (1), 2014. http://www.cybercrimejournal.com/broadhurstetalijcc2014vol8issue1.pdf

Brotherston, Lee, and Berlin, Amanda; 2017; *Defensive Security Handbook: Best Practice for Securing Infrastructure*; O'Reilly Media, Inc.

BSI; 2014; *"Bericht zur Lage der IT-Sicherheit in Deutschland 2014"*; BSI; 15 January. https://www.bsi.bund.de/SharedDocs/Downloads/DE/BSI/Publikationen/Lageberichte/Lagebericht2014.pdf?__blob=publicationFile%20

Bugcrowd; 2017; *Defensive vulnerability pricing model*. Bugcrowd report; 2017.

Business Insurance, 2017; *Growth expected in alternatives to cyber insurance*; Rob Lenihan; 3 June 2017; http://www.businessinsurance.com/article/00010101/NEWS06/912312199/Growth-expected-in-alternatives-to-cyber-insurance

Camejo C.; 2017; *The state of modern password cracking*. RSA Conference 2016, San Francisco, Moscone Center, 2017.

CBS; 2017, *"WannaCry" ransomware attack losses could reach $4 billion*; Jonathan Berr; CBS Moneywatch; May 16, 2017; https://www.cbsnews.com/news/wannacry-ransomware-attacks-wannacry-virus-losses/

CCRS and Lloyd's; 2015; *Business Blackout: The insurance implications of a cyber attack on the US power grid*; Report produced for Lloyd's by the Cambridge

Centre for Risk Studies; Emerging Risk Report – 2015; Innovation Series; Society & Security. https://www.lloyds.com/news-and-insight/risk-insight/library/society-and-security/business-blackout

CCRS; 2013; *Cyber Catastrophe: Profile of a Macro-Catastrophe Threat Type*; Simon Ruffle; Andrew Coburn; Daniel Ralph; Gary Bowman; Working Paper 201307.02; *July* 2013. https://www.jbs.cam.ac.uk/faculty-research/centres/risk/publications/space-and-technology/cyber-threat-monograph/

CCRS; 2014a, *Sybil Logic Bomb Cyber Catastrophe Stress Test Scenario*; Ruffle, S.J.; Bowman, G.; Caccioli, F.; Coburn, A.W.; Kelly, S.; Leslie, B.; Ralph, D Cambridge Risk Framework series; Cambridge Centre for Risk Studies, University of Cambridge. https://www.jbs.cam.ac.uk/faculty-research/centres/risk/publications/space-and-technology/sybil-logic-bomb-cyber-catastrophe-stress-test-scenario/

CCRS; 2014b, *China-Japan Geopolitical Conflict Scenario*; Geopolitical Conflict: Stress Test Scenario; Cambridge Risk Framework, Cambridge Centre for Risk Studies. https://www.jbs.cam.ac.uk/faculty-research/centres/risk/publications/geopolitics-and-security/china-japan-geopolitical-conflict-stress-test-scenario/

CCRS; 2016a; *Cyber Insurance Exposure Data Schema v1.0*; Cambridge Centre for Risk Studies; Judge Business School at University of Cambridge. https://www.jbs.cam.ac.uk/faculty-research/centres/risk/publications/space-and-technology/cyber-exposure-data-schema/

CCRS; 2016b; *Managing Cyber Insurance Accumulation Risk*; Cambridge Centre for Risk Studies; Judge Business School at University of Cambridge, in collaboration with Risk Management Solutions, Inc. https://www.jbs.cam.ac.uk/faculty-research/centres/risk/publications/space-and-technology/managing-cyber-insurance-accumulation-risk/

CCRS; 2016c; *Integrated Infrastructure: Cyber Resiliency in Society Mapping the Consequences of an Interconnected Digital Economy*; Cambridge Centre for Risk Studies; Judge Business School at University of Cambridge, in collaboration with Lockheed Martin; https://www.jbs.cam.ac.uk/faculty-research/centres/risk/publications/space-and-technology/integrated-infrastructure-cyber-resiliency-in-society/

CCRS; 2017a; *Cyber Risk Landscape 2017*; Cambridge Centre for Risk Studies; Judge Business School at University of Cambridge, in collaboration with RMS, Inc.; https://www.jbs.cam.ac.uk/faculty-research/centres/risk/publications/space-and-technology/crs-rms-cyber-risk-landscape-2017/

CCRS; 2017b; *Cyber Terrorism: Assessment of the Threat to Insurance*; Cambridge Centre for Risk Studies; Judge Business School at University of Cambridge, in collaboration with Pool Re. https://www.jbs.cam.ac.uk/faculty-research/centres/risk/publications/geopolitics-and-security/cyber-terrorism-assessment-of-the-threat-to-insurance/

CCRS; 2018a; *2018 Cyber Risk Outlook*; Cambridge Centre for Risk Studies in collaboration with Risk Management Solutions, Inc. https://www.jbs.cam.ac.uk/faculty-research/centres/risk/publications/space-and-technology/cyber-risk-outlook-2018/

CCRS; 2018a; *Probabilistic Cyber Insurance Loss Estimation: Survey of Insurance and Cyber Specialist Expertise on Loss Likelihood*; Cambridge Centre for Risk Studies; Judge Business School at University of Cambridge, in collaboration with RMS, Inc.

CCRS; 2018b; *Company-Specific Cyber Risk Rating: An Evidence-Based Approach*; Coburn, A.W.; C. Mitas, C.; Daffron J.; Awan, M.; Copic, J.; Leverett, E.; Cambridge Centre for Risk Studies, in collaboration with Risk Management Solutions, Inc.

CCRS; 2018b; *Probabilistic Cyber Insurance Loss Estimation: Survey of Insurance and Cyber Specialist Expertise on Loss Likelihood*; Cambridge Centre for Risk Studies; Judge Business School at University of Cambridge, in collaboration with Risk Management Solutions, Inc.

CCRS; 2018c; *Cloud Outage: The Potential for Catastrophic Loss*; Daffron, J.; Coburn, A.W.; Centre for Risk Studies, University of Cambridge, in collaboration with Risk Management Solutions, Inc.; Cyber Risk Research Whitepaper.

CCRS; 2018d; *Threat Actors in the Cyber Black Economy*; Smith, A.; Coburn, A.W.; Daffron, J.; Leverett, É.; Quantrill, K.; Centre for Risk Studies, University of Cambridge, in collaboration with Risk Management Solutions, Inc.; Cyber Risk Research Whitepaper.

CCRS; 2018e; *Insider Threat*; Daffron, J.; Cambridge Centre for Risk Studies white paper.

CCRS; 2018f; *Contagious Malware Payload Categorisation and Attributes*; Smith, A.; Daffron, J.; Cambridge Centre for Risk Studies white paper. in collaboration with Risk Management Solutions, Inc.

CCRS; 2018g; *Company-Specific Cyber Risk Rating: An Evidence-Based Approach*; Coburn, A.W.; C. Mitas, C.; Daffron J.; Awan, M.; Copic, J.; Leverett, E.; Cambridge Centre for Risk Studies white paper, in collaboration with Risk Management Solutions, Inc.

CERT; 2016; *"The Shadow Brokers auctions cyber weapons from Equation Group"*. TLP: White. Version 1.5. 26 August 2016.

Cetin, O.; Ganán, C.; Korczynski, M.; and van Eeten, M.; 2017; *"Make notifications great again: Learning how to notify in the age of large-scale vulnerability scanning"*, in 16th Workshop on the Economics of Information Security (WEIS 2017)

Cisco, 2017, *Security Capabilities Benchmark Study, as reported in Cisco 2017 Annual Cybersecurity Report*; https://blogs.cisco.com/security/cisco-2017-annual-cybersecurity-report-the-hidden-danger-of-uninvestigated-threats

Clark, Ben; 2013; *RTFN: Red Team Field Manual*; v1.0;

Clayton, Richard; 2011; *Might governments clean-up malware?*.

Cloud Security Alliance; 2017; *The Treacherous 12: Top Threats to Cloud Computing + Industry Insights*; https://downloads.cloudsecurityalliance.org/assets/research/top-threats/treacherous-12-top-threats.pdf

CNBC; 2018; Warren Buffett: *Cybersecurity risk 'is uncharted territory. It's going to get worse, not better'*; Investing; Tae Kim; 5 May 2018. https://www.cnbc

.com/2018/05/05/warren-buffett-cybersecurity-risk-is-uncharted-territory-its-going-to-get-worse-not-better.html

CNN Tech; 2017; *FTC sues maker of routers, baby monitors over security*; Jose Pagliery; January 5, 2017. http://money.cnn.com/2017/01/05/technology/ftc-d-link-lawsuit/index.html

Coburn, A.W.; Woo, G.; 2004; *Cyber Attack Scenario: Pentecost Worm Unleashed On Computer Networks*; Top 10 Risks: Cyber Attack; Risk & Insurance Magazine; May 15, 2004.

Cocks C.C.; 1973; *A note on non-secret encryption.* www.gchq.gov.uk.

Cole E.; 2015; *Detect, contain and control cyberthreats.* SANS whitepaper; June 2015

Coles, Cameron; 2017; *"Overview of Cloud Market in 2017 and Beyond"*. Skyhigh. https://www.skyhighnetworks.com/cloud-security-blog/microsoft-azure-closes-iaas-adoption-gap-with-amazon-aws/

ComputerWeekly (2015), *Mandarin Oriental hack highlights security risk of legacy point of sale systems* Warwick Ashford, 6 Mar 2015. http://www.computerweekly.com/news/2240241827/Mandarin-Oriental-hack-highlights-security-risk-of-legacy-point-of-sale-systems

Conheady, Sharon; 2014; *Social Engineering in IT Security: Tools, Tactics, and Techniques*; McGraw Hill Education, New York.

Conley, John M., and Robert M. Bryan.; 1985; *"Software escrow in bankruptcy: an international perspective."* NCJ Int'l L. & Com. Reg. 10 (1985): 579.

Constantin L.; 2015; *Software applications have on average 24 vulnerabilities inherited from buggy components.* InfoWorld. June 16, 2015.

Constantin, L. (2016); *"Hackers found 47 new vulnerabilities in 23 IoT devices at DEF CON"*. CSO. 13 September 2016. http://www.csoonline.com/article/3119765/security/hackers-found-47-new-vulnerabilities-in-23-iot-devices-at-def-con.html

Cox, J.W. (2016) *"MedStar Health turns away patients after likely ransomware cyberattack"*. The Washington Post. 29 March 2016. https://www.washingtonpost.com/local/medstar-health-turns-away-patients-one-day-after-cyberattack-on-its-computers/2016/03/29/252626ae-f5bc-11e5-a3ce-f06b5ba21f33_story.html?utm_term=.73849bd25e54

CREST; 2013; *Cyber security incident response guide.* www.crest-approved.org

Crossley, Simon; 2016; *EU regulation of health information technology, software and mobile apps*; Eversheds LLP; Thompson Reuters Practical Law. https://uk.practicallaw.thomsonreuters.com/2-619-5533?transitionType=Default&contextData=(sc.Default)&firstPage=true&bhcp=1

Cyber Risk Aware, 2017; *Cyber Risk is a Human Risk*; https://www.cyberriskaware.com/cyber-risk-is-a-human-risk

Cybereason; 2017; *NotPetya Still Roils Company's Finances, Costing Organizations $1.2 Billion In Revenue*; Fred O'Conner; Nov 9, 2017. https://www.cybereason.com/blog/notpetya-costs-companies-1.2-billion-in-revenue

Cybereason; 2017; *Paying the Price of Destructive Cyber Attacks*; Whitepaper. https://hi.cybereason.com/hubfs/Content%20PDFs/Paying-the-Price-of-Destructive-Cyber-Attacks.pdf?t=1514002191846

CyberGreen (2017), *Global DDoS: Level of Risk Posed to Others*, Website mapping and data. https://stats.cybergreen.net/

CyberScoop; 2017; *Interpol identifies 9,000 computers in Asia owned by hackers, used to launch ransomware*; Chris Bing; Apr 24, 2017. https://www.cyberscoop.com/interpol-identifies-9000-computers-asia-owned-hackers-used-launch-ransomware/

Cybersecurity Ventures, 2017; *Cybersecurity Market Report*; 2017 Q2; https://cybersecurityventures.com/cybersecurity-market-report/

Cybersecurity Ventures; 2018; 2018 *Cybersecurity Market Report*; https://cybersecurityventures.com/cybersecurity-market-report/

d'Ancona, Matthew; 2017; *Post-Truth: The New War on Truth and How to Fight Back*; May 2017;

Dark Web News, 2018; *Empire Market: A Clone of AlphaBay Market Launched*; March 9, 2018. https://darkwebnews.com/darknet-markets/empire-market-alphabay-clone/

Dark Web News; 2017; *The Value of Stolen Data on the Dark Web*; Richard; 1 July 2017. https://darkwebnews.com/dark-web/value-of-stolen-data-dark-web/

Digital Trends (2015); DoS Attacks hit Record Numbers in Q2 2015, August 19, 2015. http://www.digitaltrends.com/computing/ddos-attacks-hit-record-numbers-in-q2-2015/

DLA Piper; 2018; *Data Protection Laws of the World*; Data Protection and Privacy Group. https://www.dlapiperdataprotection.com/

DoD Software Tech News; 2016; *Software Quality Assurance (SQA)*; Vol 6-No 2 – CSIA. C https://www.csiac.org/wp-content/uploads/2016/02/stn6_2.pdf

Drinkwater D.; 2016; *These CISOs explain why they got fired*. CSO; April 20, 2016.

Duggan, Berg, Dillinger and Stamp; 2005; *"Penetration Testing of Industrial Control Systems,"* Sandia National Laboratories.

Economist; 2017; *Counterfactual underwriting*, October 21-27 2017.

Edwards B., Furnas A., Forrest S., Axelrod R.; 2017; *Strategic aspects of cyberattack, attribution, and blame*. PNAS, Vol. 114, No. 11; 2017.

EIOPA; 2017; *EIOPA's supervisory assessment of the Own Risk and Solvency Assessment: First experiences*. EIOPA-BoS/17-097.

E-ISAC, (2016), Analysis of the Cyber Attack on the Ukrainian Power Grid; Electricity Information Sharing and Analysis Center, SANS-ICS Industrial Control Systems; TLP: White. Defense Use Case, March 18, 2016. https://ics.sans.org/media/E-ISAC_SANS_Ukraine_DUC_5.pdf

Europol; 2017; *"Organised Crime Groups (OSGS) And Other Criminal Actors"*. https://www.europol.europa.eu/socta/2017/organised-crime-groups.html

Europol; 2017; *Internet Organised Crime Threat Assessment*. https://www.europol.europa.eu/iocta/2017/index.html

EYC3; 2013; *"The Cost of Bad Data,"* 06 March 2013. http://c3integrity.com/blog/posts/the-cost-of-bad-data.

FBI IC3; 2016, *2015 Internet Crime Report; Internet Crime Complaint Center*, Federal Bureau of Investigation; US Bureau of Justice Assistance. https://pdf.ic3.gov/2015_IC3Report.pdf

Filkins B.; *2016; IT security spending trends.* SANS survey report; 2016.

Financial Times; 2010; *Special Report: Productivity and IT.* Paul Taylor, Sept 28, 2010. https://www.ft.com/content/882c56b4-c9fe-11df-87b8-00144feab49a

Financial Times; 2017; *Cyber attacks lead Yahoo to accept price cut on $4.8bn Verizon deal;* Feb 15, 2017. https://www.ft.com/content/ed743ace-f3a9-11e6-8758-6876151821a6

FindLaw, 2018; *Protecting Consequential Damages Waivers In Software License Agreements;* Corporate Counsel. http://corporate.findlaw.com/intellectual-property/protecting-consequential-damages-waivers-in-software-license.html

FireEye; 2014; *Stealing Insider Information for an Advantage in Stock Trading;* Threat Intelligence; November 30, 2014; Kristen Dennesen, Jordan Berry, Barry Vengerik, Jonathan Wrolstad. https://www.fireeye.com/blog/threat-research/2014/11/fin4_stealing_insid.html

Forbes Tech; 2016; *Here's How Much Businesses Worldwide Will Spend on Cybersecurity by 2020;* Market Intelligence; Oct 13, 2016. http://fortune.com/2016/10/12/cybersecurity-global-spending/

Forbes; 2014; *Target Profit Falls 46% On Credit Card Breach And The Hits Could Keep On Coming;* Feb 26, 2014; https://www.forbes.com/sites/maggiemcgrath/2014/02/26/target-profit-falls-46-on-credit-card-breach-and-says-the-hits-could-keep-on-coming/#561812577326

Forbes; 2015; *J.P. Morgan, Bank of America, Citibank And Wells Fargo Spending $1.5 Billion To Battle Cyber Crime;* Dec 13, 2015. http://www.forbes.com/sites/stevemorgan/2015/12/13/j-p-morgan-boa-citi-and-wells-spending-1-5-billion-to-battle-cyber-crime/#4d035ab01112

Forbes; 2016; *Bank of America's Unlimited Cybersecurity Budget Sums Up Spending Plans In A War Against Hackers;* Jan 27, 2016. http://www.forbes.com/sites/stevemorgan/2016/01/27/bank-of-americas-unlimited-cybersecurity-budget-sums-up-spending-plans-in-a-war-against-hackers/#6a2a07e9434b

Fortune; 2018; *A Cyber Gang Stole $1 Billion by Hacking Banks and ATMs. Now Police Say They've Caught the Mastermind;* David Meyer; March 26, 2018. http://fortune.com/2018/03/26/carbanak-europol-arrest-spain-malware-banks/

Fox-Brewster T.; 2018; *Advanced hackers infect X-Ray machines in healthcare espionage.* Forbes, April 23, 2018.

Freund J., Jones J.; 2015; *Measuring and managing information risk;* Elsevier, Amsterdam.

FTC (2017), *FTC Charges D-Link Put Consumers' Privacy at Risk Due to the Inadequate Security of Its Computer Routers and Cameras*: Federal Trade Commission, Jan 5, 2017. https://www.ftc.gov/news-events/press-releases/2017/01/ftc-charges-d-link-put-consumers-privacy-risk-due-inadequate

FTSE Global Markets, 2016; *Is cyber risk uninsurable? Its 50/50 says PwC; 5* October 2016; http://www.ftseglobalmarkets.com/news/is-cyber-risk-uninsurable-its-50-50-says-pwc.html

Gallagher C.; 2018; *Telling it like it wasn't.* Chicago University Press, Chicago.

Gander, Kashmira; 2015; *"Neil Moore: Con artist jailed for escaping from prison by sending staff a fake email"*; The Independent; 20 April 2015. http://www.independent.co.uk/news/uk/crime/neil-moore-con-artist-jailed-for-escaping-from-prison-by-sending-staff-a-fake-email-10191080.html

Gartner; 2016; *"Gartner Says Worldwide PC Shipments Declined 8.3 Percent in Fourth Quarter of 2015."* Gartner Newsroom. 12 January 2016. http://www.gartner.com/newsroom/id/3185224

Gartner; 2017; *"Gartner Says Worldwide Public Cloud Services Market to Grow 18% in 2017"*. 2017. https://www.gartner.com/newsroom/id/3616417

Geer, D., 2015. *For good measure: The undiscovered login*: the magazine of USENIX & SAGE, 40(2), pp.50-52.

George T.; 2016; *The truth about penetration testing vs. vulnerability assessments.* Security Week, July 13, 2016.

Gibbs, Stephen; 2011; *Keeping Your Data Secure: 101 Tips You Must Know*; Snappy Titles; NSM Training Ltd.;

Global Banking & Finance Review; 2017; *Could a Large-Scale Cyber Attack on The World's Financial Institutions Crash An Economy?*; Sept 15, 2017. https://www.globalbankingandfinance.com/could-a-large-scale-cyber-attack-on-the-worlds-financial-institutions-crash-an-economy/

Gnatek, Michal, and Karen Miller; (2016); *"Changing the Game: An HPR Approach to Cyber."* presented at the RIMS 2016 Annual Conference & Exhibition, San Diego, CA, April 13, 2016. https://www.rims.org/Session%20Handouts/RIMS%2016/CRM007/CRM007FINAL%20Wed.pdf.

Goodman; 2015; *Future Crimes: Inside the digital underground and the battle for our connected world*; Corgi Books.

Gordon L.A., Loeb M.P.; 2002; *The economics of information security investment.* ACM Transactions on Information and System Security. Vol. 5, No. 4; 2002.

Greenberg, Andy; 2016; *"Hackers Claim to Auction Data They Stole From NSA-Linked Spies"*. 15 August 2016. Wired. https://www.wired.com/2016/08/hackers-claim-auction-data-stolen-nsa-linked-spies/

Greenberg, Andy; 2017; *The Biggest Dark Web Takedown Yet Sends Black Markets Reeling.* Wired. July 14, 2017. https://www.wired.com/story/alphabay-takedown-dark-web-chaos/

Grimes Roger, A.; 2016; *Why it's so hard to prosecute cyber criminals.* CSO, December 6, 2016.

Grimes, Roger, A.; 2012; *Why Internet crime goes unpunished*; InfoWorld; Jan 10, 2012. http://www.infoworld.com/article/2618598/cyber-crime/why-internet-crime-goes-unpunished.html

Grossman L.; 2017; *The worst passwords of 2017.* Time magazine, December 19, 2017.

Halperin, D.; Heydt-Benjamin, T.S.; Ransford, B.; Clark, S.S.; Defend, B.; Morgan, W.; Fu, K.; Kohno, T. and Maisel, W.H.; 2008, May. *Pacemakers and implantable cardiac defibrillators: Software radio attacks and zero-power defenses.* Security and Privacy, SP 2008. IEEE Symposium on; IEEE.

Harding L.; 2014; *The Snowden files.* Guardian books, London.

Harmer B.; 2017; *Equifax proves the CISOs right.* CSO, October 9, 2017.

Harris R., Sirrell J.; 2016; *West Midlands Regional Cyber Crime Unit presentation to British Computer Society.* https://www.bcs.org/upload/pdf/rocu-presentation-120416.pdf/ (Accessed on May 4, 2018).

HelpNetSecurity; 2017; *After a data breach is disclosed, stock prices fall an average of 5%;* May 16, 2017. https://www.helpnetsecurity.com/2017/05/16/data-breach-stock-price/

Heninger N., Durumeric Z., Wustrow E., Haldeman J.A. *Mining your P's and Q's: detection of widespread weak keys in network devices.* Proc 21st USENIX Security Symp., 205-220, USENIX, 2012.

HM Government (2017). Internet safety strategy – green paper. UK Government Assets Publishing Service. https://www.gov.uk/government/consultations/internet-safety-strategy-green-paper

HM Government and Marsh; 2015; *UK Cyber Security: The Role of Insurance in Managing and Mitigating the Risk;* March 2015. https://www.gov.uk/government/uploads/system/uploads/attachment_data/file/415354/UK_Cyber_Security_Report_Final.pdf

Hoffmann, Bruce; 2006; *Inside Terrorism;* Columbia University Press

Hofmeyr, Steven, Tyler Moore, Stephanie Forrest, Benjamin Edwards, and George Stelle; 2013; *"Modeling internet-scale policies for cleaning up malware."* In Economics of Information Security and Privacy III, pp. 149-170. Springer, New York, NY, 2013.

Hollnagel E., Woods D.D., Leveson N.; 2006; *Resilience engineering.* Ashgate, Aldershot.

Howard, Michael, and Steve Lipner.; 2006; *The security development lifecycle.* Vol. 8. Redmond: Microsoft Press, 2006.

https://www.statista.com/statistics/471264/iot-number-of-connected-devices-worldwide/

Huang F., Liu B.; 2017; *Software defect prevention based on human error theories.* Chinese Journal of Aeronautics, 30(3), 1054-1070.

Hutchings, Alice, and Clayton, Richard; 2016; *"Exploring the provision of online booter services."* Deviant Behavior 37, No. 10 (2016): 1163-1178. https://www.cl.cam.ac.uk/~ah793/papers/2016booter.pdf

IDC; 2015; *Determining how much to spend on your cyber security: the Canadian perspective.* IDC InfoDoc Report.

InfoSEC Institute, 2016, *"Panama Papers – How Hackers Breached the Mossack Fonseca Firm".* 20 April 2016. http://resources.infosecinstitute.com/panama-papers-how-hackers-breached-the-mossack-fonseca-firm/#gref

InfoSecurity; 2017; *Stock Prices Average Significant Drops After a Breach;* Tara Seals; May 15, 2017.

*International Journal of Cyber Criminology*; Editor in Chief K. Jaishankar; http://www.cybercrimejournal.com/

Jaishankar, J.; 2011; *Cyber Criminology: Exploring Internet Crimes and Criminal Behavior*; CRC Press. https://www.amazon.co.uk/Cyber-Criminology-Exploring-Internet-Criminal/dp/1439829497

Johnson A.; *Microsoft's perspective on cyber resilience*; http:// cloudblogs.microsoft.com; August 23, 2017.

Johnson, Blake; Caban, Dan; Krotofil, Marina; Scali, Dan; Brubaker, Nathan; Glyer, Christopher; 2017; *"Attackers Deploy New ICS Attack Framework "TRITON" and Cause Operational Disruption to Critical Infrastructure"* Fire Eye Blog. https://www.fireeye.com/blog/threat-research/2017/12/attackers-deploy-new-ics-attack-framework-triton.html

Kahneman D.; 2011; *Thinking, fast and slow*. Allen Lane, London.

Kaspersky Lab; 2014; *Energetic Bear-Crouching Yeti*. Kaspersky Lab Global Research and Analysis Team. https://securelist.com/files/2014/07/EB-YetiJuly2014-Public.pdf

Kaspersky Labs; 2017; *Chasing Lazarus: A Hunt for the Infamous Hackers to Prevent Large Bank Robberies*; https://www.kaspersky.com/about/press-releases/2017_chasing-lazarus-a-hunt-for-the-infamous-hackers-to-prevent-large-bank-robberies

Keeney, M., Kowalski, E., Cappelli, D., Moore, A., Shimeall, T., and Rogers, S.; 2005; *Insider threat study: Computer system sabotage in critical infrastructure sectors*. National Threat Assessment Center Washington DC. https://resources.sei.cmu.edu/asset_files/SpecialReport/2005_003_001_51946.pdf

Kennedy R.; 2017; *Cyber security basics*. Intersec journal of international security, November, December.

Kim, Peter; 2015; *The Hacker Playbook 2: Practical Guide to Penetration Testing*; Secure Planet LLC.

Kopp, Emanuel; Kaffenberger, Lincoln; and Wilson, Christopher; 2017; *Cyber Risk, Market Failures, and Financial Stability*; International Monetary Fund Working Paper WP/17/185; August 7, 2017. http://www.imf.org/en/Publications/WP/Issues/2017/08/07/Cyber-Risk-Market-Failures-and-Financial-Stability-45104

KrebsOnSecurity, 2013, *Non-US Cards Used at Target Fetch Premium*; Krebs, B.; Dec 22, 2013; https://krebsonsecurity.com/2013/12/non-us-cards-used-at-target-fetch-premium/

Kriesel, D.; 2013; *"Xerox scanners/photocopiers randomly alter numbers in scanned documents,"* 2013. http://www.dkriesel.com/en/blog/2013/0802_xerox_work centres_are_switching_written_numbers_when_scanning?

Kshetri, Nir. (2010), *The Global Cybercrime Industry: Economic, Institutional and Strategic Perspectives*. Springer, 2010. https://www.springer.com/us/book/9783642115219

Kyle C.; 2013; *American gun: a history of the US in ten firearms*, William Morrow, New York.

Lamport, L., Shostak, R. and Pease, M.; 1982;. *"The Byzantine generals problem"*. ACM Transactions on Programming Languages and Systems (TOPLAS), 1982.

Landler, Mark. *"A Filipino Linked to "Love Bug" Talks About His License to Hack."* The New York Times. Oct. 21, 2000. (Aug 12, 2008) http://www.ny times.com/2000/10/21/business/a-filipino-linked-to-love-bug-talks-about-his-license-to-hack.html

Lee, Edward A.; 2007; *"Computing foundations and practice for cyber-physical systems: A preliminary report."* University of California, Berkeley, Tech. Rep. UCB/EECS-2007-72 (2007).

Levenshtein V.; 1966; *Binary codes capable of correcting deletions, insertions, and reversals.* Soviet Physics Doklady, 10.

Leverett, Eireann, and Aaron Kaplan; 2017; *"Towards estimating the untapped potential: a global malicious DDoS mean capacity estimate."* Journal of Cyber Policy 2, No. 2: 195-208.

Leverett, Eireann; and Wightman, Reid; 2013; *Vulnerability Inheritance in Programmable Logic Controllers*; In Second International Symposium on Research in GreHack 2013, Grenoble, France. http://grehack.org/files/2013/GreHack_2013_proceedings-separate_files/3-accepted_papers/3.6_E_Leverett_and_Reid_Wightman_-_Vulnerability_Inheritance_in_Programmable_Logic_Controllers .pdf

Li, F., Durumeric, Z., Czyz, J., Karami, M. , Bailey, M., McCoy, D., Savage, S., and Paxson, V. ; 2016; *'You've got vulnerability: Exploring effective vulnerability notifications.'*; in 25th USENIX Security Symposium; USENIX Association

Lim, Joanne; 1998; *An Engineering Disaster: Therac-25*; October 1998. http://www .bowdoin.edu/~allen/courses/cs260/readings/therac.pdf

Lions, J.L.; 1996; *Ariane 5 Flight 501 Failure*; Report by the Inquiry Board; The Chairman of the Board: Prof. J. L. LIONS; Paris, 19 July 1996. http://www-users.math.umn.edu/~arnold/disasters/ariane5rep.html

Lloyd's (2016); *Cyber-Attack Scenarios: Scenario Specifications*; August 2016.

Lloyd's, 2018; *Realistic disaster scenarios: Scenario specification*; January 2018. EM 218 v1.0; https://www.lloyds.com/~/media/files/the-market/tools-and-resources/exposure-management/rds-scenario-specification-2018.pdf?la=en

Lloyd's/AIR; 2018; *Cloud Down: Impacts on the US economy*; Emerging Risk Report 2018: Technology. Lloyd's of London in collaboration with AIR World-wide; https://www.lloyds.com/~/media/files/news-and-insight/risk-insight/2018/cloud-down/aircyberlloydspublic2018final.pdf

Lloyds/Cyence, 2017; *Counting the Cost: Decoding Cyber Exposure*; Emerging Risks Report: Technology; Lloyd's of London in collaboration with Cyence; https://www.lloyds.com/~/media/files/news-and-insight/risk-insight/2017/cyence/emerging-risk-report-2017---counting-the-cost.pdf

London School of Economics; 2017, *Hacking the market: Systemic contagion from cybersecurity breaches*; LSE Business Review; Constantin Gurdgiev and Shaen Corbet; November 28, 2017. http://blogs.lse.ac.uk/businessreview/2017/11/28/hacking-the-market-systemic-contagion-from-cybersecurity-breaches/

Los Angeles Times, (2016); *Hollywood hospital pays $17,000 in bitcoin to hackers*; FBI investigating; Feb 18, 2016. http://www.latimes.com/business/technology/la-me-ln-hollywood-hospital-bitcoin-20160217-story.html

Loukas, George, 2015, *Cyber-Physical Attacks: A Growing Invisible Threat*, Butterworth-Heinemann; ISBN 978-0-12-801290-1

Luan S.; 2016; *Exploit two hypervisor vulnerabilities*. www.blackhat.com/docs/us-16/materials/..

MacKay N., Price C., Wood A.J.; 2016; *Weighing the fog of war: illustrating the power of Bayesian methods for historical analysis through the Battle of the Dogger Bank*. Historical Methods, 49(2), 80-91.

Maillart T., Zhao M., Grossklags J., Chuang J.; 2017; *Given enough eyeballs, all bugs are shallow? Revisiting Eric Raymond with bug bounty programs*. J. Cybersecurity.

Market Watch, 2017; *Equifax outlook lowered to negative by Standard and Poor's*; Sept 11, 2017, Max A. Cherney. https://www.marketwatch.com/story/equifax-outlook-lowered-to-negative-by-standard-and-poors-2017-09-11

Markman J.; 2018; *GDPR is great news for Google and Facebook, really*. Forbes, May 22, 2018.

Marsh & McLennan Companies; 2014; *Cyber Gap Insurance – Cyber Risk: Filling the Coverage Gap*; Global Energy Practice. http://www.oliverwyman.com/content/dam/marsh/Documents/PDF/US-en/Cyber%20Gap%20Insurance%20for%20the%20Global%20Energy%20Sector-06-2014.pdf

Marsh, 2016; *Captive Benchmarking Report: Creating Security in an Uncertain World*. https://www.marsh.com/us/insights/research/captive-benchmarking-report-2016.html

Martindale J.; 2017; *Meet the bug bounty hunters making cash by finding flaws before bad guys*. Digital Trends, www.digitaltrends.com/computing/bug bounty-hunters/ August 12, 2017. Accessed on May 5, 2018.

Mateski M., Trevino C.M., Veitch C.K., Michalski J., Harris J.M., Maruoka S., Frye J.; 2012; *Cyber threat metrics*; Sandia report SAND2012-2427; 2012

McAfee, 2014; *Analyzing the Target Point-of-Sale Malware*; McAfee Labs, Jan 16, 2014; https://securingtomorrow.mcafee.com/mcafee-labs/analyzing-the-target-point-of-sale-malware/

McGuire, Michael, 2012; *Organised Crime in the Digital Age*. 2012. London: John Grieve Centre for Policing and Security.

McNab, Chris; 2017; *Network Security Assessment: Know Your Network*; 3rd Edition; O'Reilly Media, Inc.

Micklethwait J., Wooldridge A.; 1997; *Drucker: the Guru's guru*. Mckinsey Quart., No. 3; Summer.

Microsoft (2014). International cybersecurity norms. Microsoft Download Center. https://www.microsoft.com/en-us/cybersecurity/content-hub/international-cybersecurity-norms-overview

Mitnick K.D., Simon W.L.; 2002; *The art of deception*; Wiley, Indianapolis.

Moe, Marie and Leverett, Eireann; 2015; *"Unpatchable"*; Chaos Communications Congress; Hamburg.

Moody's Investors Service; 2015; *Cross sector: global cyber risk of growing importance to credit analysis*. November 23, 2015. www.moodys.com,

Moritz and Womack; 2016; *Verizon plans bid to buy Yahoo's Web business, sources say*; The Washington Post; April 7, 2016. https://www.washingtonpost .com/business/economy/verizon-plans-bid-to-buy-yahoos-web-business/2016/ 04/07/91fb0cec-fd03-11e5-80e4-c381214de1a3_story.html?noredirect=on& utm_term=.1aecf7952ba6

Mower M.; 2017; *Sherlock Holmes: the Baker Street Files*, MX Publishing, 2017.

MSN, 2017; *Equifax sued over massive hack in multibillion-dollar lawsuit*; Sept 8, 2017; Polly Mosendz. https://www.msn.com/en-us/money/companies/equifax-sued-over-massive-hack-in-multibillion-dollar-lawsuit/ar-AArvtWk?li=BBnb7Kz

Murray A., Mejias M., Keiller P. (2017) *Resilience methods within the software development cycle*. Int'l. Conf. Software Eng. Research and Practice. CSREA Press. https://csce.ucmss.com/cr/books/2017/LFS/CSREA2017/SER6068.pdf

Nance, Malcolm; and Sampson, Chris; 2017; *Hacking ISIS: How to Destroy the Cyber Jihad*; Skyhorse Publishing.

National Audit Office, 2017, *Investigation: WannaCry Cyber Attack and the NHS*; Report by the Comptroller and Auditor General, Department of Health. HC 414 Session 2017–2019 October, 27, 2017. https://www.nao.org.uk/wp-content/ uploads/2017/10/Investigation-WannaCry-cyber-attack-and-the-NHS.pdf

NCA; 2017; *Hacker stole satellite data from US Department of Defence*. UK National Crime Agency public newsroom.

New York Times; 2014; *Reporting from the Web's Underbelly*; Perlroth, N.; Feb. 16, 2014. https://www.nytimes.com/2014/02/17/technology/reporting-from-the-webs-underbelly.html?hpw&rref=business&_r=0

New York Times; 2018a; *Cyberattacks Put Russian Fingers on the Switch at Power Plants, U.S. Says*; Nicole Perlroth and David E. Sanger; March 15, 2018; https://www.nytimes.com/2018/03/15/us/politics/russia-cyberattacks.html? action=click&contentCollection=Europe&module=RelatedCoverage&region= Marginalia&pgtype=article

New York Times; 2018b; *U.S.-U.K. Warning on Cyberattacks Includes Private Homes*; David D. Kirkpatrick and Ron Nixon; April 16, 2018. https://www .nytimes.com/2018/04/16/world/europe/us-uk-russia-cybersecurity-threat .html

New, Charlotte; 2014; *"Hacking at the Royal Institution"*; Blog; The Royal Institution; 7 September 2014. http://www.rigb.org/blog/2014/november/hacking-at-the-royal-institution

NIST; 2002; *Software Errors Cost U.S. Economy $59.5 Billion Annually: NIST Assesses Technical Needs of Industry to Improve Software-Testing*; National Institute of Standards and Technology; Department of Commerce; United States Government. https://web.archive.org/web/20090610052743/http://www .nist.gov/public_affairs/releases/n02-10.htm

NIST; 2014; *Framework for improving critical infrastructure cyber security*. NIST report. February 12, 2014.

NIST; 2018; *Cybersecurity Framework version 1.1*; April 2018; National Institute of Standards and Technology; US Department of Commerce. https://www.nist .gov/cyberframework/framework

NIST; 2018b; *National Vulnerability Database*; Information Technology Laboratory; National Institute of Standards and Technology, U.S. Department of Commerce. https://nvd.nist.gov/vuln-metrics/cvss#

Norvig, P.; 2016; *Google AI expert explains the challenge of debugging machine-learning systems: 'The methodology for scaling machine learning verification up to a whole industry is still in progress.'*; Network World; 25 May 2016. https://www.networkworld.com/article/3075413/software/google-ai-expert-explains-the-challenge-of-debugging-machine-learning-systems.html

Ollam, Deviant; 2016; *"Breaking into a bank with whiskey"* YouTube video, 0:17. Posted by "DeviantOllam" upload Sep 3, 2016. https://www.youtube.com/watch?v=SDl4AO4ancI

Osborn P.; 2018; *Intelligence and information advantage in a contested world.* RUSI lecture, May 18, 2018.

Ozment, A. and Schechter, S. E.; 2006; *'Milk or wine: Does software security improve with age?'*, in 15th USENIX Security Symposium, USENIX Association.

Panko, R.; 2014; *Human Error in Software Development and Inspection*; Pay Panko's Human Error Website. http://panko.com/HumanErr/Software.html

PAS (2017). *PAS announces $40 million Investment to fuel Its industrial control system cybersecurity business.* https://www.prnewswire.com/news-releases/

Penenberg A.; 2013; *Play at work: how games inspire breakthrough thinking.* Portfolio.

Pironio S.; 2018; *The certainty of randomness.* Nature, Vol. 556, 176-177, 2018.

Polyakova A., Boyer S.P.; 2018; *The future of political warfare: Russia, the West, and the coming age of global digital competition.* Brookings Report, March 2018.

Ponemon Institute; 2014; *Understaffed and at risk: today's IT security department.* HP Enterprise Security report.

Ponemon Institute; 2015; *2014: a year of mega breaches.* Ponemon Institute Research Report. January 2015.

Ponemon Institute; 2017; *Cost of cyber crime study: Insights on the security investments that make a difference.* Accenture report; 2017.

Ponemon Institute; 2017; *The Impact of Data Breaches on Reputation and Share Value: A Study of U.S. Marketers, IT Practitioners and Consumers*; May 2017. Sponsored by Centrify. https://www.centrify.com/lp/ponemon-data-breach-brand-impact/?utm_campaign=ponemon study&utm_medium=pr&utm_source=press release&utm_content=&utm_term=&ls=930-005-pr

Pool Re; 2017; *Pool Re to extend cover to include physical damage from cyber terrorism from April 2018*; November 2017 Press Release; https://www.poolre.co.uk/pool-re-extend-cover-include-physical-damage-cyber-terrorism-april-2018/

President D. Trump, (2017) *National security strategy.* US White House; December 2017.

PYMNTS, 2017; *Dark Web Down But Not Out.* August 21, 2017 https://www.pymnts.com/markets/2017/dark-web-down-but-not-out/

Rawlinson, K. (2014); *"HP Study Reveals 70 Percent of Internet of Things Devices Vulnerable to Attack".* HP. 29 July 2014. http://www8.hp.com/us/en/hp-news/press-release.html?id=1744676#.WIpDj33LFP0

Reading University; 2014; *Turing test success marks milestone in computing history*. http://www.reading.ac.uk/news-and-events/releases/PR583836.aspx

Refsdal, Atle; Solhaug, Bjørnar; Ketil Stølen; 2015; *Cyber-Risk Management*; SpringerBriefs in Computer Science; Springer.

Reinhart, Carmen M., and Rogoff, Kenneth S.; 2011; *This Time Is Different: Eight Centuries of Financial Folly*. https://press.princeton.edu/titles/8973.html

Reinsurance (2018), 'PCS: NotPetya insured losses now $3bn+'; News Sept 4, 2018. https://reinsurance.cmail19.com/t/ViewEmail/i/3B7BA06B2FDD08292540EF2 3F30FEDED/B5F3C5129DB8FB7BE89F0E32AAFB68BF

Reinsurance News (2017), 'Total WannaCry Losses pegged at $4 billion', 25 Sept 2017. https://www.reinsurancene.ws/total-wannacry-losses-pegged-4-billion/

Reuters, 2016, *Massive cyber attack could trigger NATO response*: Stoltenberg; June 15, 2016; https://www.reuters.com/article/us-cyber-nato/massive-cyber-attack-could-trigger-nato-response-stoltenberg-idUSKCN0Z12NE

Rid, Thomas; 2013; *"Cyberwar will not take place"*; Oxford University Press.

Right Scale (2018); *State of the Cloud Report*. https://www.rightscale.com/lp/state-of-the-cloud

Right Scale; 2017; *State of the Cloud Report*. https://assets.rightscale.com/uploads/ pdfs/RightScale-2017-State-of-the-Cloud-Report.pdf

Riley, M. and A. Katz. *"Swift Hack Probe Expands to Up to a Dozen Banks Beyond Bangladesh"*. Bloomberg Technology. https://www.bloomberg.com/ news/articles/2016-05-26/swift-hack-probe-expands-to-up-to-dozen-banks-beyond-bangladesh

RMS; 2016; *Managing Cyber Insurance Accumulation Risk*; Risk Management Solutions, Inc., in collaboration with Cambridge Centre for Risk Studies. http:// forms2.rms.com/rs/729-DJX-565/images/RMS-Managing-Cyber-Insurance-Accumulation-Risk-05142016.pdf

RMS; 2017; *2017 Cyber Risk Landscape*; Risk Management Solutions, Inc., in collaboration with Cambridge Centre for Risk Studies. http://forms2.rms.com/rs/ 729-DJX-565/images/RMS_CyberReport_20170427.pdf?utm_source=slipcase

RMS; 2018; *Cyber Risk Outlook*; Risk Management Solutions, Inc., in collaboration with Cambridge Centre for Risk Studies. http://forms2.rms.com/ CyberRiskLandscapeReport2018.html

Romanosky, Sasha; Ablon, Lillian; Kuehn, Andreas; and Jones, Therese; 2017; *Content Analysis of Cyber Insurance Policies: How do carriers write policies and price cyber risk?* RAND Justice, Infrastructure, and Environment; WR-1208; September 2017. https://www.rand.org/content/dam/rand/pubs/working_papers /WR1200/WR1208/RAND_WR1208.pdf

Rowley, Olivia, 2017; *Analysis: Pricing of goods and services on the deep & dark web*; Flashpoint Analysis Whitepaper; December 05, 2017; https://go .flashpoint-intel.com/docs/analysis-pricing-of-goods-and-services-on-the-ddw

RSA; 2017; *The Carbanak/Fin7 Syndicate: A Historical Overview of an Evolving Threat*; 10/17 White Paper H16817. https://www.rsa.com/content/dam/en/ white-paper/the-carbanak-fin7-syndicate.pdf

SC Magazine; 2008; *Hacker arrested in Greece for stealing, selling weapons data*; Jim Carr; Jan 30, 2008. https://www.scmagazine.com/hacker-arrested-in-greece-for-stealing-selling-weapons-data/article/554157/

Schelmetic T.; 2015; *Open-source can be more dangerous than useful.* Design hardware and software, June 20, 2015.

Schlein T.; 2015; *The rise of the chief security officer. What it means for corporations and customers.* Forbes, April 20, 2015.

Seals T. (2017) *Trump hotels hit with third data breach in three years.* Infosecurity magazine; July 12, 2017.

Search Security; 2018; *CIA attributes NotPetya attacks to Russian spy agency*; Michael Heller; 16 Jan 2018. https://searchsecurity.techtarget.com/news/450433303/CIA-attributes-NotPetya-attacks-to-Russian-spy-agency

Security (2015); *47% of the World's Credit Card Fraud Happens in the US*; June 1, 2015. http://www.securitymagazine.com/articles/86413-of-the-worlds-credit-card-fraud-happens-in-the-us

Security Week, 2014a; *Target Confirms Point-of-Sale Malware Was Used in Attack*; Lennon, M.; Jan 13, 2014; http://www.securityweek.com/target-confirms-point-sale-malware-was-used-attack

Security Week, 2014b; *How Cybercriminals Attacked Target*: Analysis; Rashid, F.Y.; Jan 20, 2014. http://www.securityweek.com/how-cybercriminals-attacked-target-analysis

Security Week, 2016; *Cyber Insurance Market to Top $14 Billion by 2022*: Report; Dec 9, 2016; Mike Lennon; https://www.securityweek.com/cyber-insurance-market-top-14-billion-2022-report

Selb G.F.; 2008; *In crisis, opportunity for Obama.* Wall Street Journal, November 21, 2008.

Serfass, Stephen A.; 2015; 'Cybersecurity in 2015'; Presentation to Reinsurance Association of America Annual Meeting; DrinkerBiddle; 23 April 2015.

Shahzad, Muhammad; Shafiq, Muhammad Zubair; and Liu, Alex X.; 2012; *"A large scale exploratory analysis of software vulnerability life cycles."*; Proceedings of the 34th International Conference on Software Engineering; IEEE Press

Shevchenko, Sergei, Hirman Muhammad bin Abu Bakar, and James Wong; 2017; *"Taiwan Heist: Lazarus Tools And Ransomware".* BAE Threat Research (Blog). October 16, 2017. http://baesystemsai.blogspot.co.uk/2017/10/taiwan-heist-lazarus-tools.html

Shor P.W.; 1994; *Polynomial-time algorithms for prime factorization and discrete logarithms on a quantum computer.* Proc. 35th annual symposium on foundations in computer science, Santa Fe, New Mexico, November, 1994.

Shostack A.; 2014; *Threat modeling: designing for security*; Wiley, Indianapolis..

Shu, X.; Tian, K.; Ciambrone, A.; and Yao, D.; 2017; 'Breaking the Target: An Analysis of Target Data Breach and Lessons Learned' arXiv:1701.04940v1 [cs.CR] 18 Jan 2017. https://arxiv.org/pdf/1701.04940.pdf

Sidaway H.; 2018; *Hacker admits international cyber attacks.* UK Crown Prosecution Service. https://www.cps.gov.uk/cps/news/hacker-admits-international-cyber-attacks (Accessed on May 4, 2018).

Sink E.; 2006; *Why we sell code with bugs*. The Guardian, May 25; 2006.

Slate; 2015; *Target Finally Agrees to Pay Up for Its Massive Data Breach*; Griswold, A.; March 19, 2015. http://www.slate.com/blogs/moneybox/2015/03/19/ target_data_breach_settlement_the_company_will_pay_out_10_million_to_ make.html

Slovic P.; 2010; *The feeling of risk*. Earthscan, London.

Smith G.; 2017; *Why your company could be wrong about cyber risks*. Fortune; February 9, 2017

Smith, Tony; 2001; *"Hacker jailed for revenge sewage attacks"*, News Article; The Register; 31 October, 2001. https://www.theregister.co.uk/2001/10/31/hacker_ jailed_for_revenge_sewage/

Sood A.K., Enbody R.; 2014; *Targeted cyber attacks*; Elsevier, Amsterdam.

Sophos; 2015; *Buh-bye Beebone! Law enforcement kills polymorphic virus-spreading botnet*. Naked security by Sophos, April 12.

Sparc FLOW, 2017; *How to Hack Like a God.*; Amazon Kindle Edition; https: //www.amazon.com/How-Hack-Like-GOD-scenarios-ebook/dp/B06Y4 HWHXC

Stajano F.; 2011; *PICO: No more passwords!*. www.cl.cam.uk/~fms27/papers/2011-Stajano-pico.pdf

Statistica (2018), *Cyber Insurance – Statistics & Facts*; https://www.statista.com/ topics/2445/cyber-insurance/

Statistica, 2017, *IoT Number of Connected Devices Worldwide.*

Stock, B.; Pellegrino, G.; Li, F.; Backes, M. and Rossow, C.; 2018; *"Didn't you hear me?—towards more successful web vulnerability notifications"*, in Network and Distributed Systems Security (NDSS) Symposium 2018,

Swiss Re; 2018; Sigma Explorer; *World Non-Life Direct Premiums Written, in USD m; 1980 – 2016*; http://www.sigma-explorer.com/

Syed, R., M. Rahafrooz and J. M. Keisler; 2018; *"What it takes to get retweeted: An analysis of software vulnerability messages"*, Computers in Human Behavior,

Symantec Security Response; 2016; *"SWIFT attackers' malware linked to more financial attacks"* Symantec Official Blog. 26 May 2016. http://www.symantec .com/connect/blogs/swift-attackers-malware-linked-more-financial-attacks

Symantec, 2013; *Hidden Lynx – Professional Hackers for Hire*; Symantec Security Response Official Blog; Version 1.0 17 Sep 2013; Stephen Doherty, Jozsef Gegeny, Branko Spasojevic, Jonell Baltazar. http://www.symantec.com/content/ en/us/enterprise/media/security_response/whitepapers/hidden_lynx.pdf

Symantec; 2014b; *Dragonfly: Cyberespionage Attacks Against Energy Supplier*. Security Response, 2014. https://www.symantec.com/content/en/us/enterprise/ media/security_response/whitepapers/Dragonfly_Threat_Against_Western_ Energy_Suppliers.pdf

Symantec; 2014c; *Emerging Threat: Dragonfly/Energetic Bear-APT Group*. Symantec Official Blog. June, 2014. https://www.symantec.com/connect/blogs/ emerging-threat-dragonfly-energetic-bear-apt-group

Target; 2013; *Target Confirms Unauthorized Access to Payment Card Data in U.S. Stores*; Press Release; Minneapolis; December 19, 2013.

TechRepublic; 2017; *NotPetya ransomware outbreak cost Merck more than $300M per quarter*; Conner Forester, October 30, 2017. https://www.techrepublic.com/article/notpetya-ransomware-outbreak-cost-merck-more-than-300m-per-quarter/

Thaler R.H., Sunstein C.R.; 2009; *Nudge*. Penguin books; 2009.

The Citizen Lab (2018); *NSO Group Infrastructure Linked to Targeting of Amnesty International and Saudi Dissident*; Bill Marczak, John Scott-Railton, and Ron Deibert; July 31. https://citizenlab.ca/2018/07/nso-spyware-targeting-amnesty-international/

The Hacker News; 2017; *US Identifies 6 Russian Government Officials Involved In DNC Hack*; Swati Khandelwal; November 02, 2017. https://thehackernews.com/2017/11/dnc-email-russian-hackers.html

The Merkle (2016); Muni First Targeted By Ransomware, Now Faces Extortion Demand By Same Hackers; Nov 29, 2016. http://www.newsjs.com/url.php?p=http://themerkle.com/muni-first-targeted-by-ransomware-now-faces-extortion-demand-by-same-hackers/

The Register; 2012; *How one bad algorithm cost traders $440m*; Dan Olds; OrionX; 3 Aug 2012. https://www.theregister.co.uk/2012/08/03/bad_algorithm_lost_440_million_dollars/

The Register; 2017, *Virus (cough, cough, Petya) goes postal at FedEx, shares halted*; The Register; Iain Thompson; 28 June 2017; https://www.theregister.co.uk/2017/06/28/fedex_tnt_express_virus_attack/

The Times, 2017, *GCHQ: British cyberweapons could paralyse hostile states*; December 21, 2017. https://www.thetimes.co.uk/article/gchq-british-cyber weapons-could-paralyse-hostile-states-zbcm3mdbt

Thompson V., Dunstone, N.J., Scaife, A.A., Smith, D.M., Slingo, J.M., Brown, S., Belcher, S.E.; 2017; *High risk of unprecedented UK rainfall in the current climate*. Nature Communications, Vol. 8, 107. Doi: 10.1038/s41467-017-00275-3; 2017.

Treadwell, James; 2013; *Criminology: The Essentials*; 2nd Edition; Sage Publications.

Turing A.M.; 1950; *Computing machinery and intelligence*. Mind, 433-460.

United States v. Azar (2:09-cr-00240-DMG); 2009; *INDICTMENT Filed as to Mario Azar (1) count(s) 1.* (sj, ) (Entered: 03/18/2009); United States Courts; 2009.

United States Whitehouse; 2017; *'Vulnerabilities Equities Policy and Process for the United States Government*; Whitehouse Declassification; 15 November 2017.

US Nuclear Regulatory Commision; 2003; *"Potential Vulnerability Of Plant Computer Network To Worm Infection"*; NRC Information Notice 2003-14; Nuclear Regulatory Commision; 29 August 2003. https://www.nrc.gov/reading-rm/doc-collections/gen-comm/info-notices/2003/in200314.pdf

USA Today; 2012; *'Top secret Visa data center banks on security, even has a moat,'* 25 March, 2012; http://usatoday30.usatoday.com/tech/news/story/2012-03-25/visa-data-center/53774904/1

Vab Rassan M.; 2018; *Comms on the battlefield*. Intersec. May, 2018.

Van der Walt, C. "*Four Lessons to Learn From the SWIFT Hacks*" Info Security. 3 August 2016. https://www.infosecurity-magazine.com/opinions/four-lessons-to-learn-from-the/

Wall Street Journal; 2013; *Target's Data-Breach Timeline*; Sara Germano, Dec 27, 2013. https://blogs.wsj.com/corporate-intelligence/2013/12/27/targets-data-breach-timeline/

Wall, David, S.; 2007; *Cybercrime: The transformation of crime in the digital age*; Polity Press, Cambridge, UK.

Weimann, Gabriel; 2004; '*Cyberterrorism How Real Is the Threat?*' United States Institute of Peace Special Report; https://www.usip.org/sites/default/files/sr119.pdf

Weimann, Gabriel; 2006; *Terror in the Internet*: The New Arena, the New Challenges; United States Institute of Peace Press, Washington D.C.

White, Alan; and Clark, Ben.; *BTFM: Blue Team Field Manual*; v1.0.

Wikipedia, The Free Encyclopedia; s.v. "*Aurora Generator Test*"; Wikipedia Article; Wikipedia; (accessed November 15, 2017); https://en.wikipedia.org/wiki/Aurora_Generator_Test

Williams K.S.; 2012; *Textbook on criminology*. Oxford University Press, Oxford.

Williams, Katie, 2016, *Judges struggle with cyber crime punishment*, The Hill, 01/09/16. http://thehill.com/policy/cybersecurity/265285-judges-struggle-with-cyber-crime-punishment

Windley, Phil; 2007; "*Blowing up generators remotely*"; Article; ZDNet; 28 September 2007. http://www.zdnet.com/blog/btl/blowing-up-generators-remotely/6451

Wired; 2008; *Polish Teen Hacks His City's Trams, Chaos Ensues*; Chuck Squatriglia; Gear; 1 Nov 2008. https://www.wired.com/2008/01/polish-teen-hac/

Wired; 2009; *Former Teen Hacker's Suicide Linked to TJX Probe*; Kevin Poulsen, Security 07 September 2009. https://www.wired.com/2009/07/hacker-3/

Wired; 2011; *How a Remote Town in Romania Has Become Cybercrime Central*; Yudhijit Bhattacharjee; 01.31.11. https://www.wired.com/2011/01/ff-hackerville-romania/

Wired; 2015; *Facebook's AI Tool for Squashing Bugs is Now Open to All*; 6 Nov 2015. https://www.wired.com/2015/06/facebooks-ai-tool-squashing-bugs-now-open/

Wired; 2018; *The Billion-Dollar Hacking Group Behind a String of Big Breaches*; Lily Hay Newman; Apr 4, 2018. https://www.wired.com/story/fin7-carbanak-hacking-group-behind-a-string-of-big-breaches/

Woo G., Maynard T., Seria J.; 2017; *Reimagining history: counterfactual risk analysis*; Lloyd's emerging risk report, London.

Woo G.; 2011; *Calculating Catastrophe*; Imperial College Press, London.

Woo, G.; 2017; *Counterfactual Analysis of WannaCry Malware Attack*. RMS Webinar, Nov 2017; and blog 'Reimagining the WannaCry Cyberattack'; http://www.rms.com/blog/2017/11/21/reimagining-the-wannacry-cyberattack/

Wood L.; 2014; *Boost your security training with gamification -really!*; Computerworld, July 16, 2014.

Woods, Daniel, Ioannis Agrafiotis, Jason R. C. Nurse, and Sadie Creese. (2017); *"Mapping the Coverage of Security Controls in Cyber Insurance Proposal Forms."* Journal of Internet Services and Applications 8 (July 14, 2017): 8. https://doi.org/10.1186/s13174-017-0059-y.

Woodward, Matt; 2018; *"How Much Does 1 Hour of Downtime Cost the Average Business?"*. RAND Group. https://www.randgroup.com/insights/cost-of-business -downtime/

World Economic Forum; 2015; *Partnering for cyber resilience: towards the quantification of cyber threats*. In collaboration with Deloitte; January 2015.

World Economic Forum; 2016; *Could a cyber attack cause a financial crisis?*; June 13, 2016. https://www.weforum.org/agenda/2016/06/could-a-cyber-attack-cause-a-financial-crisis

Wreathall J.; 2006; *Properties of resilient organizations: an initial view*. In: Resilience Engineering (Hollnagel E., Woods D.D., Leveson N. (Eds)), Ashgate, Aldershot; 2006.

Wright J.; 2018; *Cyber and international law in the 21st century*. Lecture at Chatham House, May 23, 2018.

Yar, Majid, 2013; *Cybercrime and Society*; Second Edition; Sage Publications.

York, K. (2016) "Dyn Statement on 10/21/2016 DDoS Attack". Dyn. http://dyn.com/ blog/dyn-statement-on-10212016-ddos-attack/

ZD Net; 2012; *Anonymous launches 'Operation Global Blackout', aims to DDoS the Root Internet servers*; Dancho Danchev, February 17, 2012. https://www .zdnet.com/article/anonymous-launches-operation-global-blackout-aims-to-ddos-the-root-internet-servers/

ZD Net; 2017; *A massive cyberattack is hitting organisations around the world*; Danny Palmer, June 27, 2017. http://www.zdnet.com/article/a-massive-cyber attack-is-hitting-organisations-around-the-world/

Zetter, Kim (2016b); *Why Hospitals Are the Perfect Targets for Ransomware*; Wired.com; 03.30.2016. https://www.wired.com/2016/03/ransomware-why-hospitals-are-the-perfect-targets/

Zetter, Kim; 2014; *Countdown to Zero Day: Stuxnet and the launch of the world's first digital weapon*; Broadway Books.

Zetter, Kim; 2016; *"That Insane, $81M Bangladesh Bank Heist? Here's What We Know"*. Wired. 17 May 2016. https://www.wired.com/2016/05/insane-81m-bangladesh-bank-heist-heres-know/

# Index

Ways things can go wrong, 167
Weakest link, 156, 168, 197,
  208, 281, 311
Wells Fargo, 67, 340
Whistle-blowing, 38, 134, 144,
  176
Wikileaks, 38, 66, 136
Worst-case scenarios, 92, 96

**Y**
Yahoo, 30, 172, 173, 180, 219,
  271, 292, 340, 346

**Z**
Zero days, 14, 16, 104, 105,
  121, 133, 134, 150, 174, 175,
  176, 180, 220, 254, 256, 276,
  277, 278, 281, 282, 283, 304,
  333, 353
  exploiting, 104
Zerodium, 282, 283
Zipf's law, 172, 257, 333